Fundamentals of
Voice and Diction

BRENDA IRWIN   Speech 59   9-9:50A.   Rm 1001

Fundamentals of
Voice and Diction

Fifth Edition

Lyle V. Mayer

Ferris State College

WM. C. BROWN
COMPANY PUBLISHERS
Dubuque, Iowa

contents

Barbara Titus

preface

The student, not the professor, is the center of the academic universe, and this revision of *Fundamentals of Voice and Diction* reemphasizes that idea.

The majority of students who take a course in voice and diction, or any course which emphasizes voice and speech improvement, are seeking just that—improvement of the speaking voice. They are generally not as concerned with theory as they are with practical exercises and drill material which will help them develop effective voice and speech. Yet, to make something function with maximum efficiency, it is important to understand how it is made and how it functions. With this in mind, the theoretical material has been expanded. If the written word has not always been successful in adding understanding and making clear that which is complex, it is hoped that the additional drawings especially prepared for this fifth edition will be helpful.

This revision also reflects an interesting change in attitude among most speech teachers regarding dialects and pronunciations. Until recently we were inclined to describe certain dialects and pronunciations as "unacceptable" or "substandard." Both of these terms are somewhat snobbish and patronizing—a "put-down" of a particular speaker, one might say. The word "nonstandard" will be used in this text, and it indicates only one thing—a speech style or manner may be different, but it is in no way inferior.

Theory and practice have been even more carefully integrated than before, and, in general, we have attempted to adopt a more sophisticated approach. Drill material and exercises have been reshaped, rewritten, and freshened.

No doubt, some of the exercises are unacademic and unorthodox. Let it be said at once that most of them have been used successfully for over twenty-five years in a good many voice and diction classes, which have included adult as well as college-age groups. A majority of these students made substantial improvement in their speaking voices as "before-and-after" recordings demonstrated. A lot of them, by the way, also had a good time taking the course. Any course which concentrates on a subject as fascinating as voice and speech training ought to be enjoyable—not to mention valuable—for students.

Few classes are going to find time to cover all twenty-two assignments included in this work. Few classes are going to find time to practice all of the 360 exercises. Few individuals in those classes would need to cover that many assignments or exercises. The instructor should assign on the basis of individual needs and differences.

Many individuals who have used the earlier edition of this book have suggested, and with considerable justification, I believe, that the chapter on articulation should follow chapters 3, 4, and 5 which deal with vocal quality, loudness, and expressiveness. The articulation chapter has been moved. Some instructors will prefer to get to articulation sooner, perhaps immediately after chapter 3, "Quality." The flexibility of the book will permit this arrangement.

Sometime ago, a distinguished professor addressed a conference of educators. He caused some academic eyebrows to vault upward when he commented, "It's about time that writers of textbooks write 'down' to their students, and stop writing to impress their colleagues." This revision, too, is written with that idea in mind.

acknowledgments

The author is indebted to the following individuals and publishers for their assistance and for permission to quote or reprint from their publications. Any omissions are unintentional.

Anderson House for selected lines from *Winterset*, copyright 1935 by Maxwell Anderson and Anderson House.

Ashley Famous Agency, Inc., for selected lines from *Who Was That Lady I Saw You With?* by Norman Krasna.

Brandt and Brandt for selected lines from *Gypsy* by Arthur Laurents. Book by Arthur Laurents, music by Jule Styne, lyrics by Stephen Sondheim. Suggested by the Memoirs of Gypsy Rose Lee. Copyright 1959, 1960 by Arthur Laurents, Gypsy Rose Lee and Stephen Sondheim. Reprinted by permission.

Dramatists' Play Service, Inc., for material from *You Can't Take It With You*. Copyright 1936, 1937 by George S. Kaufman and Moss Hart.

Samuel French and Paul Green for selected lines from *Johnny Johnson* by Paul Green. Copyright 1936, 1937. All rights reserved.

Harper and Brothers for "Billy," from *Ruthless Rhymes for Heartless Homes*, by Harry Graham; for a selection from "Happy Childhood Tales" from *No Poems*, by Robert Benchley. Copyright 1932 by Robert Benchley.

Ben Hecht and Charles MacArthur for selected lines from *The Front Page*.

Alfred A. Knopf, Inc., and William Seabrook for material quoted in *The Theater Book of the Year* (1946-1947), by George Jean Nathan.

Marcia Mayer for her ten drawings.

MCA Artists and Management, Ltd., for selected lines from *Picnic*, by William Inge; *All My Sons*, by Arthur Miller; *A Streetcar Named Desire*, by Tennessee Williams.

Monica McCall, Inc., Random House, Inc., and John Van Druten for selected lines from *I Am a Camera*, copyright 1952, 1955 by John Van Druten. Copyright, under the title "Sally Bowles" as an unpublished work 1951, by John Van Druten.

Random House, Inc., for selected lines from the following: *Biography*, by Sam Behrman; *The Children's Hour* and *The Little Foxes*, by Lillian Hellman; *The Man Who Came to Dinner*, by George S. Kaufman and Moss Hart; *The Women*, by Clare Booth Luce; *Waiting for Lefty*, by Clifford Odets; *Ah, Wilderness!* by Eugene O'Neill; *Boy Meets Girl*, by Samuel and Bella Spewack; Albert I. Da Silva for selected lines from *God's Favorite* by Neil Simon.

Random House, Inc., and Jess Stein for an excerpt from the preface of the *Random House Dictionary*. Reprinted from *The Random House Dictionary of the English Language*, copyright 1966, copyright 1967 by Random House, Inc., by permission.

Grateful acknowledgment is also due to those anonymous authors whose works have been quoted. In a majority of cases, unsuccessful attempts have been made to trace the holder of the copyright.

Above all, a hearty "thank you" is extended to the dozens of students who, over the years, have brought into class for their oral assignments unusually interesting and colorful material. Some of this is original; some of it will have a familiar ring: old proverbs, axioms, and famous quotes from dead but not forgotten authors. We have made use of this material extensively.

Voice and Diction: A Preview   1

If you decide to buy a new car, you must be prepared to invest quite a bit of money. Generally, before you close the "deal," you listen to the salesman at some length. He gives you a sales talk, and he spends quite a bit of time not only telling you about the outstanding features of his product, but telling you why you should own it. If you are a good buyer, you will ask questions. If he is a good salesman, he expects you to ask questions. You are tying up a substantial amount of money, and you have a right to know all about the product.

If you are reading this page, it probably means just one thing: you are enrolled in some kind of a course in voice and speech improvement. Perhaps you have elected the course; perhaps you are required to take it. In either case, it represents a substantial investment on your part. Not only money, but time. Your very first question might well be, "What am I getting into?" or "What can I expect to get out of a course such as this?"

We have jumped the gun and anticipated a few of your questions and have tried to provide a few answers.

Exactly what is a course in voice and diction? (Or maybe your college describes it as "Voice and Articulation," "Voice and Speech Improvement," or "Voice Skills.")

It is a course which deals with talking. It does not concern itself so much with what you talk about, but how you talk. In general, do the people you talk to every day react favorably to your voice? Can they understand you easily? Can they hear you? Do they find the sound of your voice pleasant and agreeable? Do they find you animated and interesting to listen to?

Another way of answering the main question is by telling you what this kind of a course is *not:* It is not an "arty" course. It is not going to make you so different that you will stand out like a sore thumb. It will not make your speech elegant. It is not a course in how-to-read-poetry, how-to-be-an-actor, or how-to-be-an-announcer.

Do I really need a course in voice and diction?

The chances are that you will profit from such a course. Most people would. Here are some interesting but alarming statistics:

Every spring many companies, firms, and industries send representatives to college campuses to interview prospective employees. Two large state universities recently asked the various firms to state their reasons for not hiring those students they had rejected. In approximately two-thirds of the cases, the reason given was that the interviewee did not "talk effectively during the interview."

Speech instructors contact and listen to many students each year. Over a period of years, the total figure may run into the hundreds. Most speech teachers agree that at least two-thirds of their students have faults of voice or diction and could benefit from some sort of course in voice and speech improvement.

And what about the post-college years? You may spend approximately five percent or less of your life in college before you enter the professional world and become a breadwinner. Bad speech habits will definitely not increase your chances for success and advancement in your chosen occupation.

Recently a woman was hired by an employment agency in a large western city. Every day she called as many as a hundred and fifty corporations, firms, or small businesses seeking job listings. She discovered that approximately one third of the receptionists or switchboard operators, the first business contact with a company, had unpleasant vocal traits or were totally unintelligible and mangled the names of the companies who paid their salaries. Marilyn Person Smith, she learned, was Merrill Lynch Pierce Fenner and Smith. The Oh Noy Lassner Vision was discovered to be Owens-Illinois Glass Container Division.

It makes no difference whether one is executive vice-president, personnel director, or custodian for General Motors. Sloppy speech or an unattractive voice, whether via telephone or face-to-face, "turns off" potential customers. First impressions, not to mention second and third, do count!

We all want friends. We all want to be liked. We all want social approval. But many people persist in thinking that an unpleasant speaking voice always signifies a disagreeable personality. A shrill, strident, grating voice, for example, is supposed to belong to an individual who is "up-tight," taut, or neurotic—a person to be avoided. Such a stereotype is not always fair, of course, but nevertheless our listeners often jump to hasty conclusions about our personalities on the basis of listening to our speech for only a few minutes. Agreeable speech habits obviously increase our chances of social acceptance and professional success.

After all, I have been talking for eighteen years, more or less. If there is something wrong with the way I talk, why haven't I found out about it before now?

The truth of the matter is that you have been told quite a few things about your talking. Your parents started giving you advice when you were a year old. "Speak up!" "Don't mumble!" "Tone it down!" "Don't talk so fast." "Sh-h-h-h!" "Read slower." "Don't talk with your mouth full!"

And like a lot of other parental advice, it may have gone quite unheeded, perhaps because you heard it so often. You may have reacted the same way towards your teachers.

You should also remember that your parents, brothers, sisters, and friends hear you a great deal. They get used to the way you speak. You may be a terrible mumbler or you may have a whiny, irritating voice, but the people you are closest to like you in spite of these faults. As far as your friends are concerned, they would not be your friends if they continually harped at you about your faults. Or, as an old advertisement goes, "Even your best friends won't tell you."

Maybe my voice isn't as good as it should be, but I have been communicating successfully with my fellow creatures for quite a few years. What is also important: I can hear myself when I speak. Doesn't that count for something?

Robert Burns, in his wise little poem, "To a Louse," has this to say:

> Oh, would some power the gift give us,
> To see ourselves as others see us!
> It would from many a blunder free us,
> And foolish notion.

If you have seen yourself in home movies, you may have been quite startled or even embarrassed. You had never realized that you walked, gestured, postured, or arched your eyebrows in quite the way the screen so realistically insists. Maybe you said, "Why, I didn't know that I acted like that!"

It is almost as great a shock the first time you hear a recording of your voice. Typically, most of us will say, "That couldn't be me!" "Do I really sound like an eighth grader?" "I don't sound like that!"

Indeed, you don't sound like that—at least, not to yourself. For when you are speaking in a conversational situation, or even when you are speaking in front of the class, how do you hear yourself? Other people can hear you only via sound waves which reach their outer ears. You hear yourself partly through the same waves, but you also hear the sounds which you are making that are conducted through the tissues of your body and the bones of your head to your hearing mechanisms. You are, of course, talking at the same instant the waves reach the ear, and you are much closer to the sound of your own voice than anyone else. Furthermore, as we have already said, you are used to the sound of your voice. You are fully aware of what you are thinking, so as a rule, you give little thought to how you sound as you speak.

This course will help you to cultivate an educated ear—an ear which not only listens to, but hears critically the world of sounds—speech or otherwise—around you. In the process of accomplishing this, you will become a far better critic-judge of your own voice.

Why is it that some people are born with good voices?

Michelangelo was not born a great sculptor, Beethoven was not born a great composer, and Muhammad Ali was not born a great boxer. They worked long and hard for what they were able to do. As the time-worn saw would have it: "Genius is 99% perspiration and 1% inspiration." This is probably exaggerated, but it is safe to say that nobody is born with a great speaking voice. Speech is a learned skill. You learned to speak when you were a small child, just as you learned to walk. You imitated your parents, brothers, sisters, friends, and later, teachers. The good voices you occasionally hear in TV, radio, movies, or on the stage were acquired by their owners only as the result of extensive work and training. Good voices are not accidents or gifts from God.

Can I actually change my voice?

Definitely yes! Perhaps "improve" is a better word. None of the physical structures which help you to produce speech sounds will be altered, nor will they be enlarged or decreased in size. You will discover, however, ways and means of taking the basic equipment you already have and using it with greater efficiency. A golfer can improve his stroke, a soprano learns how to hit high C without screeching, a track man improves his running time. When you have finished this course, you should have acquired voice and speech habits which are substantially more effective than your present manner of talking and speaking.

How do I go about improving?

The most important thing: Practice! Practice! Practice, and then more practice! Van Cliburn studies and practices a piano concerto for three years before he plays it in public. A great football team spends long, exhausting hours scrimmaging before playing its opening game, and equally long, grueling hours of practice between the rest of the games scheduled that season.

There are twenty-two assignments in this textbook. You will not have time to do all of them, nor will you need to do all of them, but your instructor will help you select the ones which will be most beneficial to you. You will note that most of the assignments ask you to concentrate on one particular aspect of voice or speech at a time, and this is by far the best way to proceed. You cannot rid yourself of every vocal fault overnight or by doing one or two assignments. Take your time, do not become impatient, and concentrate. You must learn how to listen critically and objectively to yourself.

Experience has taught that very few of us can make substantial progress or improvement with less than thirty minutes of daily practice. In many cases, forty-five minutes would be better.

I am reasonably convinced that as far as my voice is concerned there is room for improvement, and I also agree that this will take practice. Now, specifically, what kind of voice am I supposed to be working for? What are my targets or goals? In other words, just what makes effective voice and speech?

Effective Voice and Speech is Pleasant to Listen to.

This introduces us to the word *quality.*

> *Quality is the timbre, tone color, or texture of a voice.*

If a clarinetist, a trumpet player, and a violinist stand behind a screen and play "Dixie" in the key of C at the same rate of speed and the same degree of loudness, we can still distinguish between them. Each instrument has its own personality or timbre. Similarly, if we overhear two friends conversing in an adjoining room, we can invariably tell which is which.

When voices annoy us because of poor quality, we do not always use exact terms to describe the particular voice. We like to fall back on such terms as "raspy, scratchy, whiny, shrill, edgy." More accurately, we might use terms such as:

> **Breathy:** This kind of voice is feathery, fuzzy, and whispery. Breath seems to be escaping noticeably. The voice is generally too soft and does not carry well.
> **Harsh:** There are two extremes of harshness. Both are unpleasant, but in one kind, the harsh-strident, the voice is hard, brassy, and relatively high-pitched. In the other kind, the harsh-throaty, it is gravelly, raspy, and relatively low-pitched.
> **Nasal:** "Talking through the nose"—a nasal twang. It has a foghorn and sometimes a whiny quality. Singers of country western music frequently use it.
> **Denasal:** "The cold in the nose," stuffy quality. The voice sounds bottled up.
> **Hoarse-Husky:** An offensively noisy, scratchy, strained "bacon in the frying pan" quality. It often suggests that its user either has laryngitis or needs to clear his throat.

Effective Voice and Speech Is Easily Heard.

This introduces us to the word *loudness*.

> *Loudness refers to intensity (sound level), volume, or projection.*

One could have excellent enunciation and still not be able to reach his listeners. A voice which is excessively soft, weak, or thin is irritating to most people. It also suggests that its owner is timid or mousy.

Occasionally we encounter the "boomer." You may be within five feet of him, but he speaks at a level of loudness which would be ideal if he were talking without a mike in Yankee Stadium.

Effective Voice and Speech Is Varied and Flexible.

This introduces us to the word *expressiveness*.

> *Expressiveness means vocal variety: the pitch level at which we speak, our vocal movements from pitch to pitch, our rate of speaking, phrasing, emphasis, and contrast.*

An excessively high pitch can bring you the wrong kind of attention. An extremely low pitch can make your listeners edgy. If you are a "Johnny-One-Note," with little variety in pitch, you can put your hearers to sleep. A too-fast rate may possibly prevent your message from being comprehended, and a consistently slow and draggy rate is dull. Without phrasing, emphasis and contrast, your conversation or your speeches may seem rather pointless and meaningless.

Effective Voice and Speech Is Distinct, Intelligible, Clear, and Easy to Understand.

This introduces us to the word *articulation*. The words *enunciation* and *diction*, for all practical purposes, have the same meaning. All three of them refer to the accuracy and clarity of our speech.

> *Articulation involves movements of the lips, jaw, tongue, and velum (soft palate) to form, separate, and join individual speech sounds.*

Of all the problems involved with voice and speech, poor articulation is the most common. "Mumbling" is frequently used to describe careless, sluggish articulation. The mumbler does not seem to use his lips or open his mouth. He frequently drops sounds.

> *get you* is heard as *gitcha*
> *give me* comes out as *gimme*
> *thinking* becomes *thinkin'*

4

going to changes into *gunna*

recognize and *understand* turn into *rekuhnize* and *unnerstan*

The "garbler" is a close relative of the mumbler. He often substitutes an incorrect sound for a correct one, he distorts sounds or he adds extra, unwarranted sounds:

these, them, with are heard as *deze, dem, wit*

length, strength alter to *lenth, strenth*

athlete, across become *ath-a-lete, acrosst*

The other extreme of mumbling and garbling is "arty" or affected speech, less frequently encountered. Articulation is too hard and precise and calls undue attention to itself. Syllables are chopped up into individual words. A recent and well-known governor of a Middle Atlantic state favored arty speech, and his articulation of such a word as *education* resulted in a four-word phrase: *ed—you—kay—shawn.*

Effective Speech Is Unobtrusive and Appropriate.

Good speech does not attract undue attention to itself, and it should be appropriate to the speaker, the area in which he lives, and his audience.

We have already discussed arty speech in the sense of overly precise, excessively clipped articulation. Another variety of arty speech, and it is definitely obtrusive, is unnatural or affected pronunciation. In affected speech the speaker is conspicuously artificial; he "puts on airs" in certain pronunciations. He attempts to attract notice with a manner of speaking which he considers to be elegant or genteel. Examples are *either* and *neither* pronounced as **eye**-*ther* and **neye**-*ther*. To talk about your Awnt Jane instead of your Ant Jane or *to*-maw-*toes* instead of *to*-may-*toes* may also make your pronunciation conspicuous.

Consider *bona fide.* Four of the major dictionaries list "bo na fi dee" (pronounced with four syllables—bō′ nə fī′dē) as standard.[1] Yet it might, under some circumstances, make the user, if not the listener, uncomfortable. It is less conspicuous to pronounce it with three syllables: "bo na fid" (bō′ nə fīd).

Grammatical errors—and the subject does not quite fall within the scope of this book—can also make your speech obtrusive. The *I seen, he come home,* and *we ain't* phrase-dropper is suffering from verbal acne.

The subject of appropriate speech recalls a quotation from St. Augustine: "When I am here, I do not fast on Saturday; when at Rome, I do fast on Saturday." In other words, "When in Rome, do as the Romans do." The idea may be slightly suspect, and this area of pronunciation must be approached with caution.

A United States senator, running for reelection, addressed his constituents in a mountainous section of West Virginia. He quickly adopted several of the local speech mannerisms as he spoke, but later, on the floor of the Senate, he discarded them. Using the phrase *right here,* for example, he gave it a little mountain color: *ri-cheer* (rī cher′). This kind of tactic is a bit snobbish and condescending.

Chapter 6, "Articulation," will examine many regional and social differences. In the meantime, let us examine briefly "dialect." We frequently speak of a Texas or an Eastern accent. A better word would be dialect.

By dialect we mean a variety of language which is distinguished from other varieties of the same language. It is used by a group of speakers in a certain area who are set off from others geographically and socially.

There are three major regional dialects in the United States:

General American is spoken by the greatest number of people in America. Boundary lines between the various dialects are by no means sharp and rigid. In general, however, this dialect is most commonly

1. A section dealing with certain aspects of standard and nonstandard pronunciation will be found in the Appendixes.

spoken in the Midwest (as far south as the Mason-Dixon line), the West and parts of the Southwest. It is the dialect most often heard in TV, radio, and movies.

Eastern includes the New England and the Middle Atlantic states, although the dialects of New York City, Philadelphia, and Baltimore are difficult to categorize.

Southern is used in the region which approximates the states of the old Confederacy. It extends as far west as Arkansas and part of Texas.

Is one of these dialects better than the other two? Definitely not. The educated, cultivated New Yorker can be understood in Atlanta just as easily as the cultured Texan can be understood in Butte, Montana. Furthermore, it should be pointed out that while both Boston and New York are classified as Eastern, there are remarkable differences between them.

No section of the United States has a monopoly on good or correct speech. Nor is there any reason why we should all sound alike any more than we should all look or dress alike. It is more important that you attempt to emulate the well-educated and the cultured people in your area.

Each of the major dialects has several dozen subdialects. These are sometimes regarded as nonstandard or they are labeled as provincial. The Brooklynite who talks about his *goil* (girl) and the previously quoted lawmaker who insisted on saying *ri-cheer* (right here) are both using provincialisms. Such subdialects are colorful and folksy and are certainly standard within the relatively small area of their usage. Outside of that area, however, the user may possibly be tagging himself as a rather quaint character.

Listening Objectively

A play written about seventy-five years ago contains this interesting little speech: "I have never for one instant seen clearly within myself. How then would you have me judge the deeds of others?" We are going to rework this quotation and apply it to a point we now wish to make: "I will not be able to judge myself unless I first learn to judge others."

As you listen critically to the speech of other people and note their bad as well as their good points, you may discover that you yourself share some of their vocal weaknesses and virtues. Learn how to identify vocal traits in others, learn how to analyze and evaluate their voices, and you will soon become more sensitive to your own vocal personality.

The following exercises will help us listen critically to the voice and speech of others. (In working with these exercises, you may wish to use an analysis chart to help you evaluate voices. Refer to Analysis Charts 1-6, pages 273-83. A chart will be particularly appropriate for Exercise 4.)

1. Listen to a radio drama or try this interesting experiment: "listen" to a TV drama such as a soap opera, but keep the picture off the screen. Concentrate as intensely as you can on the sounds of the voices rather than on the story which is being told. Many of these plays have stereotypes—the "bad guy," the "good guy," the "other" woman, the ne'er-do-well, the long-suffering wife. Can you identify them by their vocal traits? Do you like or dislike them? Why?

2. Listen to, rather than watch, other types of programs: panels and talk shows, interviews, hearings, newscasts. Compare voices. Why do you react favorably to some and unfavorably to others?

3. There are numerous recordings available of prominent personalities reading poetry, prose, or scenes from plays, or giving speeches. Robert Frost and Carl Sandburg have recorded some of their own poetry. Sir Laurence Olivier, Richard Burton, Glenda Jackson, George C. Scott, and many other fine actors may be heard in plays. Recordings of the interesting voices of Franklin Roosevelt, Harry Truman, John Kennedy, Richard Nixon, Jimmy Carter, and Coretta King are also available. Undoubtedly your library has many of them. By referring to the elements of effective speech already listed and described in this chapter and restated in the analysis charts, evaluate these voices.

4. Evaluate the voices of the individuals listed below:
   a. A favorite professor.
   b. A professor you do not like.
   c. A close friend.
   d. An acquaintance you dislike.
   e. Somebody you know who possesses an unusual voice.
   f. A TV newscaster, actor, or actress.

5. Record your own voice. This should be done at least three times during the course, and more if possible. If time permits only three recordings, the first one should be made at the beginning of the course. The second should be made at approximately midterm, and the final one should be made at the end of the course. By doing this, you will be able to check your own progress. Your instructor will arrange for you to hear your recorded performances privately or in class.

Voice and Speech Analysis Charts 7-12, pages 285-95 are convenient ways of focusing your attention on some of the most important aspects of voice and speech. The charts will be especially useful in evaluating recorded performances, but they may also be used for nonrecorded performances. It is suggested that initially your instructor use the charts to evaluate your reading or speaking, but later in the course, perhaps you will have the opportunity to appraise your own recorded voice or the voice of a classmate.

Be sure that part of each recording is devoted to informal, conversational, and unrehearsed material. An interview with another classmate or the instructor, or a brief impromptu talk is suggested.

Read some of the material you are recording. As a rule, this should be unrehearsed. Although your instructor may ask you to record material with which you are unfamiliar, the following selections are offered as typical examples of effective recording material. They contain all of the sounds of the English language commonly found to be defective.

It is advisable to begin each recording with a sentence or two of identification:

My name is_____. This is a sample of my speaking voice as recorded during the course in ___(Voice and Diction)___ at ___(Smith College)___, ___(September, 19)___ .

1. A mouse went into a lion's cave by mistake, and before he knew what he was doing, he ran over the nose of the sleeping lion. The lion reached out his paw and caught the mouse and was about to eat him when the mouse said: "Forgive me, King of Beasts, I did not know where I was. I should never have been so proud as to come into this cave if I had known it was yours."
   The lion smiled at the poor frightened little mouse and let him go. Not long after this, the lion fell into a rope net left for him by some hunters, and his roars filled the forest. The mouse recognized the voice and ran to see if he could help him. He set to work nibbling the ropes, and soon the lion was free.
   [Aesop]

2. Love: An itch around the heart that you can't scratch. It is a power too strong to be overcome by anything but flight. In love, everything is true and everything is false. It is the only thing about which one cannot be absurd. Love is a fire. But whether it is going to warm your hearth or burn down your house, you can never tell. Someone has described it as "sentimental measles," or worse, as "a temporary insanity curable only by marriage." Love is to the moral nature exactly what the sun is to the earth. It is the wisdom of the fool and the folly of the wise. It seems the swiftest, but it is the slowest of all growths. No man or woman really knows what perfect love is until they have been married a quarter of a century. Love can canonize people. The saints are those who have been most loved. Love does not consist in gazing at each other but in looking outward together in the same direction.

3. We have all heard the saying: "Laugh and the world laughs with you. Weep and you weep alone." Laughing is the sensation of feeling good all over, and showing it mostly in one spot. Nothing shows a man's character more than what he laughs at. To laugh means to love mischief, but with a good conscience. We are in the world to laugh. In purgatory or in hell we shall no longer be able to do so. And

in heaven it would not be proper. Man is the only animal that laughs and weeps, for he is the only animal that is struck with the difference between what things are and what they might have been. If animals suddenly got the gift of laughter, they would begin by laughing themselves sick about man, that most ridiculous, most absurd, most foolish of all animals. But if we cannot be happy what can we be? Life is not any use at all unless we find a laugh here and there.

4. Once there was a prince, and he wanted to marry a real princess. He travelled all around the world to find one, but always there was something wrong. There were princesses enough, but he found it difficult to make out whether they were real ones. One evening a terrible storm came along. Suddenly a knocking was heard at the gate. It was a princess. But what a sight she was after all the dreadful weather. The water ran down her hair and clothes. And yet she said she was a real princess.

"We'll soon find out," thought the old queen. She went into the bedroom, took all the bedding off the bedstead, and laid a pea at the bottom. Then she took twenty mattresses and laid them on the pea. On this the princess slept all night. In the morning she was asked how she had slept.

"Terribly!" said the princess, "heaven knows what was in the bed, but I was lying on something hard. I am black and blue all over."

Nobody but a real princess could be as sensitive as that. So the prince married her, for now he knew that he had a real princess. [Fairy Tale]

Class Discussion: The Beginnings of Voice
(Use this page and the next one for note-taking)

The Beginnings of Voice 2

It is so easy for us to say, "Let's go to a movie or let's watch TV," that most of us rarely disturb ourselves by thinking how difficult life might be if we couldn't say it. Not that one couldn't exist without motion pictures or television. But for most of us, an existence in which we found ourselves deprived of the ability to talk would be extremely dull. As individuals we have been grunting and gurgling meaningfully since we were a few weeks old. Rarely, however, do we consider the interesting organ which produces the grunts and gurgles, as well as the more cultured sounds. If we do, we are apt to refer to it as the "thingamabob" in the throat, the voice box or, now and then, the Adam's apple. It is more correctly known as the larynx.

The larynx is the principal organ of sound and, as we shall see, it serves in other capacities, too. The vocal folds in the larynx are muscular flaps (muscle tissue and ligament) which can come together and keep foreign particles out of the windpipe. Also, when closed, they temporarily impound the air in the chest cavity. We must be able to hold our breath, of course, for any kind of strenuous work, such as lifting heavy objects, swimming underwater, and for such biological necessities as bearing down or elimination.

The various mechanisms we commonly associate with speech may, on occasion, give priority to other functions. Recall an experience in which you ran a race or swam fifty yards as rapidly as you could. Immediately after you had finished, was it possible for you to speak coherently? Probably not. More unpleasantly, remember the time that your car went out of control on an icy highway and almost skidded into a deep ditch or an oncoming diesel monster. If your heart wasn't literally in your mouth, your vocal mechanisms were for the moment at least almost as iced over as the road on which you skidded, and you may have found yourself speechless. All of us have swallowed particles of food down the "wrong" or "Sunday" throat. A coughing reflex helped to expel the foreign matter but, during the process of coughing, conversation was all but impossible.

Is Speech an "Overlaid" Function?

An interesting theory holds that the larynx was originally intended, not as a sound-making organ, but as a valve. Accordingly, consider the remarkable discovery made by a primitive man who may have lived two-and-a-half million years ago. Bending over one day to pick up a stone which he intended to use as a weapon, he inadvertently emitted a residual grunt—"Ugh!" To him, the biological explanation for making the sound was of no matter. But in his foggy logic, he decided to term, thereafter, all stones which he bent over to pick up as "Ughs." More importantly, according to the overlaid theory, he was adapting a valve in his throat to a new function.

All of the organs and structures which help us make speech sounds serve in a double capacity. We speak as we exhale air from the lungs, yet the lungs are not primarily organs of speech. The vocal folds are obviously important in speaking, but a basic function is to assist other structures in preventing foreign matter—fish bones, for example—from entering the lungs. The tongue, teeth, and lips help us to mold and shape speech sounds, but if we must eat and drink in order to live, these organs, too, carry a double load.

In one sense, speech is an overlaid function. It is like the old cliché, "Which came first, the chicken or the egg?" Speech is a product of the child's social environment. In the process of learning to make speech sounds he is making use of organs and structures of the body primarily intended to serve biological needs. The function of making speech sounds is superimposed on the biological functions of the larynx as a valve.

Likewise, a basic function of the lungs is to ventilate the blood and carry off waste products. Originally the mouth was intended to take in and chew food. In other words, the primary and older functions of the lungs, vocal folds, teeth, and lips are to help us maintain life. Yet man has been able to adapt these same parts of the body to speech. The ability and need to communicate can hardly be regarded as something of secondary importance. An organ as unique and perfect as the larynx, for example, is no mere afterthought in the evolution of man. It developed with a double purpose—for speech and as a protective device.

The specific beginnings of speech and the origins of language nobody knows. But man alone among the animal race has developed a complete, flexible, and growing verbal code of communication, and he has done so because: (a) he has been endowed with a large and responsive brain and a magnificently complex nervous system, and (b) he is sociable and gregarious.

How Is Sound Produced?

Back to the Adam's apple, which is actually nothing more than a frontal protuberance of the larynx. Hum *m* or say *ah*. Place your thumb and forefinger on the side of your "apple." You will feel a slight vibration. What is vibrating and what causes the vibration?

M and *ah* are sounds, and any sounds must have a motivating force. Breath, of course, is the sum and substance of sounds we make in the throat. After the breath is expelled from the lungs via the bronchial tubes, it passes through the windpipe (trachea). At the top of the windpipe, which is about four inches long and one inch in diameter, rests the larynx (fig. 2.1 and 2.2).

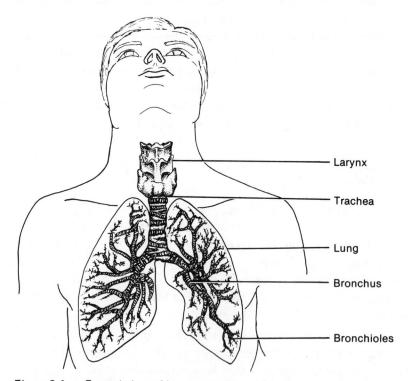

Larynx

Trachea

Lung

Bronchus

Bronchioles

Figure 2.1.   Frontal view of larynx, trachea and lungs

The lowest of these cartilages is called the cricoid. Actually it is the topmost ring of the trachea. It resembles a signet ring, being wide at the back but narrow in front, and it forms a base for the rest of the larynx.

A long time ago, Greek scientists decided that each of the two connected sides of the larynx resembled a shield. Their word for "large shield" was *thyreos*, and from this we have derived *thyroid*. The shield-shaped thyroid cartilage is the largest cartilage of the larynx, and it rests upon the cricoid. With your thumb and forefingers you can partially trace the outlines of the thyroid.

At the top and front of the thyroid your finger will hit a small depression or notch. The vocal folds, which are also known as vocal lips, bands, or cords (but never chords!) are attached just behind and below this V-shaped notch. From here, extending back along each side wall of the thyroid, they slope slightly downward. At the rear they are attached to two small ladle-shaped and movable cartilages which are known as *arytenoids*. The arytenoids, in turn, rest upon the larger signet portion of the cricoid.

When you swallow, your larynx bobs up and down. This action is controlled by the *extrinsic* muscles. One of these, for example, attaches the larynx above to the hyoid bone which lies at the base of the tongue. Thus, food or liquids pass over rather than into the larynx. The leaf-shaped epiglottis, at the base of and just behind the tongue, has no important function in speech. When we swallow, the larynx rises and the epiglottis moves backward, acting as a protective flap or covering over the larynx. This action also prevents foreign matter from entering the lungs.

Place your finger on your Adam's apple and swallow two or three times. Then try humming a high note. Jump quickly to a low note. You will notice that the larynx also jumps or shifts position. What controls the movements of the voice box? As we have already noted, the extrinsic muscles do, and they are able to raise or to lower as well as support the larynx. Extrinsic muscles have attachments outside the larynx, many of them being attached to the hyoid bone.

The *intrinsic* muscles are attached entirely to various points within the structure of the larynx. These muscles are more directly concerned with the process of making sounds, and they are therefore of more interest to us.

Listening to the voices of Richard Burton or Beverly Sills, we are profoundly impressed with the powerful, rich sonorities rolling out so effortlessly. One would almost be inclined to think that the owners of these golden voices, by some miracle, have giant pipe organs instead of small voice boxes hidden in their throats. It is incredible that such voices as these, as well as yours and mine, originate within the larynx and, more specifically, from a series of complicated movements of the two tiny intrinsic muscles which we commonly refer to as vocal folds. The average length of the folds in men is about 9/10 of an inch; in women it is approximately 7/10 of an inch.

These remarkable flaps of muscle are somewhat triangular or wedge-shaped in cross section. This means that they are thicker toward the sides where they are attached. The free, inner edges along the glottis are thinner. The inner edges are of a pearly-white, fibrous material, and they are covered with mucous membrane.

During quiet breathing the vocal folds are drawn apart leaving an opening, the glottis, between them. In this relaxed position, the folds form a V-shape with the point of the V at the front.

If we were to dissect a larynx and then cleave it, from top to bottom, from right to left, we could then remove the back half and look at the front half. This will help us to form a better idea of the interior mechanisms of the larynx (fig. 2.3).

The midsection of the larynx is of particular interest. The shelflike vocal folds (true vocal folds) have already been described. Directly above them are two small caverns, the ventricles. The ventricles contain tiny glands which secrete the mucous substance which helps to moisten and soothe the folds. The false vocal folds apparently have nothing to do with normal phonation (sound-making), but as we swallow food or liquid, they tend to pull together, thus serving as an additional barrier in keeping such matter out of the trachea.

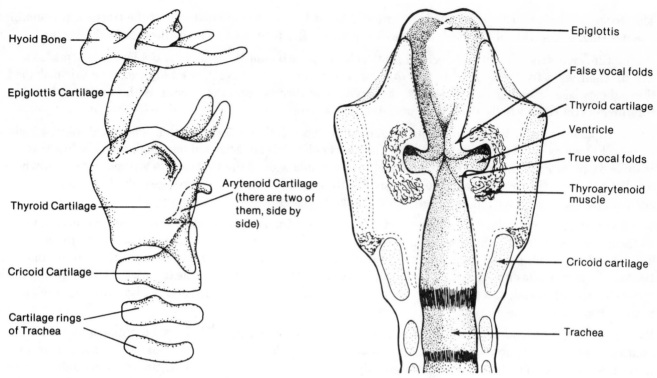

Figure 2.2. Cartilages of the larynx

Figure 2.3. Front section of the larynx

How Do the Vocal Folds Produce Sound?

Relaxed, the folds are relatively quiet and immobile, but when we are speaking, these intrinsic muscles are vibrating or fluttering with incredible speed. If you sustain middle C, the frequency of the vibration is approximately 256 times per second! What is the nature of this vibration?

Ask somebody in a pleasantly comfortable room to demonstrate how an extremely cold person acts and sounds. The chances are that he will arch his shoulders, pull in his neck, and make a peculiar noise which sounds something like "br-r-r-r." Or if you have ever studied a brass instrument such as a trombone or a trumpet, you may recall that your initial efforts were confined largely to vibrating your lips rapidly, as you might do during the unpleasantly expressive Bronx cheer, except that while you are blowing into your mouthpiece, your tongue would be entirely inside of your mouth. In any case, either example will give you a rough idea of how the vocal folds open and shut. Let us describe a cycle of opening and closing.

The vocal folds are apart during quiet breathing. Before phonation can take place, the folds, something like combination swinging and sliding doors, come together thus closing the glottis (fig. 2.4).

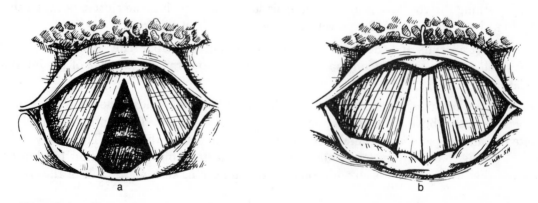

Figure 2.4. The vocal folds in position for (a) quiet breathing, and (b) phonation or vocalization

The folds are tightly closed, and air pressure is built up in the trachea beneath the glottis. When the pressure is sufficient, the now-taut folds are forced apart momentarily and a puff of air escapes. With this release of pressure, a sound wave is created, because as the folds are separated, they are set into vibration (they move back and forth).

The bands are elastic, and as the air pressure beneath them decreases, they spring back together again. As soon as the bands are closed, the pressure beneath them builds up once more, and again the folds are forced apart.

This cycle occurs again and again. The successive escaping puffs of air, as we know, set the folds into vibration; and they, in turn, cause the column of air in the voice tract to vibrate. It is this vibration which when heard by the listeners is recognized as sound.

This is an oversimplified description of how vocal tone is produced. It is true that the faster the folds vibrate, the higher the pitch. We have already noted that if you sing middle C, your vocal folds are vibrating at a rate of approximately 256 complete cycles per second. A professional tenor can generally hit "high" C, and this is one octave higher than middle C. In this case, his folds would be vibrating about 512 times per second. A first rate soprano can go up to the next higher C: this means a frequency of 1,024 vibrations per second.

The slower the bands vibrate, the lower the pitch. A baritone can easily sing a C below middle C—a frequency of 128 cycles.

It is obvious that the process of vibration is a complicated one. The tone which we recognize as high C or low C is by no means a simple tone. Either one results from a highly complex phenomenon: the overall vibration of the folds produces a fundamental tone which we recognize as the basic pitch of the tone. But, at the same time, the vocal folds vibrate in small parts or segments. These vibrations produce tones which are higher than the fundamental: overtones. The sound which eventually reaches the listener's ear is actually a blending together or an interacting of the fundamental plus the overtones.

Even if you are not a pianist you have probably made a few accurate observations about the strings inside a grand piano. The longest and heaviest string produces the lowest pitch. The shortest and lightest produces the highest. Too, you have probably watched a piano tuner tighten a string to raise the pitch. The vocal folds, however, do not operate exactly in the same manner as piano strings. The length and thickness of the vibrating edges of the folds help to determine pitch. Low frequencies are produced if the folds are short and comparatively lax. But, the shorter the folds, the thicker they are. Higher frequencies are produced if the folds are longer and more tense; the longer the folds, the thinner they are.

Length, weight, and tension are interesting and important enough to be given further consideration in a subsequent chapter which will deal with specific problems of pitch. For a moment, we might recall the legendary cattail fiddle. Allegedly it was played by holding a cat by the neck and the tail, sawing upon it in violin-fashion, and increasing the tension on the tail to increase the pitch of the cat.

Breathing for Speech

If you have taken a course in physics, you may have been quite intrigued with that section of the course which dealt with sound. But even if you made straight As, you probably would not sit through a performance of *A Chorus Line* or Beethoven's *Fifth Symphony* analyzing what you heard in terms of decibels, harmonics, and forced vibrations. You would certainly be aware that the pleasant sounds which greeted your ears emanated from a group of skilled musicians seated in the orchestra pit or on the stage, some of whom bowed, plucked, or struck their instruments, and some of whom blew air into them. All of this might remind you of a simple law of physics: Sound has as its source an object which vibrates.

What makes such an object vibrate? The violinist runs his bow across the strings of his Stradivarius. The harpist plucks the strings of his instrument. The xylophonist strikes tuned metal bars, and the French horn player, by blowing into a mouthpiece, sets into motion a column of air in about twelve feet of metal tubing.

But what about the singer, actor, or speaker who must produce his sounds without the aid of strings, bars, or metal tubing? He has, of course, the most remarkable instrument of all in his throat: the larynx which houses the vocal bands. As we know, the outgoing breath passing between these vocal bands sets them into vibration. To produce sounds successfully then, we must regulate and control this flow of air. This brings us to a consideration of the nature of breathing.

If you will take a deep breath, you will notice that your chest seems to expand and lift. To understand how this is accomplished, we must know something of the general structure of the chest or thorax.

The framework of the thorax, also referred to as the rib cage, consists of the spinal column (backbone), the sternum (breastbone), the shoulder blades and collarbones, and twelve pairs of ribs. It is the movement of the ribs which is of most interest to us.

All the ribs are attached to the backbone. The seven upper pairs are joined in front, by means of cartilages, to the sternum. Each of the next three pairs directly below is joined by cartilage to the rib above. The two lowest pairs, because they are not directly attached in front, are called free or floating ribs. It is obvious that the rib cage is not a rigid structure and that the lower part is more flexible in outward movement. The whole thorax can be lifted and enlarged from front to back as well as from side to side.

Within the thorax are two large cone-shaped lungs. They are not hollow sacs but spongy, porous organs which almost completely fill the cavity except for the heart and esophagus. The base of each lung is in contact with the upper surface of the diaphragm. It is interesting to note that breathing does not consist of "sucking in" or "pushing out" air. The lung tissues are passive. Actually, the lungs serve as reservoirs for air.

The chest and abdominal cavities are separated by the diaphragm, a tough, double-domed muscle which plays an active and important role in inhalation. This muscular partition is not a solid and unbroken sheet. There are openings in it which permit the esophagus, various nerves, and an important blood vessel (the aorta) to pass through it (fig. 2.5).

When you inhale, this is what happens:

> The muscles of the diaphragm tense and contract, and it moves downward and flattens slightly. In normal respiration the movement is less than an inch.
>
> This descending movement compresses the visceral organs (the stomach, liver, and kidneys) causing a slight bulge of the abdominal walls.
>
> The ribs are raised upward and outward.

The chest capacity is now increased in three directions: top to bottom, side to side, and front to back. Because of this increase in size, the air pressure within the lungs is decreased (a partial vacuum is also created in the chest), and air from the outside rushes in to equalize the pressure.

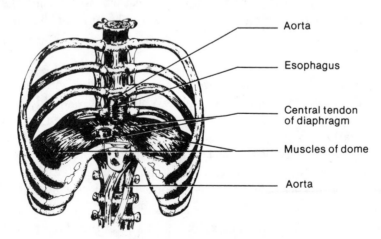

Aorta

Esophagus

Central tendon of diaphragm

Muscles of dome

Aorta

Figure 2.5. The diaphragm

If you are not talking but are only breathing quietly, this is what happens when you exhale:

The relaxation of the various muscles of the diaphragm permits that organ to move upward.

The visceral organs which have been under slight pressure now return to their uncompressed position.

When the muscles relax, the ribs move downward and inward by the pull of gravity.

These movements decrease the size of the chest cavity and compress the air in the lungs. The internal air pressure is now greater than that outside the body, and the air is expelled through the mouth and nose. This kind of exhalation requires no conscious control or awareness. It is basically a process of muscular relaxation rather than tension.

When we are talking, however, exhalation is a somewhat modified process. It must now be consciously controlled. Greater pressure and push are involved. There are four powerful sheaths of muscle which form the front wall of the abdomen. When they contract, they push in on the visceral organs which, in turn, push up against the diaphragm. The diaphragm has now returned to its arched position. This action shortens the chest cavity and, consequently, increases the pressure on the air within the lungs (fig. 2.6).

Breathing to sustain life is automatic and unconscious. In breathing for speech we make vocal sounds during the active process of exhalation. It is especially necessary that this process be controlled.

Here are several of the differences between breathing for speech and life (nonspeech) or biological breathing:

Life (Nonspeech) Breathing	Breathing for Speech
Inhalation is active. The diaphragm plays an active role.	Inhalation is active.
Exhalation is passive. The diaphragm plays a passive role.	Exhalation is active.
Breathing is comparatively shallow.	Breathing is somewhat fuller and deeper, depending upon the needs of the speaker (length of sentences to be spoken, increases in loudness).
Inhalation and exhalation occur smoothly and rhythmically, approximately fourteen to seventeen times per minute.	Inhalation occurs quickly between phrases. About 1/6 of our time is spent taking in air as we speak. Exhalation is generally slow and irregular. About 5/6 of our time is spent in letting air out.

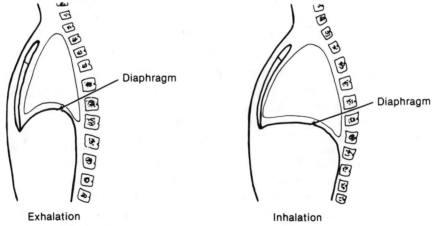

Exhalation   Inhalation

Figure 2.6.   Diagram showing changes in thoracic cavity during breathing and positions of the diaphragm

In breathing for speech, then, an easy and flexible control will help us achieve maximum effectiveness for voice production. But is there any method of breathing which enables us to acquire the proper degree of control? Often we hear that "diaphragmatic breathing" is the correct way to breathe. It would be impossible, of course, to breathe normally without the diaphragm, at least as far as inhalation is concerned. Actually, there are four general types of breathing, and the diaphragm functions to some degree in each type:

1. Clavicular-Shoulder (Extreme Upper Chest)
   Most of the movement consists of raising and lowering the collarbone and shoulders during the inhalation-exhalation cycle.
2. Thoracic-Chest
   Most of the expansion-contraction activities occur in the upper portion of the chest. (If one were to use a tape measure to determine the extent of expansion-contraction, the measurements would be made as high under the armpits as possible.)
3. Medial-Central
   Most of the expansion-contraction activities occur in the area of the lower ribs or the lower part of the thorax. (Measurements would be made at the base of the breastbone or sternum.)
4. Abdominal-Diaphragmatic
   Most of the expansion-contraction activities occur in the abdominal area. (Measure the waistline.)

Of course, there are variations and modifications of these types, and many individuals with good speaking voices as well as many fine singers, actors, and professional speakers, often use combinations, especially of the last three types discussed. Any of these will most likely promote sensitivity, flexibility, ease, and comfortableness in the control of breathing. At the same time, it should be noted that none of the last three types will necessarily guarantee one a louder, a more audible, or a more pleasant voice.

Observation and research would indicate, however, that superior voices are found infrequently among individuals using a predominantly clavicular-shoulder type of breathing. This type does not provide for sensitivity or flexibility of control. (It should be noted that in certain extreme activities—the 100-yard dash and the Olympic swimming races—this kind of breathing supplements the other types under discussion. In doing this, the individual is able to take in even more oxygen.)

Under most circumstances, however, clavicular-shoulder breathing may impede the development of good voice. Here are some comparisons:

Clavicular-Shoulder Breathing	Thoracic-Chest / Medial-Central / Abdominal-Diaphragmatic } Breathing
Clavicular breathing is shallow rather than deep breathing. The movements of the upper chest are too slight to provide an adequate amount of air. There is rarely sufficient power or strength to sustain speech tones.	The control of the breath stream rather than the amount of air inhaled is of primary importance. Expansions and movements in these areas are more natural and unlabored. A greater ease of control is possible.
Inhalation may become too frequent. Speaking rhythm is apt to be jerky. The individual is forced to pause for breath too often and at places where phrases are incorrectly chopped into awkward, meaningless chunks.	Inhalations will generally be less frequent. The speaker does not have to gasp for breath. He can utter longer phrases and avoid jerky rhythms.
It promotes excessive tensions in the muscles of the throat and larynx. There is a marked degree of tension and constriction of the larynx, and this condition may lead to a harsh, unpleasant vocal quality.	If most of the expansion and movements are in or near the midregion of the body, the throat and larynx are likely to remain free of unnecessary tensions. (Experience has shown that if individuals have unpleasant voice quality and then change their breathing habits by eliminating clavicular breathing and adopting some kind of medial breathing, voice improvement generally results.)

These exercises will make you aware of the differences between efficient and inefficient breathing, and they will help you acquire efficient habits.

1. Stand comfortably erect and try each of the four methods of breathing, but deliberately exaggerate the movements involved.

   a. **Clavicular-Shoulder:** Get the feel of raising and lowering the collarbones and shoulders.
   b. **Thoracic-Chest:** Place your hand on the breastbone (sternum). Inhale deeply.
   c. **Medial-Central:** Place the palms of your hands against the lower ribs and breathe.
   d. **Abdominal-Diaphragmatic:** Place your hand below the lower ribs in front. Inhale. Exhale.

   Which of the four ways seem the most natural to you?

2. Try each of the four types of breathing again, but this time repeat the following sentences aloud with each kind of breathing:

   a. God made the country, and man made the town.
   b. All hope abandon, you who enter here.
   c. Those who want the fewest things are nearest the gods.
   d. Let your speech be better than silence, or be silent.
   e. The finger that turns the dial rules the air.
   f. To make a mountain of a molehill.
   g. Nothing great was ever achieved without enthusiasm.
   h. A bad beginning makes a bad ending.
   i. A woman's work is never done.
   j. People who make no noise are dangerous.
   k. Life is made up of marble and mud.
   l. Only for the happy man does the tree of life flower.

If you seem to be using any one or a combination of the three types mentioned in Exercise 1 (*b, c,* or *d*), your breathing habits are probably efficient. If you are using clavicular breathing, however, try to eliminate it. Exercises 3 and 4 will help you get rid of extreme upper chest breathing.

3. Place your hands on your upper chest with the thumbs aimed at the collarbone. Take a deep breath, and then count from 1 to 10. If you are aware of any pronounced upward movement of the shoulders, repeat the exercise and deliberately use the pressure of the hands to prevent this kind of movement. Repeat this procedure saying the months of the year: January through June, and then July through December.

4. Sit comfortably erect in an armless chair. Grab the bottom of the chair seat firmly. Your shoulders should not be able to rise. Inhale and exhale, concentrating on movements in or near the midregion of the body.

5. Repeat this procedure. As you do so: count from 1 to 10, and then say the months of the year. If you are still using clavicular breathing, practice Exercise 6, which follows, at home.

6. Lie flat on your back. Place your right hand on your abdomen and your left hand on the upper part of your chest. Breathe as naturally as possible. You will notice a slow and regular expansion and contraction of the area under your right hand and very little movement of the area under the left hand.

Exercises for general practice:

7. Stand comfortably erect and as you breathe, try to keep most of the movement in the center of the body. Place your hands on your waistline, the fingers extended to the front and the thumbs to the rear. Notice the general expansion in this area.

8. Place a book against your abdominal area below the ribs. Inhale. The expansion in this area should force the book out from 3/4 to 1 1/4 inches. Exhale. The contraction permits the book to go back in. Get the "feel" of the action.

9. With the book pressed against the abdomen, try the following. Again, make certain that most of the movement is in the middle of the body.
    a. Inhale slowly, hold the breath two or three seconds, exhale slowly.
    b. Inhale slowly, hold, exhale quickly.
    c. Inhale quickly, hold the breath for five or six seconds, exhale slowly.
    d. Inhale quickly, hold for five or six seconds, exhale slowly.
    e. Inhale quickly, hold for five or six seconds, exhale slowly.

10. Assume an easy standing position with the hands at the sides. Count silently to four on the inhalation and the same on the exhalation. Count to six on each phase of respiration. Continue prolonging the count until you are taking only three or four breaths a minute.

11. Repeat the previous exercise as you walk along the street, synchronizing the counts with the steps you take.

    We make sounds, of course, as we exhale. Thus it is especially important that we control the outgoing breath. Exhale frugally; that is, in a sense you must ration or dole out the breath. Breath must not be wasted. Do not allow air to escape before you start to make a sound or a word, between words or phrases, or within a word itself.

These exercises will help you acquire control over the flow of breath:

12. Hold the sound of *ah* as long as you can. Do not let any breath leak out before you start to make the sound. Try to keep the tone smooth and steady.

13. Repeat this procedure, but this time deliberately keep the ribs raised as long as you can, allowing the abdominal wall to come back in before the ribs are lowered. Work for an even steady *ah*.

14. Sustain *ah*, beginning quietly, and let the sound swell in loudness, but do not raise the pitch. Then diminish to as soft a tone as possible. Work for steadiness and easy control of tone.

15. Reverse this process, beginning loudly, then decreasing the loudness and once again increasing the loudness.

16. Take a deep breath and release it slowly, making the sound *s*. Keep it even and regular, free of jerkiness and bumpiness.

17. Try the same procedure with the sound *f*.

18. An interesting experiment: Hold a small, lighted candle about six to eight inches in front of the mouth. Sustain *s* and then try *f*. Keep the exhalation regular and constant. The flame should not flicker and certainly should not go out.

19. With the second hand of a watch to guide you, allow yourself approximately thirty-five seconds to count aloud to fifty. Now try it on one breath and be sure that you do not allow breath to escape between numbers.

20. You will notice that some words are relatively hissy, noisy, and wasteful of breath. The *s* in "six," the *th* in "thirteen," the *f* in "forty-four," for example, are apt to be offenders, especially if you allow too much breath to escape on these sounds. Now repeat Exercise 19, and avoid producing any "hissers." You will probably be able to increase your count.

21. Substitute the letters of the alphabet for numbers. Try to say the alphabet twice on one breath.

22. Conserve your breath as you read the following. Each selection should be read on a single breath.
    a. He whom the gods favor dies in youth.
    b. Courage in danger is half the battle.
    c. His only fault is that he has no fault.
    d. For fools rush in where angels fear to tread.

e. He sleeps well who knows not that he sleeps ill.

f. Some persons make promises for the pleasure of breaking them.

g. Submit to the present evil, lest a greater one befall you.

h. Liquor talks very loudly when it gets loose from the jug.

i. We desire nothing so much as what we ought not to have.

j. Life is made up of sobs, sniffles, and smiles, with sniffles predominating.

k. I believe the future is only the past again, entered through another gate.

l. Let a fool hold his tongue and he will pass for a sage.

m. The worst use that can be made of success is to boast of it.

n. What men commonly call their fate is mostly their own foolishness.

o. A great deal of talent is lost in this world for the want of a little courage.

p. A community is like a ship; everyone ought to be prepared to take the helm.

q. Cold: Ailment cured in two weeks with a doctor's care, and in fourteen days without it.

On some occasions you may have to speak louder than you would when you are indulging in everyday chitchat with the person seated next to you or in a telephone conversation. Achieving adequate loudness is an important phase of voice production, and it will be discussed later in the book. In brief, however, when we find it necessary to increase our level of loudness, we are primarily increasing the breath pressure beneath the larynx. This means that the force and the power which produce loud, firm tones come from the muscles of breathing, mostly in the middle areas of the body, rather than from the muscles of the throat.

23. Repeat Exercise 14. As you increase the loudness, do not raise the pitch. Keep the pitch level constant.

24. Say the alphabet from A to J. Increase the loudness of each letter of the alphabet. Avoid tightening the throat, think of the support coming from the muscles of breathing, and check your pitch level. The final J should not be appreciably higher in pitch than the initial A.

25. Pretend that you are in a room large enough to seat about 100 people. Say the phrase, *Halt! Who goes there!* three times:

a. The first time, address it to the persons seated in the first row. They are 6-8 feet away from you.

b. The second time, speak to the people in the middle of the room: 20-25 feet from you.

c. The third time, speak to the people at the rear of the room: 40-50 feet from you.

As you say these, keep the throat relaxed, let the abdominal muscles give you the extra push, and do not let your pitch zoom upward.

26. Say the following briskly and forcefully, but keep the throat as relaxed as possible. Notice the sudden contraction of the abdominal muscles as you project the phrases.

a. Ha ha ha! Ho ho ho!

b. Help! Hey! Halt!

c. Stop! Go! Fast! Slow!

d. Ready! Aim! Fire!

e. Forward, march!

f. One! Two! Three!

g. All aboard!

h. Ship ahoy!

i. Rah! Rah! Rah!

j. Open in the name of the law!

k. Hands up!

l. To the rear, march!

m. Company, halt!

n. Right face!

o. Left face!

p. Stop, or I'll shoot!

q. Get set! Go!

r. Help! Help! Help!

s. On the double!

t. All ashore!

27. Read each of the following sentences three times using the procedure described in Exercise 25, sections *a*, *b*, and *c*.

a. It is not enough to do good; one must do it the right way.

b. The eye of each man sees but what it has the power of seeing.

c. Double, double, toil and trouble; fire burn and cauldron bubble.

d. Out, damned spot! Out, I say!

e. The great man is the man who does a thing for the first time.

f. Is life so dear, or peace so sweet, as to be purchased at the price of chains and slavery?

g. Oh, wind, if winter comes, can spring be far behind?

h. Look to this day! For it is life, the very way of life!

i. Gold! Gold! Gold! Gold! Bright and yellow, hard and cold!

j. 'London!' It has the sound of distant thunder.

Breathing and Speech Pauses

In speaking aloud we break up our sentences into phrases, and we generally inhale during the pauses between phrases.

What is a phrase? A phrase is a group of words expressing a thought unit—an idea or occasionally several ideas. The length and variety of pauses and phrases are determined by several factors. These will be considered in chapter 5. But one of the things which determines how often we must pause is our need for breath, and we shall consider that factor now.

We must, of course, pause often enough so that we can replenish our breath supply and always keep a reserve supply in the lungs while speaking. Otherwise, we may find ourselves gasping for breath in the middle of a phrase, with the last two or three words of the phrase sounding like a series of strained grunts.

It has been suggested that from seven to fourteen words per phrase is ideal, but we should remember that as we read material aloud, our phrases tend to contain more words and syllables than our nonread speeches.

For the reader, punctuation is an excellent guide to the eye, but we do not necessarily pause and breathe every time the eye comes across a comma, semicolon, dash, or period. As a matter of fact, some phrases are not set off for us at all with punctuation marks. Periods and semicolons, however, are often a better indication of a natural place to pause than commas.

28. Read the following. Pause briefly and breath wherever you see a comma:

a. A B C D E F , G H I J K L

b. A B C D E F , G H I J K L , M N O P Q R

c. A B C D E F , G H I J K L , M N O P Q R , S T U V W X

29. Repeat the preceding exercise. Pause briefly, but do not breathe at the commas.

30. Practice the following. Pause wherever you see two vertical lines. Breathe only when it is necessary for you to do so.

a. A drunkard: When he is best ‖ he is little worse than a man ‖ and when he is worse ‖ he is little better than a beast.

b. The difference between a rich man and a poor man is this ‖ the former eats when he pleases ‖ and the latter when he can get it.

c. If you want enemies, excel others ‖ if you want friends, let others excel you.

d. It is not the quantity of the meat ‖ but the cheerfulness of the guests which makes the feast.

e. Old friends are best ‖ King James used to call for his old shoes; they were easiest on his feet.

f. That which is good to be done, cannot be done too soon ‖ and if it is neglected to be done early, it will frequently happen that it will not be done at all.

g. Man is the only creature endowed with the power of laughter ‖ is he not the only one that deserves to be laughed at?

h. The atomic bomb in the hands of a Francis of Assisi would be less harmful than a pistol in the hand of a thug ‖ what makes the bomb dangerous is not the energy it contains ‖ but the man who uses it.

i. The superior man understands what is right ‖ the inferior man understands what will sell ‖ The superior man loves his soul; the inferior man loves his property ‖ The superior man always remembers how he was punished for his mistakes; the inferior man always remembers what presents he got ‖ The superior man is liberal toward the opinions of others ‖ but does not completely agree with them ‖ the inferior man completely agrees with the opinions of others ‖ but is not liberal toward them ‖ The superior man is firm, but does not fight; he mixes easily with others, but does not form cliques ‖ The superior man blames himself ‖ the inferior man blames others ‖ The superior man is always candid and at ease with himself or others; the inferior man is always worried about something ‖ A man who has committed a mistake and doesn't correct it ‖ is committing another mistake.

31. Study the following selections, marking them for breathing pauses, and read them aloud:

a. Chang and Chung had strolled onto the bridge over the river when the former observed, "See how the small fish are darting about! This is the happiness of the fish."

"You not being a fish yourself," said Chung, "how can you know the happiness of the fish?"

"And you not being I," retorted Chang, "how can you know that I do not know?"

"If I, not being you, cannot know what you know," urged Chung, "it follows that you, not being a fish, cannot know the happiness of the fish."

"Let us go back to your original question," said Chang. "You asked me how I knew the happiness of the fish. Your very question shows that you knew that I knew. I knew it, from my own feelings, on this bridge." [Chuangtse]

b. A great ox, grazing in a swamp, put down his foot on a family of young frogs, and crushed most of them to death. One escaped and ran off to his mother with the terrible news. "Mother," he said, "you never saw such a big beast as the beast that did it."

"Big?" said the foolish old mother frog. She puffed herself to twice her size and said, "Was it as big as this?"

"Oh, much bigger," said the little frog.

She puffed herself some more, and said, "As big as this?"

"Oh, no, Mother, much, much bigger."

So she puffed again, and puffed so hard that suddenly with a great POP! she burst into little pieces. Moral: Small men can destroy themselves by striving to be bigger than they are. [Aesop]

Our final objective is an easy and natural control of breathing. This means that we should not be consciously aware of how or when we breathe as we read, speak in class, or as we talk to people. In order to reach that goal, however, we must first put together and practice several techniques:

Breath control must be coordinated with phonation (the making of speech sounds). It must never interfere with phonation.

Breath control must be coordinated with phrasing. Inhalation must be accomplished quickly when a pause permits.

The outgoing breath must be used economically and not wasted. An adequate and easy support for the tone, in short or in long phrases, in relatively quiet or relatively loud passages, must be achieved.

32. Practice the following selections. At first you may find it necessary to concentrate on synthesizing or putting together the techniques suggested in the foregoing paragraphs. Continue practicing until you have established an effortless and supple control of your breathing processes, and you find yourself concentrating on the material rather than the techniques.

a. In the central part of the churchyard of Nigg there is a plain, undressed stone, near which the sexton never ventures to open a grave. A wild tale connects the strange stone with a merchant fleet of three vessels which eighty or a hundred years ago lay in a nearby port. The plague, the story goes, was brought to the place by one of the vessels, and one day it was seen flying along the ground in the shape of a little yellow cloud. The whole country was alarmed, and groups of people were to be seen on every hilltop, watching with anxious horror the progress of the little cloud.

They were relieved from their fears, however, by a clever citizen of Nigg, who, having provided himself with an immense bag of linen, fashioned somewhat in the manner of a huge balloon, cautiously approached the yellow cloud, and with a skill which could have owed nothing to previous practice, succeeded in enclosing the whole of it in the bag. He secured it by wrapping it up carefully, fold after fold, and then he fastened it down with pin after pin. As the linen gradually started to change color, as if in the hands of a dyer, from white to yellow, the brave fellow consigned it to the churchyard, where it has slept ever since. [Folk Tale]

b. On the first day of Christmas my true love sent to me a partridge in a pear tree.

On the second day of Christmas my true love sent to me two turtledoves, and a partridge in a pear tree.

On the third day of Christmas my true love sent to me three French hens, two turtledoves, and a partridge in a pear tree.

On the fourth day of Christmas my true love sent to me four calling birds, three French hens, two turtledoves, and a partridge in a pear tree.

On the fifth day of Christmas my true love sent to me five gold rings, four calling birds, three French hens, two turtledoves, and a partridge in a pear tree.

On the sixth day of Christmas my true love sent to me six geese alaying, five gold rings, four calling birds, three French hens, two turtledoves, and a partridge in a pear tree.

On the seventh day of Christmas my true love sent to me seven swans aswimming, six geese alaying, five gold rings, four calling birds, three French hens, two turtledoves, and a partridge in a pear tree.

On the eighth day of Christmas my true love sent to me eight maids amilking, seven swans aswimming, six geese alaying, five gold rings, four calling birds, three French hens, two turtledoves, and a partridge in a pear tree.

On the ninth day of Christmas my true love sent to me nine ladies dancing, eight maids amilking, seven swans aswimming, six geese alaying, five gold rings, four calling birds, three French hens, two turtledoves, and a partridge in a pear tree.

On the tenth day of Christmas my true love sent to me ten lords aleaping, nine ladies dancing, eight maids amilking, seven swans aswimming, six geese alaying, five gold rings, four calling birds, three French hens, two turtledoves, and a partridge in a pear tree.

On the eleventh day of Christmas my true love sent to me eleven pipers piping, ten lords aleaping, nine ladies dancing, eight maids amilking, seven swans aswimming, six geese alaying, five gold rings, four calling birds, three French hens, two turtledoves, and a partridge in a pear tree.

On the twelfth day of Christmas my true love sent to me twelve drummers drumming, eleven pipers piping, ten lords aleaping, nine ladies dancing, eight maids amilking, seven swans aswimming, six geese alaying, five gold rings, four calling birds, three French hens, two turtledoves, and a partridge in a pear tree. [Traditional]

c. Once upon a time in a small village there was a haunted house. The house had been haunted about ten years, and several people had tried to stay there all night. But before midnight they would be scared out by the Haunt.

The local preacher decided to investigate and he went to the house. He built a good fire, lit a lamp, and sat there reading the Bible. Then all at once, just before midnight, he heard something walking back and forth in the cellar. Then it sounded as if somebody was trying to scream but got choked off. Everything was quiet for a few seconds, and then he heard steps coming up the cellar stairs. He watched the door to the cellar, and the steps kept coming closer and closer. Step! Step! Step! Closer and closer. Step! Step! Step! It was right at the door. The preacher froze. He saw the doorknob turn. The door creaked open. The preacher jumped up and dropped his Bible. "Who are you? What do you want?" he shouted.

She came straight to him and took hold of his coat lapels. She was about twenty years old. Her hair was torn, and the flesh was dropping off her face so that he could see the bones underneath. She had no eyeballs but there was sort of a strange, blue light back in her eyesockets. She started talking in a voice that sounded like a howling wind. She told the preacher how her lover had killed her for her money, and had buried her in the cellar. She said if he'd dig up her bones and give her a Christian burial she could rest. Then she commanded him to take the end joint of the little finger of her left hand, and lay it in the collection plate in church next Sunday, and he'd find out who it was that had murdered her.

"After that," said the Haunt, "come back to this house once more, and I will tell you where my money is hidden, and you can give it to the church." The Haunt sobbed and seemed to sink through the floor.

The preacher found her bones and buried them in the churchyard. The next Sunday he put the fingerbone in the collection plate, and when a certain man happened to touch it—it stuck to his hand. The man jumped up, rubbed and scraped and tore at the bone trying to get it off, and then he started to scream. He confessed to the murder, and they took him to jail.

After he was hanged, the preacher went back to the house at midnight and the Haunt's voice told him to dig under the hearthrock. He did, and found a big sack of money. And where that Haunt had taken ahold of his coat lapels, it looked as if the print of her bony fingers had burned right into the cloth. It never did come out. [Folk Tale]

Assignment 1 (See suggested Checklist for this assignment)

For home practice, select any of the preceding exercises which you feel will be particularly helpful to you. In future meetings of the class you will be checked individually to see if you are acquiring efficient breathing habits.

Also, prepare and practice material to be read in class. Prose is almost always preferable to poetry for this kind of an assignment. (It is for most assignments.) Select interesting material. You will do a better job with something you genuinely enjoy. You will also elicit a better response from your listeners, and this too may help you perform more effectively. A short, short story, a folk tale, or a cutting from a delivered speech are suggested. Work for a natural, inconspicuous, and effective control of the breathing processes.

Suggested Checklist for Assignment 1

As you practice you may want to work with this checklist. Listen carefully to yourself, perhaps watch yourself in a mirror as you read. If it is feasible, get a classmate or a friend to observe and listen to you, too. Eventually your goal will be to have a check mark in the **Yes** column for each category.

(Optional: Perhaps your instructor will want to use the checklist to evaluate you during your classroom presentation.)

	Yes	No
Maintains alert, comfortably erect posture.		
Upper chest and shoulders relatively motionless.		
Most expansion-contraction activities occur in medial areas of body.		
Inhalation is silent, quick, unobtrusive.		
Avoids tense, harsh, unpleasant vocal quality which may result from clavicular, upper-chest breathing.		
Avoids running out of breath in the middle of a word or phrase.		
Avoids overbreathing: taking in too much breath, taking too much time to inhale.		
Conserves breath: avoids breath leaks before or after sounds or during pauses.		
Conserves breath: avoids breath leaks on such sounds as *s, sh, th, f.*		
Coordinates phrasing and breathing so that the material is meaningful, natural, and interesting.		

Additional comments or suggestions:

Class Discussion: The Sound of Voice

(Use this page and the next one for note-taking. You will find a voice quality analysis chart on pp. 265-66 and you may find it helpful to you as you begin your work in this unit.)

The Sound of Voice 3

Is my voice pleasant to listen to?

Mr. Robert Merrill of the Metropolitan Opera, and Frank Sinatra and Dean Martin of less Olympian heights have at least one thing in common: each of them is a baritone. Yet, if each of them made recordings of "America, the Beautiful" and sang it in the same key, few of us would confuse one singer with the other.

Likewise, if a trumpet player, a violinist, and a saxophonist played middle C and sustained the tone for the same length of time and at the same level of loudness, we would have no problem in recognizing which was which. And so it is that if a close friend calls us on the phone, we can generally identify him at once. There is a warmth, a richness, a pleasantness about his voice. Another friend, however, has a rather hard and brassy quality. Still another has a hoarse, raspy quality, and a fourth friend who calls us has a breathy, fuzzy, whispery voice.

All of these terms help us identify quality or, as we occasionally say, the texture, tone color, or timbre.

> *Quality, then, is the characteristic of a tone which may distinguish it from another tone having approximately the same pitch, duration, and loudness.*

In short, quality is the aspect of voice that causes us to judge or rate a voice as pleasant or unpleasant.

Personality is many things, of course, but certainly part of our acceptance or rejection of other people depends on how they sound. People we respond favorably to often have pleasant voices. The people we avoid may possibly have voices that jar us or "get on our nerves." The voice can often be a reliable index of character. The world of movies, radio, and TV has insisted on this point so emphatically that we have come to associate a certain type of voice with a certain type of individual. We see a timid, anemic-looking character—Charlie Brown or Don Knotts—and we more or less expect a thin, mousy little voice to come out of him. We watch Jackie Gleason or Telly Savalas characterize an aggressive loud-mouth, and we expect a gruff and raucous voice.

There are certainly exceptions, but we must remember that we are constantly being judged by how we sound. Our voice quality can be an asset or a liability to us. First impressions, right or wrong, are still highly persuasive. Certain aspects of vocal quality cannot be changed, but some aspects of quality can be substantially improved, and it is with these that we are concerned.

Two things determine quality:

1. The production of the original tone by the vocal folds (phonation).
2. The process of selection, reinforcement, and enrichment of this tone by the resonators (throat, mouth, and nasal cavities).

We are all interested in developing a pleasing and agreeable voice quality. We are already aware, however, that our voice is partly a reflection of our personality: our physical vitality and our emotional balance and well-being. Specifically, the vocal mechanism is an integrated and not an isolated part of our bodily structure. In other words, things which affect us mentally or physically may also affect, directly or indirectly, our speech processes. Simply stated, good mental and physical health are generally necessary before we can produce effective voice. Poor or inadequate voice may be promoted by flabby or unsatisfactory mental and physical health.

Most of us are blessed with good health. Does it follow, then, that most of us should also be blessed with "pleasant" speaking voices? Oddly enough, an individual might be in the "pink" of health but still be, as far as voice quality is concerned, the owner of a voice which is quite irritating and annoying to others. What is happening in this case?

In the first paragraph of this chapter we described four hypothetical voices. To select two examples, one voice was described as hard and brassy, another one as having a hoarse, raspy quality. Let's assume that both young men are in excellent health. Why, then, do they make vocal sounds which may arouse unfavorable responses or reactions in others?

It may have something to do with tension and strain. There are occasions which make any of us tense.

The football player who fails to score the extra point after the touchdown, later in the showers, complains that he "got all tense." On the following Monday morning he gets up in front of his speech class and explains what happened to him on Saturday afternoon. But he may "get all tense" here, too, and all of a sudden his voice breaks, and for an embarrassing moment or two, he sounds like the boy soprano he used to be. On his way back to his seat, he mumbles something about stage fright.

Some varieties of tension and stage fright are, fortunately, temporary, and even though they interfere with performance we will bypass them for a short discussion of a related variety which is less temporary.

We have all heard the advice to "let go" or "relax completely." Either one of them is impossible. If we did not have some muscular tension, we could not walk, talk, or kick a football. The well-meaning individuals who give such advice really mean: "Relax those muscles not needed to perform your task," or "Try to get rid of unnecessary tension in those muscles not needed to perform your task."

Part of the difference between the experienced professional and the inexperienced novice may well be the ability to distinguish between what is necessary and unnecessary in tension. The student of voice, consequently, is concerned with freeing himself from undue or abnormal tensions which hamper voice improvement, and such tensions are present in most of us—to a relative degree, of course. He is concerned with finding the right kind of relaxation, but he does not confuse relaxation with inertia or laxness. He knows that relaxation is selective, conscious and controlled.

You cannot isolate and then relax the relatively small muscles of the vocal mechanism if old bodily hypertension (excessive tension) persists. Furthermore, the large muscles of the body are easier to get at and relax than the smaller ones, so it is with these that we begin:

1. Stand comfortably erect. Deliberately tense the larger muscles of the body and then let go. Repeat several times this pattern of muscular contraction and tenseness followed by short periods of relative relaxation.

2. While you are standing, have somebody raise one of your arms slowly and then release it. There should be no resistance, and the arm should fall limply to the side. Repeat this procedure, but this time offer some resistance while keeping the rest of the body relaxed. Gradually relax the resisting arm.

3. Sit erect. Tense the body as completely as you can. Then relax, allowing the head to fall forward and the arms to dangle loosely at the sides.

Try Exercise 4 at Home

4. Select a quiet, comfortable room and assume a reclining position, face up, on a sofa or bed. Be as mentally relaxed as possible. (Some individuals find a background of quiet music helpful. Others prefer to relive a previously relaxing experience.)

   a. Stretch and yawn. The stretching should be intense, but the yawning should be gentle.
   b. Deliberately tense the larger muscles of the body and then let go. Repeat several times this pattern of muscular contraction and tenseness followed by relatively complete relaxation.
   c. Lie on the left side and rotate the right shoulder slowly and tensely. After a few seconds relax the shoulder and continue to rotate it.
   d. Repeat this procedure, lying on the right side and rotating the left shoulder.
   e. Slowly and tensely flex the right leg and raise it until the knee touches the shoulder. Then relax and let the leg fall limply.
   f. Repeat this procedure with the left leg.
   g. Extend the right arm rigidly into the air. Relax it and let it fall limply.
   h. Repeat this procedure with the left arm.
   i. Repeat Exercises b through h several times until you are able to differentiate clearly between tension and relaxation.

The following exercises are specifically designed to help you relax the sound-producing mechanisms:

5. Stretch the neck forward and downward, deliberately tensing the jaw and neck muscles. Let your head drop forward so that your chin touches the chest. Move your head slowly to your right shoulder, to the rear, to the left shoulder and forward to the chest again. Rotate the head in this manner several times, maintaining muscular rigidity and tightness.

6. Repeat this procedure, but now as you rotate the head, gradually begin to relax the jaw and neck muscles. When the head is rotated to the rear, you will notice that the mouth is partly open and the jaw relaxed.

7. Continue rotating the head in as relaxed a manner as possible, but take your hand and move the jaw easily back and forth and then up and down, making the sound of ah. Drop the head forward, then shake it from side to side, letting the jaw flop back and forth.

8. Start an easy and gentle yawn, but finish with a quiet and sustained sigh.

   a. Repeat, substituting ah for the sigh.
   b. Say the following as though sighing. The vowel sounds should be prolonged:

   aw-haw-arm-cot-caw-maw-palm-tall-up-mush-mum-sup-fun

9. The following selections may help you relax. Read them quietly, easily, and slowly. Prolong the vowel sounds slightly. You will note that most of them in the following material are easily produced sounds. They require a minimum of tension in the throat and tongue. Try to concentrate on a general feeling of laxness and ease.

   a. No seed shall perish which the soul hath sown.
   b. God is our refuge and strength, a very present help in trouble.
   c. Sadness is not a sin, but no sin hardens the heart so much as sadness.
   d. Death's but a path that must be trod, if man would ever pass to God.
   e. As a well-spent day brings happy sleep, so a life well used brings happy death.
   f. The Lord is in His holy temple; let all the earth keep silence before Him.
   g. Life's a short summer—man a flower; he dies, alas, how soon he dies!
   h. The night is already advanced, and we must obey night, which sets a limit for the works of men.
   i. Run, if you like, but try to keep your breath; work like a man, but don't be worked to death.
   j. Whenever a man has become a spirit he does not know that he has died, but believes that he is in the same body that he had in the world.
   k. If I must die I will encounter darkness as a bride and hug it in my arms.

l. God dwells wherever man lets Him in.

m. Lord, make me to know mine end, and the measure of my days, what it is, that I may know how frail I am.

n. Happiness settles the spirit, but sorrow drives it into exile.

o. Men resemble the gods in nothing so much as in doing good to their fellow creatures.

p. One was asked, "What is hell?" And he answered, "It is heaven—that has come too late."

q. The best way to know God is to love many things.

r. God listens not to your words save when He himself utters them through your lips.

s. Oh, Lord, support us all the day long, until the shadows lengthen and the evening comes, and the busy world is hushed, and the fever of life is over, and our work is done. Then in thy mercy grant us a safe lodging, and a holy rest, and peace at last.

t. The Lord is my shepherd; I shall not want. He makes me lie down in green pastures; he leads me beside still waters. He restores my soul; he leads me in paths of righteousness for his name's sake. Even though I walk through the valley of the shadow of death, I fear no evil; for thou art with me. Thy rod and thy staff they comfort me. Thou preparest a table before me in the presence of my enemies; thou anointest my head with oil. My cup overflows. Surely goodness and mercy shall follow me all the days of my life, and I shall dwell in the house of the Lord forever.

Resonance

A popular daytime TV program recently presented a fascinating experiment in sound. The audience was shown three musical instruments: a bassoon, a cello, and a trombone. Then we listened as each of three musicians played a simple tune, "Twinkle, Twinkle, Little Star," on his instrument. At once we were struck with the great dissimilarities of quality: the growling bassoon, often used by composers for comic effects; the rather plaintive cello with its husky richness; and the brassy trombone, alternately brilliant and mellow.

The commentator then asked the audience to listen to a series of four special recordings of each instrument playing the same tune. The sound, he added, had been tampered with. As we listened to the first of these recordings, it was easy to tell that the bassoon had lost some of its growl, but it still sounded like a bassoon. The cello and the trombone, respectively, had lost some of their huskiness and brilliance, but not their identity. But when we arrived at the fourth and final recording, the three instruments had not only lost all traces of their identifying characteristics, they sounded exactly alike! What had happened here? In the first of the special recordings, a number of overtones had been eliminated. In recordings 2, 3, and 4, more and more of the overtones had been erased until only the fundamental remained.

Now, let's look again at the cello. As the cellist draws his bow over a string he sets it into vibration. If the full length of the string is vibrating at a frequency of about 256 cycles per second, the ear interprets the resulting sound as the pitch of middle C. Tone which results from vibration over the full length of the string is known as the **fundamental**. It is the fundamental which tells us the pitch of the note. However, not only does the cello string vibrate over its full length, it also vibrates simultaneously in halves, thirds, fourths, or fifths. Each of these vibrating segments produces a pitch which is higher and weaker than the fundamental. These tones are known as **overtones** or **partials**. Thus, the tone we actually hear is not a pure, simple, or single tone, but it is a composite type of tone, a blending together of a fundamental and overtones.

The vocal folds, being far more complex than a cello string, produce a greater number of different simultaneous vibrations. The number and the relative strength of the overtones in combination with the fundamental help us identify voices as well as instruments. As a simple example, very few overtones are produced in the piccolo or flute. Their tone quality is relatively pure and simple. But that sometime musical clown, the bassoon, produces a good many overtones, and its tone quality is much more complex and difficult to describe.

We have used the phrase "blending together." Resonance has something to do with this process of blending, but it likewise involves several other interesting factors.

If we remove a string from the body of the cello and stretch it tightly between two chairs, the world's finest cellist could produce only indifferent and feeble musical scratchings and scrapings. Or if you remove the reed mouthpiece of a saxophone and blow into it, the sound you now hear will be puny and wan. The sounding board could also be stripped from a piano, and you could still sit down and play. But the rich, lush tones will no longer be there, and your selection will sound as though it is being played on a series of tuned tin cans.

Unaided, sound-producing vibrators—the detached cello string, the saxophone reed and the piano without the sounding board—produce, as we have noted, sounds which are weak and ineffective. Some additional type of vibrator must be present to aid in reinforcing and enriching the original tone. Similarly, the vocal folds obviously need the throat, mouth, and nasal cavities, and perhaps the chest. The cello string needs the body of the instrument. The piano keyboard and strings need their sounding boards.

Resonance, then, refers to this process of:

Reinforcement and amplification of sound.

The selection and emphasis (blending and modification) of particular groups of overtones. Different parts of the original tone are emphasized or built up, and other parts are damped or filtered out.

The enrichment of sound.

Reinforcement, *amplification*, and *enrichment* are three key words important to our understanding the resonating process. How are these brought about?

Sound begins with the vibration of the vocal folds in the larynx. The sound waves pass up through the cavities of the throat (pharynx), mouth (oral cavity), and the nose (nasal cavities). These three cavities are the human resonators (see fig. 3.1).

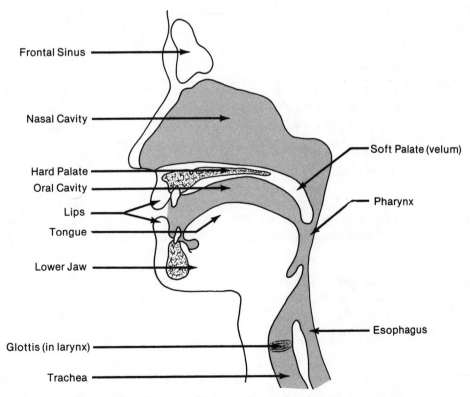

Frontal Sinus

Nasal Cavity

Soft Palate (velum)

Hard Palate
Oral Cavity

Pharynx

Lips

Tongue

Lower Jaw

Esophagus

Glottis (in larynx)

Trachea

Figure 3.1.   Section of head and neck showing resonance tract

Sound waves are reinforced or amplified by being reflected or bounced off the surfaces of the cavities approximately in the manner of a megaphone. Simultaneously the sounds are being enriched and modified by changing the size, shape, and surface tensions of the throat and mouth. A person may also use or completely close off the nasal cavities. All of these changes and adjustments produce characteristics which we identify as the individual's voice quality.

The Pharynx (Throat) as a Resonator

Description

A tubelike muscular passageway, about 5 inches long with soft side and rear walls, extending from the tops of the larynx and the esophagus to the cavity behind the nasal passage. The upper portion of the pharynx connects with the oral and nasal cavities.

Adjustability

The pharynx may be shortened or lengthened slightly by raising or lowering the larynx. This may occur in swallowing. In speech, the larynx tends to rise on higher pitched tones and shorten the pharynx. This activity may result in an increased brightness of the resonated tone. The larynx depresses on lower pitched tones and lengthens the pharynx. This activity may result in an increased mellowness and richness of the resonated tones.

The pharynx may also be shortened by raising the velum against the back wall of the throat. The diameter can be altered by contracting or relaxing constrictor muscles which form the sides of the pharyngeal cavity. The action of the muscles also influences surface textures and tensions.

Function as a Resonator

A tight, constricted throat and tense, rigid walls will possibly emphasize and give prominence to the higher overtones and frequencies. The resulting vocal quality may be strident, harsh, or metallic.

Openness of throat, relative relaxation of the constrictor muscles, walls, and surfaces will emphasize and give prominence to the fundamental and lower overtones and damp out some of the higher overtones and frequencies. The resulting vocal quality may be relatively mellow, full, and rich.

A word of caution: When the throat seems to be open and relaxed, the walls are somewhat soft and spongy. For certain types of voice, it is entirely possible that there can be too much relaxation of the constrictor muscles. If too many of the overtones are blotted out or absorbed, the voice will lack a certain degree of brilliance and thrust. Specific problems and exercises will be presented later in the chapter.

The Oral Cavity (Mouth) as a Resonator

Description

This cavity is the most variable in size and shape of all the resonance chambers. It is bounded at the front by the lips and the jaws, below by the tongue, the sides of the mouth, the hard and soft palates.

Adjustability

The size may be increased or decreased by lowering or raising the tongue or jaw. The cavity may also be altered by many movements of the tongue which can be lengthened, shortened, thickened, thinned, broadened, arched, or grooved. The shape and size of the mouth opening can be determined by the position of the lips: closed, spread, or rounded, as in puckering.

Function as a Resonator

As the most versatile and the largest cavity resonator, the mouth acts as a "balancer" or a kind of "coordinator" for the other resonators. The hard palate (arched roof of the mouth) probably acts as an efficient reflector of sound. The soft, inner surfaces of the cheeks, the lips and the tongue, on the other hand, may have an absorbing or damping effect on certain overtones. The possibilities and the combinations are as complex as they are infinite. The vowel sounds, of course, are produced by the changing size and shape of the oral cavity. If you will compare the vowel [i] in *eat* with the vowel [a] in *calm* you will feel the difference in your mouth. Most likely the vowel in *eat* makes greater use of certain overtones than the vowel in *calm*.

In a selective capacity, then, the oral cavity acts to accentuate particular overtones, which are primarily responsible for the distinguishing characteristics of the vowel sounds.

Nasal Cavity as a Resonator

Description

This cavity actually consists of two cavities. The dividing wall of thin bone and cartilage between the nostrils extends back to where the velum is joined to the hard palate.

Adjustability

The nostrils may be slightly dilated or contracted. (A famous Hollywood actress of some years back was noted for her nostril "flaring" in her highly emotional scenes.) The action of the velum can close off the rear or posterior opening of the nasal chambers.

Function as a Resonator

It is the least versatile resonator, and is primarily responsible for resonating [m, n, and ŋ]. Its total contribution to resonance is somewhat limited.

Other Resonators

If you sing or speak on a low tone, you can easily feel vibrations in your ribs and chest. Occasionally, public speakers, teachers of voice, and actors like to talk about "chest" resonance. However, the cushioning effect of flesh, tissue, and muscles, not to mention clothing, probably diminishes considerably the effectiveness of the chest as a resonator.

It is also possible that the facial bones are set into forced vibration by the action of the vocal folds. The terms "head" or "sinus" resonance are not uncommon, but here again it is unlikely that bones of the forehead or the sinuses themselves contribute significantly to the resonating process.

Both Donald Duck and Walter Cronkite have resonance in their voices but, and we may all be quite thankful, Mr. Cronkite's voice quality is vastly different from that of the famous cartoon character. Donald's voice, in reality, emanates from the throat of a quite human and unducklike gentleman, Clarence Nash, who is the voice of many cartoon characters—human and animal. Mr. Nash and Mr. Cronkite initiate fundamentals and overtones with their vocal folds, of course, and in both instances, the process of resonation selects, reinforces, amplifies, and enriches the fundamentals and overtones. Therefore, we shouldn't say that Mr. Cronkite has more resonance than Donald. He probably has more of the right kind of resonance than Donald. Or we might say that Donald has too much of the wrong kind of resonance. Actually, Mr. Nash creates Donald's file-on-sandpaper voice by deliberately interfering with and impeding resonance. He bunches his tongue toward the rear of his mouth and tightens the constrictor muscles. (Mel Blanc, who is the voice of Bugs Bunny and many other cartoon characters, uses similar techniques.)

The sound which finally comes out of the mouths of Nash and Blanc, and which we hear, is identified not as resonance but as quality. In other words, then, quality is the hearer's interpretation of resonance. Thus, one voice does not have more quality than another, but a different type of quality.

How, then, do we develop the proper kind of resonance? Perhaps the Nash-Blanc techniques give us a clue. If bunching the tongue toward the rear of the mouth and tightening the constrictor muscles of the throat help to produce a disagreeable quacking or a comic animal voice, would certain other techniques, exactly opposed to those, help to produce a desirable quality? Very likely.

There are certain conditions which are necessary before we can successfully develop a satisfactory vocal quality:

The throat and mouth passageways must be relatively open, "selectively" relaxed and free of unnecessary tension.

The lips and the jaw and, of course, the tongue must be agile and flexible.

Tone must be "projected" to the front of the mouth.

Before you practice the following, repeat Exercises 1-9 at the beginning of the chapter.

To open and relax the throat and mouth passageways:

10. Deliberately tense the throat and jaw muscles and then swallow. Maintaining this extreme tension for a few seconds, say *ah*. What happens to your vocal quality?

11. Again, tense the throat muscles, pull your tongue back to the rear of your mouth in a bunched position. Say *ah*.

12. Now, for contrast, place the tip of your tongue behind the lower front teeth. Relax the jaw, and yawn gently as you inhale. With the same degree of easiness, say *ah* on exhalation.

13. Drop your head forward onto the chest. Say *ah*, hold it, and as you do so gently drop your head to the right shoulder, to the rear, to the left shoulder, and to the front again. Repeat.

14. Repeat Exercise 13, this time substituting *oo* as in "cool." The tongue muscles will be relatively tense for this sound, but try to sustain *oo* with the same degree of laxness you used to hold *ah*.

15. Repeat Exercise 12 but watch yourself in a mirror. Note that the back of your tongue lowers, the soft palate rises and the throat opens and widens. Try to achieve the same conditions without yawning.

16. Maintaining a feeling of relaxation and openness, say the following as though sighing:

who	now	odd	up	too	arm
how	moo	oh	mush	oat	cod
awl	rue	sue	call	loll	aunt
coo	saw	shawl	lass	sum	dot

17. Allow the jaw to remain open and as motionless as possible, and keep the tip of the tongue behind the lower front teeth as you say the following:

a. yah-yah-yah-yah-yah-yah-yah-yah

b. you-you-you-you-you-you-you-you

c. yoh-yoh-yoh-yoh-yoh-yoh-yoh-yoh

d. yea-yea-yea-yea-yea-yea-yea-yea

e. hah-hah-hah-hah-hah-hah-hah-hah

f. hoo-hoo-hoo-hoo-hoo-hoo-hoo-hoo

g. hoh-hoh-hoh-hoh-hoh-hoh-hoh-hoh

h. hey-hey-hey-hey-hey-hey-hey-hey

i. yah-you-yoh-yea-hah-hoo-hoh-hey

18. Sustain *ah* by beginning it softly and gradually increasing the loudness without permitting the throat to tighten.

19. Repeat the previous exercise, but after you have built up the *ah* in loudness, decrease it so that it once again becomes soft.

20. Sing *ah* and after a few seconds merge it with *oo* (as in "moon"). There should be no break between the vowels. Repeat several times.

21. Sustain *oo*, gradually melding it into *ah* and then into *oh*. Keep the throat relaxed.

22. Read the following with an open and relaxed throat, prolonging the vowels and diphthongs[1] slightly:

a. Come up into the hills, O my young love.

b. The river is a tide of moving waters.

c. Come to us through the fields of night.

1. A diphthong is a rapid blending of two vowel sounds within the same syllable. Examples: "i" in Mike; "ou" in out.

d. The lights were sown like flung stars.

e. The light was brown-gold like ground coffee.

f. Darkness melted over the town like dew.

g. The day was like gold and sapphires.

h. The blue gulf of the sky was spread with light, massy clouds.

i. The soft rays of the sun beat the gentle earth.

j. The hush of dawn washed the murmuring brook in glowing pink.

k. The quiet music of the stars nudged the heavy clouds of night.

l. Froth and foam trickled through the thawing mash.

m. The mountains were said to be in labor, and uttered the most dreadful groans. People came together far and near to see what birth would be produced; and, after they waited a considerable time, in expectation, out crept a mouse. [Aesop]

n. My beloved speaks, and said unto me, Rise up, my love, my fair one, and come away. For, lo, the winter is past, the rain is over and gone; the flowers appear on the earth; the time of the singing of birds is come, and the voice of the turtle is heard in our land; the fig tree putteth forth her green figs, and the vines with the tender grapes give a good smell. Arise, my love, my fair one, and come away. [The Song of Solomon]

To develop agility and flexibility of the lips and jaw:

23. Pronounce the following words, opening the mouth widely on the initial sounds:

opera	owl	always	hour	awl
awful	oddly	ouster	army	ought
almond	otter	office	ostrich	auk
auger	oxen	alder	object	ocelot

24. Read the following rapidly, exaggerating lip movements:

a. we-we-we-we-we-we-we-we

b. re-re-re-re-re-re-re-re

c. me-me-me-me-me-me-me-me

d. hoo-hoo-hoo-hoo-hoo-hoo-hoo-hoo

e. haw-haw-haw-haw-haw-haw-haw-haw

f. hoo-haw-hoo-haw-hoo-haw-hoo-haw

g. woo-woo-woo-woo-woo-woo-woo-woo

h. waw-waw-waw-waw-waw-waw-waw-waw

i. woo-waw-woo-waw-woo-waw-woo-waw

j. row-row-row-row-row-row-row-row

k. raw-raw-raw-raw-raw-raw-raw-raw

l. row-raw-row-raw-row-raw-row-raw

25. Exaggerate mouth opening, jaw activity, and lip agility in the following:

a. Will Oona wipe the auto wheel with the weak wobble?

b. We always keep our cool on weary holidays.

c. He who woos Augusta and weakens will wed in October.

d. The otter chased the owl into the alder trees.

e. Raleigh rowed the rubber raft for three hours.

f. Peter Wheeler put peanuts and grog on the wobbly hall table.

g. Oliver Alden fed an ounce of almond candy to the wounded auk.

h. Although cookouts are wonderful, they may widen your waistline.

i. If your cup runneth over, let someone else runneth your car.

j. "Ouch," said Otto as Oscar dropped the wood on his wrist.

    k.   William, the outlaw, wandered to the Southern outlands.

    l.   Who said we hauled the wood to Rome?

    m.   Oxen prefer green reeds to raw meat.

One often hears teachers of speech and singing, and play directors use such phrases as "Place your voice to the front," "Focus your tone," "Bounce your voice off the back wall of the room," or as one speech textbook would have it, "Focus your voice on a pencil held 18 inches in front of the mouth!"

From a purely scientific point of view you cannot "place, focus, or bounce" your voice. For that matter, ventriloquists do not "throw" their voices either. Nevertheless, such words should not be rejected for being "gimmicks." If we give some thought to these terms and phrases, they may possibly make us more conscious of using the forepart of the mouth. If we are told to "project" or "focus" the voice, we will generally respond by opening the mouth somewhat wider than we would normally do. Our articulation may also become more nimble.

As you drill, concentrate deliberately on projecting, directing, or aiming tones forward, against the hard palate, the upper gum ridge or the upper front teeth. This kind of drilling often proves helpful in giving us greater clarity of tone and brilliance of quality.

To project the tone to the front of the mouth:

26. Chant the following:

    a.   ee-ee-ee-ee-ee-ee-ee-ee

    b.   oh-oh-oh-oh-oh-oh-oh-oh

    c.   aw-aw-aw-aw-aw-aw-aw-aw

27. Repeat *b* and *c*, but this time try to give *oh* and *aw* the same frontal placement and brilliance of *ee*.

28. Say the second and third syllable in each group with the clarity and firmness of the first syllable:

    a.   wee-woh-waw   *d.*   lee-loh-law

    b.   mee-moh-maw   *e.*   bee-boh-baw

    c.   tee-toh-taw   *f.*   dee-doh-daw

29. Using the pattern suggested in Exercise 28, strive for brightness of tone and forward placement on the second and third sentences of each group. Keep the throat relaxed. Build up the vowel tones, but avoid any hint of harshness or stridency.

    a.   Edith, Edie, and Lee each kneeled as the bells pealed.

         Moe sowed oats, potatoes, and cocoa beans in Ohio locales.

         John Ball taught the tall squaw all the psalms.

    b.   Pete, the wee thief, seized the tea, wheat, and green beans.

         Opal, the goat, tried to eat the old, yellow hoe.

         Paul shot awkwardly at Lottie as she locked the stall.

    c.   We heard Dee sing "Green Grow the Lilacs" last evening.

         The rolled overalls and robes were soaked in oceans of soap.

         The fawn gnawed and pawed the auburn alder on the lawn.

    d.   The leaping sheep cleared the wheels and machines.

         Lois rowed the low oak boat with her own oar.

         Charles and Bart sobbed when the sauce was dropped on the shawls.

    e.   Please take a seat in the leaves under the tree.

         Crows and does hope to find oats in the snow.

         If you call the officer, all the outlaws will crawl under the hall.

    f.   The teacher eagerly agreed to seek the green seals.

         I know the odor of dough came through the open window.

         John sought to muzzle the jaw of the squawking hawk.

g. The wee bee fell into the green seaweed.
   Joe stole the load of gold from the local postman.
   Hello, Dolly had a long, profitable run on Broadway.

h. If he keeps the key we must steal the seal.
   Rowboats and showboats go slowly on oceans.
   Otto caught a cod off the bottom of Salt Lake.

i. Deacon Wheeler wrapped his feet in the pleated sheets.
   He soaped the rope hoping the boat would not float.
   The calm cop was lost in the smog and fog.

j. We feel that beans, beets, and cream are cheap.
   The Roman loaded his coat pockets with gold bowls.
   " 'God is not dead' is a mod proverb," said Rod.

30. As we attempt to improve our resonance and develop a pleasing vocal quality, we do not think of the resonators as functioning in isolation from each other. Actually, their functions must be coordinated and integrated. The throat, the mouth, the lips, and the jaw are all essential parts of the speech megaphone. The material below will give you the opportunity to blend together, to harmonize many of the processes involved in resonation. As you practice, keep reminding yourself of the necessity of maintaining:

Openness and selective relaxation of the throat and mouth passageways.

Easy flexibility of the jaw and lips.

Forward projection of tone.

a. No man's credit is as good as his money.
b. Time is a sort of river passing events, and strong is its current; no sooner is a thing brought to sight than it is swept by and another takes its place, and this too will be swept away.
c. Wealth hardens the heart faster than boiling water an egg.
d. It is not death, it is dying that alarms me.
e. If you pick up a starving dog and make him prosperous, he will not bite you. This is the principal difference between a dog and a man.
f. A bee is never as busy as it seems; it's just that it can't buzz any slower.
g. The words of his mouth were smoother than butter, but war was in his heart.
h. If one person tells thee thou hast ass's ears, take no notice; should two tell thee so, procure a saddle for yourself.
i. One should eat to live, not live to eat.
j. The evil man is but a child grown strong.
k. Art is the daughter of pleasure.
l. Some people are so fond of ill-luck that they run half way to meet it.
m. When people agree with me I always feel that I must be wrong.
n. Snobs talk as if they had begotten their own ancestors.
o. A nation which robs Peter to pay Paul can always depend on the support of Paul.
p. Wherever I climb I am followed by a dog called "Ego."

Is my voice pleasant to listen to?

We are repeating the question that was stated at the beginning of this chapter. A pleasant voice, we know, is one which impresses us as being agreeable, satisfying, or gratifying. Perhaps even such a weak word as "nice" helps to define the term.

Selective relaxation will help you develop a more pleasant voice. You have been given some suggestions and exercises to aid you. Developing the right kind of resonance will certainly improve the sound of your voice, and here, too, specific exercises have been presented as a guide.

It has been said that "a pleasing quality of voice consists in the absence of unpleasant characteristics."

It follows, then, that if the voice has an *unpleasant* quality, certain unpleasant characteristics must be present. There are terms and phrases which label and partially describe most of these unpleasant vocal traits, but before we can discuss them, we should point out that there is quite a bit of confusion and disagreement over the exact meaning of many of the terms.

Perhaps you remember a poem by John G. Saxe. It begins this way:

> It was six men of Indostan
> To learning much inclined,
> Who went to see the elephant
> (Though all of them were blind),
> That each by observation
> Might satisfy his mind.

The side of the elephant felt like a wall to the first blind man. Number two grabbed a tusk and declared the elephant to be a spear. To the others, the trunk suggested a snake, the knee felt like a tree, the ear and the tail resembled a fan and a rope.

And, as Mr. Saxe says later in his jingle, ". . . each was partly in the right, and all were in the wrong!"

Five hundred students in voice and diction classes listened to recordings of the voices of two well-known political personalities. They were asked to jot down a few words or phrases describing their impressions of the voices. The results are interesting.

The voice of a famous Republican was variously described as "oily," "pleasing," "cellolike," "slimy," "coarse," "hard," "metallic," and "whiny."

The voice of a prominent Democrat was variously described as "edgy," "warm," "muffled," "twangy," "brassy," "thin," and "rough."

Obviously such descriptive terms are rather subjective and influenced considerably by the political bias of the listener. What is "gravelly and growly" to one listener is possibly "vibrant and sonorous" to another. Yet, many of these terms help to describe or label a certain kind of voice. Specifically, there are approximately nine or ten terms which are widely used by teachers of speech and writers of speech textbooks.

The remainder of this chapter will use and discuss these terms. They are:

> Breathiness
> Glottal shock (or attack)
> Harshness (harsh-strident, harsh-throaty)
> Nasality
> Denasality
> Hoarseness (huskiness)

In the following discussions we are concerned only with the improper functioning of normal structures and mechanisms.

Note: Flexibility is desirable in the choice of assignments contained in this chapter. Assignments should be selected according to individual needs. If you can, listen to recordings of your voice. Your instructor, of course, will help you acquire an awareness of the "sound" of your voice. He will tell you if you have any specific problems pertaining to voice quality, and he will then recommend those units in this chapter which will most help you improve.

Important: If the exercises do not seem to help you eliminate a specific problem, or if you become aware of any vocal strain or discomfort, discontinue the drill material. You should seek professional assistance, and your instructor will advise you to contact a speech pathologist or a physician.

Breathiness

When we are not talking, the vocal folds are in a relaxed position. The triangular-shaped opening between them, as we remember, is called the glottis. However, if we do not bring the bands together closely enough, unused (unvocalized) breath escapes between them. The resulting tone is fuzzy, whispery and feather-edged. A breathy voice is not always an unpleasant one. Indeed, we notice with rather monotonous frequency the number of TV and radio actresses who apparently have cultivated this type of vocal cloudiness. It allegedly makes the voice sound "sexier." Raquel Welch frequently uses it. The late Marilyn Monroe was decidedly breathy. Zsa Zsa Gabor cultivates a breathy quality, and in the nonentertainment world, Jackie Onassis has this vocal smog. Breathiness is less common among male voices, although Lee Marvin often resorts to it.

However, a breathy voice is too often a comparatively weak voice. Without a mike it rarely carries well, and it is sometimes monotonous. It may also suggest inertia, laziness, or ill health in its possessor.

Overrelaxation or inadequate tension may be responsible for the failure of the vocal folds to be brought together completely during tone production. Exercises 31, 32, and 33 will make you more aware of muscle adjustments in the throat and help you acquire the right degree of tension.

31. Sit erect in your chair. Grip the sides of the chair and tense your body, especially the arms and shoulders. Say the pronoun "I" half a dozen times, using a strong voice. You should be able to feel tension in the throat, and hear a firmer tone quality. Repeat.

32. Following the procedure suggested in Exercise 31, substitute the following sentences for the "I."
    a. Eat an old apple.
    b. Eight eggs are under us.
    c. Ask Andy and Emil.
    d. Oh, it is eerie.
    e. Am I in India?

33. Stand erect. Extend your arms rigidly in front of you. Hold a fairly heavy book in your hands. Say "I" several times, and then repeat the short sentences in Exercise 32.

34. Read the following groups of sentences. As you read the first sentence in each trio, deliberately exaggerate and work for a breathy, fuzzy, and whispery quality. Read the second sentence somewhat louder and try to eliminate some of the featheriness. The third sentence should be read in a firm voice and all traces of fuzziness and cloudiness should be eliminated.
    a. Some people speak from experience. Others—from experience—don't speak.
       Hank said sadly, "Helen, run downstairs and heat up some stew."
       Alice and Albert added acorns to the old dough.
    b. Everything in the modern home is operated by switches except the children.
       When one is catching fish, a silent companion is best of all.
       "I am going downtown," yelled Abe to Una.
    c. Prayer does not change God, but changes him who prays.
       God defend me from myself.
       Eddie Bracken was great in the Broadway comedy, *The Odd Couple*.
    d. Trifles make perfection, and perfection is no trifle.
       Beware the fury of a patient man.
       We will never go into the Bear Bar again.
    e. There is a time of speaking and a time of being still.
       Let him speak now, or else forever hold his peace.
       Appreciate a sunset. Maybe even God has a need for approval.
    f. He had occasional flashes of silence that made his conversation perfectly delightful.
       He knew the precise moment when to say nothing.
       Mildred always burned magazines in yellow cans.

g.　He that spareth the rod hateth his son.

　　　Saint: a dead sinner revised and edited.

　　　Ronnie Reagan would rather not remember his old movies.

h.　Joy and sadness are as close as day and night.

　　　How awful to reflect that what people say of us is true.

　　　Oh, I eat oats, beans, and onions only in Autumn.

i.　He that falls in love with himself will have no rivals.

　　　Self-love is the greatest of all flatterers.

　　　Fun is like life insurance: the older you get, the more it costs.

35. Sustain each of the following vowel sounds on one breath. Begin the sound with an exaggerated breathy quality, and then without stopping, change to a moderately loud sound, and finally as you near the end of your breath, without stopping, shift to a strong and clear vowel:

a.　ah (ɔ) as in all

b.　oh (o) as in go

c.　eh (ɛ) as in end

d.　oo (ʊ) as in look

e.　uh (ʌ) as in up

f.　i　(ɪ) as in in

g.　oo (u) as in moon

h.　a　(æ) as in add

36. Using the vowel sounds listed in Exercise 35, try this pattern: Begin the sound at a very loud level, and then without stopping, change to a loud level. Again, without a break, shift to a medium loud level. Be sure that the third level is unbreathy.

37. Certain consonants are "breathier and hissier" than others: s, f, th, h, sh, k, p, and t. These are voiceless sounds; they are simply molded puffs of air, and in every respect, quite useful sounds. The problem arises if the individual carries over the breathy or hissy sound to an adjacent vowel or consonant. In the word "shall," for example, the feathery, whispery quality you rightfully produce on sh should not continue over and color the rest of the word: "-all." Exaggerate the underlined sounds as you say the following:

a.	say	latch	wish	calf	sick
b.	hill	hiss	him	kid	thin
c.	fad	should	fine	rope	tale

38. Repeat these words, but this time cut each underlined sound extremely short. Do not prolong them. As a reminder, a diagonal line dissects each consonant. Cut the words "in two."

a.	say	latch	wish	calf	sick
b.	hill	hiss	him	kid	thin
c.	fad	should	fine	rope	tale

39. Read the following word clusters at a moderately loud level. Keep each word entirely free of breathiness. The third and fourth words in each group need special attention.

a.　I-die-sigh-high

b.　am-dam-Sam-ham

c.　ow-bow-sow-how

d.　at-bat-fat-sat

e.　ope-dope-soap-hope

f.　aw-daw-saw-haw

g.　ale-bale-pale-sail

h.　air-bare-tear-hair

i.　eyed-bide-side-hide

j.　all-doll-Paul-hall

k.　Ike-bike-tyke-hike

l.　eat-meat-seat-heat

40. Whisper ah. Gradually add phonation to the whisper, and build it in loudness, but avoid breathiness.

41. Sustain the following sounds by beginning with a quiet, but nonbreathy tone and increasing the loudness of each.

ah　　　　　　　　oh　　　　　　　ee　　　　　　　oo　　　　　　　uh

42. Read each of the following sentences twice. The first time, exaggerate the breathiness. The second time, read the sentence in a firm voice and without breathiness.

a. What we don't understand we don't possess.

b. Husky Howard, standing on the cliff, held the huge horse by the harness.

c. Silence in times of suffering is the best.

d. Rich man down and poor man up—they're still not even.

e. A fool can no more see his own folly than he can see his ears.

f. The busy bee has no time for sorrow.

g. There is more pleasure in building castles in the air than on the ground.

h. It is good to be without vice, but it is not good to be without temptations.

i. I regard that man as lost, who has lost his sense of shame.

j. Where there's no shame before men, there's no fear of God.

k. I like a friend better for having faults that one can talk about.

43. Read aloud the following pairs of words. Allow the first word in each pair to be breathy, but attack the second word with firmness, keeping it free of breathiness. Exaggerate the difference.

hate-ate	think-ink	corps-ore	foe-oh
hill-ill	hale-ale	hand-and	hurl-earl
shawl-all	pail-ail	heel-eel	Sam-am
had-add	high-eye	harm-arm	thin-in
fin-in	told-old	sheer-ear	fat-at
sill-ill	hair-air	churn-urn	hope-ope

44. Repeat the words in Exercise 43, this time reversing the words in each pair, but eliminating breathiness on all vowels and diphthongs.

45. Read the following. Start as loudly as you can, but after you have read a line or two, gradually reduce the loudness until you attain a moderate level of volume, but one which is completely free of breathiness.

a. The boy called out "Wolf, Wolf!" and the villagers came out to help him. A few days afterward he tried the same trick, and again they came to his help. Shortly after this a wolf actually came, but this time the villagers thought the boy was deceiving them again and nobody came to his help. A liar will not be believed, even when he speaks the truth. [Aesop]

b. It is recorded of Samuel Butler that on his death bed he made it plain that he wanted to say something, and what he wanted to say was that he had written that life was ninety-nine percent chance and he wished to correct this figure to one hundred percent.

c. Nothing could have been more obvious to the people of the early twentieth century than the rapidity with which war was becoming impossible. And as certainly they did not see it. They did not see it until the atomic bombs burst in their fumbling hands.

d. If you have once planted a tree, you always have a peculiar interest in it. You care more for it than you care for all the forests of Norway or America. You have planted it, and that is sufficient to make it peculiar amongst the trees of the world.

e. Three characters can be found in a man about to perform a good deed: If he says, "I shall do it soon," his character is poor. If he says, "I am ready to do it now," his character is of average quality. If he says, "I am doing it," his character is praiseworthy.

f. Ideals are like stars: you will not succeed in touching them with your hands. But like the seafaring man on the desert of waters, you choose them as your guides, and following them, you will reach your destiny.

46. Read the following in clear, "solid" tone—one which is free of breathiness.

a. There is hardly anything in the world that some man cannot make a little worse and sell a little cheaper.

b. A man of sixty has spent twenty years in bed and over three years eating.

c. He serves his party best who serves the country best.

d. He too serves a certain purpose who only stands and cheers.

e. City Life: Millions of people being lonesome together.
  f. God has two dwellings: one in heaven, and the other in a meek and thankful heart.
  g. Americans are people with more time-saving devices and less time than any other people in the world.
  h. Just think of what God can make from something when He made this whole world from nothing.
  i. After you hear two eyewitnesses to an automobile accident, you're not so sure about history.
  j. We should often be ashamed of our very best actions, if the world only saw the motives which caused them.
  k. The hardest tumble a man can make is to fall over his own bluff.
  l. It is not only fine feathers that make fine birds.
  m. I like my universe as immense, grim, icy, and pitiless as possible.
  n. Grow up as soon as you can. It pays. The only time you really live fully is from thirty to sixty.
  o. The most important secret of salesmanship is to find out what the other fellow wants, then help him find the best way to get it.
  p. I expect to pass through this world but once. Any good therefore that I can do, or any kindness that I can show to any fellow creature, let me do it now. Let me not defer or neglect it, for I shall not pass this way again.
  q. Mahomet made the people believe that he would call a hill to him. The people assembled. Mahomet called the hill to come to him, again and again. And when the hill stood still he was never a whit abashed, but said, "If the hill will not come to Mahomet, Mahomet will go to the hill."
  r. He could open either door he pleased. If he opened the one, there came out of it a hungry tiger, the fiercest and most cruel that could be procured, which immediately sprang upon him, and tore him to pieces, as a punishment for his guilt. But if the accused person opened the other door, there came forth from it a lady, the most suitable to his years that his majesty could select among his fair subjects. So I leave it with all of you: Which came out of the opened door—the lady or the tiger?

Breathiness is often related to other voice problems. An inadequately loud voice, for example, is frequently breathy. If such is the case, the student should work with both problems conjointly, and the exercises in chapter 4 will be particularly helpful. A voice which is improperly pitched, especially one which is excessively low, may occasionally have a breathy quality. A bass-baritone voice coming from a feminine larynx perhaps enhances TV commercials and the like, but away from mikes and echo chambers it can be a surprisingly weak voice. There is a serviceable and agreeable pitch level for most of us, and if we use it, we will generally not be breathy. This is the optimum pitch level. See chapter 5.

Assignment 2 (See suggested Checklist for Assignment 2)

Select interesting material and as you practice it, use a relatively moderate level of loudness. Make your vowel sounds forceful and clear. Do not let breath escape between words or during pauses, and avoid "blasting" on voiceless sounds. When you perform before the class, you should be able to do so in a voice which is free of breathiness and vocal fuzz.

Glottal Shock

Read aloud the following sentences, inserting a slight pause between words:

  Andy and Opal invited Eve to the eerie island in April.

  Ask Ann and Arthur to open the old apple with an axe.

  The owl eyed the eel and ate the olive in August.

If you noticed a raspy little bark or a sharp, staccato click on the vowels at the beginning of each word, you probably have glottal shock (also known as glottal click or attack). In one sense, glottal shock is the opposite of breathiness, because the latter condition is often apparent if breath is allowed to escape before initial vowels are begun. In glottal shock, however, the glottis is closed firmly before the initial vowel is begun. The subglottal breath pressure builds up and the breath finally explodes its way through, blasting the vocal folds apart. Part of the problem in overcoming glottal shock, then, is a matter of timing and coordination. The air stream must begin to flow just as the vocal folds are ready to receive it.

Frequently, a tense, strained throat and larynx is responsible for glottal shock. If the vocal folds are closed completely and too tensely as phonation begins, the blast will generally be pronounced. As an example, tense your throat muscles and repeat the three sentences above, deliberately attempting to initiate each word with a glottal shock. Repeat this until you are able to hear this attack.

47. Begin *aw* on a whisper, but gradually begin phonation with the softest and gentlest tone you can achieve. Be especially careful when your voice changes from a whisper to vocal tone that there is no clicking sound or rasp. Hold the nonwhispered sound for 5 or 6 seconds and then repeat.

48. Repeat Exercise 47 using *oo, ee, uh, oh, aa* (as in ask).

49. Try the following, working for an easy, relaxed attack.

   a. ha-ha-ha-ha-ha-ha-ha-ha
   b. ho-ho-ho-ho-ho-ho-ho-ho
   c. he-he-he-he-he-he-he-he
   d. hi-hi-hi-hi-hi-hi-hi-hi
   e. hoo-hoo-hoo-hoo-hoo-hoo-hoo-hoo
   f. hay-hay-hay-hay-hay-hay-hay-hay

   Repeat these syllables, dropping the h.

50. As you drill with the following word pairs you will notice again that it is easy to produce a clickless vowel if it follows <u>h</u>. Try to keep this easy, "doing-what-comes-naturally" approach as you say the second h-less word in each pair.

Hal-Al	holly-Ollie	ham-am	hoe-owe
hold-old	hide-ide	hunk-unk	hair-air
hide-I'd	honk-onk	hope-ope	hun-un
hat-at	heat-eat	handy-Andy	had-add
hoop-oop	hall-all	howl-owl	heel-eel

51. As we read aloud or speak conversationally, we do not generally place pauses or breaks between each of the words. We naturally tend to link or blend words together in phrases or clusters. Read the words in the following columns, and do not permit a break between the words in the second column. For example, *an* and *apple* are blended together just as the syllables are in *Annapolis* in the first column. Avoid glottal shock as you read.

Annapolis	an apple	tiara	tee are
thrash	three ashes	trio	tree oh
theater	the account	beautify	be at
Newark	new ark	Neanderthal	knee and
trapeze	trap easy	meander	me and
triad	try and	Fiat	fie ate
iota	I owe it	neon	knee on
fiancé	fee aunts	beater	bee eater

52. Read each of the following phrases in one continuous and uninterrupted flow of breath. Be especially careful of the attack on the initial vowels.

a. in-an-open-alley
b. evening-April-air-is-elegant
c. add-an-owl-and-an-ogre
d. Enid-eats-onions-and-omelettes
e. oodles-of-acres-are-up
f. oats-and-apples-are-extra
g. I-am-in-agony
h. ill-in-old-office
i. odes-in-October-are-awesome
j. in-an-active-army

53. As you read the sentences below, pay close attention to the initial sounds and work for an easy, "shockless" attack. Do not chop off the words, but blend them together without interruption. (Note: Occasionally speakers and actors find a glottal attack useful in separating vowel sounds, as in "law and order" or "coordinate" and in giving greater emphasis and force to a vowel, as in "Why do *I* always have to be the one?" Used infrequently, the attack is effective.)

a. Adam, an excellent actor, sang an aria from an opera.
b. Oscar and Ella owed oats to their allies.
c. Accidents often occur in amateur athletics.
d. "The edict is awful," insisted Judge Isaac Evans.
e. Adolph and Aggie adored oysters anointed in olive oil.
f. We ought to oust owls from elm trees.
g. If Andy idolizes Eve, why didn't Irma accept Ike?
h. The idle oaf ignited the apple cart.
i. Emma asked if eggs and onions are enough.
j. Eagles' eyes and ears are all but invisible.
k. Eels and otters are agile under water.
l. The elderly author was outlawed in Akron, Ohio.

Assignment 3 (See suggested Checklist for Assignment 3)

Prepare material in which most of the words begin with vowels or diphthongs. You may use nonsense material. As you practice, link the words together, but be certain that the initial words are free of glottal shock.

Harshness

There seems to be general agreement that a harsh voice is one which is offensively noisy, grating, and strained. A breathy voice doesn't necessarily jar the listener, but a harsh voice can often "set the teeth on edge." Although harshness is frequently regarded as a defect of resonance, there are types which are associated with defective action of the folds. Harshness may be described as an unpleasant quality which results from excessive muscular tensions in the area of the throat. There is hypertension and constriction, not only within the larynx, but in the muscles and tissues which are adjacent to the larynx.

To proceed beyond those generalizations, we are apt to fall into a maelstrom of confusing terms, descriptions, and evasions. Therefore, in this textbook we will arbitrarily state that a harsh voice may be more specifically described as one which is either strident or throaty. A precise definition of those words is probably needed here, but instead, we have taken a peek into approximately thirty other speech textbooks to see how their authors define or describe harshness. Here are some of the results:

Harsh-strident: Raspy, shrill, sharp, metallic, thin, cutting, piercing, tinny, hard, grating, strained, whiny, tense, screechy, pinched, brassy, blatant, edgy, scratchy, high-pitched, raucous.

Harsh-throaty: Raspy, husky, gravelly, glottal fry, pectoral, coarse, grating, muffled, hollow, heavy, mushy, sepulchral, rumbling, swallowed, pinched, flat, rough, dead, mouthy, grainy, hoarse-husky, cracking, sexy, guttural, cavernous, dark, vocal fry, crackling, gargling.

What may we conclude from these groups of descriptive terms?

A *harsh-strident* voice is offensively noisy, brassy, and relatively high-pitched.

A *harsh-throaty* voice is offensively noisy, gravelly, and relatively low-pitched.

The Harsh-Strident Voice

Personality often plays a determining role here, and we generally associate this type of voice with the nervous, high-strung, jittery, and hypertense individual. We are only too familiar with the type: The harassed young mother with three small children underfoot, nagging spouses, and a shrilly ranting Adolph Hitler.

These are extremes, of course, and we must admit that we have encountered many high-strung individuals who did not have harsh-strident voices; similarly, we have heard extremely strident voices coming from individuals who were seemingly relaxed, poised, and nerveless. Stridency can also be rather fickle. The individual with the agreeable, pleasant everyday voice who suddenly finds himself giving a speech to a roomful of people or who becomes involved in other intensely emotional situations may become temporarily strident.

If the strident quality is chronic, however, it may possibly have its roots in an emotional or personality disturbance. Perhaps psychological assistance is needed here. As far as a course in voice improvement is concerned, we may say that stridency is attributable to one or a combination of several factors:

The individual is using not only too much loudness, but, more importantly, too much of the wrong kind of loudness. He is squeezing and rasping the tone out of the throat with no feeling of bodily support. The chapter immediately following will consider a proper way to achieve the right kind of loudness.

Shallow breathing. Clavicular breathing, we have noted, promotes tension in the throat.

Improper (too high) pitch level.

Excessive tensions and constrictions of the pharynx and soft palate. In some instances harshness may result from undue prominence given the higher overtones. Hard, tense surfaces, we recall, tend to give too much emphasis to too many overtones.

Tensions of the extrinsic muscles of the larynx may uptilt the larynx to an abnormal position. Such tensions draw the vocal folds together too tightly and interfere with the free vibrations of the vocal folds.

(Review breathing Exercises 1-11 in chapter 2. In the present chapter, review relaxation Exercises 1-9; Exercises for glottal shock, 47-53. See also chapter 5, Exercises 1-13, for determining pitch level.)

54. Say this sentence at a comfortably low pitch level: "She and he weeded the wiry seaweed." As you say it several times, locate the V-shaped notch at the top of your Adam's apple. If you cannot find the notch, you may be raising the larynx too high in the throat. This often results from excessive tensions of the extrinsic muscles. Continue practicing until you are able to lower the larynx to its normal position.

55. Whisper each of the following sounds. Gradually add voice to the whisper, and build it to a moderately loud level. Try to keep the tone quality free of harshness:

oh   ah   ou   oo   oi   aye

56. With the tongue on the floor of the mouth, start an easy, gentle yawn. The throat area should now be reasonably relaxed. Say ah and hold it for about five seconds. Do not allow a feeling of tightness or tension to creep into your throat. Repeat until you have an easy control of the sound, then try the exercise with these sounds:

oo   ee   oh   ou   uh

57. Read aloud the following word groups, sustaining each vowel or diphthong for about three seconds. The sounds which are capitalized and underlined should deliberately be read in a strident voice. Make the sounds tense, hard, and pinched. The nonunderlined, noncapitalized sounds should be produced in a nonstrident, tension-free voice. Work for the easy, open-throated quality that you used in the previous exercise.

a. EEl-on-saw-rEEk-off-all-loss-knEE
b. sot-tOO-how-do-so-mEEt-wrong-my
c. mat-cool-dAY-cUE-fEEd-odd-up
d. bOY-fall-feel-mEAn-ask-mAsk-round-ray
e. full-fIle-hit-hIde-bat-bAIt-fight-fAte
f. cUbe-coy-calm-plow-lEAp-rod-hod-lawn
g. can-bEE-joy-low-saw-kIte-cAge-pOd
h. hot-palm-push-tooth-drum-dawn-fade-cross

58. Read the first sentence in each of the following groups in a *relatively* strident manner. Deliberately squeeze the tone out of the throat, tighten the constrictor muscles, and uptilt your larynx. Read the second sentence with a breathy quality. Read the third sentence with a relatively "normal" quality, which is as free as possible of harsh-stridency.

a. (strident) The wheel that squeaks the loudest is the one that gets the grease.
   (breathy) A conquered foe should be watched.
   (normal) Any man may make a mistake, but none but a fool will continue it.

b. (strident) A cynic: a man who knows the price of everything and the value of nothing.
   (breathy) The burnt child shuns the fire until the next day.
   (normal) Man sees your actions, but God your motives.

c. (strident) Avenue: A street that formerly had trees on it.
   (breathy) God can't be everywhere, and, so, invented mothers.
   (normal) The greatest of faults, I should say, is to be conscious of none.

d. (strident) One catches more flies with a spoonful of honey than with twenty casks of vinegar.
   (breathy) The fly sat upon the axle-tree of the chariot and said, "What a dust do I raise!"
   (normal) He who can take advice is sometimes superior to him who can give it.

e. (strident) There are men who are happy without knowing it.
   (breathy) Let not thy will roar, when thy power can but whisper.
   (normal) There's a time to wink as well as to see.

f. (strident) It is very foolish to insist on being the only one who is right.
   (breathy) Conscience is the inner voice which warns us that someone may be looking.
   (normal) Happiness is a way-station between too little and too much.

g. (strident) We do not what we ought; what we ought not, we do.
   (breathy) At night an atheist half believes in God.
   (normal) They learn in suffering what they teach in song.

h. (strident) "Be yourself!" is about the worst advice you can give some people.
   (breathy) It is through the cracks in our brains that ecstasy creeps in.
   (normal) It is by acts and not ideas that people live.

i. (strident) The tree of liberty grows only when watered by the blood of tyrants.
   (breathy) A man should live if only to satisfy his curiosity.
   (normal) Everything comes to him who waits—among other things, death.

j. (strident) We do not count a man's years until he has nothing else to count.
   (breathy) It is hard for an empty bag to stand upright.
   (normal) Perhaps there is no happiness in life so perfect as the martyr's.

    k.   **(strident)** What's one man's poison is another's meat or drink.

           (breathy) A bee is not a busier animal than a blockhead.

           (normal) Praise the sea, but keep on the land.

    l.   **(strident)** Ambition is like hunger; it obeys no law but its appetite.

           (breathy) We don't know life; how can we know death?

           (normal) Fellows who have no tongues are often all eyes and ears.

59. Inhale deeply and then sigh. After you have done this several times, vocalize *ah* on the sigh. Start with a relatively high tone, and then glide downward to a low tone. Your vocal folds should become more relaxed as you lower the pitch.

60. Repeat the above procedure with the following words:

well	law	full	show	shop	want
our	dart	fool	boy	prowl	hope
who	boil	not	cart	doll	loss
round	mellow	brawl	lodge	warm	time

61. Sing *oo.* Be sure that you are properly relaxed, and work for a tone which is free of harshness. Repeat this procedure, using *ah* and *oh.*

62. Carefully avoid stridency as you read the following. Prolong the principal vowel sounds and give each one a downward inflection so that it sounds like a vocalized sigh, thus:

       \   \   \   \ \   \

The years flowed by like water.

    a.   The heart of the fool is in his mouth, but the mouth of the wise man is in his heart.

    b.   Where your treasure is, there will your heart be also.

    c.   The heart has its reasons which reason does not know.

    d.   An honest man's the noblest work of God.

    e.   The strongest man in the world is he who stands most alone.

    f.   I would rather sit on a pumpkin and have it all to myself than be crowded on a velvet cushion.

    g.   With malice toward none, with charity for all, with firmness in the right, as God gives us to see the right.

    h.   If there be a hell upon earth it is to be found in a melancholy man's heart.

    i.   Blessed are the merciful: for they shall obtain mercy.

    j.   Those who hope for no other life are dead even for this.

    k.   "Let us cross the river," he said, "and rest under the shade of the trees."

    l.   The empty vessel makes the greatest sound.

    m.   People born to be hanged are safe in water.

    n.   Nothing can happen more beautiful than death.

    o.   No man loves life like him that's growing old.

63. In reading the following, prolong the vowels slightly, but avoid extreme exaggeration. Read slowly and cautiously, paying careful attention to breathing and pitch level. Work for proper relaxation, an unconstricted throat, and, of course, a vocal quality which is not harsh-strident.

    a.   After enough time has passed, all memories are beautiful.

    b.   The smallest feelings are worth more than the most beautiful thoughts.

    c.   Night whose sable hand hangs on the purple skirts of flying day.

    d.   Let no man fear to die: we love to sleep, all, and death is but the sounder sleep.

    e.   My soul is sailing through the sea, but the past is heavy and hinders me.

    f.   Was I deceived, or did a sable cloud turn forth her silver lining on the night?

    g.   Excess of grief for the deceased is madness; for it is an injury to the living, and the dead know it not.

h.   Let prayer be the key of the morning and the bolt of the evening.

i.   Rest is the sweet sauce of labor.

j.   Dreams surely are for the spirit what sleep is for the body.

k.   No evil can happen to a good man, either in life or after death.

l.   Our days on the earth are but as a shadow.

m.   I like the dreams of the future better than the history of the past.

n.   Stolen waters are sweet, and bread eaten in secret is pleasant.

o.   After silence that which comes nearest to expressing the inexpressible is music.

p.   Let us be silent that we may hear the whispers of the gods.

q.   To lie still and think little is medicine for the soul.

r.   There is no light in souls in which there is no warmth.

s.   Every one is a moon and has a dark side which he never shows to anybody.

t.   Man that is born of a woman is of few days, and full of trouble.

u.   Silence is the language of all strong passions: love, anger, surprise, fear.

v.   What is remorse? A great regret that we are what we are.

w.   This thing called rain can make the days seem short and the nights seem long.

The Harsh-Throaty Voice

If the harsh-strident voice is sometimes associated with a high-strung, taut type of personality, a harsh-throaty voice occasionally identifies a lazy and careless individual, and, now and then, a shy, hesitant type of person. However, the exceptions to this statement are often more interesting to study than the nonexceptions. Movie and TV "toughs" or "heavies" like Orson Welles and John Wayne often use guttural, growly qualities in their characterizations.

A throaty voice can be irritating to listeners because it frequently lacks carrying power. It sounds "swallowed." It is dull, lackluster, and gravelly.

What causes throatiness? One or a combination of several factors:

The individual may be speaking with inadequate loudness. Many people with throaty voices have shown substantial improvement as they learned to speak more energetically and with the proper kind of loudness, projection, and tone placement.

Too low a pitch level. It is occasionally necessary to raise the habitual level (the pitch level you most frequently use) two to four semitones.

Poor breath control. If the breath supply has been exhausted, the last few words of a thought unit or phrase may be squeezed out of the throat with a raspy quality.

Excessive tension and constrictions of the lower part of the pharynx.

The tongue humps up into the throat. This tongue retraction muffles the tone and contributes to foggy, mealy-mouthed articulation, particularly with many vowel sounds.

The extrinsic muscles pull the larynx down into an abnormally low position. The individual who permits this to happen often buries his chin in his neck as he speaks.

Excessive relaxation (laxness) of the throat may result in an overemphasis of pharyngeal resonance.

(Review Exercises 1-11 in chapter 2. In the present chapter, review Exercises 10-30, to assure openness of the throat and mouth passageways, flexibility of the jaw, and forward projection of tone. See also the exercises in chapter 5 for determining pitch level: 1-13.)

64. Read the first sentence in each of the following groups with as throaty a quality as you can achieve. Deliberately lower your pitch, let the words fall back into the throat and speak with as little energy as possible. For a complete and purposeful contrast, read the second sentence in each group in a higher pitched and relatively hard, strident manner. Read the third sentence with a "normal" quality, that is, one which is free of throatiness.

a. (throaty) For dust thou art, and unto dust shalt thou return.
    (strident) He who is a slave to his belly seldom worships God.
    (normal) Doing easily what others find difficult is talent; doing what is impossible for talent is genius.

b. (throaty) The hour of midnight fills the soul with quiet unease.
    (strident) I like trees because they seem more resigned to the way they have to live than other things do.
    (normal) A dwarf standing on the shoulders of a giant may see farther than the giant himself.

c. (throaty) Thou art weighed in the balances and art found wanting.
    (strident) If one plays good music people don't listen, and if one plays bad music people don't talk.
    (normal) Fate makes our relatives, choice makes our friends.

d. (throaty) Let us crown ourselves with rosebuds before they be withered.
    (strident) Fortune does not change men; it only unmasks them.
    (normal) Blessed are the forgetful: for they get the better even of their blunders.

e. (throaty) He who laughs best today will also laugh last.
    (strident) A fanatic is one who can't change his mind and won't change the subject.
    (normal) Even the best things are not equal to their fame.

f. (throaty) The fatal realm of memory—men call it heaven—and hell.
    (strident) There is nobody who is not dangerous for someone.
    (normal) Bad men excuse their faults; good men will leave them.

g. (throaty) The door of death is made of gold that mortal eyes cannot behold.
    (strident) No one loves the man whom he fears.
    (normal) All is to be feared where all is to be lost.

h. (throaty) Death had shaken out the sands of thy glass.
    (strident) Think in the morning, act in the noon, eat in the evening, sleep in the night.
    (normal) Never read any book that is not a year old.

i. (throaty) A good cause makes a strong arm.
    (strident) Examine what is said, not him who speaks.
    (normal) None but the brave deserve the fair.

j. (throaty) Man is a noble animal, splendid in ashes and pompous in the grave.
    (strident) When a man diets, he eats oatmeal in addition to everything else he usually eats.
    (normal) Genius does what it must, and talent what it can.

k. (throaty) Behold, God is my salvation: I will trust and not be afraid.
    (strident) If the world's a vale of tears, smile till the rainbows span it.
    (normal) The seed dies into a new life, and so does man.

l. (throaty) All men think all men mortal but themselves.
    (strident) And when we think we lead, we are most led.
    (normal) There are heroes in evil as well as in good.

65. Many individuals who are not chronically or consistently throaty have an irritating vocal mannerism. At the end of a phrase or a sentence, they will drop the pitch of the voice—a downward inflection—and frequently the final sound or two has the "growling" or "bacon-frying" quality. Slightly more energetic projection, a "brighter" degree of loudness will generally eliminate this gargling sound.

Start each of the following words on a relatively high pitch, and then inflect your voice downward. When you have reached the lowest pitch that your voice can attain without a rasp or a growl, prolong the vowel or diphthong.

die	how	who	lie	do	pie	nay
roe	they	me	lay	doe	tea	sue
maw	why	sea	no	play	raw	tie
boy	new	low	buy	too	fee	sow

66. Reversing the procedure suggested in Exercise 65, place a rising inflection on each of the following words. At the beginning of the inflection, deliberately let the voice fall back into the throat and rumble. Raise the pitch slowly and as soon as you can hear and feel the disappearance of the growling quality, prolong the vowel sound for a few seconds on that particular pitch level.

awe	sow	at	isle	keen	soup	aid
all	plow	add	ode	ire	file	put
caught	ow	ask	eel	mop	jeep	ear
sought	now	aunt	ore	sop	ale	eat

67. In this exercise we will combine the procedures suggested in Exercises 65 and 66. Each of the following sentences is divided by diagonal lines into three sections. In the first section, using the techniques outlined in Exercise 65, place a falling inflection on each vowel sound (deliberately beginning each phonation with a strident quality), and when you reach the lowest pitch you can attain without harshness, prolong the vowel sound on that pitch. In the second section, using the technique outlined in Exercise 66, place a rising inflection on each vowel sound (deliberately beginning each phonation with a throaty rumble), but as soon as you reach a pitch level at which all traces of harshness disappear, prolong the sound at that particular level. In the third section, avoid any greatly exaggerated inflections, but read the material with a normal, harsh-free quality which is a compromise between the extremes suggested for the first two sections.

a. A person who can't pay / gets another person who can't pay / to guarantee that he can pay.

b. The leader must know / must know that he knows / and must be able to make it abundantly clear to those about him that he knows.

c. It is a common rule with primitive people / not to waken a sleeper, because his soul is away / and might not have time to get back.

d. I'll not listen to reason. / Reason always means / what someone else has to say.

e. Life is a jest, / and all things show it; / I thought so once, but now I know it.

f. Death, the most awful of evils, is nothing to us. / So long as we are alive, death has not visited us. / Once we are dead, we are no longer alive.

g. Life is not lost by dying / Life is lost minute by minute / day by dragging day, in all the thousand, small, uncaring ways.

h. If life is miserable, it is painful to endure. / If it is happy, it is frightful to lose. / Live as if you expected to live a hundred years, but might die tomorrow.

i. One night he dreamed that he was in a crowd, / when someone recognized him as the president, / and exclaimed in surprise, "He is a very common-looking man." Whereupon he answered, "Friend, the Lord prefers common-looking people. That is the reason he makes so many of them."

j. Upon the first goblet he read this inscription: monkey wine. / Upon the second: lion wine. Upon the third: sheep wine. Upon the fourth: swine wine. / These four inscriptions expressed the four descending degrees of drunkenness. The first, that which enlivens, the second, that which irritates. The third, that which stupefies. Finally the last, that which brutalizes.

68. Read aloud the following pairs of sentences. The first sentence in each pair is loaded with front vowel sounds and so-called "tongue tip" consonants. (The front part of the tongue is most active.) To say

them clearly and sharply you will have to move your tongue quite far forward. Exaggerate this forward tongue movement, and work for clear, bright and vigorous sounds.

As you read the second sentence in each pair, concentrate on maintaining the same degree of brightness and vigor.

a. Pete, the seal, eats veal and other meats soaked in beet juice.
    It's more important to get in the first thought than the last word.
b. The dazed dancer dipped the dill pickle into the dish.
    A man in armor is his armor's slave.
c. It is only the fear of God that can deliver us from the fear of man.
    It is a proverb of our fathers that there is in every god an element of the divine.
d. Dean Reed was deaf to Dale's plea about the theme in the test.
    In law, nothing is certain but the expense.
e. Kate's date had seen me dig into the deep pail with a thin nail.
    He who has butter on his bread should not go into the sun.
f. She ripped ten pleats out of the beaded sheet.
    Oh, Life! Thou art a galling load, along a rough and weary road, to wretches such as I.
g. It is better to have a lion at the head of an army of sheep, than a sheep at the head of an army of lions.
    Nobody talks so constantly about God as those who insist that there is no God.
h. Where God has a temple, the devil will have a chapel.
    When the Colosseum falls, Rome will fall, and when Rome falls—the world falls.
i. In life there are meetings which seem like a fate.
    Custom is the law of fools.
j. Death opens the gate of fame and shuts the gate of envy after it.
    Clever men are good but they are not the best.
k. No man is weak by choice.
    To know how to suggest is the art of teaching.
l. Tact consists in knowing how far we may go too far.
    The public is an old woman. Let her maunder and mumble.

69. The following material contains many front vowels and tongue-tip sounds. Again, deliberately concentrate on tongue placement: it should be further forward than usual. Work also for brightness of tone and crispness of articulation. Avoid all traces of a harsh-throaty quality.

a.

team	teepee	deacon	tame	tell
tip	dint	kneel	nip	date
deer	tail	creed	theory	theme
eke	needs	thimble	eager	weasel
leak	keyed	nick	eel	west
seen	weed	tizzy	deb	Nate

b. He who wants to do everything will never do anything.
c. Without red cells, blood would bleed to death.
d. "When I use a word," Humpty Dumpty said, "it means just what I choose it to mean—neither more nor less."
e. The eyes of the dead are closed gently; we also have to open gently the eyes of the living.
f. Edible: Good to eat, and wholesome to digest; as a worm to a toad, a toad to a snake, a snake to a pig, a pig to a man, and a man to a worm.
g. If we had no defects ourselves, we should not take pleasure in noting those of others.
h. If you live in Rome, don't quarrel with the Pope.
i. Some men are like musical glasses: to produce their finest tones you must keep them wet.

    j. I like trees because they seem more resigned to the way they have to live than other things do.

    k. Eel: a seagoing snake.

    l. The devil and me, we don't agree. I hate him, and he hates me.

   m. The more help a man has in his garden, the less it belongs to him.

   n. If you don't read any books, you have no advantage over the man who can't read.

   o. One meal a day is enough for a lion, and it ought to be for a man.

   p. Who purposely cheats his friend would cheat his God.

   q. Scorn the proud man that is ashamed to weep.

   r. A man is a worker. If he is not that he is nothing.

   s. Preach not to others what they should eat, but eat as becomes you, and be silent.

   t. Men are never so likely to settle a question rightly as when they discuss it freely.

   u. The unpleasant man is one who will come in and awake a person who has just gone asleep, in order to chat with him.

   v. "No doubt I now grew very pale. But I talked more fluently and with a heightened voice. Yet the sound increased—and what could I do? It was a low, dull, quick sound—much such a sound as a watch makes when enveloped in cotton. I gasped for breath—and yet the officers heard it not. I talked more quickly, more vehemently, but the noise steadily increased. Oh God! What could I do? I foamed—I raved—I swore! I swung the chair upon which I had been sitting, and grated it upon the boards, but the noise arose overall and continually increased. It grew louder—louder—louder! And still the men chatted pleasantly, and smiled. Was it possible they heard not? Almighty God!—no, no! They heard! They suspected! They knew! They were making a mockery of my horror! But anything was better than this agony! Anything was more tolerable than this derision! I could bear those hypocritical smiles no longer! I felt that I must scream or die! And now—again! Hark! Louder! Louder! Louder! Louder!

    " 'Villains!' I shrieked, 'I admit the deed! Tear up the planks! Here, here! It is the beating of his hideous heart!' " [Poe, *The Tell-Tale Heart*]

Assignment 4 (See suggested Checklist for Assignment 4)

If your voice has been adjudged harsh-strident, prepare material which is quiet and reflective. Devote some of your practice period to the procedure suggested in Exercise 58: read a few lines in a deliberately strident manner; read several lines in a breathy voice; then reread the entire selection using a quality which is devoid of harshness and stridency. Most of your practice time should be allotted to the third and most important step. In your classroom presentation, of course, it will not be necessary to use the first two steps. Read all of the material in a manner which avoids any suggestion of stridency.

If your voice has been adjudged harsh-throaty, prepare material which is lively and vigorous. If you write your own, be sure that you include many front vowels (m<u>e</u>, <u>i</u>t, b<u>e</u>d, t<u>a</u>ke) and tongue-tip consonants (ti<u>p</u>, <u>d</u>ay, <u>n</u>igh<u>t</u>).

In your classroom presentation, read your material in an unexaggerated manner and strive for a quality which is free of the harsh-throaty.

Nasality

Three of our most pleasant and musical sounds are the nasals: *m*, *n*, and *ng* (as in "sing"). If you will hum *m* for a few seconds and then pinch your nostrils with thumb and forefinger, you will completely cut off the sound. But if you sing *ah* for a few seconds and then close your nostrils, you will note that you can sustain *ah* as long as your breath supply lasts.

What happens when we produce a nasal consonant?

The breath stream must be blocked at some point in the mouth.

The velum must be lowered and relaxed. If these conditions are present, tone will be directed through the nasal passages.

However, what happens when we say *ah* and permit the velum to hang relaxed and slightly open? The nasal passages act as supplementary resonators, and in this capacity they may accentuate the overtones of other vowels, diphthongs, and consonants as well as *ah*. Is nasal resonance desirable on nonnasal sounds and, if so, to what degree? In recent research, high-speed motion picture X-rays indicate that some speakers with normal voices leave the velum partially lowered during the production of vowel and diphthong sounds. The degree to which the velum is lowered or raised for the production of nonnasal sounds obviously varies from individual to individual.

At this point the poem, "Six Blind Men of Indostan," comes into the picture again. What actually constitutes too much or too little nasal resonance is frequently rather difficult to describe objectively. We hear speakers whose vowels and diphthongs apparently have a lot of nasal resonance; some of these voices are quite agreeable. We hear individuals whose vowels and diphthongs have little nasal resonance; yet some of these voices are also pleasant.

The proper amount of nasal resonance, then, perhaps represents a balance between too much or too little nasal resonance. To aid us in achieving such a balance we must first consider the undesirable extremes.

It must be admitted that our manner of describing the sound of nasality (also described as positive, general, or excessive nasality) is somewhat hazy and nonspecific. Most students of voice fall back on the old reliables: "foghorn," "talking through the nose," "whiny," "bottled up."

Not at all infrequently the individual with excessive nasality also has slovenly, mush-mouthed articulation. There is a suggestion of carelessness and laziness in the speaker.

Nasality is caused by any one of a combination of several factors:

The tongue is permitted to hump in the rear of the mouth. It is pulled back and up. This kind of a tongue position probably blocks sound from the oral cavity, and sound would then be directed into the nasal cavities.

The jaw is excessively rigid and the teeth are clenched or nearly closed. Stated simply, the individual does not open his mouth sufficiently for sound to get out. Again, if the sound "backfires," it does so through the nasal passages. A wider mouth opening, more vigorous articulation and a greater degree of loudness often help to decrease nasality.

Air is permitted to flow more freely through the nasal passage than it is able to flow out through the nostrils. This generally happens if the soft palate hangs to the point at which the opening into the nasal cavities is greater than the anterior opening at the nostrils. (This type of resonance is often referred to as cul-de-sac—blind alley—resonance.)

Excessive relaxation of the velum, of course, is a principal cause of nasality. The individual must learn to gain control of the velum.

70. If it has been determined that you have undesirable nasality, listen to a recording of your voice and try to detect excessive nasality on vowels and diphthongs. You may even notice it on certain consonants other than *m*, *n*, and *ng*. Perhaps your instructor or a classmate can imitate your vocal quality. Listen carefully to voices of various personalities in movies, radio, and TV, and pick out the voices with too much nasality. Lily Tomlin, for example, frequently uses it as a laugh-getting device in many of her sketches. If your nasality is caused by tongue humping, narrow mouth opening, or a rigid jaw, review Exercises 10-25.

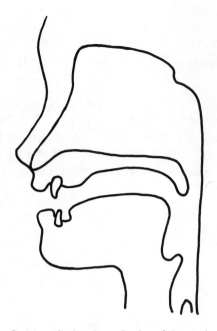

Position of velum is production of the nasal consonants: m, n, ng.

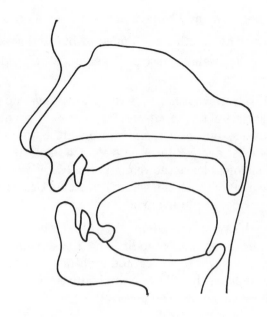

Position of velum is production of oral sounds. (For many individuals, the velum will be completely raised.)

Figure 3.2. Positions of the velum

A voice which is pitched too high may also be unpleasantly nasal. The so-called "nasal twang" is often associated with an improper pitch level. Check Exercises 1-13 in chapter 5.

71. Watching yourself in a mirror, open your mouth widely and say *aw—ng* (as in "ring"): *aw—ng, aw—ng, aw—ng.*

What happens to the velum?

To produce *aw* you must raise the velum. To produce *ng* you must lower the velum. (See fig. 3.2.) Repeat until you get the feeling of this action.

72. Start to sound *b*, building up air pressure behind closed lips, but then let the air escape through the nose for *m*. Can you feel the action of the velum? Repeat this procedure, using *d* and *n* as a combination and then *g* and *ng*.

73. In this exercise nasal and nonnasal sounds are listed in alternate order. Practice saying them until you can differentiate clearly between them:

m-aw-n-ee-ng-i-m-oh-n-eh-ng-oo-m-b-n-d-ng-g

74. Deliberately produce and sustain a very nasal *aw*. You may find this tricky at first, but it will help you lower your velum if you think of the consonant *m* as you are vocalizing the *aw*. After you are able to do this, raise the velum and sustain a normal, nonnasal *aw*.

Repeat the two kinds of *aw* until you can feel and hear the contrast: (nasal) *aw—*(nonnasal) *aw—*(nasal) *aw—*(nonnasal) *aw*.

75. Repeat the word "out" twelve times, beginning with a normal and, if possible, completely nonnasal quality. Gradually make the word more nasal until you arrive at an exaggerated, muffled nasality on the twelfth repetition.

76. In the following exercises do not permit the vowels to become unduly nasal:

   a.   Sustain *aw* for a few seconds, pause briefly, and then add a nasal consonant, likewise sustaining it. Then repeat the process without pausing between *aw* and the nasal.

        aw . . . . . . m   aw . . . . . . n   aw . . . . . . ng
        awn   awn   awn

   b.   Repeat this procedure, placing the nasal consonant in the initial position.

        m . . . . . . aw   n . . . . . . aw   ng . . . . . . aw
        maw   naw   ngaw

   c.   Place the nasal consonant between the vowels.

        aw . . . m . . . aw   aw . . . n . . . aw   aw . . . ng . . . aw
        awmaw   awnaw   awngaw

   d.   Place the vowels between the nasal consonants.

        m . . . aw . . . m   n . . . aw . . . n   ng . . . aw . . . ng
        mawm   nawn   ngawng

   e.   Repeat Exercises *a*, *b*, *c*, and *d*, substituting for *aw* the following:
        ee, ou, i, oh.

77. Sustain the vowel tones for a few seconds in each of the following. The difference, if any, between the quality of the vowel following a nasal consonant and the quality of a vowel following a nonnasal consonant should be slight:

bee-mee	dee-nee	lap-nap
boh-moh	bore-more	bad-mad
bay-may	doh-noh	bought-naught
baw-maw	daw-naw	bud-mud
dale-mail	day-nay	die-nigh

78. The first sentence in each of the following pairs contains no nasal consonants. The second sentence is saturated with them. Exaggerate the nonnasal quality in the initial sentences, and as you read the second sentences, try to force the tone through the nasal passages. Repeat until you can feel and hear the differences.

   a.   The gray crow flew over the oak tree.
        Amy and Hank ran around the merry-go-round.

   b.   The actor boiled the fresh, ripe cherries.
        Am I going mountain climbing soon?

   c.   Dot threw the book at the cat.
        Tom met Nancy near New Haven.

   d.   The icy oil oozed over the sidewalk.
        The noisy mob awakened Mike and Jan.

   e.   "Toot, toot, toot," said the factory whistle.
        The bowling team ran down the muddy ramp.

   f.   The furious coach choked the quarterback.
        Does rain fall mainly on the plain in Maine?

   g.   The tough hood shook the pebbles out of his boots.
        Nan mixed tuna and green onions.

   h.   Bert ducked before Jack tossed the rice.
        June moons are nicer than snow in March.

i. I doubt if Al will go with Ida.
   The mean man wanted to maim Arnie.
j. He poured barley soup over the rye bread.
   I'm in the mood for a new James Bond movie.
k. The Irish ship hit a large iceberg.
   Jean found diamonds under the sink.
l. "I'll huff, I'll puff," the wicked wolf growled.
   Mighty Mouse appears nightly on channel nineteen.

79. The following words do not contain nasal consonants. Read each one twice, first in the ordinary way and then pinching the nostrils with your thumb and forefinger. There should be no appreciable difference in the sound of the two words. A slight difference is of no great importance, but if you detect a considerable difference and feel an unpleasant sensation in your nose, you are probably too nasal. Wider mouth opening and "athletic" articulation will help you.

cat	hip	coat	lot	hat
rate	did	hot	sat	how
take	task	pipe	you	ask
loss	took	loose	buck	you
far	fell	beep	pore	rude

80. Repeat this procedure as you read each of the following sentences twice. Again there should be no conspicuous difference in voice quality between the two readings.

a. The four black roses wilted three days ago.
b. Jack the Ripper liked to cut up actresses.
c. The shark was hooked as he chased the playful goldfish.
d. As David dragged the deep ditch he discovered a box of rare jewels.
e. Bill's biceps bulged as he beat the baby-blue carpet.
f. Hetty Cook sits or sews by the water cooler all day.
g. Gorgeous George wrestled with Killer Capp yesterday, but he lost the bout.
h. Joe, the juggler, tossed the white disks to the old acrobat.
i. To get the sap to drip, you should tap the bark of the tree.
j. Beef or veal should be cooked for a half hour.

81. Read the following selections in the ordinary manner (without pinching the nostrils). Have somebody listen to you, and continue practicing the selections until you are adjudged free of unpleasant nasality.

a. Several years ago I heard a preacher who was powerful good. I decided to give his church every dollar I had. But he refused to quit. A little bit later I decided to keep the bills but just give a few loose quarters. A quarter hour later I decided to keep the quarters, too. A half hour later he stopped; the plate was passed. I was so exhausted that I took out five dollars out of sheer spite. [Mark Twain]

b. A Hare said to a Tortoise, "You are stupid because you are so slow." The Tortoise laughed. "We'll just see about that," he said. "Let's have a race."

"Good!" said the Hare. "I'll show you what real speed is."

They decided to race to the big forest which stood far away. The Tortoise started right away at his steady pace, but the Hare said boastfully, "I feel tired so I'll sleep for a little while. It'll still be easy to beat that stupid Tortoise."

He stretched out, fell asleep, but woke up just as the daylight had started to fade. He raced to the edge of the forest as fast as he could go, but he was very surprised to discover that the Tortoise was already there. [Aesop]

c. "Hats off to the Greeks" but "Hats off to baseball," too. The Greeks had their day, a day that existed for ages, shall exist for ages. But baseball, too, has its age. Perhaps it has created so far little poetry, little sculpture, little art, but who dares predict what lies ahead?

Baseball has revitalized our culture. We owe a great debt to the Greeks, to be sure, but what a debt we owe to baseball! The Halls of Greek Art, at our galleries, are good places to visit, we hear, but just hoist the flag at our ball park. Watch the crowds flow toward the bleachers. What's the Discus Thrower got that our favorite player fails to duplicate at a double-play? What Greek orator would try to out-argue the boss of, let us say, the Dodgers or the Braves as he protests a doubtful verdict?

Radio, as well as TV, takes the crucial World Series to every house, to every garage, to every drug store. Juke boxes are stilled. All the world holds its breath as play after play is reeled off. The pulse of each loyal rooter skips a beat at every pitch.

Perhaps "Casey at the Bat" is just the start of the epoch of the Baseball Epic.

Assimilation Nasality

If you pronounce *nan* and *lap* you will notice that the vowel sound in the first word shows more nasality than the same vowel sound in the second word. Obviously, then, if a vowel is preceded or followed by a nasal sound, there may be a tendency for its production to be influenced by its neighboring nasal consonant. This is often referred to as an assimilation nasality. The velum must move very rapidly in a word such as *nan*, and if it does not perform quickly, nasal tone will spill over to the adjacent vowel.

Say the word *nan*. Your velum must be lowered for the *n*, raised for *a*, and lowered again for the final *n*.

Efficient, prompt control of the velum is essential. The following exercises will be of aid to you.

82. As you read the first column of words, prolong the nasal consonants as indicated. Pause slightly and then pronounce the vowel or diphthong. As you read the second column, do not prolong the nasal sounds, but pause briefly before you say the final sound. As you read the third column, eliminate the pause.

mmmmmmm / / y	m / / y	my
mmmmmmm / / e	m / / e	me
mmmmmmm / / oo	m / / oo	moo
mmmmmmm / / ap	m / / ap	map
mmmmmmm / / ay	m / / ay	may
nnnnnnn / / ight	n / / ight	night
nnnnnnn / / ail	n / / ail	nail
nnnnnnn / / o	n / / o	no
nnnnnnn / / ay	n / / ay	nay

83. Practice the following. The first time you should exaggerate and prolong the nasal consonants. The second time, avoid any exaggeration, and be sure that assimilated nasality is avoided.

am	ma'am	moat	next	mate	amber
ran	mantle	nil	mouse	mask	ran
Dan	nag	banned	mouth	mitt	Don
pan	hang	ream	mound	met	pain
sand	mangle	nine	noun	knee	sand
lamb	mad	now	mount	Nat	lamb
ant	mass	cane	renown	nap	and
Jim	knack	round	hound	jam	ample

84. Exaggerate the overall nasality the first time you read the following. Then repeat, trying to avoid a generally nasal quality or a nasality which spills over from a nearby *m*, *n*, or *ng*.

    a. The nine dancers planned to do the cancan on the sanded planks.
    b. Ann sang "The Man I Love" as she leaned on the piano.
    c. Randy the mountain climber asked the man to make a path in the snow.
    d. Good manners and good morals are sworn friends and fast allies.
    e. The tame robin sang a pleasant tune.
    f. Max and Manny hung the laundry on a frame.
    g. Mac gave Nell the sparkling diamond ring.
    h. Ben Hanson sang snappy rounds about knights and damsels.
    i. The hungry men ate ham and beans at the strange banquet.
    j. Do down-in-the-mouth students drink milk while cramming for exams?
    k. Andy Morton counted the frantic lambs as they ran around the mound.
    l. Vance and Randy threw the net over the nearby mink.
    m. If there are no books in this world, then nothing need be said, but since there are books, they must be read; if there are no famous hills, then nothing need be said, but since there are, they must be visited; if there are no flowers and no moon, then nothing need be said, but since there are, they must be enjoyed; if there are no talented men and beautiful women, then nothing need be said, but since there are, they must be loved and protected.

Denasality

If you develop a bad case of sniffles in the spring and can't do your speech assignment, you possibly say to your instructor, "Good bawdig. Sprig has cub, ad I have a bad cold id the dose."

Your cold is a temporary condition, of course, and your nasal sounds will be the primary sufferers. However, we are more concerned with the persistent, chronic type of negative or inadequate nasality (denasality) in which the vowels sound stuffy, dull, and "cold-in-the-headish." Such denasality generally results from some type of obstruction in the nasal passages. A small amount of air or perhaps no air at all is allowed to enter the nasal passages. Enlarged adenoids, broken nose, deviated septum, and allergies (such as hay fever) are commonly responsible for denasality. In such cases, surgical repair or medical treatment should generally precede speech training. Unfortunately, even after such treatment, some individuals remain denasal. In other cases, the individual becomes markedly nasal, and in rarer instances, he may talk with a combination of negative and positive nasality. In this type of speech the vowel sounds become excessively nasal, but the nasal sounds are muffled and distorted.

Most persistent cases of negative nasality (after the cause has been removed) will benefit from a careful and selective program of vocal retraining. Essentially, such a program must teach the individual to gain vigorous control of the soft palate, to emphasize the nasal consonants, and to develop a keen auditory awareness of what is pleasant or unpleasant in voice quality.

85. Hum *m* vigorously up and down the scale. You will feel vibrations and tinglings on your lips and in the nasal passages.

86. Hum *n* and *ng* (as in "ring") similarly.

87. Practice with the following word pairs. As you say the first word in each pair, you should not be able to feel any vibration in the nasal cavity. When you hit the nasal consonant of the second word, however, you should be able to feel nasal vibrations. You will become more aware of the differences if you prolong each *m*, *n*, and *ng*.

bay-May	dell-Nell	bag-bang
bad-mad	day-nay	rug-rung
bail-mail	dill-nil	big-bing
bake-make	door-nor	log-long
bike-Mike	dip-nip	gag-gang
but-mutt	deck-neck	tag-tang
beet-meet	dial-Nile	rig-ring
bear-mare	deuce-noose	lug-lung

88. Prolong the nasals in the following nonsense syllables:

   a. ahm—ahm—ahm—ahm—mee—mee—mee—mee
   b. ahm—nah—nahm—nahng—ahm—nah—nahm—nahng
   c. ding—dong—ding—dong—ning—ning—ning
   d. ahm—ahn—ahng—ahm—ahn—ahng
   e. mee—may—my—moh—mee—may—my—moh
   f. nee—nay—ny—noh—nee—nay—ny—noh
   g. ngee—ngay—ngy—ngoh—ngee—ngay—ngy—ngoh

89. Read the following words twice, the first time slowly and the second time rapidly. In both readings make the nasal consonants as prominent as you can:

an	lime	noon	moll	length
sign	bone	mat	bend	strength
aunt	rhyme	moon	chin	finger
mom	plain	dawn	bring	ring
send	lawn	wean	king	thing
man	nine	mingle	linger	ginger

90. Read this material twice. On the first reading, prolong the nasals slightly so that you are definitely aware of vibrations in the nasal cavities. At the same time, can you make the tone quality of the vowels and diphthongs as vibrant and ringing as it is on *m*, *n*, and *ng*?

On the second reading, eliminate the exaggeration, but be certain that the *m*, *n*, and *ng* consonants have normal and adequate nasality, and that the vowel and diphthong sounds have enough nasal resonance to give them a little luster.

   a. Many male monkeys would make too much noise.
   b. Ned and Nina nodded dreamily over math problems in the moonlight.
   c. The mighty army moved from Canada into Northern Michigan.
   d. Melvin Nero, the dancing minstrel, chanted a new melody.
   e. Maple and elm leaves have a bronze sheen in the summer time.
   f. The moon never beams without bringing me dreams of merry Annie Miller.
   g. Martha and Maggie met the naval cadets in Annapolis, Maryland.
   h. Moe mumbled nonsense when he ran the frisking hound around the pen.
   i. Mac married Millie on the second Monday of March.
   j. Nature and wisdom always say the same.
   k. We live under a government of men and morning newspapers.
   l. Classical music is the kind that we keep thinking will turn into a tune.
   m. Applause is the spur of noble minds, the end and aim of weak ones.
   n. An artist is the only one who has normal vision.
   o. Any fool can answer when he is asked for advice, but only a great man can ask.

Balanced Resonance

If nasality or denasality (negative nasality) has been one of your vocal characteristics, by now you are definitely aware of the nature of your individual problem. Perhaps you have already begun to modify the unpleasant traits often associated with the extremes of nasal resonance. Any such process of modification is, in reality, only another way of developing balanced resonance. Balanced resonance does not mean eliminating nasal resonance, but rather, making whatever adjustments are necessary so that we can produce desirable and pleasant resonance. It might be added that such adjustments have their beginnings in the ear and not the resonators. The exercises in this section look simple, and they are—deceptively so. You will need to listen to yourself and be listened to more intently than ever before. A recorder, a classmate, and your instructor will be valuable adjuncts to your ears.

91. Read each of the following selections twice. The first time read with exaggerated slowness and concentrate on the openness of the resonators, freedom from any constrictions, adequate control of the soft palate, and pushing the tone forward. The second time read with conversational rapidity but try to carry over the favorable conditions you established during the first reading. The objective should not be the so-called "pear-shaped" tones, which are apt to be distortions, but ease and naturalness.

   a. Be not forgetful to entertain strangers: for thereby some have entertained angels unawares.
   b. Remember that the most beautiful things in the world are the most useless: peacocks and lilies, for example.
   c. What is beautiful is good and who is good will soon be beautiful.
   d. You cannot fly like an eagle with the wings of a wren.
   e. What nobody seeks is rarely found.
   f. He was like the rooster who thought the sun had risen to hear him crow.
   g. All I mean by truth is the road I can't help traveling.
   h. It is a great folly to wish only to be wise.
   i. Those who try to lead the people can only do so by following the mob.
   j. Conversation should touch everything, but should concentrate on nothing.
   k. A hen is only an egg's way of making another egg.
   l. Silence is deep as eternity; speech is shallow as time.
   m. Music is well said to be the speech of angels.
   n. If youth is a fault one soon gets rid of it.
   o. Laughter is not a bad beginning for a friendship, and it is the best ending for one.
   p. When I was a child, I spoke as a child, I understood as a child, I thought as a child; but when I became a man, I put away childish things.
   q. The Angel of Death has been abroad throughout the land: you may almost hear the beating of his wing.

Assignment 5 (See suggested Checklist for Assignment 5)

If nasality has been one of your voice problems, prepare two brief selections. The first one should contain no nasal consonants: *m, n, ng*. The second one may contain a moderate number of nasals. Listen to yourself carefully as you practice. If possible have someone else listen, too. When you present the assignment in class, try to keep your reading free of undue nasality.

If denasality has been one of your problems, select material which is saturated with the nasal consonants. Practice with the following suggestions in mind: exaggerate the nasals (*m, n, ng*) somewhat, but try especially to make the vowels and diphthongs as bright and vibrant as the nasals.

If neither nasality nor denasality has been a problem, try this for your assignment: Select material which is relatively simple and restrained. Your practicing should be rather slow, deliberate, and careful. When you present your selection to the class, concentrate on ease and naturalness of delivery. Think of the resonators and their functions as being integrated. Openness, relaxation, nimbleness of articulation, and an easy control are essential.

Hoarseness

Some listeners may find it difficult to identify nasal, strident, or even breathy voices, but few of them would fail to label a hoarse voice as such. It is the type of voice which we often associate with sore throats, and it frequently results from acute or chronic laryngitis, as well as respiratory infection or irritation.

A hoarse voice is generally harsh, raw, and strained. It may sometimes have a foghorn quality, or it may suggest that its possessor is about to or desperately needs to clear his throat.

A bad cold and sore throat generally disappear without too much difficulty, and the voice will regain its former clarity.

Chronic hoarseness, however, is dangerous. If hoarseness persists for more than two weeks, medical assistance is imperative. Persistent hoarseness may result from organic defects of structural abnormalities. Nodes, polyps (benign, noncancerous growths on the vocal cords), or malignant tumors may be responsible for the trouble. Surgical treatment is generally required for these more serious defects.

There is some controversy regarding the causes and nature of certain of these growths, but there can be little question that vocal abuse has something to do with their presence.

The kind of shouting and yelling that some of us indulge in at football games is one of the more obvious types of vocal abuse. Prolonged or excessively loud talking is another. Actors, both amateur and professional, occasionally lose their voices because of this. A pitch level which is unnecessarily high or low is still another example.

If the hoarseness has been chronic rather than temporary and medical treatment has aided in alleviating some or all of the hoarseness, it is often necessary for the individual to embark upon a program of retraining the voice. In any case, a period of vocal rest is often prescribed. This may mean complete vocal silence for a period of several days to a period of several months. (A brilliant operatic soprano, Lucretia Bori, finding herself with chronic hoarseness, refrained from talking or singing for an entire year!) Incidentally, vocal silence means that even whispering must be eliminated. Smoking is also taboo.

Let your instructor and your doctor help you. If some kind of vocal retraining is recommended, many of the discussions and exercises listed elsewhere in this book will be of value.

The interested individual is especially invited to review the following:

> In this chapter:
>> Exercises for relaxation, 1-9
>> Exercises for harshness, 54-69
> In the next chapter:
>> Exercises for loudness, 1-11
> In chapter 5:
>> Exercises for pitch, 1-13

Assignment 6 (See suggested Checklist for Assignment 6)

Early in this manual a simple question, referring to quality, was posed: "Is the voice pleasant to listen to, or does it sound harsh, nasal, breathy, or hoarse?" The present chapter has helped you answer the question. Now, as the final assignment for this specific unit, prepare material which you especially enjoy. As you rehearse, rather than isolating any one of the several attributes of voice we have just been studying—relaxation, resonance, specific vocal faults—concentrate on the overall impression your voice is making on others. Or, as the question puts it, "Is the voice pleasant to listen to? . . ." The word "pleasant," however, does not mean artificial or exaggerated. For our purposes, it means agreeable, comfortable, and natural. The techniques which you use to produce this type of voice should be subdued and in no way call attention to themselves.

Note: Some may prefer to follow this chapter with chapter 6 ("Articulation") and then proceed to chapters 4 and 5 ("Loudness" and "Expressiveness").

Suggested Checklist for Assignments 2-3-4-5-6

As you practice by yourself you may want to work with this checklist. Listen carefully to yourself. If it is feasible, record the assignment or get a classmate or friend to listen to you as you read the material. Eventually your goal will be to have a check mark in the **Yes** column for each category which applies to you. (Optional: Perhaps your instructor will want to use the checklist to evaluate you during your classroom presentation (s).)

	Yes	No
Breathiness		
Avoids inefficient breathing habits, such as shallow or clavicular breathing.		
Avoids rigid or sloppy posture which may interfere with inhalation.		
Avoids noisy inhalation.		
Avoids overbreathing: taking in too much breath.		
Avoids excessively low loudness level.		
Avoids excessively low pitch level.		
Avoids wasting breath on voiceless consonants such as [s f th-θ h sh-$\int$ k p t].		
Avoids carrying over breathy quality from the voiceless consonants to adjacent vowels and consonants.		
Glottal Shock or Attack		
Avoids excessive tension or strain in throat or larynx.		
Avoids too high pitch level (which sometimes accompanies glottal shock).		
Harshness		
Strident		
Avoids excessive tensions and constrictions of pharynx and soft palate.		
Avoids shallow or clavicular breathing.		
Avoids excessive or improper loudness.		
Avoids too high pitch level.		

	Yes	No
Harshness		
Throaty		
Avoids too low loudness level.		
Avoids too low pitch level.		
Avoids pulling chin back against neck.		
Avoids excessive relaxation (laxness) of throat.		
Avoids excessive tensions and constrictions of lower part of pharynx.		
Avoids shallow or clavicular breathing.		
Nasality (Positive or Excessive Nasality)		
Avoids attitude of carelessness and general muscular sluggishness.		
Avoids permitting tongue to hump in rear of mouth.		
Avoids excessively rigid jaw and clenched teeth.		
Apparently maintains efficient control of the velum.		
Avoids nasalizing vowels before or after nasal consonants.		
Avoids too high pitch level.		
Avoids too low loudness level.		
Denasality (Negative or Inadequate Nasality)		
Apparently maintains efficient control of the velum.		
Avoids excessive tension in nasopharynx.		

Additional comments or suggestions:

Class Discussion: Loudness

(Use this page and the next one for note-taking. You will find a loudness analysis chart on pp. 267-68, and you may find it helpful as you begin your work in this unit.)

Loudness 4

Is my voice easily heard?

Most of us genuinely enjoy an exciting football or basketball game or a homecoming rally. Swept along by the enthusiasm of the crowd, we find ourselves shouting at the "top of our lungs." In more than one sense, the noisemaking is half the fun of attending a sports event. Now and then, however, some of us report to classes or our job the following Monday morning with a vocal "hangover." The throat is raw and inflamed, and the voice—what is left of it—is unpleasantly hoarse. It hurts us to talk. When this happens, we generally attribute our sore throats to excessive yelling, shrug it off, and assume that in a day or two most of the hoarseness and rawness will disappear. Vocal hangovers are by no means confined to sports enthusiasts. Lawyers, teachers, actors, and speakers—more often the green, inexperienced novice than the seasoned professional—become victims of acute hoarseness.

On the other hand, there are thousands of individuals whose jobs or professions require them to speak or sing loudly enough to be heard successfully over relatively large areas and not always with the help of a public address system. Consider the teacher who lectures several hours daily in a good-sized classroom. Consider the Broadway actor who must get his voice across to his audience as often as eight times a week. Consider the election year politician and his door to door, stump-to-stump electioneering, or the drill sergeant or the football coach, not to mention professional public speakers. Seldom do these individuals come down with vocal hangovers. The logical conclusion, then, is that it is the quality rather than the quantity of loudness which leads to hoarseness.

In this chapter we are primarily concerned with helping you develop a voice which is sufficiently loud for most normal, speaking situations rather than showing you how to cheer or shout at football games. Perhaps you have already felt a sense of irritation in listening to some of your friends, classmates, and professors because their voices simply do not carry or "get across." They are weak and unintelligible, even though the speaker seems to be moving his lips and jaw. Now and then, too, we are annoyed by the individual whose voice is constantly and painfully booming and roaring in our ears. Who has not encountered the telephone "blaster"? When this one calls us, we have to preserve our eardrums by holding the instrument at arm's length. Thus, we are not interested in developing loudness merely for the sake of loudness as such. Loudness must be adequate for the situation and it must be tempered and varied.

In reality, loudness is a comparative term which describes the strength of the sensation we receive through our hearing apparatus. The sound of rustling leaves has relatively little carrying power. We might describe such a sound as having weak or low intensity. The sound of a jet plane taking off has relatively great carrying power. We might describe such a sound as having strong or high intensity. (The noise of a jet plane taking off may range up to 140 decibels, a decibel being a unit to express the intensity of a sound wave.) Our ears interpret intensity as soft or loud or in other terms which fall some place in the range between. Loudness is often referred to as intensity (as already noted), volume, force, strength, or projection. All of these terms express some relationship to loudness, but a more detailed study of that relationship, although interesting, is not essential here.

What are some of the factors which will help us achieve adequate loudness?

1. *Openness of mouth.* Stated simply, some of us with weak voices do not open the mouth widely enough as we speak. The voice doesn't carry because, in a sense, it doesn't have much of a chance to get out of the mouth in the first place. It is perhaps true that convicts or prisoners in concentration camps have been forced to communicate with each other in this ventriloquist, not-moving-the-lips fashion, but it is a poor practice for the rest of us.

   As an experiment, try the old tongue twister, "Peter Piper picked a peck of pickled peppers" in three different ways:

   a. The first time, say it with as little lip or jaw activity as possible.
   b. The second time, say it with normal lip and jaw activity.
   c. The third time, exaggerate the oral activity.

   Can you feel the differences? If you feel that your voice is weak because of a bottled-up sound, you will need to review lip and jaw Exercises 23-25 in chapter 3 (or preview Exercises 1-7 in chapter 6).

2. *Proper pitch level.* Pitch levels which are too low sometimes go hand-in-hand with weak intensity. Likewise, a too-high pitch level is occasionally associated with weak intensity. You should use your best pitch level. This, of course, does not refer to a single tone but to a cluster of tones somewhere within your total speaking range. If you have a loudness problem and believe that it is related to a problem of pitch, you may wish to jump ahead to the next chapter, Exercises 1-13.

   Under some circumstances, even if an individual is using his best pitch level, he may still permit his pitch to jump upward as much as five or six tones when he is attempting to speak with considerable loudness.

3. *Maximum use of resonance.* Loudness, in part, results from the reinforcement of the original tone by the resonators. Hence, openness of throat and freedom from undue muscular constrictions are essential in developing loudness. If you need to, review Exercises 10-22 in chapter 3.

4. *Increase in breath pressure below the vocal folds.* A hardy and seasoned marine sergeant whose job was teaching potential drill instructors once told the writer, "I don't tell 'em anything scientific about shoutin' commands. I just tell 'em to pack the tone from the guts. And it works!"

   It probably does, too. To express it more delicately, however, the sergeant very likely saw to it that his students got their propulsive power from the muscles near the midregion of the body. The pressure of the muscles of exhalation must be firm and sustained. There must always be enough air in the lungs to maintain pressure.

   Should your breathing habits be rechecked at this point? See Chapter 2, Exercises 1-27.

5. *Clear tone quality.* Inadequate loudness is frequently paired with breathiness, hoarseness, or a harsh-guttural quality.

6. *Conscious control of rate and articulation.* "Speak slower" is obvious advice, but it is incomplete. To some, slowing down means putting longer pauses between words or phrases. More significantly, as far as loudness is concerned, it should mean slowing down on the words, that is, giving greater emphasis and duration to the vowels and diphthongs. Articulation, in general, will need to be more crisp and exact.

7. *Sufficient energy and animation.* The complex problem of personality threatens to becloud the picture again at this point. It might be emphasized, however, that shy, bashful individuals aren't always the only ones who are unable to get their voices across. Vocal laziness, not to mention indifference, inevitably hinders good projection.

   Another complication stymies our attempt to help the vocally lazy individual. At the moment you have made this type of person speak loudly enough, he invariably protests: "But I'm screaming!"

We must then convince him that to his hearers he probably is not screaming. If his mental and physical health is good, his projection will be helped immeasurably if he deliberately attempts to speak with more strength, force, and energy. Such communication is not a haphazard by-product of the breathing mechanisms, the resonators and the articulators. It is an integrated, overall process in which the entire body must respond. He will also discover that enthusiam and animation are not unattainable to one who has something to say, a purpose in saying it and, above all, a strong desire to say it.

What are some of the factors, concerned with the situation and the material being presented, which will help us to achieve adequate loudness?

Room or area: size and acoustical qualities. It almost borders on the absurd to say that our loudness will have to be greater if we speak in a 2,000 seat auditorium than it will be in a 9′ x 12′ living room. And yet we have all been exposed to the kind of speaker who finds himself in an unfamiliar room or area, and, without the aid of a mike, cannot be heard. His problem is lack of experience or an inability to adapt rather than laziness. After all, he himself is close to the source of the sound, and he has no difficulty comprehending what he is saying.

Audience size and proximity. We should not have to "turn up the volume" in a coke or coffee conversation with three friends in a booth to the same extent that we do if we talk to thirty or 300 in a large assembly room.

The nearness of the audience is also important. To a partner five feet away we can pitch a baseball with a mere flick of the wrist. If he is standing fifty feet away, more energy and strength are required.

Competing noises. It must be noted regretfully that the general noise level in cities is rising. One study has indicated that background noises are apparently increasing at the rate of one decibel a year.

Record players and radios, low-flying aircraft, motorcycles, cars, and, always, the sounds that the human animal makes offer us frequent competition. In the face of this, you must try to be heard without screaming or straining your voice. Undoubtedly, under some circumstances, silence is the best solution.

Nature of material being presented. Material which expresses relatively strong and forceful emotions or ideas (happiness, elation, rage, anger, conviction) is often more effective if relatively loud levels are used. Material which expresses sadness, despair, profundity, moodiness, or sincerity is frequently more effective if relatively quiet levels are used.

Later in the chapter we will examine in greater detail variations in loudness.

In the following exercises we will arbitrarily use four relative levels of loudness: (a) soft (avoid whispering), (b) medium loud, (c) loud, (d) very loud.

1. As a sergeant in charge of a squad, you are about to give the command, "Ready! Aim! Fire!" four times. The first time, you are standing next to your squad. The first level of loudness will do. The second time, you stand about ten yards from your squad. The second level of loudness will do. The third and fourth times, you stand about twenty and thirty yards away, necessitating the use of the third and fourth levels. As you give the command four times, deliberately tighten the throat muscles, do not try to control the pitch levels and, especially the fourth time, let the sound "blast."

    As a result of this negative practice (and don't try it more than once) you will certainly feel or hear several things: an excessive upward swoop in pitch, a strangled and strident vocal quality on levels three and four, and a possible slight strain or irritation in the throat. All of these are highly undesirable elements in achieving loudness.

Here are some exercises which use a proper and positive approach:

2. Begin *ah* softly, and then increase it to your loudest tone of good quality. Sustain the loud tone for a few seconds, and then decrease it to your softest tone of good quality. Repeat several times, keeping the pitch constant.

3. Using the procedure suggested in Exercise 2, substitute these sounds: *ee, oh, aye, oo, uh.*

4. Sustain *ah* at a comfortable pitch level for about five seconds. Keep the throat open, keep the pitch steady, and avoid strain. Try it at the four levels of loudness.

5. Repeat this procedure, using the sounds listed in Exercise 3.

6. Count as far as you can on one breath, beginning softly and gradually building a crescendo. Reverse the pattern by starting with the number you previously reached, counting backward, and gradually decreasing the loudness.

7. Musicians are concerned with signs and symbols as well as notes. The sign ⟨ indicates a gradual increase in loudness or intensity (a crescendo). The sign ⟩ indicates a gradual decrease in loudness or intensity (a decrescendo). Borrowing these convenient signs, read the following as indicated:

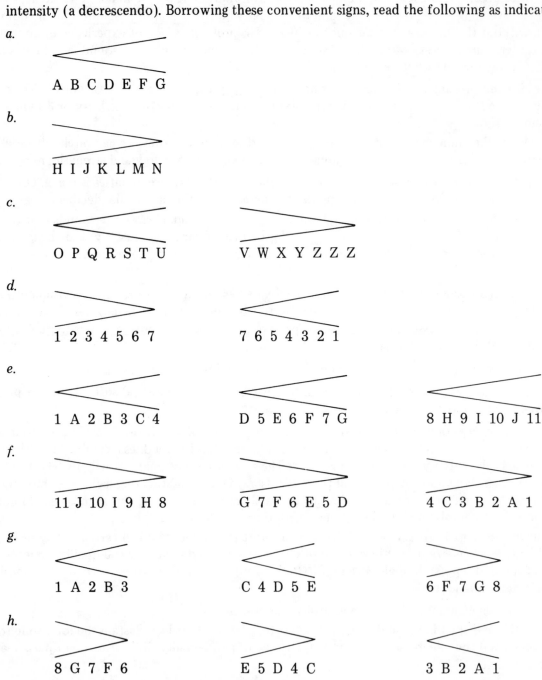

a.

A B C D E F G

b.

H I J K L M N

c.

O P Q R S T U V W X Y Z Z

d.

1 2 3 4 5 6 7 7 6 5 4 3 2 1

e.

1 A 2 B 3 C 4 D 5 E 6 F 7 G 8 H 9 I 10 J 11

f.

11 J 10 I 9 H 8 G 7 F 6 E 5 D 4 C 3 B 2 A 1

g.

1 A 2 B 3 C 4 D 5 E 6 F 7 G 8

h.

8 G 7 F 6 E 5 D 4 C 3 B 2 A 1

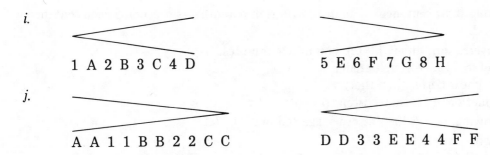

i.

1 A 2 B 3 C 4 D   5 E 6 F 7 G 8 H

j.

A A 1 1 B B 2 2 C C   D D 3 3 E E 4 4 F F

8. In reading each of the following at the four levels of loudness, inhale deeply and quickly. Release the breath suddenly and with a quick contraction of the abdominal muscles. Do not squeeze the words out of the throat, but keep the throat as "open" as possible.

a.	Hey!	*h.*	About face!
b.	Halt!	*i.*	Port arms!
c.	March!	*j.*	Shoulder arms!
d.	Stop!	*k.*	Order arms!
e.	Left face!	*l.*	To the rear, march!
f.	Right face!	*m.*	Ready! Set! Go!
g.	Eyes right!	*n.*	Ahoy there!

9. In the following selections, as a reminder:

    (1) indicates the first level of loudness: *soft.*
    (2) indicates the second level: *medium loud.*
    (3) indicates the third level: *loud.*
    (4) indicates the fourth level: *very loud.*

For practice purposes, be careful to sustain the loudness quite evenly at the specified level. Avoid the tendency, especially at the third and fourth levels, to punch the beginning of the line and then let the final words of each phrase fade away.

a.   (1) He that fights and runs away
     (2) May turn and fight another day;
     (3) But he that is in battle slain
     (4) Will never rise to fight again.

b.   (1) Stand! the ground's your own, my braves!
     (2) Will ye give it up to slaves?
     (3) Will ye look for greener graves?
     (4) Hope ye mercy still?

c.   (1) What's the mercy despots feel?
     (2) Hear it in that battle peal!
     (3) Read it on yon bristling steel!
     (4) Ask it,—ye who will.

d.   (1) In the God of battles trust!
     (2) Die we may, and die we must:
     (3) But, Oh, where can dust to dust
     (4) Be consigned so well?

     [Pierpont, "Warren's Address at Bunker Hill"]

10. Drill with the following short sentences. The instructions in parentheses preceding each sentence will suggest a loudness level.

   a. **(Telephone conversation: quiet)** I'll see you in five minutes.
      (Casual, face-to-face) He's a rough grader.
      (Vigorous) You know better than that!
      (Strong determination) I refuse to listen to you!

   As you read the following, repeat the pattern suggested in *a*, above:

   b. I have no idea where she is.
      Let's go on a picnic tonight.
      He always cheats in tests.
      I've never been so mad.

   c. Sorry, but I'm busy tonight.
      Sorry, but I'm busy tonight.
      Sorry, but I'm busy tonight.
      Sorry, but I'm busy tonight.

   d. I was just taking a nap.
      Where did you get that good looking tie?
      Boy, I can't wait for vacation!
      I want my money, and I want it now.

   e. I haven't seen you in months.
      Why is that card up your sleeve?
      I don't care what you think.
      I don't care what anyone thinks.

   f. Do you know what I saw today?
      They used to go together.
      I do not believe that God is dead.
      Don't bother me. Let me alone!

   g. I don't watch TV any more.
      I heard that she was seriously ill.
      I do believe that God is dead.
      I'll never wait for you again.

   h. I'm getting a new roommate.
      Isn't the food around here terrible?
      You've said that a hundred times.
      Listen to me: We're all through!

11. To practice the following material, go to a large room or auditorium if possible. The members of the class should be scattered around the room. Stand at one end and read each of the following lines at the four levels of loudness. The first level should easily reach those seated nearest to you. The second level should easily reach those who are seated somewhat farther away, etc. As you continue practicing, you should be able to develop the ability to project material read at the first level of loudness to those seated the greatest distance from you. It is true that they may not hear your first and second levels as comfortably as your last two levels, but if you are doing a good job, you will find that even a whisper can be made to carry over a considerable area.

   The lines should be read under the following conditions:

   Speak at a comfortable pitch level. Carefully avoid excessive increase of pitch.

   Get the support, not from the throat itself, but from below the larynx, that is, from or reasonably near the central portion of the body.

Strive for maximum, controlled relaxation.

Prolong the accented vowels and diphthongs slightly.

a. And soon I heard a roaring wind: it did not come anear.
b. Arm! Arm! It is the cannon's opening roar!
c. Cry "God for Harry, England, and Saint George!"
d. Roll on, thou deep and dark blue ocean, roll!
e. O World, I cannot hold thee close enough.
f. A fig for those protected! Liberty's a glorious feast!
g. Life is real! Life is earnest! And the grave is not its goal.
h. Alas! Alas! With me the light of day is o'er.
i. Ring, happy bells, across the snow; the year is going, let him go.
j. The long light breaks across the lakes, and the wild cataract leaps in glory.
k. Break, break, break, on thy cold, gray stones, O sea!
l. I am the master of my fate: I am the captain of my soul.
m. O Captain! my Captain! rise up and hear the bells.
n. Lord God of Hosts, be with us yet, lest we forget!
o. I must go down to the seas again, to the lonely sea and the sky!
p. Flame out, you glorious skies; welcome our brave!
q. A horse! a horse! my kingdom for a horse!
r. March we along, fifty score strong; great-hearted gentlemen, singing this song!
s. Heave at the windlass! Heave all at once, with a will!
t. A Yankee ship and a Yankee crew! Ye ho, ye hoo! Ye ho, ye hoo!
u. Ye crags and peaks, I'm with you once again.
v. The anchor heaves! The ship swings free! To sea, to sea!
w. Come live, be merry and join with me to swing the sweet chorus of "Ha, ha, ha!"
x. "Forward, the light brigade! Charge for the guns!" he said.
y. Who cares for nothing alone is free—sit down, good fellow, and drink with me!
z. Fifteen men on the dead man's chest—Yo-ho-ho, and a bottle of rum!
aa. Into the jaws of death, into the mouth of hell rode the six hundred.
bb. Put your trust in God, my boys, and keep your powder dry!

Projection

The term "projection" has already been used. Obviously, it has something important to do with loudness, but because it also has a rather special meaning, we will give it some extra consideration.

A bride tosses her bouquet. Customarily, she throws it in the general direction of the bridesmaids, not necessarily at a specific young lady. A baseball pitcher throws a ball, but he aims it in the direction of a specific individual—the catcher.

If we speak of loudness, we are, in a sense, "tossing" our voice in a general direction and over a general area with sufficient strength and power so that most of those present can hear and understand what we are saying. If we speak of projection, we are beaming the voice to a particular individual, group or a rather specific area.

Projection is a difficult term to define, and it is all but impossible to approach it from a "scientific" point of view.

Projection is controlled energy which gives impact and intelligibility to sound. On the part of the speaker, it also involves a deliberate concentration and a strong desire to communicate with his listeners.

Athletic, crisp articulation is essential, but, additionally, one makes maximum use of resonance to aid in "beaming" and focusing the sound. Breath control must be flexible but firm. A projected voice does not merely reach its hearers, it penetrates them.

Directors and actors use the word constantly, and it is well that they do. We have all attended amateur and professional plays and complained that we could not "hear" the actors. Perhaps what we really meant was that we did not "understand" them. Their loudness may have been adequate—perhaps they were even shouting—but their voices only reached, rather than penetrated us. Yet the actor who knows how to project rather than merely speak loudly can be understood easily even when he is speaking sotto voce—in a low, soft voice.

The concluding scene of Edward Albee's hell-raising *Who's Afraid of Virginia Woolf?* finds the two principal actors, after more than two hours of shouting profanity and semihysteria, in a mood of quiet, hushed exhaustion. They spoke their lines at the loudness level of a semiwhisper. But every word they said was heard at the rear of the Broadway theater.

Another example of successful projection in the theater: Have you ever attended a play produced in "theater-in-the-round," arena or central staging? Here the audience is often seated on four sides of a centrally placed platform. This means that regardless of where an actor stands, he has some part of his audience which cannot see his face. The actor who projects will be easily heard and understood by that same segment of the audience.

Exercises can hardly provide the student with psychological "know-how" to project: the motivation to want his hearers to understand his every word. But exercises can help the student with certain purely mechanical aspects of projection. Resonance, breath control, and articulation have already been mentioned in this discussion, and it is quite possible that articulation is the most important.

12. Here is an approach which is different from the ones used in the chapter dealing with articulation:

   For an assignment in loudness, a student, as requested, brings in vigorous material. Three of his lines are, for example:

   > Listen, my children, and you shall hear,
   > Of the midnight ride of Paul Revere.

   > I must go down to the seas again, to the lonely sea and sky.

   Such material is well suited to energetic projection. The problem is that it is so obviously familiar to most of us that even if the performer garbles it, swallows his words, and completely fails to project, our memories step in as prompters and recall some of the lines for us anyway. As a result, it is our memory that supplies the intelligibility and not the student. So we may give him an A or a B for what actually may have been a rather slovenly and unprojected performance. We might argue that he should use unfamiliar material. As a matter of fact, he could even write his own "stuff." But even here, the student will almost inevitably rely upon rather common word associations, groupings, and clusters. And once again our memories, guided by habits and patterns of verbalization that we have acquired over the years, often tend to make the indistinct distinct, the unintelligible intelligible.

   A partial solution, and a more interesting challenge to us, is the use of nonsense material. Such material may be constructed of, for example, real words combined or used in grammatically illogical combinations and groupings. In reading nonsense material you will discover that loudness alone will not put your material over. You will be constrained to round out and prolong the vowels and diphthongs and, above all, to attack the consonants with sharpness, precision, and accuracy.

   Your immediate goal, then, in projecting such a line of gibberish as: *Foam, the riddled has-been, snapped a rose to a now fly,* is obviously not that of getting across specific meanings, thoughts, or ideas. Your objective should be the intelligible and forceful projection of speech sounds.

   As you practice the following, use a comfortable level of loudness, but read energetically and with "athletic" articulation:

   a. Cora, the crust, sat on the noise by the she-ram.
   b. The gulp hid the perch over the smasher in the saddle.
   c. Bruce canned his riddles and docks by painting smog.

d. The foot vandal met Art's suet in Gunner's great acre.
e. It grabbed mush and hiked buzz from no side, they sang.
f. Oafs roped tan oil bombs from a silt cutter tomorrow.
g. The flip frame wolfed up groups of pepper cottons with Ida.
h. The candied bandana was real George on your quiet moon.
i. Will Jumbo ride the blue calf at the track pudding deck?
j. The limp forest reeked of hoofing owls and warped whistles.
k. Wells of soda gurgled toward doghats and green oxen.
l. The lead feather washed a fish snorkel on no sneezy axe.
m. Did Jay rake wires and tar toes with omens?
n. On, three, on, four, and do not sniff cliffs of old, young corks.
o. Tap the brick when the blue tack rides too low-high in prunes.

Obviously we do not spend our lives communicating with fellow creatures through the use of nonsense sentences. But perhaps the previous exercise has made you more sensitive to the need for energetic and forceful articulation in order to project intelligibly. Can you carry over this awareness into non-nonsense material, some of which is conversational? It is not always the public speaker who fails to project; it is frequently the person in private or "everyday" conversation.

13. Speak the following energetically and enthusiastically. In addition to resonating the tone as richly as you can and giving yourself strong and sturdy breath support, you must have an urgent desire to project your feelings and sincerity.

a. When angry, count ten before you speak. If very angry, count a hundred.
b. If mankind had wished for what is right, they might have had it long ago.
c. There will never be any peace for those who resist God.
d. You cannot put a great hope into a small soul.
e. Keep cool and you command everybody.
f. Judge no one before you have been in his place.
g. Many a truth sprang from an error.
h. Nobody ever commits a crime without doing something stupid.
i. Why stand we here idle? What is it that gentlemen wish? What would they have? Is life so dear, or peace so sweet, as to be purchased at the price of chains and slavery? Forbid it, Almighty God! I know not what course others may take; but as for me, give me liberty, or give me death!
j. You shall not press down upon the brow of labor this crown of thorns. You shall not crucify mankind upon a cross of gold.
k. We shall fight on the beaches, we shall fight on the landing grounds, we shall fight in the fields and in the streets, we shall fight in the hills; we shall never surrender.
l. While there is a lower class I am in it; while there is a criminal element I am of it; while there is a soul in prison, I am not free.
m. There is a homely adage which runs, "Speak softly and carry a big stick; you will go far."
n. Books cannot be killed by fire. People die, but books never die. No man and no force can abolish memory. In this or any war, we know, books are weapons.
o. America: It is a fabulous country, the only place where miracles not only happen, but where they happen all the time.
p. A man said to the prophet, "Give me a command." He said, "Do not get angry." The man repeated the question several times, and he said, "Do not get angry."
q. Never shrink from doing anything which your business calls you to do. The man who is above his business may one day find his business above him.
r. With malice toward none; with charity for all; with firmness in the right, as God gives us to see the right, let us strive on to finish the work we are in; to bind up the nation's wounds: to care for him who shall have borne the battle, and for his widow, and his orphans—to do all which may achieve and cherish a just and lasting peace among ourselves, and with all nations.

Assignment 7 (See suggested Checklist for this assignment)

Prepare vigorous and energetic material which lends itself to forceful projection. Divide your material into four sections, and present it using the four levels of loudness (soft, medium loud, loud, very loud). If possible, your performance should be given in a large room or auditorium.

or

Prepare nonsense material (you may wish to write your own) or select serious material which is suitable for lively projection. Again, your presentation should be made in a large room or auditorium. "Beam" it at individual members or sections of your group, but before you have finished you should make sure that each listener feels that you have spoken to him personally at least once.

Levels of Loudness

Loudness, as we have previously said, must be adequate for the situation, and it must be tempered and varied. Obviously, we will need to use something akin to the fourth level of loudness if we call a friend a block away. In the telephone booth, however, something akin to the first level will do. But what of the speaker or the actor in a large room? Must he use the fourth level exclusively? By no means. It would not only be unnecessary, it would also become extremely monotonous.

In reality, to deal with loudness in terms of four levels is a rather artificial device. There are probably forty or perhaps four hundred levels. In other words, the nuances and shadings are infinite. As a rough approximation of what is meant, it might be presented this way:

Level 1: Soft	Soft soft Medium loud soft Loud soft Very loud soft	
Level 2: Medium Loud	Soft medium loud Medium loud medium loud Loud medium loud Very loud medium loud	
Level 3: Loud	Soft loud Medium loud loud Loud loud Very loud loud	
Level 4: Very Loud	Soft very loud Medium loud very loud Loud very loud Very loud very loud	

Such arbitrary classifications are, of course, relatively ridiculous, or as one student put it, "ridiculously relative." But perhaps they might serve to remind us of the innumerable gradations and subtleties possible for us to achieve within any one level—indeed, within one sentence or even a phrase.

14. What helps us determine variations within the general levels of loudness? A few suggestions are offered here. In the following chapter, vocal variations of all kinds will be explored in greater depth.

The Need for Accent, Stress, or Emphasis

Accent: *The degree of prominence of a syllable within a word. The syllable is made louder and frequently higher in pitch than adjoining syllables. We accent syllables because English is a subtle language, and because it is often an aid to intelligibility. There are obvious differences between convict and convict, between project and project.*

Read the following words and make the underlined syllables louder than the other syllables in the same word:

li . brary   con . clu . sive   dis . crim . i . na . tion
re . bel   ev . i . dence   va . ca . tion . ist
re . bel   prob . a . bly   Mis . sis . sipp . i . an
cav . al . ry   po . di . um   re . pub . li . ca . tion
con . cern   neg . li . gee   prop . a . gan . da
quar . ter   u . til . i . ty   oc . ca . sion . al
re . proach   guar . an . tee   re . spect . a . bil . i . ty

Stress: *The degree of prominence of a word within a phrase or sentence. The word is made louder and frequently higher in pitch than adjacent words. We stress words to make meaning and feeling clear. Nouns and verbs, as well as their modifiers, adjectives and adverbs, often carry the meaning of a sentence. Such words are generally given more loudness than the less important articles, prepositions, conjunctions, and occasionally pronouns.*

Read aloud the following, observing the differences in meanings as you stress the underlined words:

a. What did you say to him?
b. What did you say to him?
c. What did you say to him?
d. What did you say to him?
e. What did you say to him?

Emphasis: *The degree of prominence given to a phrase or thought-grouping. An important phrase, or one containing a key idea, is made louder, and sometimes the pitch will be higher or lower than neighboring phrases or sentences.*

Read the following twice. The first time, emphasize the underlined sections. The second time, emphasize a different section. Do you notice differences in meaning?

a. I'll give you the money tomorrow. But not today.
b. I forgot all about it. I refuse to apologize.
c. I told you this would happen. I knew it would happen.
d. Professor Jones, from what I hear, is a terrible grader.
e. When Jack hit Joe, he lost control of the car, and it rolled over.
f. The telephone rang, so I answered it.
g. They didn't understand *Hamlet*, because they talked all the way through it.
h. You can fool some of the people all of the time, and all of the people some of the time: but you can't fool all of the people all of the time.

The Need for Psychological Contrast

A charming legend tells us that the 18th century composer, Franz Joseph Haydn, tried an unusual stunt in his "Surprise" Symphony. Fearing that the audience might snooze during the performance and especially during the quiet section of the work, he inserted several extremely loud, crashing chords where they would be least expected. "That's sure to make them jump," he said.

The story is probably not altogether true, but Haydn was a clever musical psychologist, and he knew the value of dramatic contrast.

An experienced speaker or reader may be presenting his ideas or material at a relatively low volume level for a few minutes. Then he comes to a key idea or punch line, and his volume level is suddenly raised to a near-shout. Conversely, he may be speaking at a moderately loud or loud level, and just before he gets to his major point, he drops the volume to a near-whisper. In the first case, the hearers may be jolted; in the second, the hearers may lean forward, feeling that they are being taken into the speaker's private confidence and are sharing information of dramatic importance.

It must be emphasized that either device involves a certain degree of showmanship. Their constant use would make them quite ineffective. They should be used sparingly.

Far more subtle is the method in which the loudness is gradually increased over a short period of time. Here, too, an audience will sometimes lean forward expectantly, waiting for the climactic moment. This device, when reversed—going gradually from the loud-loud to the soft-soft—is also quite effective.

15. As an experiment, read the following selection at a moderately loud level—loud enough to carry easily in your classroom. Pause when you reach the pause marks: / /. Deliberately read the final phrases, after the pause marks, at your most comfortable very loud level (level 4):

The manuscript? Well . . . I have torn the manuscript into a thousand pieces. I have torn my own life to pieces. So why should I not tear my lifework, too? Yes, I tell you! A thousand pieces—and scattered them on the fjord. There is cool sea-water at any rate—let the pieces drift on it, drift with the current and the wind. / / And then presently they will sink—deeper and deeper—as I shall, Hedda. [Ibsen, *Hedda Gabler*]

16. Reverse the procedure and read the selection again. The material before the pause should be read at a relatively very loud level. The final phrases should be read at a soft level (level 1).

17. Repeat the procedures suggested in Exercises 15 and 16 as you read the following:

I can see him there . . . he grins . . . he is looking at my nose . . . that skeleton. What's that you say? Hopeless? Why, very well! But a man does not fight merely to win! No no. . . better to know one fights in vain! You there! Who are you? A hundred against one! I know them now, my ancient enemies! Falsehood! Prejudice! Cowardice! What's that? Surrender? No! Never, never! / / Yet in spite of you, there is one crown I bear away with me, and tonight when I enter before God, my salute shall sweep all the stars away from the blue threshold! One thing without stain, unblemished, unspotted . . . and that is . . . my white plume! [Rostand, *Cyrano de Bergerac*]

18. As you read the following, begin softly with level 1. Gradually increase the loudness, so that as you reach the end of the selection, you will be at level 4—very loud.

But what good does all this do me now? What good is anything to me now that you've taken away my vision of eternity? What can I do with my life, when I've lost my honor? I grafted my right arm and half my brain on to another trunk, because I thought they would all grow together . . . into one perfect tree. And then someone came along with a knife and cut off the grafted part. So I'm only a half-tree. But the other half—it keeps growing with my one arm on it and my half-brain . . . while I fade away and die because I've given the best part of myself away. I want to die now! Do what you want with me! I've ceased to exist! [Strindberg, *The Father*]

19. Reread the selection in Exercise 18, reversing the suggested procedure: Start at level 4 and gradually reduce the loudness to level 1.

20. Practice the following in various ways. Try each one with the procedures described in Exercises 15-19.

   a. Do you think it was done coldly, cunningly? I was not the same person then that I am now, standing right here and telling you this. Do you know something? I think there are two sorts of will, of desire, in everyone. I wanted that woman out of the way, but I never really thought it would happen. With every step I took, I felt as if something seemed to shriek inside me. No further! Not a step further! But I could not stop. I had to go just a little further. Just one step, and then another, always one more. And so it happened. That's the way things like that do happen. [Ibsen, *Rosmersholm*]

   b. Well, I'll be darned! What's on the schedule now? Why are all these men trying to surround me? What do you men want? What's all the commotion about? Why are you closing in on me all of a sudden? What's the rush? Where are we going? Some rumble! Hell's bells! They've grabbed me. Damn it all! Citizens, friends, to the rescue! Save me, fellow citizens! Help! Let me go, you donkeys, you asses! [Plautus, *The Menaechmi*]

c. Ye Gods! That's it! Now nobody, but nobody, is going to stop me from going straight to your wife and telling her the truth . . . the whole story about you and your little schemes. You just wait, you parasite, until this stuff starts coming back at you. That banquet you enjoyed and I never got to is going to give you bad dreams. Wait and see! [Plautus, *The Menaechmi*]

d. And Jesus replied, "Today you will be with Me in paradise. This is a solemn promise." By now it was noon, and darkness fell across the whole land for three hours, until 3 o'clock. The light from the sun was gone—and suddenly the thick veil hanging in the Temple split apart. Then Jesus shouted, "Father, I commit My spirit to You," and with those words he died. [*New Testament*]

e. He seemed so old and still he's so young. His face was as warm as spring, but his heart was as cold as winter. It was a sad thing. A weary body can always find a place to rest, but what about a weary mind? I've just had a terrible thought: I think that there are people who are unhappy, and incurably so, simply because they are alive . . . because they exist! [Buechner, *Leonce and Lena*]

f. The knife, where's the knife? I left it here. It'll give me away! What is this place? I hear something . . . something that's moving! But now it's quiet . . . so very quiet! Marie, Marie . . . why are you so pale? Where did you get those red beads that you are wearing around your neck, Marie? Did you earn them with your sins? Your sins made you black, Marie, and I made you pale. But the knife, the knife! There! I've got it. Now, into the water with it! Ha, it'll get rusty! Nobody will ever find it! But why didn't I break it first? And am I still bloody? I've got to wash myself. There's a spot, there, and there's another. [Buechner, *Woyzeck*]

g. Pardon me, but you are not engaged to anyone. When you do become engaged to someone, I, or your father, should his health permit him, will inform you of the fact. An engagement should come to a young girl as a surprise, pleasant or unpleasant, as the case may be. It is hardly a matter that she should be allowed to arrange herself. And now I have a few questions to put to you, Mr. Worthing. While I am making these inquiries, you, Gwendolen, will wait for me below in the carriage. [Wilde, *The Importance of Being Earnest*]

h. One day you will know the truth. This is tyranny! They have torn off the veil, they carry their heads high, they tread upon our corpses. I accuse Robespierre and his executioners of high treason. They will smother the Republic in blood. The tracks of the tumbrils will be the highways of invading armies into the very heart of France. You ask for bread, and they throw you our heads. You are thirsty, and they make you lick our blood from the steps of the guillotine! [Buechner, *Danton's Death*]

It is hoped that the exercises in this chapter will help you develop loudness which is sufficient for the situation as well as flexible and varied. Frankly, however, many of these exercises, in themselves, have an artificial basis. A good speaker or reader in performing does not necessarily concentrate on loudness levels 1, 2, 3, or 4, accent, stress, emphasis, or psychological contrast. These, at best, are "gimmicks" which when used judiciously will help him.

21. The following practice material is not marked in any way. As you read, concentrate—not on "gimmicks"—but on achieving sufficient and varied loudness.

a. Absolutely speaking, "Do unto others as you would that they should do unto you" is by no means a golden rule, but the best of current silver. An honest man would have but little occasion for it. [Thoreau]

b. Charles Lamb was hotly attacking the character and reputation of a certain person, when his hearer, rather surprised at this outburst, interrupted it to say that he had no idea that Lamb knew the man in question. "Know him!" Lamb exclaimed. "Of course I don't know him. I never could hate anyone I knew." [Thoreau]

c. Somebody once asked Beethoven, "Master, how, when, where did you think of the beautiful theme in your third symphony?" "Well, it was like this. I walked out to the woods, and when it got hot and I got hungry, I sat down by a little brook and unpacked my cheese and sausage. And just as I opened the greasy paper, that darn tune pops into my head!"

d. When you command a dog to "sit up," the poor idiot thinks he has to do it. The average cat throws off, pretends to be stupid and not to understand what you want. He really understands you too well, but he sees nothing in it for him. Why sit up?

e. I was thinking of an old idea of self-discipline—an old proverb of a Chinese Christian. He prayed every day—he had been taught to pray to our kind of God—and his prayer was, "Lord, reform Thy world, beginning with me."

f. An old lady was accused by her nieces of not being logical. For some time she could not be brought to understand what logic was, and when she grasped its true nature, she exclaimed: "Logic! Good gracious! What rubbish! How can I tell what I think until I see what I say?"

g. A man who had not seen Smith for a long time greeted him with these words: "You haven't changed at all." "Oh," said Smith, deeply shocked.

h. May blessings light upon him who first invented sleep! It is food for the hungry, drink for the thirsty, heat for the cold, and cold for the hot. It is the coin that buys all things, and the balance that makes the king even with the shepherd, and the fool with the wise. [Cervantes]

i. When a man suffers, he ought not to say: "That's bad! That's bad!" Nothing that God imposes on man is bad. But it is all right to say: "That's bitter!" For among medicines there are some that are made with bitter herbs. [Hasidic saying]

j. You should not anger yourself about this world: it does not care. Whatever comes, assign to its proper place in your little world and you will be happy!

k. If you are beasts, then stand here like fat oxen, waiting for the butcher's knife! If you are men, follow me! Strike down that guard, gain the mountain passes, and there do bloody work, as did your forefathers. Is Sparta dead? Is the old Grecian spirit frozen in your veins, that you do cower and shiver like frightened dogs beneath their masters' lashes? O, comrades, warriors! If we must fight, let us fight for ourselves! If we must slaughter, let us slaughter our oppressors! If we must die, let it be under the clear sky, by the bright waters, in noble, honorable battle! [Spartacus to the Gladiators]

l. If it had not been for these things, I might have lived out my life, talking at street corners to scorning men. I might have died, unmarked, unknown, a failure. Now we are not a failure. This is our career and our triumph. Never in our full life can we hope to do such work for tolerance, for justice, for man's understanding of man, as now we do by an accident. Our words, our lives, our pains—nothing! The taking of our lives—lives of a good shoemaker and a poor fish peddler—all! That last moment belong to us, that agony is our triumph! [Vanzetti to Judge Thayer]

m. My Lords, you cannot, I venture to say, you cannot conquer America. What is your present situation there? We do not know the worst, but we know that in three campaigns we have done nothing and suffered much. You may swell every expense and strain every effort; you may traffic and barter with every pitiful German Prince who sells and sends his subjects to the shambles of a foreign country. Your efforts are forever vain! For it irritates the minds of your enemies, to overrun them with the sordid sons of plunder! If I were an American as I am an Englishman, while a foreign troop was landed in my country, I never would lay down my arms!—never! never! never! [William Pitt (1777)]

n. I understand, Mady . . . There is, however, one thing I haven't had the courage to tell you until tonight . . . My dear children, devoted wife, faithful servants . . . Have any of you stopped to think why, after a lifetime of luxury and prosperity, we're suddenly living in a house that's twelve degrees colder than it is outside? Have you wondered why plumbers, electricians, supermarkets have all turned their backs on us? Why a butcher that I have personally kept in business for fifteen years, by buying the finest beef in the world, sends over meat that three of our cats walked away from? The answer is . . . I am being tested! Tested for my courage and strength. [Neil Simon, *God's Favorite*][1]

1. Excerpt from *God's Favorite* by Neil Simon © 1975 Neil Simon, reprinted by permission. All rights reserved.

Assignment 8 (See suggested Checklist for Assignments 7 and 8)

Bring to class and be prepared to read fifteen to twenty lines of material. Avoid purely descriptive or expository material. Select something which will give you an opportunity to approach loudness as subtly as you can. A narrative, especially one containing dialogue, is often effective for this type of assignment. Read it with enough overall loudness to be heard in a reasonably large room, but work for as much contrast and variety in loudness as you can.

Suggested Checklist for Assignments 7 and 8

As you practice by yourself you may want to work with this checklist. Listen carefully to yourself. If it is feasible record this assignment or get a classmate or friend to listen to you as you read the material. Eventually your goal will be to have a check mark in the **Yes** column for each category. (Optional: Perhaps your instructor will want to use the checklist to evaluate you during your classroom presentation.)

	Yes	No
Adjusts to size and proximity of audience.		
Adjusts to size and acoustical qualities of room.		
Responds to emotional nature of material.		
Varies loudness for expressiveness: demonstrates awareness of accent, stress, emphasis.		
Displays sufficient energy and animation.		
Maintains maximum, controlled overall relaxation.		
Propulsive force comes from muscles near midregion of body.		
Avoids undue muscular constriction and tension of throat.		
Avoids breathiness, harshness, hoarseness.		
Avoids breathlessness: gasping for breath.		
Avoids rigid jaw, clenched teeth, immobile lips.		
Avoids too low pitch level.		
Avoids too high pitch level.		
Avoids excessive upward jumps in pitch.		
Avoids starting on a loud tone and then fading to an inaudible one.		

Additional comments or suggestions:

Class Discussion: The Expressive Voice
(Use this page for note-taking. You will find an expressiveness analysis chart on pp. 269-70 and you may find it helpful as you begin your work in this unit.)

The Expressive Voice 5

Is my voice varied and flexible?

> Now I lay me down to sleep,
> The lecture dry, the subject deep;
> If he should quit before I wake,
> Give me a poke, for heaven's sake!
>
> Anonymous

This bit of doggerel is, unfortunately, too often the classroom prayer of too many students. The really significant phrase consists of the three words at the beginning of the second line: "The lecture dry . . . ." In a sense, that phrase is a key to what this chapter is about.

Recent surveys at 50 colleges and universities gave several thousand students the opportunity to rate their instructors on "teaching personality" and to explain or comment briefly upon their ratings. Here is a simple breakdown of some of the results:

General Ratings of Instructors	Reasons or Comments
Superior, Excellent, Good	Enthusiastic delivery, alive, brisk, peppy, alert, vocally animated, dynamic way of expressing himself, lots of personality, varied, uses lots of inflections, vivid, cool, energetic, vivacious.
Fair, Inferior	A monotone, drones and chants, indifferent, lacks animation, singsong, sluggish, stale, dull to listen to, bored with himself, sounds the same in everything he says, no enthusiasm, dead.

No doubt, many of these words and phrases are somewhat ambiguous, but in either category, do they not more or less echo labels and descriptions we ourselves have so often applied to the hundreds of voices we listen to? And as far as the second category is concerned, let it not be said that we are attempting to perpetuate the stereotype of the pompous, dull, absent-minded professor; for we remind ourselves that vocal monotony is by no means an occupational hazard peculiar to the teaching profession. Similar surveys could be conducted in such groups as ministers, lawyers, congressmen, housewives, and, it almost goes without saying, students.

Actually we are not so much interested in the identity of the drone as we are in why he is that way. In general, vocal monotony has its roots in: (a) personality characteristics, (b) purposes of the speaker, including his subject matter and the general nature of his material, (c) the attitudes, moods, and emotions of the speaker, (d) faulty habits, (e) health and hearing.

Let us set up a drone's gallery and determine in which category, if any, we belong.

Personality Characteristics

1. Somnolent Samuel. He thinks slowly, moves slowly, and speaks slowly.
2. Bashful Basil. He is shy, modest, timid, or reserved.
3. Unimaginative Undine. She is just plain dull, her greatest lack being that of imagination.
4. Slothful Sylvia. She is lazy and inert. Her principal lack is physical energy.
5. Frigid Frederick. He is a "cold fish" and emotionally unresponsive.

At this point, the obvious should be made more obvious. The drone types listed above are oversimplifications. There are surely hundreds of Bashful Basils around us, but it would be erroneous to think that all shy, modest, or reserved people are drones. Basil may be excessively bashful in his everyday social intercourse with friends and associates, but he may suddenly become super charged and emit sparks on the speaker's platform or on a stage.

Likewise, not all slow-paced people—the slow movers and speakers—are bores in front of audiences. Frigid Frederick, too, and his "cold" colleagues are sometimes able to catch fire in performance situations.

Purposes of Speaker, Including Subject Matter and General Nature of Material

6. Pious Peter. He often turns up as the minister of a church with a rather exclusive and select congregation. He fails to realize that dignity does not justify monotony.
7. Ramrod Randolph. He is a lieutenant colonel at the Pentagon. He gives three or four briefings a week. His argument is that his material is inherently dull and dry. Actually, he is not sufficiently immersed in his specific purpose for communicating with his listeners.
8. Repetitious Reginald. He teaches Economics 103 and has been teaching it for twenty years. He has slowly slid into the wrong kind of groove without being aware of it, or his argument is that it's impossible to sound lively in something you've been saying over and over again, year in and year out. In reality, he is no longer genuinely interested in what he has to say. He needs his batteries recharged.

Attitudes, Moods, and Emotions of Speaker

9. Frightened Frieda. In conversation she is a fireball, but in front of her speech class she suddenly freezes. The Bashful Basil who blossoms in front of an audience has his counterpart in the vivacious individual who "clams up" and becomes highly inexpressive in front of a group.
10. Superior Sebastian. He knows his stuff and he knows that he knows it. What is worse, he shows that he knows that he knows it. Audiences, large or small, bore him and he approaches them condescendingly.
11. Dejected Dudley. He is down-in-the-mouth about something. Specifically, he is sad, depressed, worried, or melancholy.
12. Confused Constance. Almost everything bewilders her. Her principal crime is mental flabbiness and a general inadequacy of intellectual responses.

Faulty Habits

13. Insensitive Inga. Her speech instructor has told her that she has faulty auditory discrimination or poor auditory acuity. In Inga's case, this does not mean that she suffers from a partial hearing loss. It simply means that she has developed bad listening habits. She is an indifferent and careless listener. Her argument—and it isn't a bad one—may be that her ears are bombarded hour after hour, day after day, with voices, the blare of her roommate's radio or record player and, at home, TV and her brother's new stereo set. Thus, when Inga wants to study or concentrate on something, she can't always be censured for attempting to shut out extraneous sounds. Unfortunately, however, there may be an undesirable carry-over into other more general situations.

14. Individuals suffering from general ill-health.

15. Individuals suffering from partial hearing loss.

People with problems of health and hearing generally need medical aid or the assistance of specially trained speech therapists who can help in setting up a program of hearing rehabilitation.

Individuals included in the other groups, and they are our primary concern here, need, firstly, a substantial measure of self-honesty. None of us like to be told that we are lazy, indifferent, dull, or stuffy, even though we may have had a sneaking suspicion that the fault was there long before we were specifically accused of it. We must make an honest attempt to face such a problem squarely. The old saw: "The leopard cannot change his spots" is quite true—for leopards. Secondly, if we will maintain an attitude of receptiveness as we work on the material contained in this chapter, we can make considerable progress in removing ourselves from the drone's gallery.

It is not enough, by the way, to say "be sincere." Sincerity is important. So is smiling. But neither one of them can give you a lively and expressive delivery. One could be completely sincere in the desire to sing well or become a superb golfer, and yet not make the grade. Technique is also important, and in this chapter we will deal with techniques.

Typically, many drones use a range of two, three, or four tones as they speak. The singsong drone may use many more, but his up-down-up-down vocal pattern is just as devastating as the Johnny-3-Note-Drone. The trained voice is capable of using an octave and a half or more. Almost all of us should be able to develop and use effectively a range of at least one octave. Before we can work on specific techniques which will help us achieve greater vocal flexibility, we must consider the interesting subject of pitch.

Pitch

That almost legendary tenor, Enrico Caruso, was once singing an opera somewhere in Italy. At the end of Act I, one of his colleagues, a bass-baritone, was seized with a violent coughing spasm a few seconds before his "big" aria was to begin. He couldn't negotiate it. But the performance wasn't stopped. Caruso sang it for him.

Caruso, of course, built a reputation as a great tenor and not a bass-baritone. He looked like a tenor, acted like a tenor, sang like a tenor, and had the vocal equipment of a tenor. We all understand that a tenor voice is higher in pitch than a baritone; an alto is lower in pitch than a soprano. But what, specifically, does "pitch" refer to?

Pitch refers to the highness or lowness of tone or sound. The slower the vibration cycles of the vocal folds, the lower the pitch; the faster the vibration cycles, the higher the pitch. Find middle C on the piano and hum a corresponding pitch. Your vocal folds are meeting and separating in vibratory cycles of approximately 256 times per second. If you hum the C above middle C, they are vibrating about 512 times per second.

What determines pitch? Age, sex, and general emotional states are the more obvious factors, but we must also reckon with three other relatively subtle factors. (a) length, (b) thickness and mass, and (c) degree of tension of the vocal folds.

Length: Pitch is lowered if length is increased. A man's larger vocal folds produce lower tones than a woman's smaller vocal folds. We have all observed that the longest piano strings produce the lowest bass tones; the short strings produce the highest treble tones.

Thickness and Mass: Pitch is lowered by greater weight, that is, greater thickness and mass. The strings on a bass viol are thicker and heavier than the strings on a violin.

Tension: Pitch is raised as tension of the vocal folds is increased. As we stretch a rubber band and snap it or tighten a guitar string, we can raise the pitch.

There are other complex factors involved, but at the moment let us say that it is reasonably safe to assume that pitch is largely the result of variations in tensions, and changes in pressure beneath the vocal folds.

If the mechanics of pitch are complex but interesting, far more important to us is using a pitch level which is suitable to our own voice. Voices, like musical instruments, have a range or span of tones in which they sound their best. For example, strike 3 or 4 keys at the top and bottom of a piano keyboard, and you will immediately realize why composers very rarely write compositions calling for the use of those particular keys.

We have heard the individual who speaks in a harsh growl—a sort of glottal gargle. He is probably using the lower extremes of his vocal span or range. Perhaps more irritating is the person who habitually uses the upper extremes of his range, producing a voice which can best be described as thin, squeaky, or shrill.

A good speaking voice will be pitched at a level which is most satisfactory for that particular voice. Every voice has a general pitch level at which it performs most effectively and efficiently. This level, of course, varies for different individuals, but each one of us will perform best at our optimum pitch level.

The optimum pitch level is simply our most desirable and serviceable level.

No one advocates that we chant at one pitch, of course. Vocal variety and animation are so important that a large section of this chapter will be devoted to them. But, at the moment, we are interested in finding a pitch level at which tone is the richest, the purest and has maximum carrying power. In finding and developing this level, we may also be making progress in correcting harshness, stridency and weakness of voice, disorders of quality which are sometimes associated with an improper pitch level.

Frequently, young people are interested in cultivating relatively deep-pitched voices. For years many radio announcers, disc jockeys, actors and actresses, as well as TV, movie and stage personalities have massaged our ears with sultry, bass rumbles. Favorite female performers have voices reminding us of the younger Marlene Dietrich, Bea Arthur in "Maude," or Elizabeth Taylor with a bad cold. Their male counterparts bring to mind the younger Orson Welles, perhaps Lee Marvin or a Paul Newman. All of these voices seem to emerge from cavernous depths.

There is surely nothing wrong with a well-used bass or contralto voice. At the same time, there is nothing wrong with a well-used tenor or soprano voice. It should be noted that a large number of successful speakers or performers in the areas already mentioned have voices which might be considered relatively high pitched.

Your business with this section of the chapter, then, should assuredly not be that of developing a "low," enticing or commercial voice. Your business should be discovering how to make the best of what you already have.

You will notice that as you speak or read a few lines of material the pitch of the voice varies in highness or lowness. The upward and downward inflections, however, seem to cluster about one average or central pitch level. It is the pitch level which you most frequently use. You may move up or down from it, but you most often return to this level. It is generally described as the habitual or customary pitch level. Another term which refers to it is average pitch level.

Finding Your Habitual Pitch Level

1. Sit comfortably erect in a chair. Inhale deeply two or three times, and then sigh audibly. (Vocalize! Do not whisper.) Listen carefully to the pitch level of the sigh. Repeat this process and vocalize a sigh several times. You will probably discover that the sighs are being vocalized at approximately the same pitch level. This level is close to your habitual level.

2. Read the sentences below in a normal and relaxed manner. The underlined words are to be emphasized, but you should try to concentrate on the unemphasized words. You will be quite close to your habitual pitch level on the unemphasized words. (The final syllable or word in a sentence, however, is often pitched lower than the habitual level.)

a. I <u>must</u> go home for lunch.

b. The black dog tried to <u>bite</u> me.

c. It is too <u>hot</u> in the house today.

d. Jim says that it will <u>rain</u> or <u>snow</u> through most of <u>March</u>.

e. <u>They</u> came early and were the last to leave.

3. Read the following story three or four times. During the first reading, use as much variation as you wish. Then, read it again, gradually working toward a monotone, narrowing and compressing the range until you have eliminated the upward and downward inflections. When you arrive at a level, sustain *ah* at that level, and find the corresponding note on the piano. You are probably at or near your habitual pitch level.

There was a villager whose business caused him to travel every day to a nearby seaport. As his neighbors rarely travelled, he was their newspaper. Each night he told them about some strange sight he had seen until finally the time came when he had exhausted all of the seaport's novelties. As he hated to return without a story, he made up one about a fish so large that it filled the entire harbor. His amazed but trusting listeners were so impressed by the story that they set out to see the fish. On the way they overtook their storyteller who, carried away by his own invention, was also hurrying to see the amazing sight.

4. Starting with the *ah* that you levelled off with in Exercise 3 (and be sure that you check this again with a pitch pipe or piano) sing "one" on the *ah* and then down the scale with "two," "three," "four," "five" to the lowest note you can produce comfortably and with reasonably good quality.

Repeat this exercise several times. It will be the basis of another exercise we will use to help you locate your optimum pitch level. We have already said that the optimum pitch level is our most desirable and serviceable level. It is the best for effective speaking.

Finding the Optimum Pitch Level

5. Repeat Exercise 4, singing down the scale to the lowest good note you can produce without scraping. This time sing "one" on that note, and then go back up the scale with "two," "three," "four," "five." Sustain the "five" for a few seconds. (Actually, you will be prolonging the "i" sound.) With the help of a piano or pitch pipe, determine what note you are sustaining. Using this level, say monotonously, "The day is dark and cold and dreary."

Repeat the sentence one tone higher and then one tone lower. In this general area is your optimum pitch level.

6. Hold your hands over your ears and hum up and down the scale several times. You will notice that one tone has an increased intensity; it sounds fuller. This particular tone should be very close to your optimum pitch level. Now, compare the results of this exercise with the results of Exercise 5.

7. Start again at your lowest comfortable pitch, this time singing *ah.* You do not have to cover your ears. Then move up and down the scale several times. Again you will hear and feel that one particular note seems to be the strongest and richest and easiest to produce. It should be the same or almost the same tone you discovered in Exercise 6, and also at or very near your most efficient pitch level.

Repeat Exercises 3, 4, 5, and 6 until you are able to tell the difference, if any, between your habitual and your optimum pitch levels. If you find a difference of approximately one or two tones between the two levels, the pitch level you are using is probably quite satisfactory. If the difference is greater, you should try to make your optimum pitch level habitual.

A word of warning: Your instructor or a speech therapist is by far the best judge of this. Let them make recommendations before you embark on any kind of a program of changing your pitch level. The truth of the matter is that a large majority of us do not have problems as far as optimum pitch is concerned. Our habitual pitch in most cases is also our optimum pitch. Attempts to raise or lower the habitual level are possibly dangerous. Vocal abuse and damage could easily result from misguided attempts to acquire a better pitch level. An old Roman axiom says, "You cannot put the same shoe on every foot."

If you are advised by a competent authority that your habitual pitch level is too high or too low, the following exercises will help. (If your habitual level is satisfactory, skip Exercises 8-13, and continue with the section on Pitch Range.)

Making the Optimum Pitch Level Habitual

8. Once again locate your optimum pitch. A piano or pitch pipe will be necessary. Sing *ah* on the optimum pitch and hold it for approximately six seconds.

9. Chant the following sentences with deliberate monotony at your optimum pitch level. In other words, you are to concentrate on how you sound as you read these lines rather than what you are reading:
   a. The shades of night were falling fast.
   b. They also serve who only stand and wait.
   c. Where ignorance is bliss, it is folly to be wise.
   d. Where is death's sting? Where, grave, thy victory?
   e. "Beauty is truth, truth beauty"—that is all you know on earth, and all you need to know.
   f. I never hear the west wind, but tears are in my eyes.
   g. All I ask is a merry yarn from a laughing fellow-rover, and quiet sleep and a sweet dream when the long trip is over.
   h. Now I lay me down to sleep, I pray the Lord my soul to keep; if I should die before I wake, I pray the Lord my soul to take.

10. Chant the following words at your optimum pitch level. Practice with maximum, controlled relaxation.

dawn	lot	feet	bath
murmur	hope	boat	all
hush	men	match	tip
moth	mar	tar	mail
call	took	cap	round
sad	gain	while	chill

11. Repeat the columns of words in Exercise 10, pronouncing each word twice. The first time deliberately use your old habitual level—the one you are now trying to modify. Check this with a pitch pipe or piano.

The second time, read the words at your newer optimum level—the one you are now trying to make permanent. Be certain that it is your optimum level.

12. Chant monotonously the first sentence in each of the following pairs at the optimum pitch level, and the second one at the habitual level. Do not raise or lower the pitch within the sentence.
   a. When day is done and my work is finished, I turn my feet homeward once more.
      Amid the noisy and unending roar and screeching of the city, I come to you.
   b. You never speak and yet I sense something because your eyes have always spoken for you.
      I know what it is. You'd have me tarry before I go. Am I right?
   c. So I linger for a moment, and then I join the rushing swarms of people.
      But somehow, I know that you and I will meet again another night.
   d. No words have ever passed between us, yet I understand you so well.
      And I always wait until you turn green, Oh, Traffic Light!

13. The following exercise is probably the trickiest one in this chapter. It is interesting, however, and it has been found extremely helpful to individuals with a wide discrepancy between the habitual and the optimum levels.

Each of the following lines is to be read differently:

MH: Chant it monotonously at the old, habitual pitch level.

MO: Chant it monotonously at the new, optimum level.

NO: Read it naturally with simple vocal inflections (pitch changes during a phonation.) In other words, avoid chanting. But read the NO material at or near your optimum pitch level.

a. MH: God created the world because he could create it.

b. MO: A great part of courage is the courage of having done the thing before.

c. NO: Rum is good in its place, and hell is the place for it.

d. MH: All are apt to shrink from those who lean upon them.

e. MO: It is more moral to be behind the age than in advance of it.

f. NO: Friendship is the only cement that will ever hold the world together.

g. MH: A person with a bad name is already half-hanged.

h. MO: Yea, though I walk through the valley of the shadow of death, I will fear no evil.

i. NO: I had rather men should ask why no statue has been erected in my honor, than why one has.

j. MH: Beware equally of a sudden friend and a slow enemy.

k. MO: My dwelling was small, and I could hardly entertain an echo in it.

l. NO: If you have to keep reminding yourself of a thing, perhaps it isn't so.

m. MO: I have met in the street a very poor man who was in love. His hat was old, his coat worn, his cloak was out at the elbows, the water passed through his shoes, and the stars through his soul.

n. NO: There is something about saying "O.K." and hanging up the telephone with a bang that kids a man into feeling that he has just pulled off a big deal, even if he has only called up the operator to find out the correct time.

o. MO: When Bach's wife died, he had to make funeral arrangements. But the poor man had been used to having everything done by his wife, so when his old servant asked him for money to buy black crepe, he said tearfully, with his head buried: "Ask my wife."

p. NO: We are students of words: we are shut up in schools, and colleges, and recitation rooms for ten or fifteen years, and come out at last with a bag of wind, a memory of words, and do not know a thing. [Emerson]

q. MO: One day the bear met the fox, who came slinking along with a string of fish he had stolen. "Where did you get those?" asked the bear.

"Oh, I've been out fishing and caught them," said the fox.

So the bear had a mind to learn to fish, too, and bade the fox tell him how he was to set about it.

"Oh, it's an easy craft for you," answered the fox, "and soon learned. You've only got to go upon the ice, and cut a hole and stick your tail down into it. You must hold it there as long as you can. You're not to mind if your tail stings a little. That's when the fish bite. The longer you hold it there the more fish you'll get; and then all at once out with it, and with a cross pull sideways, and with a strong pull, too."

Yes, the bear did as the fox had said, and held his tail a long, long time in the hole, till it was fast frozen in. Then he pulled it out with a sharp pull, and it snapped short off. That's why the bear goes about with a stumpy tail to this very day. [Folk Tale]

r. **NO:** One summer evening, a sentinel who stood leaning on his spear at the entrance to the Han Ku Pass—for this was many years before the building of the Great Wall—beheld a white-bearded traveller riding toward him, seated cross-legged upon the shoulders of a black ox.

Said the elderly stranger, when he drew near and halted: "I am an old man, and wish to die peacefully in the mountains which lie to the westward. Permit me, therefore, to depart."

But the sentinel threw himself to the ground and said, in awe: "Are you not that great philosopher?"

For he suspected the traveller to be none other than Lin Tang, who was known to be the holiest and wisest man in China.

"That may or may not be," replied the stranger, "but I am an old man, wishing to depart from China and die in peace."

At this, the sentinel realized that he was indeed in the presence of the great Lin Tang, who had for more than a hundred years, sat in the shadow of a plum tree, uttering words of such extreme simplicity that no man in the whole world was learned enough to understand their meaning.

So the sentinel threw himself in the ox's path and cried out:

"I am a poor and ignorant man, but I have heard it said that wisdom is a thing of priceless worth. Spare me, I beg of you, before you depart from China, one word of your great wisdom, which may enrich my poverty or make it easier to bear."

Whereupon Lin Tang opened his mouth, and said gravely: "Wow." [Seabrook]

Assignment 9 (See suggested Checklist for Assignments 9-13 at end of this chapter)

Prepare 12-15 lines of material. Mark it as selections a-l, Exercise 13, are marked: **MH, MO,** and **NO.** (**MH:** to be read monotonously at the habitual pitch level. **MO:** to be read monotonously at the optimum pitch level. **NO:** to be read with simple inflections at the optimum pitch level.) Divide your practice sessions into two periods each. During the first period, practice your material as you have marked it, reading it in the three different ways. During the second period, practice your material at the NO level only. When you present it in class, use this level. Practice with maximum, controlled relaxation.

Pitch Range

The drone characteristically reads or speaks using a range of 2-4 tones. Effective speakers are frequently capable of using a range of 12-14 tones, or slightly more than two octaves.

The objective of this section, therefore, will not be merely widening your range, unless you are an extreme monotone, and such types are encountered infrequently. We will try, however, to help you use effectively, expressively, and flexibly the range you already have. In a sense, you are being asked to sweep away the vocal cobwebs from the upper and lower extremes of your range.

14. Hum a tone which is easy and comfortable for you to sustain. From here hum down the scale to your lowest good tone. Then reverse the procedure and hum back up the scale to your highest acceptable tone. You will most likely discover that your range is at least an octave and quite possibly more.

15. Relocate your optimum pitch level. Hum down the scale from it. You should be able to hum approximately three tones below it. Hum up the scale from your optimum level. You should be able to reach five or six tones above this level. If you have difficulty reaching these extremes, repeat the exercise.

16. Read the material in this exercise as monotonously as you can. The first time, read it at your optimum level. Repeat it a tone lower, and then reread it a tone higher than the optimum level. Continue the reading, expanding or extending your range outward from the original level. Do not scrape rock bottom, and do not strain at the top. Maintain an easy relaxation.

   Rings and jewels are not gifts, but apologies for gifts. The only gift is a portion of yourself. Therefore, the poet brings his poem; the shepherd, his lamb; the farmer, corn; the miner, a gem; the sailor, coral and shells; the painter, his picture; the girl, a handkerchief of her own sewing.

17. Read the following selection three times.

   The first time read it monotonously at your optimum pitch level.
   The second time read it with a pitch range of 2-4 tones.
   The third time read it with as wide a range as you can.

   May I be no man's enemy, and may I be the friend of that which is eternal. May I never quarrel with those nearest me; and if I do, may I be reconciled quickly. May I devise no evil against any man; and if any should devise evil against me, may I escape uninjured and without the need of hurting him. May I love, seek, and attain only that which is good. May I wish for all men's happiness and envy none. May I never rejoice in the ill-fortune of one who has wronged me .... When I have done or said what is wrong, may I never wait for the rebuke of others, but always rebuke myself until I make amends .... May I win no victory that harms either me or my opponent. May I reconcile friends who are wroth with one another. May I never fail a friend in danger. May I always keep tame that which rages within me. May I accustom myself never to be angry with people. May I never discuss who is wicked and what wicked things he has done, but know good men and follow in their footsteps. [Ancient Pagan Prayer]

18. Repeat the selection in Exercise 17.

   Read it monotonously at your optimum pitch level.
   Read it monotonously at the highest tone of satisfactory quality that you can produce. Avoid strain.
   Read it monotonously at the lowest tone of satisfactory quality that you can produce. Avoid strain.

19. Read each of the following on an ascending scale. Say the first word in each line on a comfortably low pitch, and pitch each succeeding word a half-tone or whole tone higher.

   a. Sink or swim.
   b. As good as gold.
   c. Little things affect little minds.
   d. That most knowing of persons—gossip.
   e. To eat is human; to digest, divine.
   f. The vagabond, when rich, is called a tourist.
   g. It is better to wear out than to rust out.
   h. No sooner said than done—so acts your man of worth.
   i. How awful to reflect that what people say of us is true.
   j. To be a leader of men one must turn one's back on men.
   k. It seems sort of significant that we have two ears and only one mouth.
   l. He was not merely a chip off the old block, but the old block itself.
   m. Diet: A system of starving yourself to death just so that you can live a little longer.
   n. If people are unwilling to hear you, better it is to hold your tongue than them.
   o. A doctor is a man who tells you that if you don't cut out something, he will.
   p. The more anyone speaks of himself, the less he likes to hear another talked of.
   q. One big vice in a man is apt to keep out a great many smaller ones.

20. Repeat Exercise 19, but this time as you read the material, use a descending scale. Say the first word on a comfortably high pitch, and pitch each succeeding word a half tone or a whole tone lower.
21. Singers commonly use a warming-up exercise which is also helpful in developing flexible range. To sing a scale you would sing "do re me fa sol la ti do" (or if it is easier, "one two three four five six seven eight"). In our little exercise we will use only "do me sol do" (or one three five eight). Do this exercise many times and experiment by placing the first note on different tones.

Intonation

The overall pattern or melody of pitch changes and movements in phrases and sentences is described as intonation. As we are speaking, our voice moves from sound to sound with an almost continuous rise and fall in pitch. Such descriptive phrases as "speech or sentence melody," and "pitch contour" also relate to intonation.

For our purposes, we will consider these aspects of intonation: Key, inflections, and steps. Stress and emphasis, strictly speaking, are adjuncts of intonation, and they will be touched upon briefly.

Key

As we will use the word here, "key" refers to the general pitch level, ranging anywhere from high to low, used at any given moment in talking or reading. In conversational situations, key is largely determined for us by our physical and emotional status and the specific nature of what we are saying. If we feel well and happy, and our ideas are concerned with light, humorous, cheerful, or frivolous topics, the key in which we speak may tend to be in the relatively higher part of our voice range. Too, in anger and fear our voice may soar into a higher key. If we do not feel well or are sad or depressed or our ideas are concerned with dark, quiet, melancholy, or profound topics, the key in which we speak may tend to be in the relatively lower part of our voice range. Routine or relatively unemotional ideas or material, sometimes labeled "neutral," are most frequently expressed in the middle key.

In reading material aloud, we should use a key which is appropriate to the mood and spirit of our material. Hamlet's most famous soliloquy, "To be or not to be," is a meditation about death, and a low key would be more suited to its mood than a high key. The "Twenty-third Psalm" ("The Lord is my shepherd . . . ."), too, would be more expressive if read in a lower key. However, this does not mean that either selection would be delivered in a low monotone, for even within a general, overall key, there must be contrast and variation.

"Casey at the Bat" or Hamlet's "Speak the speech, I pray you . . ." would be most effective in a relatively high key, but here, too, certain lines or sections might well be read in a middle or comparatively low key. An informal talk or casual conversation about a recent trip to the seashore could conceivably be well handled in a middle key.

22. Read the following selections in a relatively low key, but be very careful to work for variation within that general range.
   a. When a man dies, he dies not just of the disease he has. He dies of his whole life.
   b. It is idle to talk to people of their faults, for, if they knew them, they wouldn't commit them.
   c. The tree which moves some to tears of joy is in the eyes of others only a green thing that stands in the way.
   d. There is, perhaps, no solitary sensation so exquisite as that of slumbering on the grass or hay, shaded from the hot sun by a tree, with the consciousness of a fresh light air running through the wide atmosphere, and the sky stretching far overhead upon all sides.

e. A man's dog stands by him in prosperity and in poverty, in health and in sickness. He will sleep on the cold ground, where the winds blow and the snow drives fiercely, if only he can be near his master's side. He will kiss the hand that has no food to offer. When all other friends desert, he remains. When riches take wings and reputations fall to pieces he is as constant in his love as the sun in its journey through the heavens. And when the last scene of all comes, and death takes the master in its embrace, and his body is laid away in the cold ground, no matter if all other friends pursue their way, there by his graveside will the noble dog be found, his head between his paws, his eyes sad but open in alert watchfulness, faithful and true even to death.

f. The day is cold, and dark, and dreary,
   It rains, and the wind is never weary;
The vine still clings to the mouldering wall,
   But at every gust the dead leaves fall,
And the day is dark and dreary.

23. Read the following selections in a middle key. Again, work for flexibility and variety within the key.

a. If I am accused of a mistake, I can only say, as Woodrow Wilson once said: "Perhaps I have made a number of other mistakes of which you have never heard." [Churchill]

b. "I have done this," says memory; "I can't have done this," says pride. In the end, memory yields.

c. When I was a boy of fourteen, my father was so ignorant I could hardly stand to have the old man around. But when I got to be twenty-one, I was amazed at how much he had learned in seven years. [Mark Twain]

d. He who does not believe that God wants this bit of sand to lie in this particular place, does not believe at all.

e. I came into this world, not chiefly to make this a good place to live in, but to live in it, be it good or bad. A man has not everything to do, but something; and because he cannot do everything, it is not necessary that he should do something wrong.

f. The crowd cheered lustily as the team trotted on the field. Eleven mighty and determined men going forth to fight for the old Alma Mater, to give their all. With them came Charlie. Everybody knew Charlie. On the campus his bubbling personality had won him many friends. He turned and faced the fans. He grinned. There was confidence as well as determination in his grin. He assumed the pose the vast crowd had seen so often. With an assuring tone in his voice he barked out: "Peanuts, popcorn, candy!"

24. Read the following selections in a relatively high key. Be careful to avoid monotony.

a. Know thyself. A Yale undergraduate left on his door a note for the janitor on which was written, "Call me at 7 o'clock; it is absolutely necessary that I get up at seven. Make no mistake. Keep knocking until I answer." Under this he had written: "Try again at ten." [Phelps]

b. Bark: This is a sound made by dogs when excited. Dogs bark at milkmen, postmen, yourself, visitors to the house, and other dogs. Some of them bark at nothing. For some reason dogs tend not to bark at burglars, salesmen, and income tax collectors, at whom they wag their tails in the most friendly manner.

c. I have sixty days for this tour and I have visited ten countries. That makes six days in each country, and when you start blocking up traffic—well, the first day people enjoy it, but by the third day they get bloody tired of it. The art of being a good guest is to know when to leave. [Prince Philip]

d. Do as your children do. They go to bed at night and sleep without worries. They don't care if they will get soup or bread tomorrow; they know that Father and Mother will take care of them. [Martin Luther]

e. Oh, you imbecile! To take a lounge lizard for a man of importance! He'll spread the story all over! And I'll be the laughing stock. That's what hurts! They'll all show their teeth in a grin and clap their hands. What are you laughing at? You're laughing at yourselves! Damn you! I'd like to tie you all in a knot and grind you into powder. I just can't get over it! Indeed, it's true that when God wants to punish a man, he takes away his reason first. Now, what was there in that lounge lizard like a government inspector? Absolutely nothing! No even half a finger's resemblance, but suddenly everybody is shouting: "The inspector, the government inspector!" Now, who was the first to let out the notion that he was a genuine government inspector? Speak up! [Gogol, *The Inspector*]

25. Analyze each of the following selections and decide which key—high, middle, or low—would be most appropriate. Read them aloud, but do not hesitate to experiment a little by trying some of the selections in more than one key. Be as expressive as you can.

a. God meets me in the mountains when I climb alone and high.
b. When you have got an elephant by the hind leg, and he is trying to run away, it's best to let him run.
c. Oh, to be in England now that April's there.
d. I am thy father's spirit, doomed for a certain time to walk the night.
e. Abide with me: fast falls the eventide; the darkness deepens. Lord, with me abide.
f. O health! health! The blessing of the rich! The riches of the poor! Who can buy thee at too dear a rate, since there is no enjoying the world without thee?
g. O, it's a snug little island! A right little, tight little island!
h. O judgment! Thou art fled to brutish beasts, and men have lost their reason!
i. The human knee is a joint and not an entertainment.
j. One of the striking differences between a cat and a lie is that a cat has only nine lives.
k. Oh, fie, Miss, you must not kiss and tell.
l. We are such stuff as dreams are made of and our little life is rounded with a sleep.
m. Man that is born of woman is of few days, and full of trouble.
n. Into each life some rain must fall; some days must be dark and dreary.
o. War is much too important a matter to be left to the generals.
p. Life is real! Life is earnest! And the grave is not its goal.
q. Stand! The ground's your own, my braves! Will you give it up to slaves?
r. Needles and pins, needles and pins; when a man marries, his trouble begins.
s. The King is dead. Long live the King!
t. It is best never to have been born. But who among us has such luck? One in a million, perhaps.
u. I haven't much doubt that man sprang from the monkey, but where did the monkey spring from?
v. "Isn't there heaven?" (she was but seven)
"Isn't there—for dogs?" she said.
w. A man who lives, not by what he loves but what he hates, is a sick man.
x. Sadness is a wall between two gardens.
y. All those who are contented with this life pass like a shadow and a dream, or wither like the flower of the field.

Inflections

A pitch change occurring within a single uninterrupted phonation or utterance is known as an inflection.

A rising inflection is an upward gliding movement of the voice, without interruption, to a relatively high pitch level. It is diagrammed:

It may express: questioning of a certain kind, hesitancy or uncertainty, doubt, curiosity, suspense, surprise, perplexity, and incompleteness of thought.

A falling inflection is a downward gliding movement of the voice, without interruption, to a relatively low pitch level. It is diagrammed:

It may express: certainty, conviction, command, emphasis, finality, and completeness of thought.

A circumflex or double inflection is any combination of the rising and the falling inflection. It is diagrammed:

It may express: uncertainty, sarcasm, irony, evasion, surprise, double or hidden meanings, and complexity of thought.

Inflections may vary in duration and range. In general, mild or moderate emotions, lack of conviction, and negativism are often expressed with inflections which are brief of duration and relatively limited in range. Strong, more positive emotions, and general conviction are often expressed with inflections which are relatively lengthy and which use a wide range.

26. Read each of the following with a rising inflection. The first time give each word a slightly exaggerated inflection. The second time use a moderately exaggerated inflection. The third time use a greatly exaggerated inflection.

a. Oh	d. No	g. Why	j. Please	m. Don't
b. Ah	e. Yes	h. Who	k. Good	n. Maybe
c. Hey	f. Well	i. Now	l. Bad	o. Here

27. Repeat Exercise 26, using a falling inflection.

28. Repeat Exercise 26, using a circumflex inflection.

29. Say "OH," suggesting the following meanings:

a. Elation	g. Sarcasm	m. Indifference
b. Fear	h. Doubt	n. Finality
c. Pity	i. Anger	o. Curiosity
d. Amazement	j. Hesitancy	p. Great surprise
e. Mild surprise	k. Disgust	q. Bashfulness
f. Horror	l. Evasion	r. Gratitude

30. Read each of the following words aloud, using an appropriate inflection. The sentences or phrases in parentheses will help you determine a specific meaning for each word, but do not read the sentences or phrases aloud.

a. So (We've caught you at last, you rascal!)
b. So (What's it to you?)
c. John (Is that you tiptoeing upstairs?)
d. John (What do you mean by coming in at this hour?)
e. Stop (Here?)
f. Stop (At once!)
g. Please (Don't hurt the puppy.)
h. Please (This is the last straw!)
i. Why (I've never heard of such a thing.)
j. Why (I'll tell you why.)
k. Yes (I'm not so sure.)
l. Yes (I'm positive.)
m. Well (This is just what I expected.)

n. Well (Have you made up your mind yet?)

o. Ah (The poor thing.)

p. Ah (I'm tired.)

q. Mary (Who?)

r. Mary (That's who.)

s. Gosh (I dropped a button.)

t. Gosh (I flunked three courses.)

u. Boy (Isn't she a beauty?)

v. Boy (I've had it!)

w. Really (Did it actually happen?)

x. Really (Don't ever speak to me again.)

y. Help! (I'm drowning!)

z. Help? (Why should I?)

Steps

A pitch change between words or syllables is known as a step or shift. The voice skips, jumps, or leaps from one pitch to another, either up or down.

The step is more emphatic and positive than the inflection. Steps enable us to give greater prominence to important words or phrases or, conversely, to give lesser prominence to unimportant words and phrases.

Say: "Good heavens!" Mary screamed. "He's dead!"

Almost instinctively you will say the "Good heavens!" at a higher pitch than "Mary screamed." You very likely paused between "heavens" and "Mary," and during this second of silence you shifted the pitch downward. You probably paused briefly between "He's" and "dead," and here you may have used an upward step.

31. Read the following twice, placing a slight pause between the two words. Use a higher pitch on the second word than on the first. The first time use a moderately exaggerated step. The second time use a greatly exaggerated step.

a. She did.	*g.* Sign here.	*m.* Of course.	*s.* Why not?
b. Don't stay.	*h.* But why?	*n.* So what?	*t.* Not now.
c. I'll go.	*i.* What time?	*o.* Try that.	*u.* I have.
d. Oh, no.	*j.* Who's there?	*p.* All right.	*v.* Try again.
e. I should.	*k.* Oh, gosh.	*q.* I'll bite.	*w.* That's it.
f. How much?	*l.* Right now.	*r.* Which one?	*x.* He's here.

32. Repeat Exercise 31, using a pitch which is lower on the second word than on the first.

33. In the following sentences the position of the word indicates the location of the step and the relative size of the jump or skip. Read them in an exaggerated manner.

a.

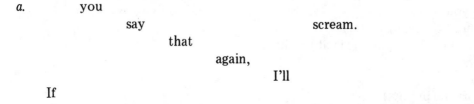

b.
   be
To   or
     not   that
       to   is the
       be,
            question.

---

c. I   won't   tomorrow.
   won't   answer
     answer
       now,   I
       and

---

d.   here?
          sitting
    home,   you
   you   were
      or
Were

---

e.   now
      forever
       hold
Speak   your
    or   peace.

---

f. I
    do   do
If say   it
     it,   fast.

---

g.   mean?
        you
      what
    to understand
   supposed
  I
Am

---

h. Smile,
     that,
  when you say
     my friend!

i. I'm
tired
of
telling
you
to
get
out.

---

j. Who, window?
broke that
may I ask,

---

k. along
Come now, soon
show be
or the will over.

---

l. Karen, me?
marry
will you

---

m. Oh, never
Jim, you and I get
would along!

---

n. Where
gracious, did
Good Helen. you
get
that
hat?

---

o. Gee,
it's spooky in here.

---

p. told
you I?
that didn't
I would happen,

---

q. What party,
a and
boy,
am
I
tired.

r.
    I   you

     don't

         think

               she   I think   pushed her.

                fell,

---

s.
  Well,

                        say

         what do you have to   for

    Hank,   yourself?

---

t.
         that   not

Don't try   again,   kidding!

                   I'm

        Jack,

          and

---

u.
  Care—   near—

     ful!   er.

        They're getting

                      Oops!

                        It's

                         too

                           late.

---

v.
               you

             certainly

I'm not ly—

      ing,

                  are!

       but

---

w.
      all

We're

      going.

        Well,

           Mike isn't.

---

x.
     pie?

Apple

          just

    Sorry, I   lost

            my

              appetite.

34. Read the sentences in Exercise 33 again, using a pattern of pitch levels and steps different from the ones indicated.

35. Analyze the following and work out a pattern of pitch levels and steps appropriate to the general meaning of each line.

    a. Mark, I hate to do this. Here's your ring.
    b. I have never liked him and I never will.
    c. When Jane comes home, we'll soon see who's boss around here.
    d. Strange—that I should run into her every place I go.
    e. Jane, darling, don't try to pull the wool over my eyes.
    f. Oh, so you think you know the answer, do you?
    g. I was afraid this would happen; I kept telling you it would.
    h. Rudy, old boy, you've had it!
    i. She's such a square—how much money did you say she's inherited?
    j. Rodney, is that lipstick on your shirt collar?
    k. Don't call us. Let us call you.
    l. Boy, did he get his comeuppance at last!
    m. Oh, Charles, a mink coat? It's just what I wanted.
    n. Somebody in this very room, I'm sorry to say, murdered poor, helpless Jim.
    o. Gosh, what a beautiful sight!
    p. She said that about me?
    q. I'm tired, I'm sick, I'm disgusted, and I'm boiling mad.
    r. Well, what do you know about that?
    s. I'm not so sure. Let me think about it.
    t. Helen, is that you? Why, Mabel, what are you doing here?
    u. It can't possibly flood here. Where's all that water coming from?
    v. All right, I'll go. Wait a second. Why are you so anxious for me to go?
    w. Jerry? Didn't you know? He died more than three years ago.
    x. Who stole my billford? Oh, here it is on the desk.
    y. Let's cross that bridge when we get to it!

Stress and Emphasis

We have already learned that syllables, words, or phrases may be given accent, stress, or emphasis by:

    An increase or decrease in loudness.
    Raising or lowering the pitch.
    Inflections and steps.
    Prolonging a syllable, word, or phrase.

Is there such a thing as too much emphasis? Yes, although it is not encountered too often. Too much emphasis or too much similarity in emphasis defeats its own purpose.

The frequency and quantity of emphasis should be determined by what is being spoken, of course. A word or group of words which give the key to the meaning of the sentence will naturally receive greater emphasis than less important words. As an illustration, emphasize the underlined passage:

Joe and Jane can't come to the picnic, because they're <u>flying to Mexico to get married</u>.

In general, the key or idea words which most truly reveal the meaning and thought of a passage are nouns, verbs, adjectives, and adverbs. The shorter words—pronouns, prepositions, conjunctions, and helper verbs—are less frequently emphasized. You will find important exceptions to all of the foregoing, however.

36. Your best friend has just starred in a campus production of *Hamlet*. After the performance you go back stage and say to him, "You were great! What a performance!" with the following suggested meanings:

a. He was outstanding.

b. He was outstanding. The others in the cast were atrocious.

c. He was fair.

d. He was awful.

e. He was outstanding, and you didn't think he had it in him.

f. He was a fine actor—several years ago.

g. He was satisfactory, but not as good as he told you he would be.

h. You slept throughout the entire performance, and you're asking him how effective he was.

37. In the following, stress the underlined word:

a. But—on the contrary—it has given <u>me</u> faith.

b. I haven't exactly decided <u>what</u> to do yet.

c. No matter how much the meek may be bulldozed or gypped they <u>will</u> eventually inherit the earth.

d. We'd talk about books and laugh at <u>ridiculous</u> people.

e. Of course I drink milk with that—not out of the glass—but <u>through</u> the glass.

f. He <u>is</u> thinking of something.

g. How <u>this</u> would have amused him.

h. You certainly ought to know what goes on in your <u>own</u> mind.

i. That was his favorite island; that was where <u>he</u> was going.

j. No, it's <u>I</u> who ask a favor of you.

k. Perhaps it's the last thing you <u>can</u> do for me.

l. I haven't the slightest interest in <u>what</u> you tell him.

38. Repeat the previous exercise, this time not stressing the underlined word, but stressing any other word which you consider to be relatively important.

39. Combine Exercises 37 and 38. In other words, stress two words in each sentence. Try to vary the amount of stress given to each of the two words.

Let's take another look at Exercise 33-x. We diagrammed it in this manner:

If you followed the suggestion to read it a second time with a different intonation, you may have found your own way of reading it much more expressive than the original version. You could experiment, if you wished, and possibly find ten or fifteen other ways of reading it—all of them effective. The point probably is that as far as vocal variety is concerned there isn't necessarily any one right way of reading or saying anything.

In another sense, we might say that the best rule is that there are no rules. Now and then, however, we must remind ourselves of a few general rules which may possibly be of some help to us, as long as we bear in mind that the exceptions quite often tend to disprove rather than prove the rules.

40. Statements of fact and commands generally use a falling intonation pattern. A key word, of course, may well be pitched higher than the other words in the sentence, but ordinarily at or toward the end of the line, the speech melody starts to run downhill.

A simple statement of command might be given in at least two ways, and both of them are good:

John,
     get
        out
          of
            here.

or   John, get
                          out
                             of
                               here.

In both cases, however, the sentence is completed with a falling intonation. Try the following:

a.   Ellen, I insist that you come with me.
b.   I'm tired of it all.
c.   Let's go to the lake.
d.   He doesn't live on Oak Street. He lives on Maple Avenue.
e.   Bring me some champagne.
f.   I have made it a rule never to smoke more than one cigar at a time.

41. If words or phrases are listed or enumerated, all of the items will generally take a rising or a level intonation, except the last which requires a falling intonation:

a.   Buy apples, eggs, oranges, and onions.
b.   Of the people, by the people, and for the people.
c.   Last night we saw Helen, Mart, Grace, and Agatha.
d.   The box contained a diamond, three watches, a pair of gloves, and a can opener.
e.   Russia lacks freedom of speech, freedom of religion, freedom of the press, and freedom of thought.
f.   I've owned Fords, Buicks, Chevies, and Chryslers, but never a Rolls-Royce.

42. If words or phrases are listed or enumerated, and if each of the items is given a falling intonation, a meaning of finality and deliberateness will be conveyed. Read the following, and then reread the sentences in Exercise 41, comparing the differences in meanings.

a.   Buy me pearls, rubies, emeralds, and diamonds.
b.   Of the people, by the people, and for the people.
c.   Last night we saw Tom, Dick, Harry, and Archie.
d.   Nevada mines gold, silver, tin, and copper.
e.   These he valued above all: justice, patriotism, honor, and charity.
f.   Jeff can't stand opera, ballet, plays, or movies.

43. A complex (double) intonation may be used to express sarcasm, doubt, evasiveness, and uncertainty.

a.   Well, I'm not so sure about that!
b.   Oh, no, you don't.
c.   I didn't mean to say that.
d.   I just don't know what to tell you.
e.   Gee, I really don't know who to vote for next November.
f.   If I flunk this course, I'm in trouble.

44. Repeat Exercise 43, using a falling intonation. Which is more subtle?

45. A rising intonation is generally used with questions which can be answered "yes" or "no," or with questions which are not introduced by interrogative words. Read the following, slightly exaggerating the melody pattern:

a.   Will you bring her along?
b.   Do you want to buy a Cadillac?
c.   Will you help him build the house?
d.   Did you like the movie?
e.   May I go now?
f.   Have you seen a flying saucer?

46. Read the sentences in Exercise 45 again, this time using a falling intonation. What differences in meanings do you notice?

47. Questions which are introduced by interrogative words (how, when, where, which, what, and why) often take a falling melody pattern:
    a. Why don't you do what you're told?
    b. How did he lose that much money?
    c. When will you ever learn?
    d. Who is staying and who is coming along?
    e. Which one did he finally purchase?
    f. Where did I put my old green coat?

48. Read the questions in Exercise 47 again, this time using a rising inflection. What differences in meanings do you notice?

49. Anyone of us could say, "I'm the happiest person in the world!" with an appropriate intonation and still fail to convey sincerity and enthusiasm. The key you choose, as well as your inflections, steps, stress, and emphasis, might be "coldly" correct, and yet the total overall effect could still be mechanical and false. The devices listed in the previous sentence are "gimmicks." They are helpful devices, but they are not quite enough.

    If we do not fully comprehend the nature and meaning of the ideas and material we are delivering, if we are unable to meet their emotional requirements or if we are otherwise inhibited, devices will not help us greatly in acquiring vocal variety. As an interesting illustration, study the material in Exercises 49 and 50. In your first reading, concentrate solely on the intonation pattern and everything that is included, but deliberately give a cold reading of each line. Try to avoid responding to the obvious emotional nature of the material. In your second reading, however, let the melody pattern guide you, but respond emotionally and with as much sincerity, vitality, and animation as possible.
    a. I'm frightened.
    b. Man, am I happy!
    c. He's dead! You're sure?
    d. I hate her.
    e. I'm sad.
    f. I'm suspicious of him.
    g. My, how eerie it is.
    h. I guess I'm in love.
    i. Get out of here.
    j. Please don't leave me.
    k. You're the murderer!
    l. They're going to run me for president! Me? Me?
    m. I can't stand it another minute.
    n. You're too late—he just died.
    o. This is the strangest thing that ever happened to me.
    p. I cannot fail; I must not fail.
    q. How awful.
    r. That's disgusting.
    s. What wonderful news!
    t. Go ahead! I dare you!
    u. I'm getting sick and tired of your nagging.
    v. I passed math? You must be kidding.
    w. Fasten your seat belts. We just ran out of fuel!
    x. Who could be knocking at the door at this hour of the night?
    y. You won't believe this: I've just won the million dollar lottery!

50. Using the sentence "I'd like to see you," say it in a manner which would suit each of the following situations:

 a.   The dean of men stops a student who has led riots on the campus.
 b.   The captain of the football team asks for a date with the reigning campus queen.
 c.   The reigning campus queen hints for a date with the captain of the football team.
 d.   An enthusiastic salesman to a prospective buyer.
 e.   A parent of a sick child to a doctor.
 f.   A young man who has just quarrelled with his best girl, pleads for a reconciliation.
 g.   A failing student to a professor.
 h.   A father to his five-year-old son who has just thrown a rock through the picture window.
 i.   A father to the neighbor's five-year-old son who has just thrown a rock through the picture window.

Stereotyped Pitch Patterns

Inexperienced or careless speakers and readers are sometimes guilty of using a fixed intonation or melody pattern over and over again until it not only calls attention to itself but becomes extremely irritating to the listeners.

Fond parents will pardon their fourth grader for giving a recitation on a vocal seesaw:

Listen, my   you shall
    children, and   hear
   midnight   Paul Re—
Of the   ride of   vere.

It is a little more difficult to pardon the minister who singsongs thusly:

       receive
     we   the
    as   Sunday
   now
And   offering

     bow
   all   our
  us   heads
Let   in
        prayer.

Or the student who ends every sentence with a rising intonation:

Last summer I had a very interesting experience.

One day I was walking down the street.

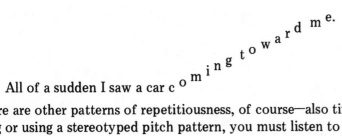

All of a sudden I saw a car coming toward me.

There are other patterns of repetitiousness, of course—also tiresome. If you have been accused of being sing-song or using a stereotyped pitch pattern, you must listen to yourself as critically and sharply as you can. A considerable amount of work with a tape recorder is essential. As you read or speak, generally avoid using the same melody pattern on two or more consecutive phrases. (As always, there are the inevitable exceptions.) Four phrases or sentences delivered in the following melody pattern, for example, would probably become quite monotonous:

a. A funny thing happened last night.

b. I went out to get a coke.

c. A fat man was standing in the doorway.

d. I tried to get by him but he wouldn't move.

But four phrases or sentences delivered in melody patterns which are varied and which differ from each other can be interesting and expressive:

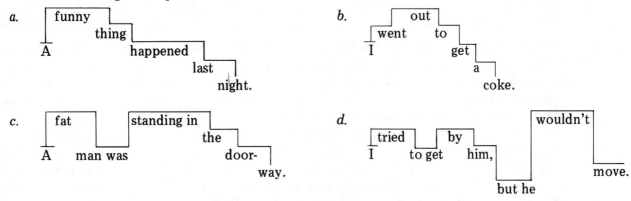

Excessive pitch pattern is sometimes related to, but not always identical with, pitch pattern. Here, there is little or no subtlety in vocal variety. Instead, the voice swoops up or down. Emphasis is too heavy and too frequent. Jumps and leaps are apt to be considerable. The circumflex inflection is used too often, and in men this may suggest effeminacy. In general, the individual whose pitch variations are extreme suggests childishness, excessive eagerness, and insincerity. The gusher is a perfect example of the latter.

According to the dictionary a gusher is one who expresses himself extravagantly or emotionally. Some people would classify Carol Channing, Paul Lynde, and Charles Nelson Reilly as gushers.

51. If it has been determined that you are a singsonger, a gusher, or use another kind of pitch pattern stereotype, through the use of a recorder, experiment with the following selections. The first time you read them, make no attempt to correct repetitious or excessive pitch patterns. Deliberately over-use double inflections, unduly heavy emphasis on too many words, swooping inflections, and steps of considerable size.

Then, analyze the same selections, marking them with diagrams or lines—any of the devices already used in this chapter—and work for a more subdued and subtle melody pattern. Record and compare with your previous performance.

a. Ring out, wild bells, to the wild sky,
    The flying cloud, the frosty light:
    The year is dying in the night;
Ring out, wild bells, and let him die.

Ring out the old, ring in the new,
    Ring, happy bells, across the snow:
    The year is going, let him go;
Ring out the false, ring in the true.

b. "Mercy on me, Beth loves Laurie!" she said, sitting down in her room, pale with shock of the discovery which she believed she had just made. "I never dreamt of such a thing! What will mother say? I wonder if he—" there Jo stopped, and turned scarlet with a sudden thought. "If he shouldn't love back again, how dreadful it would be. He must! I'll make him!" and she shook her head threateningly at the picture of the mischievous looking boy laughing at her from the wall. "Oh, dear, we are growing up with a vengeance. Here's Meg married, and a ma, Amy flourishing away in Paris, and Beth in love. I'm the only one that has sense enough to keep out of mischief." Jo thought intently for a minute, with her eyes fixed on the picture. Then she smoothed out her wrinkled forehead, and said, with a decided nod at the face opposite, "No, thank you, sir! You're very charming, but you've no more stability than a weathercock; so you needn't write charming notes, and smile in that insinuating way, for it won't do a bit of good, and I won't have it." [Alcott, *Little Women*]

c. "Mr. Worthing, I confess I feel somewhat bewildered by what you have just told me. To be born, or at any rate bred, in a handbag, whether it had handles or not, seems to me to display a contempt for the ordinary decencies of family life that reminds one of the worst excesses of the French Revolution. And I presume you know what that unfortunate movement led to? As for the particular locality in which the handbag was found, a cloakroom at a railway station might serve to conceal a social indiscretion—has probably, indeed been used for that purpose before—but it could hardly be regarded as an assured basis for a recognized position in good society. You can hardly imagine that I and Lord Bracknell would dream of allowing our only daughter—a girl brought up with the utmost care—to marry into a cloakroom and form an alliance with a parcel? Good morning, Mr. Worthing!" [Wilde, *Importance of Being Earnest*]

Assignment 10 (See suggested Checklist for Assignments 9-13 at the end of this chapter)

The ideas suggested below have proven most effective in helping individuals whose reading and speaking tend to be somewhat dull and monotonous. They are also quite enjoyable, and the shy, reserved type of person may find any one of them conducive to "letting himself go."

Short, Short Story
Select narrative prose which contains conversation. A short, short story or a paragraph or two taken from a short story is suggested. Choose material which is exciting or dramatic. Analyze it carefully, taking into consideration the various aspects of intonation: inflections, steps, key, stress, and emphasis. In your performance before the class, however, concentrate on the story you are trying to tell and the ideas and emotions you are attempting to get across.

A Commercial
We are probably inclined to agree that many radio and TV commercials are irritating. Part of our irritation is caused by the dull and repetitious material which they contain. However, we may also agree

that many superior announcers deliver commercials with considerable effectiveness, as far as vocal variety is concerned. Their presentations are frequently lively, colorful, and enthusiastic.

Using original material, preferably selling a commodity or service which is fictitious, prepare a one minute commercial. You must be so familiar with your script that even though you read your material when you perform, you are still able to inject into it a lot of animation, vigor, and spontaneity. Sell your audience, and enjoy yourself while you're doing it.

A Fairy Tale

If you have ever been exposed to small, preschool age children you have discovered that a favorite phrase is, "Tell us a story!" Delicate nuances and shadings may be too subtle for an audience of small-fry, so the experienced storyteller generally tends to use a somewhat exaggerated melody pattern with considerable pitch variation and relatively heavy stress and emphasis. (If excessive pitch variation is one of your problems, you will do well to substitute another assignment for this one. Deliberately select something quiet, moody, perhaps even sad.)

Prepare a two-three minute fairytale or children's story. In performance do not read it but tell it in your own words, using a rather exaggerated melody pattern. Present it as though the age level of your audience is approximately three-five.

Rate

If you have studied music appreciation, you have learned that the typical piano concerto consists of three sections or movements. Customarily, the opening movement is moderately fast. The second movement is slow and the final movement is rapid. The very popular Tchaikovsky Concerto *No. 1* is no exception to the general format. But does this mean that when the composition is performed only three different tempos are used: moderately fast, slow, and rapid? Hardly. For the general effect would be sheer boredom. As a matter of fact, in the first section alone, Tchaikovsky indicates 44 different tempo variations. In the second and third sections, 28 tempo patterns are suggested. Thus, in listening to a 36-minute performance of the concerto, you will hear about 72 different tempos or, theoretically speaking, approximately two contrasting rates of speed per minute.

Time or rate variations are as essential in reading and speaking as they are in music. We have all heard the speaker who has sufficient pitch variation but who is, nevertheless, guilty of monotony, a certain repetitiousness and evenness. Listen to him carefully and you may discover that his speaking rate rarely changes. He is possibly aware that 150 words per minute is a good general speaking rate, and this means that in ten minutes he will have uttered, with almost no change in pace, approximately 1,500 words.

Rate, as the term will be used here, includes speed of utterance, quantity or duration of sounds, and length and number of pauses. In general, time and rate variations will be determined by the personality and the mood of the speaker, the nature of the material being spoken and the total audience situation: the number of listeners, the size of the room, and general acoustical conditions.

How do we measure rate? The simplest, but not necessarily the most accurate method is to count the number of words read or spoken per minute (w.p.m. = words per minute). The problem here is obvious.

If you were to read this kind of material for one minute and then count the words:

> "He wanted quantitative observational evidence and tested the implications through observations of the moon, whose monthly revolution constituted an instance of his law of gravitation."

or read this kind and count:

> "When she heard the siren she ran into the old house. The hallways were black with clouds of smoke. A thin trickle of flame licked at her feet."

You will quickly conclude that the speaker of the first example, loaded as it is with big words, will read fewer words per minute than the reader of the second example. A better way to measure would be syllables, rather than w.p.m.

Nevertheless, we think in terms of w.p.m. In the selections which follow, the language will be moderately simple. The extremes—excessive use of either multisyllabic or monosyllabic words—will be avoided.

52. A rate of 120-140 w.p.m. is in many circumstances regarded as excessively slow. It can irritate the listener even more than the "faster-than-a-speeding-bullet" rate which some individuals use. The habitual use of this rate might suggest that the user is ill, lazy, extremely shy, or a stuffed shirt.

Under certain circumstances 120-140 w.p.m. might be used for relatively short periods of time. Extremely complex or technical matter or material which is profound or sad might justify this rate. A large audience in an acoustically poor area or the presence of competing noises could also force a speaker to an excessively slow rate.

Even though you may rarely have occasion to read at this rate "get the feel" of it. This may help you gain more flexibility and sensitivity to rate. The following selection will give you an idea of this general rate. It contains exactly 140 words. The number of words up to the diagonal line totals 120. Thus, a maximum and a minimum are established. Practice the selection, timing yourself, until it takes you approximately one minute to read to either terminal point.

> How lonely sits the city that was full of people. How like a widow has she become, she that was great among the nations! She that was a princess among the cities has become a vassal. She weeps bitterly in the night, and her tears are on her cheeks. Among all her lovers she has none to comfort her. All her friends have dealt treacherously with her. They have become her enemies. Is it nothing to you, all you who pass by? Look and see if there is any sorrow like my sorrow which was brought upon me, which the Lord inflicted on the day of his fierce anger. He has left me stunned and faint all the day long. / / The Lord is in the right, for I have rebelled against him; but hear, you people, and behold my suffering. [The Bible]

53. A rate of 140-180 w.p.m. is generally regarded as satisfactory.

Material which expresses sorrow, gravity, meditation, and quietness or material which is technical and difficult for the hearers to absorb might be effectively read at an approximate rate of 140 words per minute.

Relatively unemotional material (for example—descriptive or simple expository) might be read at an average rate of approximately 160 words per minute.

Material which expresses happiness, humor, lightness, and, on occasion, anger, might be read at an average rate of approximately 180 words per minute.

The following selection will give you an idea of this general rate. It contains exactly 180 words. The diagonal line is placed after the 140th word. Repeat the procedure suggested for reading the selection in Exercise 52.

> A traveler with a donkey and a horse, who carried merchandise from town to town, was in the habit of letting the donkey carry all of the load. One hot day the donkey was feeling quite weak and sick, and he begged the horse to carry some of the load. "For," she said, "if I have to carry all of it today I am going to collapse for good. But if you will help me carry part of it, I will soon get well again and then I'll be able to carry it all." But the horse was very proud and stubborn, and said that he didn't wish to be bothered with the complainings of a mere donkey. The donkey jogged on in silence. But soon, what with the great heat and the heavy load, she fell down and died. / /
>
> When this happened, the master fastened the whole load on the horse, and made him carry the dead donkey besides, as far as the next tannery. The moral of the fable is obvious: An unwilling partner is his own undoing.

What about purely conversation situations? The 140-180 w.p.m. rate is generally acceptable, although most of us tend to use a slightly faster pace: 150-185 w.p.m.

Our best public speakers often choose rates ranging from 135-185 w.p.m., with 160 w.p.m. a very comfortable and effective average. It is safe to state that speaking rates are generally somewhat slower than reading rates.

If you are interested in timing your speaking rate, you will have to give a short, informal speech on a casual topic. Do not read it. Record it, count the words and determine your rate.

54. A rate of 160-170 w.p.m. is generally regarded as superior. Professionals as well as experienced and talented amateurs often favor this range.

The following selection will give you a general idea of this rate. It contains exactly 170 words. The diagonal lines are placed after the 160th word.

> May blessings light upon him who first invented sleep! It is food for the hungry, drink for the thirsty, heat for the cold, and cold for the hot. It is the coin that buys all things, and the balance that makes the king even with the shepherd, and the fool with the wise. It is said, "Sleep is death enjoyed." There is, perhaps, no solitary sensation so marvelous as that of slumbering on the grass or hay, shaded from the hot sun by a tree, with the consciousness of a fresh light air running through the wide atmosphere, and the sky stretching far overhead upon all sides. Sleep falls like silence on the earth. It fills the hearts of ninety million men. It moves like magic in the mountains. It walks like night and darkness across the plains and rivers of the earth, until low upon lowlands, and high upon the hills, flows gently sleep, smoothsliding sleep—oh, sleep, sleep! / /
>
> It is a gentle thing, beloved from pole to pole.

55. A rate of 180-200 w.p.m. is in many circumstances regarded as unsatisfactory. Occasionally, in oral reading or public speaking we might use it if our material is exceptionally energetic or forceful, expresses great elation, excitement, fear, or anger. But extended reading or speaking at this rate, unrelieved by slower rates, might possibly exhaust the listeners, if not the speaker. Constant rapid reading or speaking might also suggest that the individual is highly nervous, extroverted, unsure of himself, or otherwise emotionally disturbed.

If you wish to go into this range, you should ask yourself a question: "How is my articulation?" If it is clear and clean-cut, you could probably communicate intelligibly at a rate of 210 w.p.m. If it isn't, you will perhaps be unintelligible even at 180 w.p.m. or somewhat less.

The following selection will give you a general idea of this rate. It contains exactly 200 words. The diagonal line is placed after the 180th word.

> What is it, then? What do you want? What have you come for? What do you mean by this flightiness? Bursting in all of a sudden, like a cat having a fit! Well, what have you seen that's so surprising? What kind of an idea has gotten into your head? Really, you know, you act like a three-year-old child and not in the least like what one would expect from a girl of eighteen. I wonder when you'll get more sensible, and behave as a well brought-up young lady should and learn a few good manners? Oh, your head's always empty! You're copying the neighbor's girls. Why are you always trying to be like them? You've no business using them as models. You have other examples, young lady, right in front of you—your own mother. I repeat—your own mother! That's the model you ought to imitate! There, now you see—it was all because of you, you silly child, that our guest was on his knees in front of me—and then you blunder in. / /
>
> You come snooping around, just as though you'd gone completely out of your mind. Just for that, I refused him! [Gogol, *The Inspector General*]

56. Determine a general rate which would be appropriate for each of the following. As you read them aloud, however, be sure that you vary the rate.

   a. I have paid no poll tax for six years. I was put into jail once on this account, for one night. And, as I stood considering the walls of solid stone, two or three feet thick, the door of wood and iron, a foot thick, and the iron grating which strained the light, I could not help being struck with the foolishness of that institution which treated me as if I were mere flesh and blood and bones, to be locked up. I wondered that it should have concluded at length that this was the best use it could be put to, and had never thought to avail itself of my services in some way. I saw that, if there was a wall of stone between me and my townsmen, there was a still more difficult one to climb or break through before they could get to be as free as I was. I did not for a moment feel confined, and the walls seemed a great waste of stone and mortar. I saw that the state was half-witted, that it did not know its friends from its foes, and I lost all my respect for it, and pitied it. [Thoreau, *Civil Disobedience*]

   b. VOLPONE: Ah, Mosca, you clever puppy, what a fool you are, how little you have learned of me! Do you really think you have to let the ducats fly in order to have everything? No, you fool! Let them rest quietly, side by side. Then, people will come of their own accord to offer you everything. Get this through your head: the magic of gold is so great that its smell alone can make men drunk. They only need to sniff it, and they come creeping here on their bellies; they only need to smell it, and they fall into your hands like moths in a flame. I do nothing but say I am rich—they bow their backs in reverence. Then I make a pretense at mortal illness. Ah, then the water drips off their tongues, and they begin to dance for my money. Ah, how they love me: Friend Volpone! Best beloved friend! How they flatter me! How they serve me! How they rub against my shins and wag their tails! I'd like to trample the life out of these cobras, these vipers, but they dance to the tune of my pipe. They bring presents! Who, I ask you, does a more thriving business here in Venice and has a juicier sport to boot? [Jonson, *Volpone*]

   c. MARGARET: No, no . . . I die, but you must live. I'll tell you carefully how to prepare the graves. The best place you must give to mother, and lay my brother close beside her. Somewhere to one side . . . a little space apart . . . let me lie. And here, on my right side, lay my little one . . . my baby . . . for no one else will ever lie near me! What happiness, what sacred joy it was to nestle in your arms. But that will never be again! Hurry! Hurry! Save your child! Go, now! Follow the path down by the brook . . . there . . . there by the bridge in the woods, to the left, where the plank lies . . . there, in the pool. Quickly! Seize it! Quickly! It's trying to rise . . . it's struggling still. Save it, save it! [Goethe, *Faust*]

   d. CYRANO: My nose is very large? Young man, you might say many other things, changing your tone. For example—Aggressively: "Sir, if I had such a nose, I'd cut it off!" Friendly: "You'd have to drink from a tall goblet or your nose would dip into it." Descriptive: " 'Tis a crag . . . a peak . . . a peninsula!" Graciously: "Are you so fond of birds that you offer them this roosting place to rest their little feet?" Quarrelsome: "When you smoke a pipe and the smoke comes out of your nose, doesn't some neighbor shout 'Your chimney is on fire'?" Warning: "Be careful, or its weight will drag down your head and stretch you prostrate on the ground." Tenderly: "Have a small umbrella made to hold over it, lest its color fade in the sun." Dramatic: "It's the Red Sea when it bleeds!" Countrified: "That's a nose that is a nose! A giant turnip or a baby melon!" My friend, that is what you'd have said if you had had some learning or some wit. But wit you never had a bit of. As for letters, you have only the four that spell out "fool!" [Rostand, *Cyrano de Bergerac*]

   e. HECUBA: Child, how mournful was your death! You might have fallen fighting for your city, grown to a man's age, and married, and with the king's power like a god's, and died happy, if there is any happiness here. But no. Now you lie broken at the wrists before my feet. You are dead; and all was false when you could lean across my bed and say: "Mother, when you die I will cut my long hair in your memory, and at your grave bring companies of boys my age to sing farewell." It did not happen. Now I, a homeless, childless, old woman must bury your poor corpse, which is so young. Alas for all the tenderness, my nursing care, and all your slumbers gone. What words will the poet inscribe upon your monument? "Here lies a little child the Argives killed, because they were afraid of him." That? The epitaph of Greek shame. You will not win your father's heritage, except for this, which is your coffin now. [Euripides, *The Trojan Women*]

Assignment 11 (See suggested Checklist for Assignments 9-13 at end of chapter)

If your reading or speaking has been adjudged excessively rapid or slow, you may want additional practice in making yourself feel comfortable with a 160-170 w.p.m. range. Choose some informal material from a lit book or a magazine and place diagonal marks after word 160 and word 170, and again after word 320 and word 340. Your performance should take approximately two minutes.

Duration

Duration refers to the length or amount of sound. Syllables and words might be likened to accordions, inasmuch as they can be stretched out or compressed. As a rule, we hold vowels longer than consonants, but there might be an appreciable difference in the length of the same vowel used in two different words. You will note that you tend to hold the *aw* in "law" longer than you do the *o* in "log." You will also note that both vowel sounds are longer than the *g* of the second word.

As we have discovered in our work in articulation, for some of the sounds the articulators move quite rapidly; certain sounds tend to be relatively short in duration. But with other sounds the articulators move rather slowly, and the resulting sounds are comparatively long in duration. These, of course, are the physical characteristics of sound and sound production. Additionally, at least two other factors may determine quantity:

> **General rate of speaking.** The rapid speaker is often prone to cut, clip, or shorten his sounds or words. This is a habit, by the way, which is frequently characteristic of poor readers or speakers. The slow speaker, on the other hand, is often inclined to draw out and elongate his sounds or words. If carried to excess, this can also result in monotony for the listener.

> **Basic meanings of words or ideas.** Earlier in this chapter it was mentioned that key words or phrases, words which are especially significant or meaningful, are often emphasized by stressing their sounds or syllables. Stress is accomplished by a combination of several elements: loudness, raising (sometimes lowering) the pitch, and prolonging the sound.

57. Often greater stress is given to nouns, verbs, adverbs, and adjectives than to the other parts of speech. Read the following, stressing the underlined words:
    a. Put the money on the table.
    b. He ran into the alley, lurched and stumbled over the curb, and collapsed in the gutter.
    c. Although she played lightly and rapidly, she certainly made no errors.
    d. He lives in the blue house—not the green one.

58. In most instances relatively little stress is given to articles, prepositions, conjunctions, and auxiliary verbs. Read the following, unstressing the underlined words:
    a. The lad gave an apple and a sausage to the old man.
    b. Some of us in our haste say, "To who do you wish to speak?" instead of "To whom do you wish to speak?"
    c. Joe and Sally left early, but they'll run into snow or rain.
    d. The thief has escaped and is hiding, but the bloodhounds are chasing him.

The amount of stress given to a word or phrase is also subject to a good deal of subtle variation, depending upon the emotional nature of what is being said. If you discover that your house is burning down about your ears, how would you shout these lines? "Hey! The house is on fire! Quick, somebody, call for help!"

You could build up quite a case for at least two key words: "fire" and "help." And very likely you would give them a split second greater stress than the other words. We'll agree, however, that our general approach to all of the words would probably be to cut them short and attack the sounds rather briskly. This might be compared to touching a piece of red-hot metal. One does not linger long. For such brisk, brief, and abrupt attacks we might borrow the word staccato from musical terminology. A staccato utterance of words is often effective in material which expresses comparatively extreme emotional states such as rage, fear, excitement, and elation.

Opposed to staccato is the word legato which describes a smooth and connected style. In speech perhaps a more accurate term, as far as sound duration is concerned, is "prolonged." It implies that words are lengthened, extended, or "drawn out." As we already know, the vowels and diphthongs are particularly capable of being stretched. A prolonged utterance of words is often effective in material which expresses less violent emotional states such as contentment, weariness, reverence, awe, complexity, and deep grief. An interesting exception: an enraged person, ordering the object of his wrath to leave the premises, might say between clenched teeth—"Get out!" and exaggerate considerably the length of the *e* in "get" and the *ou* in "out."

Utterance which is neither staccato nor prolonged may be described as average, normal, or regular. It is the kind we use most frequently, and it is often appropriate for matter-of-fact, casual, routine conversation and speech or for relatively unemotional material.

Give this line a staccato reading. Cut the vowels and diphthongs extremely short. Think of touching a hot stove as you attack each word:

I've never been so insulted in my life!

Give this line a prolonged reading. Draw out the important vowels and diphthongs.

The la-a-a-a-ake is sa-a-a-ad and ca-a-a-a-alm.

Give this line a regular reading. This would be like chatting with a classmate before the class begins.

I might go home this weekend. Want a ride?

59. The following lines are marked S for Staccato, P for Prolonged, and R for Regular. Read them accordingly, noting the contrasts.

S   *a.*   I can't stand it another minute!
P   *b.*   The sky is deep blue; the stars are tarnished silver.
R   *c.*   May I see you later this evening?
S   *d.*   Get out of here and don't ever come back.
P   *e.*   Death—awful, cruel, and weary—hung like a pall over the grim field of battle.
R   *f.*   I don't believe it will rain or snow tomorrow.
S   *g.*   Don't let them kill me, Your Honor! I'm innocent—I swear it!
P   *h.*   The silent forest stood there, cool and green and drowsy.
R   *i.*   Let's order a milk shake and a pizza.
S   *j.*   If that's the way you feel about it, all right!
P   *k.*   Relax. Close your eyes. Go to sleep.
R   *l.*   Did you order this terrible weather?
S   *m.*   Look out! He's got a gun! Duck!
P   *n.*   I don't believe one word of it.
R   *o.*   Boy, I wish I had that kind of money!

60. Reread the sentences in Exercise 59, trying a reading different from the indicated mark. For example, try the S lines with a P reading and vice versa.

61. Study the following sentences carefully before reading them aloud. Some of them might be equally effective if read in more than one of the ways previously described. If you would like to be quite subtle, "shift gears" within a line, going from a prolonged to a staccato reading.

    a.   I'm sorry, but he died quite peacefully three hours ago.

    b.   This is the last time you'll ever try anything like that, do you hear?

    c.   Go ahead! Strike me if you dare.

    d.   It's a lazy, hot and humid day.

    e.   What would you do with a million dollars?

    f.   The weary driver crawled slowly along the endless highway through the desert.

    g.   The people pushed, shoved, screamed, and acted like lunatics at the bargain sale.

    h.   It was a fine movie. I like Robert Redford.

    i.   The Shenandoah inched along, rippling quietly under the cool light of a slowly rising moon.

    j.   Excited? Who's excited?

    k.   The cold is making me numb and tired and sleepy.

    l.   Get this right. It's 2866 Harvard Road in Newark, not 2688 Harper Road in New York.

    m.   I'm afraid the news is bad. Your family has been wiped out.

    n.   I've never been so humiliated in my life! How dare you!

    o.   In the summer I enjoy reading detective stories.

    p.   John? It can't be you! You're supposed to be dead!

    q.   Don't ever let me catch you in that place again!

    r.   Oh, I wish you'd stop asking such stupid questions.

    s.   She was such a decent person . . . quiet, patient, dignified . . . we couldn't have known that she was slowly dying.

    t.   Give me three minutes to think it over and you'll have your answer.

    u.   I've been so depressed lately. I wonder why.

    v.   I've never heard of anything like this before. Have you?

    w.   I guess it would be better if we didn't see each other again.

    x.   That was the longest, dreariest bore I've ever sat through.

    y.   I thought I had told you to leave town, Partner!

62. In the following selections you will find that certain phrases or lines will be most appropriately expressed in staccato speech. Others will be more effective if read with prolonged tones or tones of regular duration. Strive for contrast and variety within each selection.

    a.   "What?" He seemed to wake up. "Oh . . . I got spattered with blood helping to carry him to his lodging. By the way, mamma, I did an unpardonable thing yesterday. I was literally out of my mind. I gave away all the money you sent me . . . to his wife for the funeral. She's a widow now, with consumption, a poor creature . . . three little children, starving . . . nothing in the house . . . there's a daughter, too . . . perhaps you'd have given it yourself if you'd seen them. But I had no right to do it, I admit, especially as I knew how you needed the money yourself. [Dostoevski, *Crime and Punishment*]

    b.   But a sort of blankness, even dreaminess had begun by degrees to take possession of him. At moments he forgot himself, or rather forgot what was of importance and caught at trifles. Glancing, however, into the kitchen and seeing a bucket half full of water on a bench, he decided to wash his hands and the axe. His hands were sticky with blood. He dropped the axe with the blade in the water, snatched a piece of soap that lay in a broken saucer on the window, and began washing his hands in the bucket. When they were clean, he took out the axe, washed the blade and spent a long time, about three minutes, washing the wood where there were spots of blood, rubbing them with soap. Then he wiped it all with some linen that was hanging to dry on a line in the kitchen and then he was a long while attentively examining the axe at the window. There was no trace left on it, only the wood was still damp. He carefully hung the axe in the noose under his coat. [Dostoevski, *Crime and Punishment*]

c. As he advanced, his feet sank in. He very soon had the mire half-knee deep, and water above his knees. He sank in deeper and deeper. The water came up to his armpits. He sank still deeper. He threw his face back to escape the water, and to be able to breathe. He made a desperate effort, and thrust his foot forward. His foot struck something solid. He reached the other side of the sewer. He rose, shivering, chilled, infected, bending beneath this dying man, whom he was dragging on, all dripping with slime. He resumed his route once more. He walked with desperation, almost with rapidity, for a hundred paces, without raising his head, almost without breathing, and suddenly struck against the wall. He had reached an angle of the sewer, and arriving at the turn with his head down, he had encountered the wall. He raised his eyes, and at the end of the passage, down there before him, far, very far away, he perceived a light. It was the light of day. He reached the outlet. There he stopped. Suddenly he felt an indescribable uneasiness, such as we feel when we have somebody behind us, without seeing him. He turned around. Somebody was indeed behind him. [Hugo, *Les Miserables*]

d. It was dark when Natty Bumpo reached the borders of the lake. Around a glittering fire he dimly saw dusky figures dancing. They were in war paint. Among them was the renowned chief, Muck-a-Muck. The chief held in his hand long prominent tufts of raven hair. The heart of Natty Bumpo sickened as he recognized the clustering curls of his love, Jennie. In a moment his rifle was at his shoulder, and with a sharp "ping," Muck-a-Muck leaped into the air a corpse. Then he dashed off to Jennie's cabin. He burst open the door. Why did he stand frozen with open mouth and distended eyeballs? Was the sight too horrible to be borne? On the contrary, before him, in her peerless beauty, stood Jennie Tompkins, leaning on her father's arm.

"You're not scalped, then!" gasped her lover.

"No. I have no hesitation in saying that I am not; but why this abruptness?" responded Jennie.

Bumpo could not speak, but frantically produced the silken tresses. "Why, that's my hairpiece!" said Jennie, turning her face aside.

Bumpo sank fainting to the floor. [Harte, *A Modern Indian Novel After Cooper*]

Pausing and Phrases

The fact that almost everybody knows exactly how *Hamlet* should be played is perhaps one of the reasons it is so seldom well played. The widely renowned Hamlets of John Gielgud, Richard Burton, and Laurence Olivier have aroused equal measures of acclaim and controversy. All three portrayals were vastly dissimilar, in whole as well as in details. Perhaps Hamlet's most universal moment is the famous "To Be or Not To Be" soliloquy. If you listen to recordings of these three actors, you will note interesting differences in the location of pauses and the length of phrases.

To be   or not to be   that is the question.
To be or not to be   that is the question.
To be or not to be   that   is the question.

Which is the most effective? Probably none is better than the others. Taste alone, not rules, can decide.

Mr. Burton, for example, in three consecutive performances, gave a completely different reading of the soliloquy each performance! He relocated the pauses and altered phrase lengths. It is rather difficult to establish specific rules governing the location and frequency of pauses and length of phrases. As long as clarity is preserved and the desired emphasis is achieved, a group of words can be phrased with the accompanying pauses in several different ways. Nevertheless, something tells us that we might be annoyed at any of the following readings.

To   be or not to   be that is the question.
To be or not   to be   that is the   question.
(With no pauses at all) Tobeornottobethatisthequestion.

What, then, is a pause? A pause is a period of silence.

What, then, is a phrase? A phrase is a group of related words (although it may consist of a single word) expressing a thought unit, a "sense" unit, an idea, or occasionally a series of ideas. Phrases are set off from each other with pauses.

Why Phrase?

63. *Phrasing is used to emphasize and convey more clearly the exact meaning of a group of related words.*

    (The phrasing in the following material is merely suggested and should not be regarded as definitive. Read each sentence twice. The first time, ignore the pauses indicated by the two vertical lines. Then reread, pausing as indicated.)

    a. Let's talk about it now ‖ and not later this afternoon, because if we don't buy ‖ we can use our money for that trip to Europe.
    b. Frieda ‖ not knowing that the class was asleep ‖ continued to write on the board.
    c. If you don't vote this time ‖ you won't vote next time ‖ because the next time is like the last time.
    d. Run home ‖ scrub your face ‖ polish your shoes ‖ eat your lunch ‖ and then come back.
    e. It was in December ‖ not January ‖ that the Joneses ‖ not the Smiths ‖ flew to Norway ‖ not Sweden.

64. *Phrasing is used to prevent the meaning of one group of words from spilling over into another group.*

    a. My best friend ‖ said Joe ‖ is in critical condition.
    b. When he had eaten ‖ the dog ran away.
    c. When a dentist begins ‖ setting his drill in the correct position is his main concern.
    d. Yes ‖ Mister ‖ Thompson screamed at the deaf old man ‖ Without Love ‖ I would venture to suggest ‖ would be a fine play for you to read.
    e. His date ‖ said Bob ‖ was quite boring.

65. *Phrasing is used to heighten emotional effect.*

    a. We shall fight on the beaches ‖ we shall fight on the landing grounds ‖ we shall fight in the fields and in the streets ‖ we shall fight in the hills ‖ we shall never surrender.
    b. Life's but a walking shadow ‖ a poor player that frets and struts his hour upon the stage ‖ and then ‖ is ‖ heard no more.
    c. Yea ‖ though I walk through the valley of the shadow of death ‖ I will fear no evil.
    d. To avoid criticism ‖ do nothing ‖ say nothing ‖ be nothing.
    e. We were never really driven out of paradise ‖ We love and work in the midst of paradise as ever ‖ we ourselves are paradise ‖ but unknowing and therefore ‖ in hell.

66. *The nature of the material itself also governs phrasing.* In general, material which is solemn, profound, complex, unfamiliar to the audience, or presented in acoustically inferior surroundings might be delivered in comparatively short phrases and at a comparatively slow rate. Material which is casual, humorous, or cheerful, familiar to the audience, or presented in acoustically superior surroundings might be delivered in comparatively long phrases and at a comparatively rapid rate.

    a. The year is dying in the night ‖ ring out, wild bells and let him die.
    b. Therefore ‖ never send to know ‖ for whom the bell tolls ‖ it tolls ‖ for thee.
    c. It is better to keep your mouth shut and appear stupid ‖ than to open it ‖ and remove all doubt.
    d. Fear death ‖ to feel the fog in my throat ‖ the mist in my face.

e. Were he not to marry again, it might be concluded that his first wife had given him a disgust to marriage; ‖ but by taking a second wife he pays the highest compliment to the first, ‖ by showing that she made him so happy as a married man, that he wishes to be so a second time.

f. Suicide thwarts the attainment of the highest moral aim by the fact that ‖ for a real release from this world of misery ‖ it substitutes one that is merely apparent.

g. How do you know love is gone? ‖ If you said that you would be there at seven, and you get there by nine, and he or she has not called the police yet ‖ it's gone. [Marlene Dietrich]

h. I expect to pass through this world but once. ‖ Any good therefore that I can do, or any kindness that I can show to any fellow creature ‖ let me do it now. Let me not defer or neglect it, ‖ for I shall not pass this way again.

67. The breath control of the speaker may also influence phrasing. If your breath supply is inadequate, you may find yourself gasping for air in the middle of a phrase. Then, of course, one occasionally hears this criticism of a speaker: "But he never stops to take a breath!" This type of individual gets wound up in his words and seemingly never runs down. Either fault, "gaspitis" or perpetual motion of the jaw, is apt to call attention to itself and detract from the significance of what is being said. Read the following in one phrase each:

a. Fear not!
b. Run, Sheep, Run!
c. Haste is of the devil.
d. Beggars must be no choosers.
e. Hatred is the madness of the heart.
f. Birds of a feather will gather together.
g. There is always someone worse off than yourself.
h. What's one man's poison is another's meat or drink.
i. They love him most for the enemies he has made.
j. A leader is best when people barely know that he exists.
k. Put your trust in God, my boys, and keep your powder dry.
l. Tell me what you eat, and I will tell you what you are.
m. You can't set a hen in one morning and have chicken salad for lunch.
n. Don't put too fine a point to your wit for fear it should get blunted.
o. Health lies in labor, and there is no royal road to it but through toil.
p. He got the better of himself, and that's the best kind of a victory one can wish for.
q. Fortune is like the market, where many times, if you can stay a little, the price will fall.
r. Thieves respect property. They merely wish the property to become their property that they may more perfectly respect it.
s. Holiness is what is loved by all the gods. It is loved because it is holy, and not holy because it is loved.

68. Study the following nonsense material, and phrase it in such a manner that it becomes relatively intelligible:

Esau Wood sawed wood. Esau Wood would saw wood. All the wood Esau Wood saw Esau Wood would saw. In other words, all the wood Esau saw Esau sought to saw. Oh, the wood Wood would saw! And oh, the wood-saw with which Wood would saw wood. But one day Wood's wood-saw would saw no wood, and thus the wood Wood sawed was not the wood Wood would saw if Wood's wood-saw would saw wood. Now, Wood would saw if Wood's wood-saw would saw wood, so Esau sought a saw that would saw wood. One day Esau saw a saw saw wood as no other wood-saw Wood saw would saw wood. In fact, of all the wood-saws Wood ever saw saw wood Wood never saw a wood-saw that would saw wood as the wood-saw Wood saw saw wood would saw wood, and I never saw a wood-saw that would saw as the wood-saw Wood saw would saw until I saw

Esau saw wood with the wood-saw Wood saw saw wood. Now Wood saws wood with the wood-saw Wood saw saw wood.

As we are already aware, a phrase is separated from other phrases by pauses. A pause, of course, is a period of silence, an absence of sound.

Pauses should not be confused with hesitations. With the latter the speaker has, as a rule, momentarily forgotten what he was going to say, is reluctant to say anything, or has tripped over a word. With the former the speaker wishes to give his listeners time to absorb or respond to what has been said or to prepare them for what is about to be said. The inexperienced individual is generally guilty of using too few pauses, and the ones he uses are either too short or too similar in duration. Or he is inclined to regard every punctuation mark as an indication that he must pause. Punctuation is generally a guide for the eye rather than the ear. It indicates meaning. It is quite true that you frequently pause where a writer has placed a comma, period, dashes, or a semicolon, but you do not always do so. Punctuation marks are generally placed between thought-groups, and pauses are most logically placed between thought-groups. Nevertheless, if we were to pause at every punctuation mark, the effect would be jerky and choppy. As an illustration of this, read the following passage, pausing at every punctuation mark:

> In England, if something goes wrong—say, if one finds a skunk in the garbage—he writes to the family lawyer, who proceeds to take the proper steps; whereas in America, you telephone the fire department. Each satisfies a characteristic need; in the English, love of order, and legal procedure; in America, what you like is something vivid, and red, and swift.

At the other extreme, twentieth century writers are using punctuation rather sparsely. Many of the short stories appearing in the New Yorker magazine, and some of the writings of Ernest Hemingway illustrate this trend. If we read this kind of prose, we may possibly have to pause more times than there are punctuation marks.

What about reading poetry? Should we pause at the end of every line or after every rhyme? Not necessarily. Note how awkward Longfellow's "The Day is Done" reads if phrased as indicated:

> The day is done, and the darkness ‖
>   Falls from the wings of Night, ‖
> As a feather is wafted downward ‖
>   From an eagle in his flight.

If we are more interested in thought content than creating a rhythmical mood or pattern, we might do better to observe these suggested pauses:

> The day is done ‖ and the darkness falls from the wings of night ‖ as a feather is wafted downward from an eagle in his flight.

Why Pause?

Pauses and phrasing are so closely integrated that much of what has been said about the latter is applicable here. Pauses, effectively used, aid us in achieving emphasis, clarity, intelligibility, and emotional quality, and, of course, they provide us with a natural opportunity to take a breath.

We often encounter the phrase "dramatic pause." Actually, this expression is one more way of describing emphasis or emotional quality, terms we have already used. The importance of the dramatic pause has long been realized by polished public speakers and actors. (George C. Scott once said that the pause is the last fundamental that the actor learns to master.) The most subtle thing about the dramatic pause, however, is not its frequency but its length. Solemn, profound, and complex material generally demands longer pauses than lighthearted, simple, or familiar material, although there are exceptions to this. A long pause after an idea or a phrase generally emphasizes or gives finality to what has just been said. A long pause before an important idea or a climactic key word generally heightens suspense. In comic material the "punch" or "laugh" word or line can often be pointed up and made funnier if it is preceded by a relatively long pause. For example, Carol Burnett, in some of her comedy sketches, is particularly adept at pointing up her lines.

69. In the following material | L | indicates a long pause, | M | indicates a medium pause, and | S | indicates a short pause. Such markings are, of course, suggested and are not necessarily definitive. "Long," "medium," and "short" are obviously relative terms.

    a. (A minister concluding a sermon) . . . and unless we destroy corruption in government, | S | I promise you that we will go down in overwhelming disgrace, defeat, and disaster! | L | Let us pray.

    b. Shall we build in our time the foundation for everlasting peace? | L | I say yes | M | and I shall tell you how.

    c. And there it lay | M | that moldy coffin | S | ugly and menacing in the bloodless moonlight. | S | We lurched forward | S | six pairs of trembling hands seized the grimy lid | S | ripped it open. | M | Something | S | somewhere shrieked. | M | Our eyes, hot and glazed, pierced the formless shadows inside the casket. | S | Again a godless scream | S | and then we knew | M | the evil box | S | was | L | empty.

    d. To be poor | S | and seem to be poor | S | is a certain way | M | never to rise.

    e. The only possible society is | S | oneself.

    f. The public is wonderfully tolerant. It forgives everything | M | except genius.

    g. The sea is calm tonight | L | the tide is full | M | the moon | S | lies fair upon the straits.

    h. Only one person could have killed her | M | and that person is | L | you.

    i. Lizzie Borden took an axe
And gave her mother | S | forty whacks:
When she saw what she had done | L |
She gave her father | M | forty-one.

    j. Free thought I now proclaim for all | S | and death to him | M | who does not think as I do.

    k. It was a lover and his lass | S | with a hey and a ho | S | with a hey nonino.

    l. Shall I | S | wasting in despair | M | die | S | because a woman's fair?

    m. You wanted the money | S | Here it is.

    n. I have only one thing to say to you | L | You are a liar.

    o. Don't take highway 40 | M | Take highway 50.

    p. Run quickly | S | Get a doctor | S | Call an ambulance!

    q. What is the most important thing in the world? | L | Love.

    r. I would have been there | L | but I was angry with you.

    s. I saw her yesterday | S | but not this morning.

    t. Should we go now | M | or should we wait for the others?

    u. When a hundred men stand together | S | each of them loses his mind | M | and gets another one.

    v. The pride of dying rich raises the loudest laugh | L | in hell.

    w. Courage consists not in blindly overlooking danger | S | but in seeing it | L | and conquering it.

    x. Economy: | M | Going without something you do want | S | in case you should someday want something | S | which you probably won't like.

    y. The black flower of civilized society | M | a prison.

70. Restudy the material in Exercise 69. Relocate and vary the length of pauses.

71. Study and analyze the following selections for location and length of pauses. Mark according to your own judgment and then read.

    a. Death, the most awful of evils, is nothing to us. So long as we are alive, death has not visited us; once we are dead, we are no longer alive.

    b. I don't like disorder, but I am exasperated by those who shout, "Don't move!" when no one is yet in place.

    c. For sleep is good, but death is better still; the best is never to be born at all.

    d. Heaven goes by favor; if it went by merit, you would stay out and your dog would go in.

    e. Experience—a fine teacher, it's true; but here's what makes me burn: Experience is always teaching me things I'd rather not learn.

    f. He that has a secret should not only hide it, but hide that he has it to hide.

    g. As it is said of the greatest liar, that he tells more truth than falsehood; so it may be said of the worst man, that he does more good than evil.

    h. There are three Johns: 1. the real John, known only to his maker; 2. John's ideal John, never the real one, and often very unlike him; 3. Thomas's ideal John, never the real John, nor John's John, but often very unlike either. [Holmes, *Autocrat*]

    i. Nothing is more gentle than smoke, nothing more frightful. There is the smoke of peace, and the smoke of villainy. Smoke, the density and color of smoke, makes all the difference between peace and war, between brotherhood and hatred, between hospitality and the grave, between life and death. Smoke rising through the trees may signify the most charming thing in the world, the hearth; or the most terrible, a conflagration. [Hugo, *Les Miserables*]

    j. The pleasure of an afternoon nap is double that of sleep at night.

    k. "If everybody minded their own business," the Duchess said, in a hoarse growl, "the world would go round a great deal faster than it does."

    l. Appearances to the mind are of four kinds. Things either are what they appear to be; or they are, and do not appear to be; or they neither are, nor appear to be; or they are not, and yet appear to be. Rightly to aim in all these cases is the wise man's task.

    m. People are always dying in *The New York Times* who don't seem to die in other papers, and they die at greater length and maybe even with a little more grace.

    n. It is perfectly monstrous the way people go about nowadays saying things against one, behind one's back, that are absolutely and entirely true.

    o. Beautiful earth, forgive me for having walked over you to no purpose. Beautiful sun, your glorious rays have shone upon an empty shell—no one within to receive warmth and comfort from you, the owner never in his house. Beautiful sun, beautiful earth, it was for nothing that you warmed and nourished my mother. Nature is a spendthrift, and the spirit is a greedy miser. One's life is a heavy price to pay for being born. I will go up—up to the highest mountaintops. I'll see the sun rise once again and gaze upon the promised land until my eyes are weary. Then the snow will fall and cover me, and on my resting-place will be written an epitaph: "The tomb of no one!" And after that, well, come what may! [Ibsen, *Peer Gynt*]

    p. The sound came again—it was a sigh. Rushing to the corpse, I saw—distinctly saw—a tremor upon the lips. In a minute afterward they relaxed, disclosing a bright line of the pearly teeth. I felt that my vision grew dim, that my reason wandered; and it was only by a violent effort that I at length succeeded in nerving myself to the task which duty thus once more pointed out. There was now a partial glow upon the forehead and upon the cheek and throat. There was a slight pulsation at the heart. The lady lived, and with redoubled vigor I betook myself to the task of restoration. I chafed and bathed the temples and the hands, and used every exertion which experience, and no little medical reading, could suggest. But in vain. Suddenly, the color fled, the pulsation ceased, the lips resumed the expression of the dead, and, in an instant afterward, the whole body took upon itself the icy chilliness, the livid hue, the intense rigidity, the sunken outlines, and all the loathsome peculiarities of that which has been, for many days, a tenant in the tomb. [Poe, *Ligeia*]

q.

MILGRIG AND THE TREE WILFS
(Something like Hans Christian Andersen)

Once upon a time there was a little girl named Milgrig, believe it or not. She lived in the middle of a deep dark forest with her three ugly sisters and their husbands, who were charcoal burners. Every night the three ugly sisters used to take little Milgrig and pull out a strand of her golden hair, so that by the time she was thirteen years old she looked something awful. And after the three sisters had pulled out her hair, their three husbands (I forgot to tell you that the three husbands were even uglier than the three sisters and much nastier) would stick pins into little Milgrig until she looked like a war map.

One night, when little Milgrig was so full of pins that she couldn't see straight, a fairy prince came riding up to the door of the charcoal burners' hut and asked if he had lost the way.

"How should I know?" replied the oldest sister, who was uglier than all the rest. "What was your way?"

"My way was to the king's castle," replied the prince, "and I must get there before midnight, for my father is torturing my mother with red-hot irons."

"Your father sounds like a good egg," replied the oldest husband, who was uglier than all the rest. "We must ask him down some night."

The prince, however, did not think that this was very funny and asked if little Milgrig might not be allowed to show him the way to the castle.

The ugly husbands and sisters, thinking that Milgrig would not know the way and would get the prince lost in the forest, agreed heartily to this suggestion, and the pins were pulled out of Milgrig to make it possible for her to walk.

"Good luck and a happy landing!" they all called out after the two young people as they set forth on their perilous journey.

But the prince was no fool, and knew his way through the forest as well as you or I do (better, I'll wager), and he took little Milgrig to the palace just as fast as his palfrey would carry him.

She wasn't particularly crazy about going, but a prince is a prince, and she knew enough to keep her mouth shut.

When they reached the palace and the prince found that his father had already killed his mother, he turned to little Milgrig and said: "Now you are the queen."

At this, little Milgrig was very pleased and immediately dispatched messengers to the charcoal burner's hut, where the three ugly sisters and three still uglier brothers-in-law were burned alive in a slow fire. Little Milgrig and the prince, happy in this termination to their little affair, lived happily ever after. [Robert Benchley]

Assignment 12 (See suggested Checklist for Assignments 9-13 at end of chapter)

Prepare 15-20 lines of material. A brief cutting from a short story or a play would be ideal. Try to choose material which contains several contrasting moods.

Analyze your selection, determining which words, phrases, or lines would be most appropriately expressed in staccato speech, which in prolonged utterance, and which in tones of regular duration.

Analyze and mark the selection into appropriate phrases and pauses of various length.

When you present your selection to the class, work for as much spontaneity as you can. The techniques you use should not call undue attention to themselves.

Integration

Lewis Carroll wrote: "Take care of the sense and the sounds will take care of themselves." As you work with the following, rather than concentrating merely on any one or two of the various elements contributing to vocal expressiveness—blend and integrate them, subordinate all of them to the general effect. Search for meaning and intelligibility. Search for contrasting moods and varied emotional states.

72. Using all the vocal versatility you can command, read as spontaneously as possible the following:

   a. Johnny: So here you sit, holy as God, and make your plans—marking up your thousands of dead and dying like cold figures on a blackboard. Know what that means? I ask you—know what that means?—all these boys—young fellows like me—like what you used to be—going out to die—shot down—killed—murdered—to be dead and stiff and rotten in a trench with rats and mud? We were meant for something better, I tell you! We want to live, and you could let us live. Only a second's time—a movement of your hand—a written word—and you could stop the war. Do it! Do it! [Green, *Johnny Johnson*]

   b. Kurt: I was a kid of fourteen. There was a strike. One day my father took me out for a walk. Sunny spring morning. We stopped to listen to an organizer. My father was a mild little man with kind of faded, tired blue eyes. We stood on the outskirts of the crowd. My father was holding me by the hand. Suddenly somebody shouted: "The Militia!" There was a shot. Everybody scattered. My father was bewildered—he didn't know which way to run. A second later he crumpled down beside me. He was bleeding. He was still holding my hand. He died like that. [Behrman, *Biography*]

   c. Countess: Oh, I wish she hadn't brought up the Alps, Lucy. It always reminds me of that nasty moment I had the day Gustav made me climb to the top of one of them. Anyhow, there we were. And suddenly it struck me that Gustav had pushed me. I slid halfway down the mountain before I realized that Gustav didn't love me any more. But love takes care of its own, Lucy. I slid right into the arms of my fourth husband, the count. [Boothe, *The Women*]

   d. Birdie: I've never had a headache in my life. You know it as well as I do. I never had a headache. That's a lie they tell for me. I drink. All by myself, in my own room, by myself, I drink. You know what? In twenty-two years I haven't had a whole day of happiness. Oh, a little like today with you all. But never a single, whole day. And in twenty years you'll be just like me. They'll do the same things to you. [Hellman, *The Little Foxes*]

   e. Alice: Oh, I wish I lived in a family that didn't always forget everything. That—that behaved the way other people's families do. I'm sick of cornflakes—and Donald—and everything! Why can't we be like other people? Roast beef, and two green vegetables, and—doilies on the table, and a place you could bring your friends to! [Kaufman and Hart, *You Can't Take It With You*]

   f. Alice: Look, Tony, this is something I should have said a long time ago, but I didn't have the courage. I let myself be swept away—because I loved you so. I want to make it clear to you. You're of a different people—a whole different kind of people. Oh, I don't mean money or socially—that's too silly. But your family and mine—it just wouldn't work, Tony. It just wouldn't work. [Kaufman and Hart, *You Can't Take It With You*]

g. Sid: You're right, Lily!—right not to forgive me! I'm no good and never will be! I'm a no-good drunken bum! You shouldn't even wipe your feet on me! I'm a dirty rotten drunk!—no good to myself or anybody else! If I had any guts I'd kill myself, and good riddance!—but I haven't—I'm yellow, too—a yellow, drunken bum! [O'Neill, *Ah, Wilderness!*]

h. Kolenkhov: He should have been in Russia when the Revolution came. Then he would have stood in line—a bread line. Ah, Grandpa, what they have done to Russia! Think of it! The Grand Duchess Olga Katrina, a cousin of the Czar, she is a waitress in Childs' Restaurant! I ordered baked beans from her only yesterday. It broke my heart. A crazy world, Grandpa! [Kaufman and Hart, *You Can't Take It With You*]

i. Henderson: Now wait a minute! I'm not here to argue with you. All I know is that you haven't paid your income tax and you've got to pay it! And let me tell you something else! You'll go to jail if you don't pay, do you hear that? There's a law, and if you think you're bigger than the law, you've got another think coming! You'll hear from the United States government, that's all I can say! [Kaufman and Hart, *You Can't Take It With You*]

j. Horace: I'm sick of you, sick of this house, sick of my life here. I'm sick of your brothers and their dirty tricks to make a dime. There must be better ways of getting rich than cheating poor people on a pound of bacon. Why should I give you the money? You wreck the town, you and your brothers, you wreck the town and live on it. Not me. Maybe it's easy for the dying to be honest. But it's not my fault I'm dying. I'll do no more harm now. I've done enough. I'll die my own way. And I'll do it without making the world any worse. I leave that to you. [Hellman, *The Little Foxes*]

k. Miriamne: You in the shadows! You killed him to silence him! But I'm not silenced! All that he knew, I know! And I'll tell it tonight! Tell it and scream it through all the streets that Trock's a murderer and he hired you for this murder! Your work's not done—and you won't live long! Do you hear? You're murderers, and I know who you are! [Anderson, *Winterset*]

l. Crystal: Now get this straight, Mrs. Haines. I like what I've got and I'm going to keep it. You handed me your husband on a silver platter. But I'm not returning the compliment. I can't be stampeded by gossip. What you believe and what Stephen believes will cut no ice in a divorce court. You need proof and you haven't got it. When Mr. Winston comes to his senses, he'll apologize. And Stephen will have no choice, but to accept—my explanations. Now, that's that! Good night! [Boothe, *The Women*]

m. Martha: Pushed around. We're being pushed around by crazy people. That's an awful thing. And we're standing here—we're standing here taking it. Try to understand this: you're not playing with paper dolls. We're human beings, see? It's our lives you're fooling with. Our lives. That's serious business for us. Can you understand that? [Hellman, *The Children's Hour*]

n. Walter: You've kicked over the whole City Hall like an applecart. You've got the mayor and Hartman back against a wall. You've put one administration out and another in. This ain't a newspaper story—it's a career. And you standin' there bellyachin' about some girl. . . . Why they'll be naming streets after you. Johnson Street! You and I and the senator are going to run this town! Do you understand that? [Hecht and MacArthur, *The Front Page*]

o. Muriel: You did, too! You're lying and you know it! You did, too! And there I was right at that time lying in bed and not able to sleep, wondering how I was ever going to see you again and crying my eyes out, while you—I hate you! I wish you were dead! I'm going home this moment! I never want to lay eyes on you again! And this time I mean it! [O'Neill, *Ah, Wilderness!*]

p. Phil: Mr. Grady, I could act this soldier part. I could build it up and act it. Make it up—Honest to God I could! I need the job—that's why I could do it! I'm strong. I know my business! You'll get an A-1 performance. Because I need this job! My wife's having a baby in a few weeks. We need the money. Give me a chance! [Odets, *Waiting for Lefty*] *q.* C. Elliot Friday: Now really, boys, I'm tolerant, but I've got to see results. I'm not one to put the creative urge in a straitjacket. But you've been fired off every lot in this industry for your pranks. Perhaps you've forgotten, Benson, but when I hired you for this job you promised me to behave in no uncertain terms. And you promised me Law would toe the line. Now, I'm warning you boys. Let's get to work. Let's concentrate. Do you realize you boys are making more than the President of the United States? [Spewack, *Boy Meets Girl*]

r. Stanley: Mr. Whiteside, these gentlemen are deputy sheriffs. They have a warrant by which I am enabled to put you out of this house, and I need hardly add that it will be the greatest moment of my life. I am giving you fifteen minutes in which to pack up and get out. If you are not gone in fifteen minutes, Mr. Whiteside, these gentlemen will forcibly eject you. And that means bag, baggage, wheelchair, penguins, octopus, and cockroaches. I am now going upstairs to smash our radio, so that not even accidentally will I ever hear your voice again. [Kaufman and Hart, *The Man Who Came to Dinner*]

s. Keller: What should I want to do? Jail? You want me to go to jail? If you want me to go, say so! Is that where I belong? Then tell me so! What's the matter, why can't you tell me? You say everything else to me, say that! I'll tell you why you can't say it. Because you know I don't belong there. Because you know! Who worked for nothing in that war? When they work for nothing, I'll work for nothing. Did they ship a gun or a truck outa Detroit before they got their price? Is that clean? It's dollars and cents, nickels and dimes; war and peace, it's nickels and dimes, what's clean? Half the Goddam country is gotta go if I go! That's why you can't tell me. [Miller, *All My Sons*]

t. Sally: Two days ago. Just after we left here. He saw us in the street . . . Mother and me, I mean— and our eyes met—his and mine, I mean—and he sort of followed me. To a tea shop, where he sat and gazed at me. And back to the hotel. And at the restaurant. He had the table next to us, and he kept sort of hitching his foot around my chair. And he passed me a note in the fruit basket. Only Mother got it by mistake. But it was in German. I told her it was from a movie agent. And I went over and talked to him, and he was! Then we met later. He's quite marvelous, Chris. He's got a long, black beard. Well, not really long. I've never been kissed by a beard before. I thought it would be awful. But it isn't. It's quite exciting. Only he doesn't speak much German. He's a Yugoslavian. That's why I don't know much about the picture. But I'm sure it will be all right. He'll write in something. And now I've got to run. [Van Druten, *I Am a Camera*]

u. Stanley: Honey, I told you I thoroughly checked on these stories! Now wait till I'm finished. The trouble with Dame Blanche was that she couldn't put on her act any more at Laurel! They got wised up after two or three dates with her and then they quit, and she goes on to another, the same old line, same old act, same old hooey! But the town was too small for this to go on forever! And as time went by she became a town character. Regarded as not just different but downright loco—nuts. And for the last year or two she has been washed up like poison. That's why she's here this summer, visiting royalty, putting on all this act—because she's practically told by the mayor to get out of town! Yes, did you know there was an army camp near Laurel and your sister's was one of the places called "Out-of-Bounds"? [Williams, *A Streetcar Named Desire*]

v. Rosemary: You think just cause you're a man, you can walk in here and make off with whatever you like. You think just cause you're young you can push other people aside and not pay them any mind. You think just cause you're strong you can show your muscles and nobody'll know what a pitiful specimen you are. But you won't stay young forever, didja ever think of that? What'll become of you then? You'll end your life in the gutter and it'll serve you right, 'cause the gutter's where you came from and the gutter's where you belong. [Inge, *Picnic*]

w. Bluntschli: Yes, but when the sergeant ran up as white as a sheet, and told us they'd sent us the wrong ammunition, and that we couldn't fire a round for the next ten minutes, we laughed out the other side of our mouths. I never felt so sick in my life, though I've been in one or two very tight places. And I hadn't even a cartridge for my revolver—only chocolate. We had no bayonets— nothing! Of course, they just cut us to bits. And there was Don Quixote flourishing like a drum major, thinking he'd done the cleverest thing ever known, whereas he ought to be court-martialed for it. Of all the fools ever let loose on a field of battle, that man must be the very maddest. He and his regiment simply committed suicide; only the pistol missed fire, that's all. [Shaw, *Arms and the Man*]

x. Margaret: The day is dawning. It is the last day for me! Why, this was to have been my wedding day! Tell no one you have already been with me. We shall see each other again . . . but it will not be at a dance. The crowd is gathering silently in the street, on the square. The death bells are tolling. The wand is snapped. They seize me, they bind me with lashes. I, alone, on the scaffold. Now I'm shoved to the block. Over each neck the keen-edged knife quivers as it quivers over mine. The sharp steel flashes . . . the world lies hushed as the grave! [Goethe, *Faust*]

y. Rose: But she says I can't make her an actress like she wants to be. The boys walk because they think the act's finished. They think we're nothing without her. Well, she's nothing without me! I'm her mother and I made her! And I can make you now! And I will, baby, I swear I will! I am going to make you a star! I'm going to build a whole new act—all around you! It's going to be better than anything we ever did before! Better than anything we even dreamed! The old act was getting stale and tired! But the new one? Look at the new star, Herbie! She's going to be beauti- ful! She is beautiful! Finished?! We're just beginning and there's no stopping us this time! [Laurents, *Gypsy*]

z. Faust: If you wish to share this room with me, dog, stop that growling and bellowing. I can't have such a noisy comrade near me. One of us must go, and as host, I'm reluctant to withdraw. But the door is open, dog, and you are free to go. Oh, God! What do I see? Can such a thing happen? Is this natural? . . . a shadow, a phantom? The dog . . . how large he grows! He rises in might! What sort of a specter have I harbored here . . . with eyes of fire and blazing jaws? How he swells and bristles now! He cowers from the spell, yet he still seems to loom like a frightful cloud, filling up the room. Down, you proud spawn of hell! The power I wield is no deceit. I'll shrivel and scorch you with holy flame. Do not wait to know the strongest art at my command! Spirit of Hell! Come, stand forth! [Goethe, *Faust*]

aa. Harpagon: Thieves! Thieves! Assassins! Murderers! I'm undone, I'm murdered! They've cut my throat . . . they've stolen my money! Who did it? Where is he hiding? Where shall I run? Where shall I not run? Aha! Who is this? Stop! (He has taken ahold of his own arm, behind his back.) Give me back my money, wretch! Ah . . . it's myself. Alas! My mind is wandering and I don't know who I am or what I'm doing. My money, my poor, poor money! My dearest friend! I have nothing to live for! I demand justice! I'll have everybody in this house put to torture . . . the ser- vants, my son, my daughter . . . and myself, too. I'll hang everybody, and if I don't find my money, I'll hang myself afterwards. Alas! It's all over with me. I can bear it no longer! I am dying! I am dead! I am buried! [Molière, *The Miser*]

bb. Harpagon: Aha! There you are, you trollop, you harlot! So this is the way you thank me for everything I've done for you? It isn't bad enough that you give your love to an infamous thief, but to make matters worse, you get yourself engaged to him—and without my consent. But I'm afraid both of you will be badly disappointed. Four stone walls and iron bars will make you change your mind, you hussy! And you, you arch criminal, a good, strong gallows will take care of you. Gallows! I was wrong to say the gallows. You'll be broken alive on the wheel. [Molière, *The Miser*]

cc. Corbaccio: I . . . hee, hee . . . like to look at dying men. I've seen so many and I enjoy each one more. I'm eighty-two. I've buried brothers, sisters, friends, enemies, but I'm still alive . . . hee, hee . . . I'll outlive 'em all. I've known many of them in the cradle, and seen 'em grow up and all at once they lie there—blue, cold, and dead . . . hee, hee. And now this one, too! He lived a merry life . . . young, could have been my son—and he's come to die already, hee, hee! I want to take a look at him. Here, stand up, carcass, face an old man. You're younger—you have better legs. Stand up . . . hee, hee! Often you've mocked poor old Corbaccio for being miserly . . . hee, hee . . . who's mocking now, you windbag, you glutton? He'll outlive you all, will old Corbaccio!

dd. Corvino: Ah, Colomba, you're crying. Have I hurt you, my little flower? Forgive me! It's only love when I torment you. And all the time I truly know what a gentle, good little wife, what a cooing turtledove I have in you. Forgive me, Colomba, if I've tormented you. You ought to see other men, who lock in their wives, have them spied on and clamp them in an iron girdle when they go on their travels. I'll give both you and me proof of my great trust in you, my angel. Come, make yourself lovely . . . I want to show you that Corvino is not the jealous spouse for whom you take him. Come!

ee. Volpone: Sour sport for me. No, Mosca, you are mistaken! I'm not acting. I still feel sick as a dog, and my stomach is turning over and over. You call that sport, you fool! For you, perhaps, but not for me. You can believe me when that Leone was fiddling with his dagger to tickle my ribs, my stomach rose up with one sweep, and I didn't need any medicine to turn the color of cheese. All my life long, I've never been so afraid. (Drinking) Ah, wonderful! Another one! Now I feel myself again. Ah, the joy of standing on two healthy legs. I'm beginning to feel happy and warm again. I feel the old Volpone stirring inside Volpone's corpse.

ff. Mosca: Be reasonable! Is the devil already driving you into new mischief? Madness! You'll tread on their poison fangs! I've had enough! Play your little joke alone. I refuse! I've had too much! I'm no bloodhound, no gallows bird. I came to you as a respectable toady to drink wine, to enjoy women, to laugh, and to make others laugh . . . but I'll play this game no longer! I tell you . . . a cold wind blew through my hair in court today. I've had too much. My flesh is creeping . . . creeping along the road that leads to the gallows. Find someone else for your little jests. I like my nice straight neck better than anything else, and I don't want to joke myself into a hempen collar.

gg. Leone: Where is the scoundrel? I'll tear him from limb to limb! I'll cut his hide to ribbons. Where is he? I was dragged through the city like a criminal . . . roped to the pillory . . . the flies, gnats, the sun . . . Ugh! And they laughed . . . those stinking people, and spit at me, me, a soldier! All that scoundrel's fault! I must choke him once more. Let me go, I'll gouge out his damned eyes with my dagger. (Tottering) Oh . . . tired . . . tired! I'm dying from thirst . . . give me something to drink. Oh . . . what shame . . . oh . . . tired, tired! [Jonson, *Volpone*]

hh. Bendix: City desk! Bendix here! I fell into the damnedest story! I was walking by Wong's Chinese restaurant, Forty-sixth, west of Broadway, when a gun went off, not ten feet from me! It hit somebody, I don't know who yet, but you better take as much of the story as I got! The woman who fired the gun is Mrs. David Williams. First she thought she'd hit her husband, and she got pretty hysterical. I got the story in chunks, but here's the important part! Her husband's an F.B.I. man, he's been an undercover F.B.I. man for years . . . and he's a plain, ordinary assistant chemistry professor at Columbia University! [Krasna, *Who Was That Lady I Saw You With?*]

ii. Martha: I have tried, oh, God, I have tried; the one thing . . . the one thing I've tried to carry pure and unscathed through the sewer of this marriage; through the sick nights, and the pathetic, stupid days, through the derision and the laughter . . . God, the laughter, through one failure after another, one failure compounding another failure, each attempt more sickening, more numbing than the one before; the one thing, the one person I have tried to protect, to raise above the mire of this vile, crushing marriage; the one light in all this hopeless . . . darkness . . . our son! [Albee, *Who's Afraid of Virginia Woolf?*]

Assignment 13 (See suggested Checklist for Assignments 9-13)

Choose two-three minutes of material which requires several contrasting moods or emotional qualities. Perhaps you might wish to restudy one of the selections from Exercise 72 and present it before the class as your assignment. Practice it thoroughly and read it with as much vocal variety as possible.
or
Select a two-four minute scene from a play involving two characters. Choose a climactic moment in the play, one which is intensely dramatic, suspenseful, or funny. Rehearse with your partner. The scene is not to be "acted" in the complete sense of the word inasmuch as movement, business and properties may be disregarded. Delineate as sharply as you can the characters you select.

Suggested Checklist for Assignments 9-13

As you practice you may want to work with this checklist. Listen carefully to yourself. If it is feasible record your assignment or get a classmate or friend to listen to you as you present the material. Eventually your goal will be to have a check mark in the **Yes** column for each category. (Optional: Perhaps your instructor will want to use the checklist to evaluate you during your classroom presentation(s).)

	Yes	No
Pitch		
Uses most desirable, serviceable pitch level.		
Uses effective pitch range.		
(Intonation)		
Keys (general pitch levels) appropriate to content and mood of material.		
Inflections appropriately varied to suit emotional demands of material.		
Steps used effectively to give greater (or lesser) prominence to words and phrases.		
Stress and emphasis used effectively to give prominence to syllables, words and phrases.		
Avoids stereotyped pitch patterns such as:		
Overuse of rising intonations to end phrases or sentences.		
Excessive pitch variations (gushing).		
Singsong.		
Rate		
Rate of reading/speaking appropriate to material.		
Overall rate varied effectively.		
Avoids excessively rapid rate.		
Avoids excessively slow rate.		
Appropriate use of staccato, prolonged, and regular durations.		
(Pausing and Phrases)		
Pauses and phrases appropriate to emotional quality of material.		
Pauses and phrases used effectively to achieve emphasis, clarity, and intelligibility.		
Responds to emotional requirements of material.		
Achieves spontaneity: does not call undue attention to techniques used.		

Additional comments or suggestions:

Class Discussion: Articulation

(Use this page for note-taking. You will find an articulation analysis chart on pp. 271-72, and you may find it helpful to you as you begin to work on this unit.)

Articulation 6

Is my speech clear, distinct, and accurate?

Overheard on the campus: a dialogue between John and Jack.

"Jeat?

Yup. D'u?

Naw. Wha'jav, f'rinsance?

Hambers 'n frenfried podados.

Same'l stuff. Guess I'na hungry. Lessgo ta show.

Can't. Gotta 'r test in Erpeen istry tomorr 'n other'n govmnt 'n poltics day aftomorr. Gonna stedy ina libary.

Cancha rlax? Ya shount stedy alla time.

Awright. Whas plain ada movie? Jest so it isn a Westin. I ate Westins.

This'n priddy good. Bedder'n las'n we saw. It's *The Go'fader.* Breakin' all box office recors.

Thatsomepin. Lessgit goin'. I kin stop ada faternity house onway home an stedy wi' Waler Jones. He barred m' book inyway."

Double talk? Mumble-itus? Call it what you will, but this type of speech represents a tediously common-place verbal disease: sloppy, indistinct, slurred, garbled, mushy speech. More formally, we refer to it as poor articulation.

Articulation—The Process by Which Speech Sounds Are Formed, Separated, Joined, and Differentiated

We will use the term *articulation* in its broadest sense and as synonymous with *enunciation* and *diction.* All of these terms refer to clarity, intelligibility, and distinctness of speech. Distinct speech is often a rather reliable indication of the mental and physical alertness of the individual. The foregoing dialogue certainly illustrates carelessness, if not out-and-out mental flabbiness. How did the two conversationalists get that way?

Like many other faults of voice or speech, mealy-mouthed enunciation might be attributed to personality or emotional disturbances (nervous tension, the temporary as well as the more persistent variety, can be included here), problems of health, dull hearing, organic abnormalities, or nerve injuries. Obviously, environment or social conditioning also have a great deal to do with it. If their parents had poor speech habits, it may well explain why John and Jack sound as they do.

We would be inclined to agree with one survey which disclosed this startling evidence: About three people in a hundred have good or superior articulation, but more than one-third speak so indistinctly that they are in need of some kind of special help. And this, in view of the fact that at least 90% of all the communicating done is oral!

131

Nor is it always a simple matter to convince John and Jack that their speech needs improvement. An individual is rarely conscious of his speech habits until his attention is called to them, and even after that, he may shrug off the accusations. After all, he is always intelligible to himself. Even if he could not hear himself, he would still know what he was thinking. As one of these mumblers once told his speech instructor: "Mebbe issa coinsdence, but se'ral a m'bes frens seem to be gittin' deaf. They kin ne'er unerstan what I say an' keep askin' me to r'peat alla time."

If slovenly speech irritates its hearers more than most other speech faults combined, only slightly less irritating is the type used by Pedantic Percy. His speech is "arty," affected, and elegant. It is far too precise and clipped. It calls undue attention to itself, and speech which does this, as we have previously noted, is generally undesirable. Good articulation requires preciseness of utterance, but it requires a precision which is not excessive. Naturalness is what we are after, and naturalness is perhaps a dangerous word if applied to speech, but less so if we remember that the word, as it is used here, avoids either of two extremes: sloppiness and artificiality. It is intended to describe that type of speech which is as clear and lucid as it is apparently easy, unforced, and effortless. The listener concentrates on what is being said rather than how it is said.

We must always bear in mind that as we speak we most often do so in phrases and sentences and not disconnected words. Our language, when properly spoken, tends to flow along smoothly, without noticeable jerkiness or choppiness. Words seemingly melt or blend into one another.

Would you really say at lunch, for example:

"Please || pass || the || bread || and || butter."?

Probably not. The chances are that you would say something like:

"Please pass the bread 'n' butter."

Connected speech, then, is not like a slow-moving, old-fashioned freight train with an open space between each boxcar. Instead, it more closely resembles the slick modern streamliners, with no perceptible break between cars.

Therefore, we must realize that speech sounds are rarely given their full value in connected speech. One sound in a word affects and modifies its neighboring sounds. This process is known as *assimilation*. Assimilation helps to make sounds and sound combinations easier to pronounce because it facilitates the various movements of the articulators. Thus, it is easier to say:

merry g'round	than	merry || go || round
horshoe	than	horse || shoe
whata ya doing?	than	what || are || you || doing?
black 'n' blue	than	black || and || blue

If assimilation is a common and necessary phenomenon in our speaking, couldn't we then use it as a defense for the previously quoted dialogue of John and Jack. These two were practicing assimilation, of course, but they were carrying it to extremes. "Jeat?" it can be seen, is an overassimilated version of "Did you eat?" If assimilation is practiced to such a degree that it interferes with intelligibility, it is wrong.

Informal, casual conversational speaking permits more assimilation than formal utterance or any kind of speaking which demands a relatively slow rate. As you practice the material in this chapter, remember that connected speech is natural. Disconnected sounds in continuous speech, as a rule, are not. Articulation, after all, also means joined.

Speech sounds are formed and molded by the movements and positions of the articulators, the most important of which are the lips, the front teeth, the lower jaw, the tongue, and the velum (fig. 6.1).

The lips may round (the position is not unlike puckering), as in *weep, wool, loon, oats, toby.*

The lips may touch together, as in *pill, beet, mean.*

The lower lip may contact the upper teeth, as in *veal, fight, feud.*

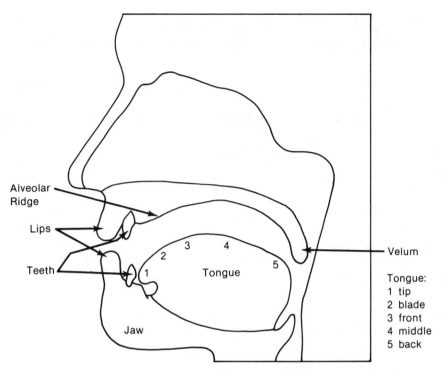

Figure 6.1. Organs of articulation

The **front teeth** assist articulation when other articulators come into contact with them.

    If you say *this theme,* you will be aware that the tip of the tongue touches the upper teeth.

    The lower lip makes a similar contact on *veal, feud.*

The **lower jaw** drops on such words as *awl, calm,* but is almost closed for *oven, few.*

The **tongue** is the most flexible, mobile, and versatile of the articulators.

    Think, there: Tongue tip touches upper front teeth.

    Bust, buzz: Blade of tongue touches alveolar ridge.

    Use, meat: Front of tongue touches or is near hard palate.

    Up, buck: Center of tongue raised slightly.

    Fool, shoe: Back of tongue close to velum.

    Noon, suit: Sides of tongue touch upper teeth.

The **velum** (soft palate) lowers, diverting the breath stream through the nasal cavities as you are making:
    my, nine, ring.

If we may return for a moment to our friends, John and Jack, let us assume that their articulators are normal. What is it, then, about their organs of articulation which makes their speech so slushy? Elsewhere in this book we will discuss tension and its probable effects on voice and speech. We have all observed and listened to the person who speaks with almost no activity of the lips. He draws them into two narrow, taut steel bands. As a rule his jaw is also tense, rigid, and unmoving. These are excellent qualities for a ventriloquist, but not for the rest of us. (Barbara Walters, prominent TV newscaster, has often been accused of speaking with tight lips and little jaw activity.) More characteristically, however, John and Jack are afflicted—not with too much tension—but too much laxness of the articulators. Sluggish activity, inaccuracy of movement and position of the tongue, lips, jaw, and velum generally yield sluggish speech.

To help us develop articulatory agility and flexibility, the following exercises are suggested:

Exercises for the Lips

1. Protrude the lips as far as you can and then pull them back tightly into an extreme smiling position. Repeat.
2. Turn the lower lip downward in an extreme pouting position and then relax. Repeat this procedure as rapidly as possible.
3. Raise the right-hand side of the upper lip and then relax it. Repeat with the left-hand side of the upper lip.
4. Exaggerate lip movements as you say the following:
    a. too-tee-too-tee-too-tee-too-tee.
    b. too-tay-tee-taw-too-tay-tee-taw.
    c. bee-boo-tee-too-bee-boo-tee-too.
    d. too-boo-boo-too-too-boo-boo-too.
    e. wee-way-wee-way-wee-way-wee-way.
    f. Would Woodrow Wheeler woo Wanda if she wore blue boots?
    g. Two bees flew away from the wooden teacup.
    h. Two teamsters tried to steal twenty-two keys.
    i. Why did William whimper when Warren wiggled the whip?
    j. Please do not praise a program in which you won prizes.
    k. We might eat more moose meat if veal is meager.
    l. Will wee Little Bo Peep flee down the beaten path?
    m. Oh, he will feel woozy when he works while reading.
    n. Robert Roper roams around the world in eighty ways.

Exercises for the Jaw

5. Drop the jaw easily as if you were going to say *aw*.
6. Move the relaxed jaw from left to right with your hand.
7. Exaggerate jaw movements as you say the following:
    a. taw-taw-taw-taw-taw-taw-taw-taw.
    b. er-aw-er-aw-er-aw-er-aw.
    c. oo-aw-oo-aw-oo-aw-oo-aw.
    d. goo-gaw-goo-gaw-goo-gaw-goo-gaw.
    e. gee-gaw-gee-gaw-gee-gaw-gee-gaw.
    f. gee-gaw-goo-gaw-gee-gaw-goo-gaw.
    g. Odd birds always gobble green almonds in the autumn.
    h. Eve shrieked and screamed all the way through the long opera.
    i. Autumn in October is often awesome and awkward.
    j. Pete yawns in the evening while Don tosses moss onto the lawn.
    k. Clowns squeal in odd, round, owl-infested houses.

Exercises for the Tongue

8. Double the tongue back against the soft palate as far as you can. Then thrust it firmly against the inside of the left cheek and then against the right cheek.
9. Extend the tongue as far as you can, pointing it toward the chin and then toward the nose. Repeat rapidly several times.
10. Double the tongue back against the soft palate and then drop it quickly to the floor of the mouth. Repeat rapidly. Open your mouth as widely as you can, press the upper surface of the tongue firmly against the hard palate, and then drop it quickly to the floor of the mouth. Repeat rapidly.

11. Exaggerate tongue movements as you say the following:
    a. taw-taw-taw-taw-taw-taw-taw-taw.
    b. law-law-law-law-law-law-law-law.
    c. daw-daw-daw-daw-daw-daw-daw-daw.
    d. raw-raw-raw-raw-raw-raw-raw-raw.
    e. yaw-yaw-yaw-yaw-yaw-yaw-yaw-yaw.
    f. Three thrifty rural rats ran through thirty-three thrones.
    g. Little lambs like to loll near the large locks.
    h. "Hooray!" roared Randolph Ramsey, racing toward the aroused rabble.
    i. The yodeler liked to eat yellow yams while sailing in Yankee yawls.
    j. Lonnie threatened to throw logs at the red lobsters.

Exercises for the Velum (Soft Palate)

12. Watch yourself in a mirror as you yawn. Note that the velum rises. Repeat the yawn.
13. Still observing yourself in the mirror, make the sound *aw*. Be sure that the soft palate is raised high. Repeat.
14. Say *m*. Your soft palate is now lowered. Repeat.
15. Try to feel the contrasting actions of the soft palate as you say the following:
    a. aw-m-aw-m-aw-m-aw-m.
    b. n-aw-n-aw-n-aw-n-aw.
    c. g-ng- (as in "ring") g-ng-g-ng-g-ng.
    d. b-m-b-m-b-m-b-m.
    e. d-n-d-n-d-n-d-n.
    f. ee-m-ee-m-ee-m-ee-m.
16. Be certain that the soft palate is lowered for *m*, *n*, and *ng*, but is in a relatively higher position for all other sounds as you read the following:
    a. Art asked Mamie to make a meat sandwich for Mort Johnson.
    b. If Gene dreams nightiy about Jean, why doesn't Jean dream about him?
    c. Irene sang nicely in *Funny Girl* but was noisy in *Carmen*.
    d. Green beans and moldy meat might ruin Mr. Alden's appetite.
    e. Morton and Barton may marry Anita and Nell on Wednesday.
    f. *Moll Flanders* is not a novel for small children.
    g. Ask God's blessing on your work but do not ask Him to do it.

Sounds and Symbols

We are now almost ready to discover, one by one, how sounds are formed and molded. Specifically, what kind of a task lies ahead of us? It couldn't be too difficult, you might say, because everybody knows that there are only two main families of sounds: vowels and consonants. The five vowels are *a*, *e*, *i*, *o*, and *u*.

That leaves twenty-one consonants, there being twenty-six sounds in the English language. You might then suggest that the logical place to begin is with the first letter of the alphabet, *a*. But what kind of an *a* do you mean? Note the underlined *a* in the following nonsense sentence:

Art asked Amy if she caught any of the bears she saw stealing bananas around the quay near the jail.

If you have a reasonably good ear, you can detect about half a dozen different *a* sounds. You discovered a long time ago that English spelling is a highly unreliable guide to pronunciation. Read the following words, and you will discover that *ough* has six pronunciations:

although,   through,   thought,   bough,   enough,   cough

While it is true that there are twenty-six letters in the English alphabet, we are concerned at the moment with sounds rather than letters. There are almost fifty different sounds in our language. At this point, what is needed is a system of symbols in which each symbol represents a distinctly different sound.

Professor Higgins, in *My Fair Lady*, gets the plot rolling when he attempts to copy down and then mimic the cockney dialect of Eliza Doolittle, the flower girl. Obviously, to capture the nuances and subtleties of the following excerpt would require a special set of sound symbols:

"Ow, eez ye-ooa san, is e? Wal, fewd dan y' de-ooty bawmz a mather should, eed now bettern to spawl a pore gel's flahrzn than ran awy athaht pyin. Will ye-oo py me f'them?" ("Oh, he's your son, is he? Well, if you'd done your duty by him as a mother should, he'd know better than to spoil a poor girl's flowers and then run away without paying. Will you pay me for them?")

The Professor is a phonetics expert, and he remarks that phonetics is the science of speech. More accurately, phonetics is the study of the sounds of spoken language.

The most widely used phonetic alphabet, the International Phonetic Alphabet, contains hundreds of symbols. If you are interested in learning the entire alphabet you could, at least in theory, transcribe phonetically any language on earth. For our practical purposes, however, we can get by with fewer than fifty symbols. A reasonable degree of familiarity with these symbols will aid us in identifying with accuracy and precision the sounds we hear and make. Until we are able to do this, we cannot improve faulty articulation.

Each symbol represents a basic unit or sound family—the *phoneme.* As an example, the "d" sound in dog and ba<u>d</u> is a phoneme. Actually we cannot produce precisely the same "d" in both words any more than nature produces two exactly identical snowflakes. But we recognize and understand both sounds as "d."

The International Phonetic Alphabet, often referred to as the IPA, consists of a set of symbols, each one representing a specific speech sound: one sound per symbol and one symbol per sound. We will need to recognize forty-eight phonemes. Twenty-five are consonants and twenty-three are vowels and diphthongs. Learning the IPA symbols is not difficult. You are already familiar with more than half of the symbols for consonants.

A majority of popular dictionaries, however, do not use the IPA. They indicate pronunciation with diacritical markings or symbols. While the dictionary markings are neither as precise nor as consistent as the IPA, in this chapter we will list the dictionary equivalents to the right of the phonetic symbols. (A more detailed presentation of dictionary symbols may be found in Appendix A—"Pronunciation and Vocabulary.")

Consonants

Phonetic Symbol	Dictionary Symbol	Key Word	Word Examples
t	t	<u>t</u>ip	<u>t</u>ow, pre<u>tt</u>y, a<u>t</u>
d	d	<u>d</u>in	<u>d</u>ay, me<u>dd</u>le, li<u>d</u>
p	p	<u>p</u>ig	<u>p</u>en, <u>p</u>a<u>p</u>er, sli<u>p</u>
b	b	<u>b</u>et	<u>b</u>ag, ro<u>bb</u>er, la<u>b</u>
k	k	<u>k</u>in	<u>ch</u>oir, li<u>qu</u>or, pi<u>ck</u>
g	g	<u>g</u>one	<u>gh</u>ost, da<u>gg</u>er, pla<u>gue</u>
h	h	<u>h</u>im	<u>h</u>all, <u>wh</u>o, a<u>h</u>ead
f	f	<u>f</u>ell	<u>ph</u>ony, di<u>ff</u>er, tou<u>gh</u>
v	v	<u>v</u>ain	<u>v</u>at, dri<u>v</u>er, li<u>v</u>e
s	s	<u>s</u>in	<u>sc</u>ene, <u>s</u>ister, ni<u>c</u>e
z	z	<u>z</u>one	<u>z</u>any, si<u>zz</u>le, ha<u>s</u>
m	m	<u>m</u>ad	<u>m</u>y, hu<u>mm</u>er, hy<u>mn</u>
n	n	<u>n</u>od	<u>n</u>ail, ma<u>nn</u>er, sig<u>n</u>
l	l	<u>l</u>ate	<u>l</u>ook, ho<u>ll</u>y, sou<u>l</u>
r	r	<u>r</u>an	<u>wr</u>eck, glo<u>r</u>y, nea<u>r</u>
w	w	<u>w</u>in	<u>w</u>ant, a<u>w</u>ay, q<u>u</u>iet

136

The remaining nine consonants may not be so familiar to you. Some of the sym[...]
familiar letters, and two symbols are borrowed from the Greek alphabet and th[...]

Phonetic Symbol	Dictionary Symbol	Key Word	
θ	th	<u>th</u>rill	t[...]
ð	t͟h	<u>th</u>em	t[...]
ʃ	sh	<u>sh</u>ell	s[...]
ʒ	zh	bei<u>g</u>e	[...]
tʃ	ch	<u>ch</u>ain	[...]
dʒ	j	<u>g</u>em	<u>j</u>ilt, sol<u>d</u>ier, e<u>dg</u>e
ŋ	ŋ or ng	ri<u>ng</u>	ki<u>ng</u>, ba<u>nk</u>er, si<u>ng</u>er
j	y	<u>y</u>es	<u>y</u>et, <u>u</u>nion, be<u>y</u>ond
hw[1]	hw	<u>wh</u>ile	<u>wh</u>ere, some<u>wh</u>at, <u>wh</u>ich

The vowel symbols represent seventeen vowels and six diphthongs. (Diphthongs are vowels which change their sound during production, beginning with one sound and shifting to another.)

Vowels

Phonetic Symbol	Dictionary Symbol	Key Word	Word Examples
i	ē	t<u>ee</u>	<u>ea</u>t, m<u>ee</u>t, b<u>e</u>
ɪ	i or ĭ	<u>i</u>t	<u>i</u>f, s<u>ie</u>ve, p<u>i</u>ty
e	ā	f<u>a</u>te	<u>a</u>pe, g<u>au</u>ge, d<u>a</u>y
ɛ	e or ĕ	b<u>e</u>t	<u>e</u>bb, m<u>a</u>ny, st<u>ea</u>dy
æ	a or ă	s<u>a</u>d	<u>a</u>t, pl<u>ai</u>d, r<u>a</u>ng
a	ȧ or ă	<u>au</u>nt	<u>a</u>ft, d<u>a</u>nce, wr<u>a</u>th
ɑ	ä	<u>a</u>h	<u>a</u>lms, f<u>a</u>r, s<u>e</u>rgeant
ɒ	o or ŏ	m<u>o</u>ss	<u>o</u>ff, st<u>o</u>p, w<u>a</u>nder
ɔ	ô or ȯ	j<u>a</u>w	<u>a</u>ll, br<u>ou</u>ght, s<u>a</u>w
o	ō	<u>o</u>bey	<u>o</u>asis, v<u>o</u>cation, <u>o</u>mit
ʊ	o͝o or u̇	p<u>u</u>t	l<u>oo</u>k, w<u>ou</u>ld, w<u>o</u>lf
u	o͞o or ü	t<u>oo</u>l	<u>oo</u>ze, fr<u>ui</u>t, wh<u>o</u>
ʌ	u or ŭ	c<u>u</u>t	<u>u</u>nder, s<u>u</u>m, fl<u>oo</u>d
ə	ə	<u>a</u>head	<u>a</u>mong, c<u>a</u>rnival, b<u>a</u>nan<u>a</u>
ɝ	ûr	m<u>ur</u>der	<u>er</u>mine, h<u>er</u>d, det<u>er</u>
			(ɝ occurs only in accented syllables; the <u>r</u> is sounded)
ɜ	ûr	m<u>u</u>rder	<u>er</u>mine, h<u>er</u>d, det<u>er</u>
			(ɜ occurs only in accented syllables; the <u>r</u> is silent)
ɚ	ər	ev<u>er</u>	p<u>er</u>form, sing<u>er</u>, err<u>or</u>
			(ɚ occurs only in unaccented syllables; the <u>r</u> is sounded)

1. (hw) is not treated in this book as a separate sound unit, but as an (h) approach to (w).

honetic Symbol	Dictionary Symbol	Key Word	Word Examples
aɪ	ī	ride	isle, while, die
aʊ	ou or aù	now	out, house, sow
ɔɪ	oi or ȯi	boy	oyster, noise, joy
ju	yo͞o	use	union, cute, few
oʊ	ō	go	snow, foe, so
eɪ	ā	say	day, weigh, hey

'When placed above and to the left of a syllable this mark indicates that this syllable is to receive the principal or primary accent.

     Example: 'dʌblɪn (Dublin)

'When placed below and to the left of a syllable the mark indicates that this syllable is to receive a secondary accent, that is, one which is weaker than the primary accent.

     Example: ,mɪsə 'sɪpɪ (Mississippi)

Consonants

As Charlton Laird has written in *The Miracle of Language:* "Consonants can be made either by stopping the breath or by disturbing it, making it explode, or making it buzz or hum." In other words—

The lips, front teeth, lower jaw, tongue, or the velum must interfere with, obstruct, or modify the outgoing breath stream to produce a sound or noise.

Consonants make for clearness and intelligibility in our speech. They act as dividing units and frequently they separate vowel sounds. Occasionally they influence the beginnings and endings of vowels.

Consonants fall into two general classifications: voiced or voiceless. Exaggerate the following sounds slightly as you pronounce them (and do not pronounce them as letters of the alphabet):

1	2
[t] t	[d] d
[p] p	[b] b
[k] k	[g] g
[f] f	[v] v
[ʃ] sh	[ʒ] zh

Place your fingertips lightly against your larynx as you pronounce the sounds in column 1. You should feel no vibrations because the vocal folds are momentarily at rest. But as you run through the sounds in column 2, you will feel a slight vibration because the vocal folds are now in movement. Thus, column 1 contains the voiceless sounds. The vocal folds are not set into vibration for their production. Column 2 contains voiced sounds. The folds vibrate for their production. All vowels in normal, nonwhispered speech are voiced.

It is also convenient to classify consonants according to their physical characteristics and the manner in which they are produced. (Dictionary symbols are listed only if they differ from phonetic symbols.)

Classification of Consonants

(Dictionary symbols in parentheses will be listed only if they differ from phonetic symbols.)

Place of Articulation	Plosives [1] Voiceless [1]	Plosives Voiced [1]	Fricatives Voiceless	Fricatives Voiced	Glides (Semi-Vowels) Voiceless	Glides (Semi-Vowels) Voiced	Nasals Voiceless	Nasals Voiced	Affricates Voiceless	Affricates Voiced
Lips (Bilabial)	p	b				w		m		
Lower Lips and Upper Teeth (Labiodental)			f	v						
Tongue and Teeth (Linguadental)			θ (th)	ð (th)						
Tongue Tip and Upper or Lower Gum Ridge (Lingua-alveolar)	t	d	s	z		l²		n		
Tongue Blade and Hard Palate (Linguapalatal)			ʃ (sh)	ʒ (zh)		r j (y)			tʃ³ (ch)	dʒ (j)
Back of Tongue and Soft Palate (Linguavelar)	k	g						ŋ		
Space Between Vocal Folds (Glottal)			h							

1. Voiceless sounds are formed of breath without tone from vibrating vocal folds. Voiced sounds are formed of tone or sound resulting from vibrating vocal folds.
2. (1) is sometimes labelled a lateral semivowel or consonant.
3. An Affricate is a combination of a plosive and a fricative.

Plosives	Fricatives	Glides (semivowels)	Nasals	Affricates
[p]	[f]	[w]	[m]	[tʃ] ch
[b]	[v]	[l]	[n]	[dʒ] j
[t]	[θ] th	[r]	[ŋ] ng	
[d]	[ð] t͟h	[j] y		
[k]	[s]			
[g]	[z]			
	[ʃ] sh			
	[ʒ] zh			
	[h]			

Plosives

The plosives (also known as stops or stop-plosives) are made by momentarily stopping the out-going air stream, thus building up air pressure. The velum is raised, thereby preventing the escape of breath through the nose. Then the tongue is dropped or the lips opened suddenly, and the impounded air is released with a little explosion.

(Dictionary symbols are listed on the right-hand side of the page only if they differ from phonetic symbols.)

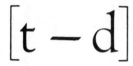

Place of
Articulation: tongue tip and upper gum ridge.

Classification: [t] voiceless.
                [d] voiced.

Examples: [t] T͟erry asked T͟homas to set͟t͟le the mat͟t͟er on the dent͟ist's yacht͟.
                 [d] D͟id͟ D͟aisy ped͟d͟le d͟iamond͟s, jad͟e, and͟ emerald͟s in Mad͟rid͟?

Typical Production:

Press the tip of your tongue against the upper gum ridge. The sides of the tongue should lie in close contact with the inner borders of the teeth. As a rule, the teeth and the lips are slightly parted. The soft palate is elevated, as it is for all sounds except [m, n, and ŋ]. The air stream is now momentarily dammed up. Lower the tongue tip quickly and suddenly (generally the lower jaw moves downward at the same time), and the breath will be released as a little explosion.

Faults or Problems:

1. The tongue tip may be allowed to fall so low that it rests against the teeth instead of the gum ridge.

    Result: *pat* [pæt] may sound something like *path* [pæθ]
               did [dɪd] may sound something like *dthid* [dðɪd]

    To correct such a sluggish [t and d] work for a vigorous upward movement of the tongue, and be sure that it is contacting the gum ridge just above the upper front teeth as you practice the following:

a. tea	until	hit	die
ten	water	get	do
tie	pity	bait	under
turn	kitty	cat	windy
day	tidy	had	rind
dine	idea	wide	tide

b. Tillie the dainty tassel twister toiled until twilight.

c. Terry the tentmaker tried to take time off on Tuesday.

d. Tina Little travels by jet to Toronto.

e. Dan tittered as Ted tapped the dented cart.

f. Tim the tuba player traded his tuba for a dusty deerskin.

g. Dora Thomas tried to dance a tango near the tilting totem pole.

h. The dreadful twister tore the old docks and domes apart.

i. Did Tippy's terrifying toothache triple in torture yesterday?

j. If Dad drops the kettledrum, will Della hide the tom-tom?

k. Tad bet Rudd that the lad would not eat pickled pig's feet.

l. Did Dot say that she was mad or glad when Bud proposed?

2. [t and d] are often swallowed or omitted when found in the medial position of a word. Occasionally the glottal stop ˀ (a glottal click or grunt) is substituted.

Result: *pretty* [ˈprɪtɪ] may sound something like *pri'y* [prɪ]
 ladle [ledl] may sound something like *la'l* [leˀl]

Stress medial [t and d] slightly in the following:

a. matter	after	wider	body
winter	history	couldn't	kettle
wouldn't	biting	Teddy	pardon
potato	shouldn't	whittle	candy
Betty	metal	certain	hadn't

b. Hedda, the fattest kitten, trotted toward the bottled butter.

c. On Saturday the water is better in the afternoon.

d. The title of toastmaster fitted Mr. Sattler perfectly.

e. Twenty naughty little tots handled twenty tempting potatoes.

f. Haughty Hetty noticed Horton standing under the oldest spindle.

g. Why wouldn't Dotty meet the children in the garden?

h. Milton pelted the wilted lettuce with muddy weed killer.

i. Looters do not find rodents, scooters, or hoarders in Scotland.

j. Metal models of buildings often put windows in shadows.

3. If [t] occurs in the medial position and especially if it is preceded and followed by voiced sounds, there is a rather common tendency to substitute [d].

Result: *pretty* [ˈprɪtɪ] may sound something like *pridy* [ˈprɪdɪ]
quarter [ˈkwɔrtɚ] may sound something like *quarder* [ˈkwɔrtɚ]

Some feel that to insist upon articulating a [t] as a [t] rather than a [d] in words with a "t" spelling is unnatural. To be sure, to say "pridy" instead of "pretty" [ˈprɪtɪ] probably does not interfere with communication. It is possible to argue that only very meticulous speakers will say [ˈprɪtɪ] and [ˈkwɔrtɚ]. Perhaps it is a matter of individual preference. If you choose to emphasize the medial [t] in the following, make it energetic, but avoid making it too prominent.

a.	ditty	Saturday	later	kettle
	booty	Hattie	latter	total
	little	cattle	metal	rattle
	petal	sooty	mister	battle
	kitty	subtle	motto	better

b. Morton and Horton had a pretty boat with a little motor.

c. Netty noticed the sprightly kitten flitting through the matted grass.

d. Pouting Letty rotated and twisted around the totem pole.

e. Mr. Hester had a watery blister after crating the teeter-totter.

f. Lottie jilted Matt Lipton because he skated faster than she did.

g. The ratty cattle ate all of Smitty's petals.

h. Peter Martin counted thirty dirty shutters littering the battlefield.

i. Did chatter among the twenty bitter citizens betray Walter Sutton?

j. Thirty Westerns interested the frantic fighter in North Dakota.

4. If [t] is preceded or followed by [s] it is commonly omitted. In general [s-t-s] combinations are tricky.

Result: *fists* [fɪsts] may sound something like *fiss* [fɪs]

             vests [vɛsts] may sound something like *vess* [vɛs]

To correct this fault, pronounce [s-t-s] slowly and carefully as separate sound units. When you are certain that you are forming a sharp clear [t], pronounce the sounds in a connected manner. As you practice the following, be sure that the [t] is not omitted when it occurs in difficult sound combinations:

a.	waists	masts	rusts	pastes
	gifts	acts	busts	erupts
	posts	lists	dusts	tastes
	crusts	wrists	rejects	bests
	chests	trusts	boosts	pasts

b. Tad insists that the lists of tests were placed in the chests.

c. Dot boasts that she fasts on crusts at feasts.

d. The crests, the masts, and the beasts could not be seen in the mists.

e. John rests while Betsy sews vests in the forests.

f. Do pets hate posts, pests, and gates?

g. Jim Reston paints masts with pots of paints.

h. I insist that he resists ghosts with his fists.

5. [t and d] are frequently omitted if they occur in final positions, especially when they are preceded by other consonants.

Result: *belt* [bɛlt] may sound something like *bel* [bɛl]

             second [ˈsɛkənd] may sound something like *secon* [ˈsɛkən]

Sound distinctly, but do not unduly emphasize, final [t and d] in the following:

a.	crept	just	world	ground
	moist	crossed	sold	fad
	pelt	quart	heard	baled
	raft	fact	hand	crazed
	fort	jolt	gagged	card
	ripped	bankrupt	lord	cold

b. Chet felt the wet pelt of the rabbit in the moist crypt.

c. Thad, the wicked lad, hit the painted boat with a quart of sand.

d. Was Mat mad at Bud because Bud had hit his granddad?

e. Won't Bert be glad when the flat belt is sold?

f. Milt would not trod the old road without part of his old raft.

g. Did Lud slide past third when Bart sat in the loft?

h. Mort will scald his hand if he welds the wood to the cardboard.

i. Kit almost slipped in the silt before he felt the mound of quicksand.

j. It was his fault that he put a quart of yeast and salt in the mild malt.

k. The only way to get rid of a temptation is to yield to it.

l. Don't knit mittens for Lot but fit the hat on his head.

m. His best friends laughed when he found the gold in the loft.

n. She kissed his hand when he passed the paste.

6. If *-ed* [əd] is used to form the past tense of a verb it is occasionally omitted or mispronounced.

   If the -ed is preceded by [t or d], it is generally pronounced as a separate syllable:

   hunted is pronounced *hun<u>tud</u>* [ˈhʌntəd]

   skidded is pronounced *skid<u>dud</u>* [ˈskɪdəd]

   If the -ed is preceded by a voiceless sound, it is pronounced as [t]:

   whipped is pronounced *whipt* [hwɪpt]

   asked is pronounced *askt* [æskt]

   mashed is pronounced *masht* [mæʃt]

   If the -ed is preceded by a voiced sound, it is pronounced as [d]:

   nagged is pronounced *nagd* [nægd]

   filled is pronounced *fild* [fɪld]

   Pronounce the -ed endings correctly in the following:

a.	lurched	matted	hoed	iced
	edged	razzed	trapped	drowned
	shaded	loved	rammed	ranted
	crashed	attacked	fitted	missed

   b. Mack backed the rusted truck into the road and loaded it.

   c. Mary attacked Jim who peeked and squealed as he tucked the money away.

   d. Jack stole the locked door and tacked a cracked sign on the filed knob.

   e. Jerry bribed and jabbed the duped and draped couple.

   f. Kent lunged at Doug before he slipped the trapped bat into the sack.

   g. Milt rubbed his tanned hide as the bottled port dripped from the faucet.

   h. If Doug had known that he was fated to have waded ashore twice, he might have waited before he faded.

   i. Bud seldom felt that he needed to heed repeated commands as ordered.

   j. After Bud was court-martialed, he passed time for five wretched years in a frayed brig where he peeled and scraped uncrated potatoes.

7. The following sentences contain [t and d] in many positions and sound combinations. Articulate these two plosives carefully and precisely. You may find it helpful to exaggerate somewhat as you read the drill material aloud. Eventually, however, you will want to strive for ease and naturalness and articulate a [t] and a [d] which are not unduly prominent or which do not call attention to themselves.

   a. We talk but little if we do not talk about ourselves.

   b. Though it be honest, it is never good to bring bad news.

   c. The most useless day of all is that in which we have not laughed.

   d. Betty Gladstone and Freddy Flint bent one hundred of the oldest candles.

   e. If the world seems cold to you, kindle fires to warm it.

   f. Let him that thinketh he standeth take heed lest he fall.

g. The constitution does not provide for first and second class citizens.
h. The captain demanded that the hordes of soldiers hold their metal shields high.
i. Softly and swiftly the costly mustard melted into the pot on the left.
j. Howard Anderson said, "Let's hide Greta Adler's old copy of *Two Years Before the Mast.*"
k. If your luck isn't what it should be, write a "p" in front of it and try again.
l. Do not waste the hours of daylight in listening to that which you may read by night.
m. A little neglect may breed mischief. For want of a nail the shoe was lost, and for want of a horse the rider was lost.

$\left[\, p - b \,\right]$

Place of
Articulation: lips.

Classification: [p] voiceless.
              [b] voiced.

Examples: [p] Portia happened to slip when Peter put pepper on the apple.
          [b] Buddy booed before Abe bounced the ball off the cupboard.

Typical Production:

Press the lower and the upper lips firmly together. As a rule, the teeth are slightly parted. The breath is compressed within the mouth. Part the lips suddenly, and the impounded air is released with a light "pop" or explosion.

Faults or Problems:

8. Some individuals permit the lower lip to make contact with the edges of the upper teeth. Occasionally this happens if the lower jaw is receding, a condition known as overbite. Consequently, a sound resembling [f or v] may be formed.

Result: *rib* [rɪb] may sound something like *riv* [rɪv]
        pat [pæt] may sound something like *fat* [fæt]

The [f and v] substitutions are also apt to occur when the [p or b] are followed by [f or v].

Result: *stop first* [stɑp fɝst] may resemble *stop virst* [stɑp vɝst]
        bib full [bɪb fʊl] may resemble *bib vull* [bɪb vʊl]

Be sure that the lips contact each other as you articulate [p and b] in the following:

a.			
plot	table	ebb	Bob votes
pry	ribbon	aptly	pop vendor
bat	sober	barber	help fight
bear	warp	cupful	drip varnish
pauper	clasp	cab full	rob Frank
corpse	bulb	cap fits	rub Victor

b. Corporal Phillip placed the pulp fiber over the sharp harpoon.
c. With a hop, a jump, and a yelp she landed in the steep stoop.
d. Pat Parker put the apple and the chop in the shop.
e. Chub let the rope fall as he blew up the bulb.

f. Did he bribe Rob to stop first and grab the cupful of herbs?

g. Wipe up the pepper from the carpet, Rip.

h. Her job was to place the tape and the tube on the lab table.

i. Don't bob under the crib if I jab your rib with my elbow.

j. Did the cop see the cab veer as his cap fell?

k. All happy families resemble one another. Every unhappy family is unhappy in its own way.

9. Foreigners, and especially those with a Germanic language background, often confuse [p and b]. If the initial sound of the word is [p], a [b] may be substituted. An initial [b] may be replaced with [p].

Result: *pay* [pe] and *bike* [baɪk] become *bay* [be] and *pike* [pɑɪk]

Remember that the initial [p] is voiceless, but the initial [b] is voiced. There will, of course, be a greater emission of breath with the voiceless [p].

For contrast practice the following, differentiating clearly between the initial voiceless [p] and the initial voiced [b]:

pun	pail	pig-big	pore-bore
but	bill	pin-bin	pet-bet
pill	pine	pot-bought	pad-bad
bop	bit	pack-back	pull-bull

Some foreigners replace medial [b] with [v], a mispronunciation which will result if the lips are not completely closed for [b].

Result: *rubbing* [ˈrʌbɪŋ] becomes *ruving* [ˈrʌvɪŋ]
fibbing [ˈfɪbɪŋ] becomes *fiving* [ˈfɪvɪŋ]

The voiceless [p] is commonly substituted for the voiced [b] in the final position, too.

Result: *cab* [kæb] becomes *cap* [kæp]
knob [nob] becomes *knop* [nop]

As you practice the following, be certain that the lips are firmly closed for medial [b]. Do not confuse the voiceless final [p] with the voiced final [b]:

a.

sober	nap-nab	lop-lob	sip-sib
habit	bop-Bob	dip-dib	rip-rib
ribbon	cap-cab	pup-pub	nip-nib
table	rope-robe	gap-gab	rep-reb

b. Rob, help Abe grab the rope crib.

c. Herb, tape the tub before you tab the map.

d. Bob the cop could not grab the sub from the ship.

e. Did the Arab nap near the pub or the cab?

f. In April he will stoop in the steep sloop and sip from the supper table.

g. The robe fits Pope Peter better than the tailor expected.

h. The happy rabbit popped the slipper into the paper shop.

i. The flabby robber hid the trap in the path near the bath.

j. The roped robber sipped a drop from the dribbling sap.

10. *Probably* [ˈprobəblɪ] is one of the most frequently misarticulated words in our language. What we so often hear is *prob'ly* [ˈproblɪ] or even *pro'ly* [ˈprolɪ]. Although we are still able to understand the word, such a mispronunciation suggests sloppiness.

Careless speakers occasionally omit [b], particularly if it is preceded by another [b], by [p or m].

Result: *probably*, as we have noted, is heard as *prob'ly* or *pro'ly*
capably [ˈkepəblɪ] is heard as *capa'ly* [ˈkepəlɪ]
number [ˈnʌmbɚ] is heard as *num'er* [ˈnʌmɚ]

Work for a firm and distinct [b] in the following sentences:

a. Some members do not remember to slumber in December.

b. He probably could handle the combination of numbers quite capably.

c. Is lumber more limber in Columbus than in Emporia?

d. Did the feeble umpire fumble when Dempsey tumbled?

e. Somebody disturbed the members as they played Scrabble.

11. Lazy lips and general sluggish activity, both of which commonly result from carelessness and indifference, are probably responsible for more poorly articulated [p and b] sounds than any other factor. As you practice the following, work for vigorous, crisp articulation. The lips should make a reasonably firm contact and then be opened quickly and simultaneously.

a. The popsicles made in Bob Popper's pantry are bad for bored people.

b. Cappy put the bottles into the blue bucket behind the bath.

c. It is a horrible habit for robbers to whimper at happy prison keepers.

d. "Mop the sloop, pin the mast, and rope the ship," yelped Captain Knapp.

e. Rupert will hobnob with Mab but snub snobs who wear drab garb in the pub.

f. Plump Barbara Appleton prepared pudding for the pastor's supper.

g. Was the ample laborer responsible for stumbling over the amber baseball?

h. To whip people with iron ribs use whips of steel.

i. He is too experienced a parent ever to make positive promises.

j. Papa, potatoes, poultry, prunes, and prism are all good words for the lips: especially prunes and prism.

k. The brave people grumbled as they stumbled over the humble rebels in Portland.

l. Most people judge others either by the company they keep, or by their fortune.

m. "You're Not the Only Pebble on the Beach" is a popular song composed by Cole Porter, Irving Berlin and the Beatles.

n. Most painters become paupers because they never paint what they see. They paint what the public sees, and the public never sees anything.

o. A ball player's got to be kept hungry to become a big-leaguer. That's why no boy from a rich family ever made the big leagues.

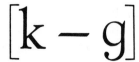

Place of
Articulation: back of tongue and soft palate.

Classification: [k] voiceless.
              [g] voiced.

Examples: [k] Kenneth wal<u>k</u>ed ba<u>ck</u> into the <u>c</u>ave after the si<u>x</u> members of the <u>ch</u>orus ate the bis<u>c</u>uits.
            [g] <u>G</u>olden ea<u>g</u>les eat bu<u>gs</u> and e<u>x</u>ist in <u>gh</u>ettos during bi<u>g</u> pla<u>g</u>ues.

Typical Production:

Press the raised back portion of the tongue firmly against the velum. This blocks off the air passageway, building up pressure. Lower the back of the tongue suddenly, releasing the air with a little puff or explosion. As a rule, the tongue tip remains momentarily on the floor of the mouth behind the lower front teeth.

<u>Faults or Problems</u>:

12. In careless speech [k and g] are often allowed to become somewhat guttural. This happens when they are distorted to resemble an exaggerated [h] sound—in other words, a kind of deformed fricative. This fault is most noticeable if the [k or g] occur in medial positions.

Result: *decorate* [ˈdɛkəˌret] reaches our ears as *dehorate* [ˈdɛhəˌret]

bigger [bɪgɚ] reaches our ears as [bɪhɚ]

As you practice the following, is the back portion of your tongue making a firm contact with the velum? Try to keep the [k and g] relatively light and clean-cut, and avoid producing a muddy, heavy sound.

a.

market	talking	cigar	haggle
deacon	liquor	buggy	nugget
acute	basket	ago	organ
picnic	naked	jigger	lingering
chicken	tobacco	burglar	aghast

b.   Do cocoa beans, sugar, and eggplant grow bigger in the darkest Arctic?

c.   Uncle Ricky put the finger cookies in the rigged locker.

d.   Is it likely that the wicked beggar would forget to anchor the luggage?

e.   "Cookie Carter fell off the rocker," said the hungry actor.

f.   The wicked worker snickered when he heard his second echo.

13. Sometimes the voiced [g] is substituted for the voiceless [k]. Foreign students may also confuse [g and k].

Result: *local* [ˈlokl̩] is pronounced as *logal* [ˈlogl̩]

pig [pɪg] is pronounced as *pick* [pɪk]

Differentiate carefully between [k and g] in the following, and be sure that you do not make [k] a voiced sound or the [g] a voiceless sound. In general, you should try to make vowel sounds longer in duration before [g] than before [k].

a.

game-came	snigger-snicker	bag-back
God-cod	stagger-stacker	nag-knack
gate-Kate	lagging-lacking	sag-sack
goat-coat	logging-locking	brig-brick
gill-kill	haggle-hackle	hog-hock
gall-call	trigger-tricker	lug-luck

b.   Did the staggering stoker get locked in the luggage compartment?

c.   Tack the tag on the log lock and tell Chuck to put the rag on the rack.

d.   The cad said, "I got caught tacking tagging onto the basket."

e.   Could you scold the barking dog who is digging on the cold, gold dock?

f.   Kate could not pick up the pegs from the sagging sack.

14. The eleventh letter of the alphabet, *k*, is not present in the following words:

cat	six	queen
liquor	accept	choir

But the phoneme [k] is present in all of them:

<u>k</u>æt	sɪ<u>ks</u>	<u>k</u>win
ˈlɪ<u>k</u>ɚ	æ<u>k</u>ˈsɛpt	<u>k</u>waɪr

The twenty-fourth letter of the alphabet, *x*, is present in such words as:

exist   exam

But how do you pronounce the letter *x* in these words? As g*z* [gz]

    ɛg ˋzɪst   ɛg ˋzæm

The strange spellings given to sounds which are actually [k and g] may, in some cases, confuse us and at the same time account for faulty pronunciation of words containing those sounds.

The principal troublemakers are words such as *accept* and many other words containing the *cc* spelling. A common fault is to omit the [k] sound in these words:

access: correctly pronounced as ˋæksɛs

             incorrectly pronounced as ˋæsɛs

accident: correctly pronounced as ˋæksədənt

             incorrectly pronounced as ˋæsədənt

Other problem words are ones such as *exert* and *exit*. In the first one, the correct sound for *x* is [gz]: ɪg ˋzɚt. In the second one, the correct sound for *x* is [ks]: ɛksɪt.

There are two simple rules which will help you distinguish between *x* words which require the [gz] pronunciation and *x* words which take the [ks] pronunciation.

If the vowel sound following the *x* is accented, the *x* will be pronounced as [gz]. Try the following:

exactly = ɪg ˋzæktl

exempt = ɪg ˋzɛmpt

exhaust = ɪg ˋzɔst

If *x* is found in the final position it will be pronounced as: [ks].

box   = bɒks

fix   = fɪks

Max   = mæks

If *x* is followed by a pronounced consonant, it will also be pronounced as: [ks].

excite = ɪkˋsaɪt

expect = ɪkˋspɛkt

extra   = ˋɛkstrə

If a word ends in [sk, sks, or skt], the spelling may be of some help to us, although there is a common tendency to omit the [k] sound in these words.

Examples: *bask* [bæsk] should not sound like *bass* [bæs]

            tasks [tæsks] should not sound like *tas* [tæs]

            asked [æskt] should not sound like *ast* [æst]

If a word begins with a [kn] or [gn] combination, the [k] or the [g] is silent:

    <u>k</u>napsack, <u>k</u>nee, <u>k</u>nife, <u>k</u>nob

    <u>g</u>narled, <u>g</u>nat, <u>g</u>neiss, <u>g</u>nomic

The following material contains many [k and g] sounds, but the various spellings assigned to these do not always tell you that [k or g] are present. If [k] is to be sounded be sure that you form it properly: the back of the tongue must make a definite contact with the velum. You should be able to feel this activity. Be sure that you hear it correctly. [k] is voiceless. In a few *x* words, [gz] is, of course, voiced. Do not pounce on the [g] element or prolong it, but give it its due value.

a.   Jinx could not accept the expensive flasks which were hidden in the desk.

b.   He asked if the accident had caused the Sphinx to expand.

c.   The exhaust pipe was in a box near the accelerator.

d.   The lynx, a cat with extraordinary instincts, is now almost extinct.

e.   Mr. Rusk makes excellent ivory discs from walrus tusks.

f.   The Scot, Mr. McFox, found the Alaska landscape to be exciting.

g. John Ruskin expected that the exotic gift would be acceptable.

h. As an example, do not exhale wax fumes from the cask.

i. The masked boxer risked his life when he slipped on the waxed floor.

j. The export whiskey exploded on the soaked docks.

15. In poor speech, final [k and g] are often almost completely dropped, making them quite inaudible. As you read the material below, do not give the final plosives too much prominence, but be certain that they are clearly and precisely articulated.

a.
dark	creek	bag	rig
shock	frock	vague	drag
talk	click	morgue	egg
chic	clique	agog	frog

b. Does Rock like to sing music on top of the bleak peak?

c. Jock took a peck of cake and put it on the attic deck.

d. With a flick of its tail the dark shark rammed the log bark.

e. Here Skugg lies snug as a bug in a rug.

f. The pig chased the bug into the keg in the bog.

g. A rogue with a log will jig but not jog.

h. Will Dick Rigg track the elk through smog and smoke?

i. Mack was agog as the hulk of the brig struck the tug.

j. Chuck tried to drink the milk and tonic.

k. Cauliflower is nothing but cabbage with a college education.

l. Every good dog has his day, and only mad dogs should be flogged.

m. Rogues and goblins eat the flecked eggs that ducks and geese lay.

n. War talk by men who have been in a war is always interesting; whereas moon talk by a poet who has not been in the moon is likely to be dull.

o. In the queer mess of human destiny the determining factor is luck. For every important place in life there are many men of fairly equal capacities. Among them luck decides who shall accomplish the great work, who shall be crowned with laurel, and who shall fall back into obscurity and silence.

16. If a plosive is followed in the same word by another plosive or consonant, the first plosive is not completely exploded or released. In other words, there should be no sound of breath release after the first plosive. Instead, the plosive sound is held momentarily and then blended or merged into the succeeding sound.

Pronounce the following words, but do not explode the underlined plosive or allow a puff of air to escape after it.

a.
cupcake	tracked	subdued	topkick
cupbearer	bagged	captain	midpoint

If a plosive ends one word and a plosive or another consonant begins the next word, the final plosive of the first word is not exploded separately nor should there be a sound of breath release after the final plosive. Again, the sound is blended into the initial sound of the following word.

Pronounce these word pairs, but do not "pop" the underlined plosives:

b.
bake popcorn	pack bottles	bad boy	rob Pete
hit Tom	dog gone	look tough	gag Kate
Big Ben	hip boot	hot dish	did push
rope trick	fake gold	wrap paper	drink coffee

17. In Exercise 16 you pronounced words and phrases which contained adjacent plosives. In the following sentences, you will find words containing two or more plosives, and adjoining words, ending and be-

ginning with plosives and other consonants. As you practice, work for light but firm plosive sounds, but do not chop adjacent plosives into separate bits:

    a.   Pat took the hot dogs and ate ten of them.
    b.   Bob bet that he could tip the street car into the camp pool.
    c.   At midnight the old dame mounted her magic carpet and took off.
    d.   The topmost blackboard fell on the white table.
    e.   The black bat and the pink beetle often hid near the back porch.
    f.   Peter Porter, the pumpkin eater, had a wife named Dot Tarr.
    g.   Ed and Tony would not permit back talk from spoiled darlings.
    h.   Mark Call said that a subdeb was not the same as a subteen.
    i.   MacDonald, the pop peddler, was subdued near the park pool.
    j.   The captured captain walked toward the blackberry bush.

<u>Practice Material for the Plosives</u>

18.   The following selections contain all of the plosives in a variety of positions and sound combinations. Practice for clear, careful articulation of the plosives, but be sure that they do not call excessive attention to themselves.

    a.   Oh, it's nice to get up in the morning, but it's nicer to stay in bed.
    b.   A man must not swallow more beliefs than he can digest.
    c.   If you do not think about the future, you cannot have one.
    d.   There'll be a hot time in the old town tonight.
    e.   God will not look you over for medals, degrees, or diplomas, but for scars.
    f.   It is easier not to speak a word at all than to speak more words than we should.
    g.   A cow is a very good animal in the field, but we turn her out of a garden.
    h.   Would you both eat your cake and have your cake?
    i.   Why should the devil have all the good tunes?
    j.   When a man resists sin on human motives only, he will not hold out long.
    k.   Character is what you are in the dark.
    l.   Men are not always what they seem—but seldom better.
    m.   Must then Christ perish in torment in every age to save those who have no imagination?
    n.   What people say behind your back is your standing in the community or on the campus.
    o.   I, John Brown, am now quite certain that the crimes of this guilty land will never be purged away but with blood.
    p.   They are blind leaders of the blind. And if the blind lead the blind, both shall fall into the ditch.
    q.   It is a common rule with primitive people not to waken a sleeper, because his soul is away and might not have time to get back.
    r.   As old wood is best to burn, old horses to ride, old books to read, and old wine to drink, so are old friends always most trusty to use.
    s.   I don't know why it is that we are in such a hurry to get up when we fall down. You might think we would lie there and rest awhile.
    t.   If all the people in the world should agree to sympathize with a certain man at a certain hour, they could not cure his headache.
    u.   If a man can write a better book, preach a better sermon, or make a better mousetrap than his neighbor, though he builds his house in the woods, the world will make a beaten path to his door.
    v.   Children, love one another, and if that is not possible, at least try to put up with one another.
    w.   Boots and shoes are the greatest trouble of my life. Everything else one can turn and turn about, and make look like new. But there's no coaxing boots and shoes to look better than they are.
    x.   The gnome gnashed his teeth when the knave gnawed the knockwurst.
    y.   The knight knows that gnus have large knuckles.

z. Not many sounds in life, and I include all urban and all rural sounds, exceed in interest a knock at the door.

aa. I hold that if the Almighty had ever made a set of men that should do all the eating and none of the work, He would have made them with mouths only and no hands. And if He had ever made another class that He intended should do all the work and no eating, He would have made them with hands only and no mouths.

bb. The friendly cow all red and white,
   I love with all my heart.
She gives me cream with all her might
   To eat with apple-tart.

Assignment 14 (See suggested Checklist for this assignment)

Prepare material which contains many examples of the six plosives: [t d p b k g] and in various positions and sound combinations. If you have found one or two of them to be unusually troublesome, be certain that your material is "loaded" with them. You may find it easier to write your own material than to attempt to find material which contains those particular sounds on which you are concentrating. Nonsense material is generally acceptable, but if you prepare your own, emphasize simplicity. Tongue twisters and complex material are rarely satisfactory for drilling.

As you practice your material aloud, at first exaggerate the plosives. Try to make firm, crisp, and relatively hard sounds. But as you continue practicing, gradually decrease the exaggeration and strive mainly for distinctness and intelligibility of speech. Remember that normal, connected speech is natural speech.

Suggested Checklist for Assignment 14

As you practice by yourself you may want to work with this checklist. Listen carefully to yourself. If it is feasible record the assignment or get a classmate or friend to listen to you as you read the material. Eventually your goal will be to have a check mark in the Yes column for each category. (Optional: Perhaps your instructor will want to use the checklist to evaluate you during your classroom presentation.)

	Yes	No
Initial plosives firmly articulated.		
Medial plosives firmly articulated.		
Final plosives firmly articulated.		
Avoids overemphasis resulting from excessive pressure.		
Differentiates between voiceless [p] and voiced [b].		
Differentiates between voiceless [t] and voiced [d].		
Differentiates between voiceless [k] and voiced [g].		
Avoids muddy, guttural production of [k] and [g].		
Differentiates between voiceless [ks] and voiced [gz] in words containing x spelling.		
Avoids omitting [t] in [s-t-s] combinations.		
Avoids omitting [d] in [ldl] or [ndl] combinations.		
Avoids substituting [θ] for [t].		
Avoids substituting [f] or [v] for [p] or [b].		
Avoids pronouncing [t] and [d] when the sound is silent.		
Pronounces "ed" endings correctly.		
Avoids adding schwa vowel [ə] to a final plosive.		

Additional comments or suggestions:

Fricatives

There are nine members in the fricative family:

[f]	[ð] th	[ʃ] sh
[v]	[s]	[ʒ] zh
[θ] th	[z]	[h]

A fricative is made by narrowing or constricting the mouth passageway with the articulators in such a manner that the outgoing breath stream is partially obstructed. The air, forced through a relatively small, narrow aperture, produces a frictionlike sound.

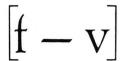

Place of Articulation: lower lip and upper teeth

Classification: [f] voiceless.
   [v] voiced.

Examples: [f] Frank coughed and offered Flora enough fudge to comfort her.
   [v] Velda shoved Stephen into the vat with more verve than love.

Typical Production:
Raise your lower lip, drawing it inward, and place it lightly against the edges of the upper front teeth. The breath stream is then forced audibly between the lip and teeth.

Faults or Problems:

19. In careless speech the voiceless [f] and the voiced [v] are occasionally confused. Individuals with foreign language backgrounds frequently tend to substitute one for the other. German students quite often produce initial or final [v] as [f].

   Result: *vine* [vaɪn] becomes *fine* [faɪn]
   live [laɪv] becomes *lif* [laɪf]

   (Germans also tend to confuse [v and w]. See Exercise 57 under [w], page 181.)

   Spanish-speaking people, learning English, often pronounce an initial [v] as [b].

   Result: *vent* becomes *bent*

   Distinguish carefully between the voiceless [f] and the voiced [v] in the following. Do not confuse [v] and [f], and do not substitute [w] or [b] for [f].

   a.

feel-veal	rifle-rival	half-have	van-ban
fan-van	strife-strive	wail-vale	vote-boat
fat-vat	safe-save	weldt-veldt	vase-base
fail-vale	raffle-ravel	wine-vine	veer-beer
few-view	duff-dove	wane-vane	veil-bail
file-vile	fife-five	safe-save	vest-best
folly-volley	surf-serve	went-vent	vane-bane

b. Did the evil elf dive into the half-hive or the rough groove?

c. Biff could not bluff or laugh his way through the twelve tough problems.

d. Marv wants proof that five knives halved his cuff and sleeve.

e. If Jeff will cuff the dove, Mr. Neff will strive to ban the van.

f. Carve the beef on the hoof in the cave above the bluff.

g. Should I forgive my love for playing her five fifes without life and verve?

h. The brave chief gave his knife and revolver to the fifty-five divers.

i. "Well," said Violet Williams, "Verna and Wanda vanished without visiting the wall."

j. Would Victor spill weak vinegar on Wilbur's Western vest?

20. The person who tells you that he has a *lotta time* [lɑtə tɑɪm] is committing an extremely simple, but careless error. The phrase should read *lot of time* [lɑt ʌv tɑɪm], but because so many of us speak rather rapidly and because the preposition *of* is rather short and inconspicuous, we often omit the [v] sound from the word.

Practice this material slowly a few times, and then gradually increase your speed to a more normal rate. Be conscious of the lip-to-teeth articulation as you make a [v] sound at the end of each *of*.

a.

full of people	bunch of girls	full of smoke
bag of peanuts	litter of pups	tired of him
lots of money	rows of seats	box of candy
half of those	can of soup	pat of butter

b. He put the loaf of bread, the bag of beets, and the quart of cream on the chest of drawers.

c. She threw the pail of water on the mob of people from the top of the house.

d. He won a hand of poker with the ace of clubs and the queen of spades.

e. Half of the time he was at the head of his class.

21. [v] in the final position of a word sometimes loses its identity if a succeeding word begins with [m, p, or b]. The incorrect substitution is closer to [b] than to [v].

Result: *have money* [hæv ˈmʌnɪ] changes to *hab money* [hæb ˈmʌnɪ]
            love Pat [lʌv pæt] changes to *lub Pat* [lʌb pæt]
            save bills [sev bɪlz] changes to *sabe bills* [seb bɪlz]

As you read the following, try to articulate clear and not too prominent [f and v] sounds. Be sure that you are not substituting other sounds for them.

a. I've decided that the five pigs weigh about forty-five pounds.

b. If you believe Pat, they've begun to save more money.

c. I've come to ask you to give me the five buttons.

d. "Love me or leave me," said the knave boldly.

e. Move Bill's stove into the hive behind the grove.

22. A clean-cut [f and v] depend mostly on the activity of the lower lip. If the lip is protruded or drawn back too far, the resulting [f and v] may become blurred and fuzzy. Be certain that the lower lip is making a light contact with the edges of the upper front teeth as you articulate these two sounds in the following:

a.

fact	valve	every	laugh
fair	very	avoid	fluff
fin	suffer	cover	above
four	tougher	saving	dove
vim	before	snuff	behave
veer	afoot	tiff	Dave

b. Footloose, fancy-free, and feather-brained, Fanny Faust found the fiddle.

c. The valuable elephant was afraid of the laughing prophet.

d. Effie carefully ate wafers and truffles before having breakfast coffee.
e. Did the rough tough inhale enough of the snuff?
f. I shall huff, puff, and cough if you cuff me.
g. Flossie and Velma finally viewed the carving of Venus.
h. The frantic voodoo man hid the very fragile firefly in the vault.
i. The fickle savage covered the seven fancy gravy spots.
j. If I leave this life, I believe you will grieve.
k. The oval vase must have faded in the cave.
l. Phil, do not fail to avoid the veiled fishwife.
m. Everything that's worth having goes to the city; the country takes what's left.
n. Fate makes our relatives. Choice makes our friends.
o. Always leave them laughing before you say good-bye.
p. A phrase has spread from civilians to soldiers and back again: "This is a phony war."
q. Many a man who thinks to found a home discovers that he has merely opened a tavern for friends.

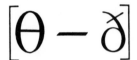 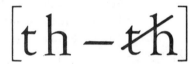

Place of
Articulation: tongue tip between teeth.

Classification: [θ] voiceless.
[ð] voiced.

Examples: [θ] Thelma thought a stealthy thief threw the bathtub into the booth.
[ð] They saw father put the lather on the smooth leather.

Typical Production:
Place the tip of the tongue lightly against the back or edges of the upper front teeth, or protrude the flattened tongue tip slightly between the teeth so that the upper side makes a gentle contact with the lower edges of the upper teeth. Force the breath between the tongue tip and the teeth.

Faults or Problems:
23. For a long time, Hollywood movies and certain popular TV programs insisted that the typical college athlete was a big, bumbling lout, only semiliterate, and possessing an accent which could only be described as "Brooklyn Mafia."

This type is apparently unable to say *these*, *them*, or *thought*. He says, instead, *deze*, *dem*, and *tought*. His not-so-distant relative, the stage Frenchman, has similar difficulties with certain *th* sounds, but when he says *these* and *them*, they may sound something like *zeez* and *zem*.

Fortunately, such rather phony characters are disappearing from movie and TV screens, but there is some truth behind these stereotypes, because very few foreign languages contain our *th*—[θ or ð]. Thus, the bona fide Frenchman, in speaking English, or any individual with a background of nonstandard American speech may substitute other sounds. Specifically, they may be permitting the tongue to make too firm a contact against the edges or the inside surfaces of the teeth. A sound like [t or d] is apt to result. It should be remembered that [t and d] require a firm tongue tip contact, but that the contact for [θ and ð] must be light.

If you are substituting [t or d] for [θ or ð], try this: Protrude the tongue so that the blade (the broad flat part directly behind the tip) is in light contact with the upper front teeth. Force out air as you gradually retract the tongue until the tip reaches the upper front teeth. When you can make a satisfactory sound, try the following. Be certain that the contact is light for good [θ and ð] sounds, but firm for good [t and d] sounds. Distinguish carefully between them.

a.

thin-tin	oath-oat	death-debt
thought-taught	thank-tank	three-tree
thigh-tie	theme-team	author-otter
through-true	worthy-wordy	lather-latter
then-den	mother-mudder	their-dare
thou-Dow	seethe-seed	breathe-breed
lather-ladder	thine-dine	those-doze

b. The thin bat and the thick rat fell into the tin bath.
c. Although his father gave him doughnuts for the fodder, he seethed when he saw the seed.
d. Miss Diss said this: "Thanks for putting the three trees in the tank."
e. Tie the sheath around his thigh and then put Luther in the den.
f. Take the time to thank Ted for both boats.

24. If you are substituting [s] for [θ] or [z] for [ð], check your manner of articulation.

To produce [s or z]:   The tip of the tongue is raised toward, but not in actual contact with, the upper gum ridge.

To produce [θ or ð]:   Place the tongue tip lightly against the back or the edges of the upper front teeth. The vocal folds vibrate for [ð], of course, but remain lax for [θ].

Check your tongue positions as you read this material. Do not articulate [s] where [θ] is required; avoid substituting [z] for [ð].

a.

thigh-sigh	think-sink	teethe-tease
myth-miss	thumb-sum	rather-razzer
thought-sought	breathe-breeze	bathe-baize
lathe-lays	seethe-seize	south-souse

b. Thor sighed and said, "My thigh is sore."
c. When Thelma danced in Selma, she would rise and then writhe.
d. I think that the sink will make Mr. Whizzer wither.
e. Do not tease a pet mouse or tickle its mouth while it teethes.

25. A three-year-old child who says, "I fro the ball," meaning "I throw the ball," is merely cute, but if an adult says the same thing, he is apt to be labeled as infantile. It is true that baby talk among adults is not frequently encountered, but the substitution of [f] for [θ] happens now and then in sloppy speech.

Compare the manner in which [f and θ] are produced:

To produce [f]:   Raise the lower lip, drawing it inward, and place it lightly against the edges of the upper front teeth.

To produce [θ]:   Review the description of this sound, and remember that the tongue tip but not the lower lip contacts the upper teeth.

Read the following, contrasting carefully between [f and θ]. Let this simple formula help you:

[f]—Lower lip against front teeth.
[θ]—Tongue tip against front teeth.

a.	thin-fin	wrath-raff	think-fink
	three-free	wreath-reef	death-deaf
	thaw-faugh	myth-miff	thrum-from

b. Fred fought for the right to throw the thread to and fro.
c. The three theater tickets were free.
d. The thin fin on the three fenders caused the death of the deaf oaf.
e. Did the fancy frills on the wreath thrill Phil as he sat near the reef?

26. The chances are that you do not pronounce the word *sixths* [sɪksθs] correctly. It is a good example of a one-word tongue twister. Many people simply say *six* [sɪks]. Try the word in slow motion:

$$[s - ɪ - k - s - θ - s]$$

and then try to say it a bit faster. You will note that the [θ] is quite difficult to pronounce in this particular word. Nevertheless, the [θ] belongs in the word. As you practice this material, be sure that the [θ] is present. Also, avoid a very common tendency to substitute [t] for the sound in question.

a.	fifths	moths	depths	earths
	sevenths	deaths	months	growths
	faiths	myths	paths	births

b. The moths flew out of the empty fifths in the north booths.
c. Ruth's oaths were taken on the eighth and not the fourth of June.
d. The mammoth's bones were found in both paths.
e. "Seth's way of saying 'sixths, sevenths, eighths, and ninths' is worthless," said Beth's sister.

27. Careless speakers may fail to distinguish between the voiceless [θ] and the voiced [ð]. In general, there seems to be a trend toward using [θ] at the expense of [ð]. With some *th* words this might be acceptable, but in others it would perhaps call attention to itself. Try to avoid confusing the two sounds as you practice these:

a. The theft of the three thick feathers happened in a leather thimble.
b. Thora said the weather soothed her smooth thumb.
c. Tell them that these things and those threads are theirs.
d. Thornton, the other Thane, thought about his brother's theory.
e. This thirty-third theme belongs to Arthur's father.
f. Faith Thurber had a toothache during the earthquake.
g. Ethel's birthday gift was smothered with hawthorn and heather.
h. Although it bothers Mother, Father would rather gather wreaths.
i. Nothing is earthier than youthful, Southern rhythm.
j. He that thinketh by the inch and speaketh by the yard should be kicketh by the foot.
k. Bertha Thompson thinks that the best ten years of a woman's life are between thirty-three and forty-three.

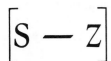

Place of
Articulation: tip or blade of tongue, gum ridge.

Classification: [s]   voiceless.
                          [z]   voiced.

Examples: [s] Sarah said she would ask the cigar-smoking singer for the next dance.

                [z] Zelda was busy raising daisies in the zoo near Zion.

Typical Production:

Raise the sides of the tongue so that they touch the inner edges or surfaces of the upper back teeth. Air is forced through a narrow, V-shaped groove along the midline of the tongue. No breath escapes except through this narrow, midline fissure. The tip of the tongue may be raised toward, but not in actual contact with, the gum ridge. The tongue tip is in a similar position for [t]. Note: The position of the tongue tip may vary. It may be raised as described, held straight forward or placed behind the lower gum ridge or incisors (the cutting teeth). A fine jet stream of air is directed toward the cutting edges of the upper and lower front teeth (the incisors).

[s] is probably the most troublesome and the most frequently defective sound in our language. (It is to be understood that whatever is said here about the articulation of [s] generally applies also to [z].) The production of an acceptable [s] sound requires not only a keen sense of hearing, but also rather precise adjustments of the articulators.

Faults or Problems:

28. [s] is the sound in the English languages which is most apt to "stick out like a sore thumb." Listen to any kind of a performance in which a group of people read material in unison—responsive readings by the congregation in church are a fine example—and you will hear waves of hisses which would be more appropriate in a snake pit.

A majority of the "hissers" are very likely articulating the sound correctly, as far as tongue positions are concerned. What they are doing is simply producing too much of the sound. Even an acceptable, normal [s] sound is noisy, and to prolong or emphasize it is to make it disagreeably obtrusive. One does not have to expel a large amount of breath to produce a satisfactory [s]. The individual who makes an [s] which sounds like air escaping from a balloon needs to reduce his breath pressure and not force the sound. Nor should the sound be sustained or held. Cut it short, touch it lightly and briefly but, of course, do not let it disappear from your speech.

For contrast and to help you hear the difference between a good, short, and a long-drawn out [s], read aloud the following word pairs. Deliberately exaggerate [s] in the first word of each pair as the spelling indicates. Prolong the sound, emphasize, and force it. In the second word of each pair, tap the sound as lightly as you can, and cut it very short, hurrying on to the following vowel sounds. Stress the vowels instead.

a.

s-s-s-s-see—see	s-s-s-s-sad—sad
s-s-s-s-so—so	s-s-s-s-saw—saw
s-s-s-s-say—say	S-S-S-S-Sue—Sue
s-s-s-s-sot—sot	s-s-s-s-sin—sin
s-s-s-s-sit—sit	s-s-s-s-sag—sag

Listen to yourself as carefully as you can while you practice the following. Work for an unobtrusive [s or z], one which is both brief and quiet.

b.

Sam	zone	zigzag	hiss
sort	Zulu	using	face
sod	zany	music	lass
sill	zest	lazy	dross
scene	lesson	lizard	fizz
sigh	gossip	busy	has
sack	faster	dizzy	craze
cell	aside	rosy	maze

zip	blister	loss	theirs
zoo	recent	guess	does
zeal	classic	miss	doze
zero	rusting	race	toes

c. The somber psalm was sung slowly by the sad sergeant.
d. Zane the zebra zigzagged around the zoo.
e. Scott soaked the sock in the sauce.
f. Mr. Francis fastened the Christmas basket to the side of the cesspool.
g. The soccer player from Zeeland received a zero in zoology.
h. The fuzzy buzzard nuzzled Lizzie the gazelle.
i. Strawberry soda mixed with Squirt and Sprite makes a nice bracer.
j. The hiss of his voice disturbed the peace of the house.
k. There is always someone worse off than yourself.
l. Every place is safe to him who lives with justice.
m. All true zeal for God is a zeal also for love, mercy, and goodness.
n. If you wish to preserve your secret, wrap it up in frankness.
o. No one means all he says, and yet so few say all they mean, for words are slippery and thought is sticky.

29. The whistling [s] is even more annoying than the prolonged or blasted [s] described in Section 28. It has often been associated with elderly people or individuals with plates, but it can also be detected fairly often in young people. It is an unpleasant sound, and a definite handicap to anyone who has occasion to work with microphones: public address systems, radio, TV, and some stage performances.

The whistler's [s] sometimes results from overprolongation—making too much of it. More often it is caused by improper placement of the tongue, a jaw which is thrust too far forward, irregularities or gaps between certain teeth or poor occlusion ("fitting together") between the upper and lower teeth.

If the blade or tip of the tongue is pressed tensely against the gum ridge or the palate, a whistling sound may result. Similarly, if the tip of the tongue is too close to, or in actual contact with, the upper teeth, a thin or sharp whistle may be produced.

Now and then an individual produces a hisser because he permits the lower lip to touch the upper teeth during the production of the sound. Bear in mind that most acceptable [s] sounds require that the lips be curled away from the teeth sufficiently to keep the edges of the teeth free.

Before you read the following, hiss [s], holding your tongue in slightly different positions. Retract the tip slightly, enlarging the space between the tongue and the gum ridge. Listen carefully as you experiment until you can find a satisfactory position.

a.
moss	hits	loose	cross
sass	mats	mace	sauce
loss	ropes	deuce	vice
less	roots	boss	toss
puss	juice	vase	rice

b. Miss Alice Moss, my niece, wore a nice, ice-blue dress.
c. After three days Rose found three ways out of the maze.
d. "This jazz puts me into a daze," Ross said to Rose.
e. We are never deceived: we deceive ourselves.
f. Sam always sings in a sad and lazy manner on Sundays.
g. Bess fixed and fastened the zipper on his flossy vest.
h. If Russell goes West will Susan go soaring over Arizona?
i. Sarah Salem spun the wrestler around so many times that he became dizzy.
j. "Say," said Mr. Zum, "will somebody trade a zircon for this fancy zither?"

k.   Heaven sends us good meat, but the devil sends cooks.

l.   In skating over thin ice our safety is our speed.

30.   Quite a few 19th and 20th century novelists, in describing the speech of small children, fall easily upon the word *lisping.* Anyone familiar with the chatter of the very young recalls that the fricatives, in general, are somewhat scrambled. For example, a *th* sound [θ] is often substituted for [s]. The voiced *th* [ð] may be substituted for [z].

The tiny tot wants to say "Sister Sue," but he comes out with something like "Thither Thue." He wants to say "Lizzie is his pup," but he comes out with "Lithie ith hith pup."

Now and then, this particular type of lisp carries over into adulthood, and "baby talk" in adults isn't especially attractive. There are several types of lisps, and the one we are presently considering is often known as a *central* or *frontal* lisp. In this case, the lisper is allowing the tip of his tongue to touch or protrude slightly beyond the edges of the upper front teeth.

An effective method of correcting this type of lisp is by using the [t] position approach.

As far as tongue positions are concerned [t and s] have much in common. Close the mouth, bring the teeth close together, and sound [t], but allow the air stream to continue without perceptibly changing the positions of any of the articulators. This is a good way to learn how to keep the tongue away from the edges of the teeth. As you continue practicing you may experiment by altering positions slightly, but be sure that the tongue is always retracted on [s and z] and does not vary greatly from its position for [t].

a.

take-sake	tip-zip	tee-see	tack-sack
tale-sail	too-zoo	tap-sap	tin-sin
till-sill	teal-zeal	tie-sigh	tear-seer
top-sop	tone-zone	taupe-soap	tick-sick
Tor-sore	tomb-zoom	test-zest	tot-sot

b.   Somber Thomas and Sally keep tallies as Saul grows tall.

c.   Ted said that Sam tried to sing tacky songs in the seething tempest.

d.   Sir Terence's serfs toil in the soil while his ten sisters ski on Tuesday.

e.   Tina saw twenty-two sailors tilt the sub and sink into the sea.

f.   Is Zoe's toe better or is it worse?

g.   Zeke passed the math test with zest.

As you practice these word combinations, listen to and try to feel the difference in making good, acceptable [θ t s] and [ð t z] sounds.

h.

thin-tin-sin	thee-tea-Zee
thaw-taw-saw	though-toe-Zoe
Thor-tore-sore	then-ten-Zen

31.   *The lateral lisp:*

The individual who talks out of the side of his mouth is apt to attract attention to himself not only because of the odd or unusual manner in which he draws back the corners of his mouth, but also because of the peculiar sound he emits. [s and z] will be completely distorted, and the resulting sound is a kind of liquid, slushy sound that is halfway between *sh* [ʃ] and a voiceless [l].

This type of lisper is probably blocking the oral outlet at or near the gum ridge or the upper front teeth. He also lowers one or both sides of the tongue, and the breath stream will be forced to escape over the sides. In other words, he is trying to produce an [s or z] with the tongue in position for [l].

Negative practice will help here. Try the following word pairs. Notice that when you produce [l], the tip of the tongue is generally placed lightly against the upper gum ridge, and the sides of the tongue are lowered. For the [s], of course, the tip of the tongue may be raised toward the gum ridge, and the sides of the tongue should touch the edges of the upper back teeth.

Deliberately read the second word in each pair with the tongue in the [l] position and note the distortion which results:

a.

lake-sake	lock-sock	loot-suit
lip-sip	law-saw	light-sight
low-sew	lad-sad	lass-sass
lay-say	lot-sot	lid-Sid
lope-soap	lee-see	lamb-Sam

b. Repeat the word pairs in Exercise a, but this time do not carry over the tongue position for [l] to the second word in each pair.

Again the [t] approach will be useful. Place your tongue in position for that sound. The sides of the tongue should lie in close contact with the inner edges of the teeth. Drop the tip of the tongue quite slowly, holding the sides against the borders of the teeth.

Say "tots" several times, and make certain that the sides of the tongue are lifted for the [s] as they are for the [t].

As you read the following, try to carry over the [t] tongue position to your articulation of [s]:

c. let-lets-letssssss (prolonging the s)-ssssss
hot-hots-hotsssssss-ssssss
pat-pats-patssssss-ssssss
lout-louts-loutsssssss-ssssss
mitt-mitts-mittssssss-sssssss
cat-cats-catssssssss-ssssss
fight-fights-fightsssssss-ssssss

Do the following, and once again check your tongue position on the [s] sounds. Is it in approximately the same position as it is for the [t] sounds? Try to feel the similarity of positions.

d.

tie-sigh-tip-sip	tog-sog-tag-sag
tang-sang-tong-song	tizzle-sizzle-till-sill
top-sop-tone-zone	tick-sick-tomb-zoom
tell-cell-tap-sap	tup-sup-tide-side
tore-sore-tack-sack	too-Sue-tear-seer
teed-seed-teen-seen	tips-zips-tum-sum

e. Don't tuck Sid's torn sash into Betsy's hats.
f. Kit seldom puts tom-toms, skates, boats, or coats on the footstool.
g. Do colts, bats, and cats eat oats, rats, and hats?
h. Ted's moods if he drinks too many cokes are quite silly.
i. Ted said, "Are Tammy and Sammy talking about Todd Sodd?"
j. When Thomas Samson plays cards he bets more chips than he needs to.
k. Nests of toads in nets are pests.
l. "Fats" treats his dates to snacks consisting of carrots, roots, and beets.
m. Mike's pet bites and fights Chad's goats.
n. Tippy zipped through the tiny zoo in Toronto.
o. Tina Sims dotes on Terry's sari and silver belts.

32. Check your [s and z] sounds carefully when they occur in consonant clusters. They are frequently distorted, and occasionally omitted altogether.

Examples of consonant clusters:

skates	risks	rusts	restrict
Spain	hips	install	streaks
else	strives	births	silks

The individual who produces a slushy [s] and who tends toward a lateral lisp must be particularly cautious articulating words which contain any kind of [s or z] sound preceded or followed by [l]. Be conscious of tongue positions for [s and l], and be sure that there is definitely a change of position between the two sounds.

The material below contains many consonant clusters. Avoid making a liquid or slushy [s] which sounds like a voiceless [l], and be certain that your [s and z] are sharp, clear, and short in duration. Do not omit the sounds.

a. If a slave rebels he will slay all the Slavs.
b. Mr. Fast could not sleep while slender sleigh bells rang in the sleeping car.
c. She boasts that the desks will sag if the sliding bolts rust.
d. Do not slander slum dwellers with slangish slogans.
e. Spike feels that the costly slide is too slick.
f. The sling was too slippery for the little sow.
g. Belle slipped the scales under the small scrabble set.
h. The slowpoke smiled as Lil Smith took smelling salts.
i. Slim slowly fell asleep at the slumber party.

33. By now we are only too well aware that spelling is not an accurate guide to pronunciation. This is painfully evident as we note the final sound, the letter *s*, in each of the following:

tips   = [tɪps]
runs   = [rʌnz]
dishes = [ˈdɪʃɪz]

How do we pronounce final *s* when it is added to a noun or verb?

In such words as *buys, boys, loves, dolls, runs, pencils, hides,* the final sound is pronounced as [z] because the sound immediately preceding it is voiced. It is easier for the vocal folds to continue vibrating the final sound. The final *s* in each of the following words is preceded by a voiced sound. Therefore, when you sound the word, articulate a [z] sound rather than [s]:

lids	fills	loves
sings	dogs	dies
Bob's	bars	bathes
sees	hams	shows
runs	times	jails

In such words as *hits, spoofs, pipes, decks, sifts,* the final sound is pronounced as [s], because the sound immediately preceding it is voiceless. It is easier for the vocal folds to remain at rest for the final sound. The final *s* in each of the following words is preceded by a voiceless sound. Therefore, when you sound the word, articulate [s]:

bats	laps	kicks	huffs

Foreign students often have difficulty with [s and z]. Most commonly they will pronounce final [s] as the voiceless [s] when, in many cases, it should be the voiced [z]. If you have a Germanic, Scandinavian, or Russian language in your background, read the following. The sound of [z], not [s], must be made at the end of each word ending in *s*.

a. Is it his or is it hers?
b. Was Tom's prize taken from these because those are like ours?
c. I will excuse you if you will close the door after you use it.
d. Does Ray's father abuse those dogs when he rubs their legs with salves?
e. He will lose his eyes if he lies about the spies.

In such words as *bosses, fizzes, fishes, churches, edges, rouges,* the final sound is pronounced as [ɪz or əz], and the ending actually becomes an extra syllable. In other words, if the preceding sound is one of these fricatives: [s z ʃ tʃ ʒ dʒ], it would be awkward to pronounce [s or z] immediately following.

(Try, for example, to pronounce *dishes* as [dɪʃz]—without an [ɪ] or an [ə] between the [ʃ] and the [z].)

Articulate the correct final sound in each of these:

f.	pits	Ruth's	hatches	masses
	glosses	foes	fakes	hymns
	funds	bits	tires	knits
	cows	wishes	crags	bibs
	passes	judges	smashes	botches

g.   The cops found no traces of the crook's braces near the trucks or sluices.

h.   She crosses bridges on the backs of old busses.

i.   The boy's boasts about taking tusks from elephants, walruses, and other beasts proved false.

j.   He stoops and scratches their backs and then runs and hides in the trucks.

34. Practice the following material which contains [s and z] in a variety of positions and combinations. Don't forget that these fricatives must be short, sharp, fine, and clear. Don't blast them. Don't prolong them. Once again, is your tongue position correct?

a.   Ask me no questions and I'll tell you no fibs.

b.   To get back one's youth one merely has to repeat one's follies.

c.   Our senses don't deceive us: our judgment does.

d.   A man gazing at the stars is always at the mercy of the puddles in the road.

e.   Three times early rising makes one whole day.

f.   They that govern must make least noise.

g.   The most rotten state has the most laws.

h.   He who listens understands.

i.   It's a good loser that finally loses out.

j.   Ladies grow handsome by looking at themselves in the glass.

k.   Secrets are things that we give others to keep for us.

l.   Everything is funny as long as it is happening to somebody else.

m.   By swallowing evil words unsaid, no one has ever yet harmed his stomach.

n.   God may forgive you your sins, but your nervous system won't.

o.   The world, which took but six days to make, is likely to take six thousand to make out.

p.   A classic is something that everybody wants to have read and nobody wants to read.

q.   As long as I have a want, I have a reason for living. Satisfaction is death.

r.   The longer one lives the more one is inclined to think that this sphere is used by other planets as a lunatic asylum.

s.   There is a time of speaking and a time of being still. Let him now speak, or else forever after hold his peace.

t.   It is with narrow-souled people as with narrow-necked bottles; the less they have in them the more noise they make in pouring out.

u.   Swan swim over the sea;
Swim, swan, swim.
Swan swim back again;
Well swam, swan.

[ʃ – ʒ]   [Sh – Zh]

Place of
Articulation: tip or blade of tongue behind gum ridge.

Classification: [ʃ] voiceless.
                   [ʒ] voiced.

Examples: [ʃ] "Sure," said Sherry, "let us rush the machines across the ocean."
              [ʒ] The Persian lady took great pleasure in pinning the corsage onto the beige dress.

Typical Production:

For an interesting approach to [ʃ], compare it with [s], as in "she" and "sea," "shy" and "sigh." If you say the sounds in isolation, you will notice that the whole tongue is drawn back slightly farther for [ʃ] than for [s]. The tongue surface is flattened somewhat, and the sides of the tongue should touch the inner borders of the upper back teeth. The air stream passes over a relatively wide but shallow central passage rather than through the narrow fissure which characterizes [s]. The lips are slightly rounded and protruded.

Faults or Problems:

35. The lisp, so commonly associated with [s and z], is not necessarily exclusive to those sounds. It frequently involves [ʃ and ʒ]. If your sound is adjudged mushy or otherwise unduly conspicuous, review Exercises 30 and 31.

    A fairly common fault is the substitution of [s] or a sound close to it for [ʃ]. Foreign students may also substitute [z] for [ʒ]. To overcome these faults, contrast again the manner in which each of the two sounds is produced. Watch yourself in a mirror as you articulate [s—ʃ] again and again. Note the obvious differences in the positions of the articulators. It is especially important that you feel the difference of greater tongue retraction and lip rounding for [ʃ] than for [s].

a.		
sack-shack	crass-crash	rues-rouge
suit-shoot	lass-lash	bays-beige
sin-shin	lease-leash	lows-loge
sore-shore	mess-mesh	lasses-lashes
seer-sheer	class-clash	puss-push
say-shay	Gus-gush	muss-mush

    b. Sheila sells shrouds and sails at the seashore.
    c. The motion of the machine exerted pressure on the cushion.
    d. The short Englishman reached for the Danish pastry.
    e. The shiny sheen of the socks shone on the brass shelf.
    f. Sid showed Sam how Charlotte shook the spark plugs in the machine.
    g. A sheaf of Swiss shawls was found in the small shed on the shore.
    h. Zane was taking a shower when the unusual invasion began.
    i. Was Shane sane when he hid the treasure in the shanty near the garage?
    j. Sol Shawn said, "Shall we shake hands for Sally's sake?"

36. Sometimes the tongue is permitted to rise too high toward the hard palate. This may also be accompanied by excessive tension of the tongue. The resulting sound is higher in pitch than an acceptable [ʃ], and it is frequently characterized by too much friction. Listen to yourself as you sound [ʃ], and experiment by lowering the tongue from a position relatively high in the mouth to one which is somewhat lower.

164

a.   Shaw shook Shawn for putting the shoes on the precious shawl.
b.   Should Charlotte shut the shop and shun the shouters at the shore?
c.   She pushed the crushed shield into the plush shop.
d.   The shark shunned the shoals and rushed toward the ocean.
e.   He should wash the squash and put it on the shelf.
f.   "Hush," said the shopkeeper, "the usher's gun is showing."
g.   Finish washing the fresh radishes and put them on the dish.
h.   To avoid social tension in Chicago drink sherry or champagne.
i.   Your vision of treasure on the azure shore is only a mirage.

Place of
Articulation: glottis (the sound is initiated here).

Classification: voiceless.

Example: Harry hated to see Helen Hanson forge ahead in her humble manner.

Typical Production:

No movement of the lips, jaw, or tongue is required to produce this sound. The vocal folds are brought close enough together to restrict the outgoing breath stream, thus producing an audible friction noise. However, they are not brought close enough together to produce tone. There is probably no one characteristic position of the articulators for [h]. Instead they are more or less preset in position for the vowel sound which is to follow the [h], and the outgoing breath stream produces a slight, whispery noise before the succeeding sound is vocalized.

Faults or Problems:

37.   Individuals with a foreign language background may omit [h], a fault which is most likely to call attention to itself if the sound occurs in a prominent, stressed word. Thus, if *"Harry is happy because Helen came home"* sounds like *" 'Arry is 'appy because 'elen came 'ome,"* the absence of [h] is rather conspicuous.

The initial and medial [h] should be present but not unduly stressed in this material:

a.	old-hold	odd-hod	it-hit	ahead	rehearse
	at-hat	is-his	ope-hope	behave	unholy
	ill-hill	am-ham	as-has	anyhow	behold
	id-hid	ode-hoed	arm-harm	inhale	inhuman
	eat-heat	air-hair	eel-heel	exhale	withhold
	ate-hate	ear-hear	ow-how	behind	somehow

b.   Hal heaved the hard-handled foghorn behind the huge halter.
c.   The unhappy Horace was hiding under the unheated house.
d.   Hugh Hess behaves as if he didn't know a hawk from a handsaw.
e.   Harriet married Hans, who inhabited the Hartford lighthouse.
f.   Henry was unhurt, but Hubie took him to the hospital anyhow.

g. Has Hilda hidden the heels under the mohair hats?

h. The hated heretic behaved badly on the hill.

i. In humid weather Horton hates to hurry while rehearsing.

38. If [h] is the initial or medial sound of an unaccented syllable or unstressed word it is often permissible to drop the sound. The rigid insistence on pronouncing every [h] may tend to make speech stilted and artificial. In the following, for example, the underlined [h] will probably fall by the wayside:

"If <u>h</u>e had known it was <u>h</u>is book, he would <u>h</u>ave returned it."

Intelligibility which is free of awkwardness and artiness should be your guide in determining which [h] sounds might be dropped in these sentences:

a. Did Herbert give his helmet to him?

b. He should have hidden him in his hamper.

c. He has always said hello when he has passed him on the highway.

d. I have fought a good fight, I have finished my course, I have kept the faith.

e. He held her hand in his for hours.

f. Many of us spend half our time wishing for things we could have if we didn't spend half our time wishing.

g. "Hello, Harry," said the homely hermit. "How can I become a shepherd?"

h. The hour has come to honor the humble heir.

39. Now and then [h] may become defective for one of the same reasons [s] so often does: there is too much of it. When [h] must be sounded to assure intelligibility, take care that it isn't blasted. Like [s], touch it lightly and briefly.

a. Hubert Higgins hired the happy sheepherder near Lake Tahoe.

b. Henceforth, the henpecked Howard will head the Harris household.

c. Perhaps Hall will behave if Hiram rides the horse to Idaho.

d. Hortense had helped Hannah heat her hotel in Hazel Park.

e. How happy Hedwig was when Hy Hanson rehearsed Hamlet in the playhouse.

f. If a man could have half his wishes, he would double his troubles.

g. There is no record in human history of a happy philosopher.

h. God help those who do not defend themselves!

i. The cuckoo who is on to himself is halfway out of the clock.

j. The man who interferes with another's habits has the worst one.

k. He who has health, has hope; and he who has hope has everything.

l. What I have been taught, I have forgotten; what I know, I have guessed.

m. He who exalts himself does not rise high.

n. The secret source of humor is not joy but sorrow; there is no humor in heaven.

Affricates

The affricates (also known as affricatives) are kissing cousins of the fricatives. However, as their symbols might indicate, each one is actually a closely and rapidly blended combination of a plosive and a fricative. The two sounds are merged, for in articulating either one of them you do not completely finish the plosive and then begin the fricative.

[tʃ] ch
[dʒ] j

The tongue momentarily blocks the breath as it does for the plosives, but then the tongue quickly assumes the fricative position and the impounded air is released somewhat explosively.

[tʃ – dʒ] [Ch – j]

Place of Articulation: tongue tip and upper gum ridge plosives combined with tongue blade and front part of palate fricatives.

Classification: [tʃ] voiceless.
  [dʒ] voiced.

Examples: [tʃ] <u>Ch</u>arles, feeling righ<u>t</u>eous, hid the ha<u>tch</u>et under the ba<u>tch</u> of pea<u>ch</u>es in the ki<u>tch</u>en.
  [dʒ] <u>J</u>oyce fed <u>g</u>inger and <u>j</u>elly to <u>G</u>eorge as he planted cabba<u>g</u>e at the ed<u>ge</u> of the lod<u>ge</u>.

Typical Production:

The tip of the tongue, as well as the flat portion immediately behind it, must be pressed quite firmly against the gum ridge. The body of the tongue assumes a position similar to that for [ʃ]. The tip is then lowered, and as it depresses, a modified explosion, less sharp than that for [t or d], is heard.

Faults or Problems:

40. If [tʃ or dʒ] are defective, generally only the fricative portions of those sounds are at fault. If necessary, review Exercises 35-36 in this chapter.

 We have previously noted that some individuals have a tendency to exaggerate the plosive qualities of [t and d] and to make [ʃ and ʒ] too conspicuous. It is not altogether unlikely then that when they approach the affricates, which are modified combinations of plosives and fricatives, they may produce minor vocal hurricanes. Be sure that the affricates are sharp and relatively delicate rather than coarse or prolonged.

a.

chill	birches	each	joke
choke	nature	march	gin
cheap	richer	hitch	gem
chant	urchin	coach	gesture
chap	pitcher	lunch	giraffe
chew	question	lurch	jack
magic	surgeon	adjust	urges
region	logic	damage	marriage
huge	lodge	rage	singe

b. Jack and Jill had orange juice, jam, and jelly in their pail.
c. Chilled cheese, chestnut, and chicken sandwiches choked the duchess.
d. The pigeon plunged from the large ledge.
e. He exchanged the chicken chowder for the cheap chili.
f. Judge Jones lodged Major Johnson in jail with the gypsies.
g. The cabbage and the orange could not be budged from the edge of the carriage.
h. Charles, the chunky merchant, jumped into the jeep.
i. Do not ask if a man has been through college; ask if a college has been through him.

41. The Scandinavian who says "Yack Yones" for "Jack Jones" and the German who says "larch" for "large" are possibly more fact than fiction. Many foreign languages, including French, lack the [tʃ] or [dʒ] or both. The weirdly inconsistent English spelling of these sounds only compounds the confusion. Note, for example, [dʒ] in: age, gem, jest, gesture, soldier, adjoin, grandeur.

Here is a partial list of sound substitutions and distortions characteristic of one or more foreign dialects. If English is your second language, you may wish to study the lists. The accompanying drill material may help you to overcome some of the difficulties with English pronunciation. Be sure that somebody with a reasonably good ear listens critically to you as you practice.

Differentiate carefully between these sounds as they occur in the following word pairs or sentences:

a. [ʃ] is often substituted for [tʃ].

share-chair	mush-much	mash-match
Shaw-chaw	wash-watch	shop-chop
Schick-chick	bash-batch	dish-ditch
shirk-chirk	cash-catch	hash-hatch
shore-chore	lash-latch	shin-chin
sheet-cheat	bush-butch	crush-crutch

b. [j] (the initial sound in "yes") is often substituted for [dʒ].

you-Jew	yip-gyp	Yale-jail
yell-jell	yoke-joke	yellow-Jello
Yap-Jap	yam-jam	yawn-John
yaw-jaw	Ute-jute	yowl-jowl
year-jeer	use-juice	yule-jewel
yet-jet	yak-Jack	yea-jay

c. [ts] and [dz] are sometimes substituted for [tʃ] and [dʒ].

mats-match	wades-wage
wits-witch	raids-rage
hits-hitch	cads-cadge
mitts-Mitch	seeds-siege
pats-patch	rids-ridge
huts-hutch	Ed's-edge

d. [ʒ] is sometimes substituted for [dʒ].
   (1) Janet put the corsage on the edge of the magenta jacket.
   (2) The Persian jigged and jested when he saw the magic vision.
   (3) Mr. Bridges, the agent, could not make his usual decision about the region.
   (4) The large lesion on the huge pigeon could just be measured.
   (5) The engineer who camouflaged the erosion on the edge of the mirage had great prestige.

e. [ʃ] is often substituted for [ʒ] in the final position.
    [tʃ] is often substituted for [dʒ] in the final position.
   (1) General Wishe ordered the barrage to crush the sabotage.
   (2) To reach the edge before lunch, the huge bunch must charge the bridge.
   (3) I shall dash into the garage and fish the corsage out of the beige-colored trash can.
   (4) A batch of cabbage is no match for fresh oranges and fudge.
   (5) Nudge anyone who puts the badge on the edge of the lodge.

Practice Material for the Fricatives and Affricates:

42. The following drill material contains all of the fricatives and affricates in a variety of positions and sound combinations. As you practice, remember that although these particular consonants have often been described as having in their midst several of the ugliest sounds in the English language, none of them have to be offensively noisy or unpleasant. They are important to our speech, and when they are handled with precision, exactness, and sensitivity, they need not sound like vocalized belching, exaggerated hissing, or buzzing.

 a. A fat paunch never breeds fine thoughts.
 b. An exaggeration is a truth that has lost its temper.
 c. A coward is one who in a dangerous situation thinks with his legs.
 d. A saint is a sceptic once in twenty-four hours.
 e. Forty is the old age of youth; fifty is the youth of old age.
 f. We are all geniuses up to the age of ten.
 g. An accident is a surprise arranged by nature.
 h. Alarm Clock: A device for awakening childless households.
 i. A bee is a buzzy busybody.
 j. An armistice is a pause to permit the losing side to breed new soldiers.
 k. A cynic is a man who, when he smells flowers, looks around for a coffin.
 l. Alas!—early Victorian for "Oh, hell!"
 m. The President of the U.S.S.R. possesses more power than any other man on earth, but he cannot stop a sneeze.
 n. A brain is that with which we think we think.
 o. A bore is the kind of a man who, when you ask him how he is, tells you.
 p. Slang is sport-model language stripped down to get more speed with less horsepower.
 q. Jazz is music which will endure as long as people hear it through their feet instead of their brains.
 r. College: a washing machine. You get out of it just what you put in, but you'd never recognize it.
 s. The objection to Puritans is not that they try to make us think as they do, but that they try to make us do as they think.
 t. Commas are used if you have to take a breath, and periods are used if you want to stop and think.
 u. California smog—it's as if God had squeezed a big onion over Los Angeles.
 v. Every normal man must be tempted, at times, to spit on his hands, hoist the black flag, and begin slitting throats.
 w. "When I get my voice back, I'll sing as well as you," the hoarse cuckoo told the nightingale.
 x. A cabbage is a familiar kitchen-garden vegetable about as large and wise as a man's head.
 y. A quotation is something that somebody said that seemed to make sense at the time.
 z. "George," said his father, "do you know who killed that beautiful little cherry tree yonder in the garden?" Looking at his father with the sweet face of youth brightened with the inexpressible charm of all-conquering truth, he bravely cried out: "I cannot tell a lie. I did it with my little hatchet."

Assignment 15 (See suggested Checklist for this assignment)

Select material which contains many examples of the nine fricatives and the two affricates in a variety of positions. If you have been experiencing difficulty with one or more of these sounds, be especially certain that the material includes a lot of them. Don't shy away from the fricatives and affricates, but give them their due prominence. Articulate them with as much care and finesse as you can, however, and avoid excessive noisiness and prolongation.

Suggested Checklist for Assignment 15

As you practice by yourself you may want to work with this checklist. Listen carefully to yourself. If it is feasible, record the assignment or get a classmate or friend to listen to you as you read the material. Eventually your goal will be to have a check mark in the **Yes** column for each category. (Optional: Perhaps your instructor will want to use the checklist to evaluate you during your classroom presentation.)

	Yes	No
Initial fricatives short, sharp, and clear in articulation.		
Medial fricatives short, sharp, and clear in articulation.		
Final fricatives short, sharp, and clear in articulation.		
Avoids omitting initial fricatives.		
Avoids omitting medial fricatives.		
Avoids omitting final fricatives.		
Differentiates between voiceless [f] and voiced [v].		
Differentiates between voiceless [θ] and voiced [ð].		
Differentiates between voiceless [s] and voiced [z].		
Differentiates between voiceless [ʃ] and voiced [ʒ].		
Avoids excessive pressure in production of fricatives.		
Avoids lateral, slushy articulation of [s z ʃ] or [ʒ].		
Pronounces correctly final *s* or *es* as added to verbs and nouns.		
Avoids substituting fricatives for nonfricatives.*		
Avoids substituting nonfricatives for fricatives.*		

*If there are substitutions, a few of the more commonly used ones are listed below. Check or indicate as needed:

[b] for [f] or [v] _____ [t] for [θ] or [ð] _____   [s] for [θ] _____   [w] for [v] _____
[d] for [θ] or [ð] _____   [v] for [f] _____   [s] for [ð] _____   [z] for [s] _____
[f] for [θ] or [ð] _____   [v] for [w] _____   [s] for [z] _____   [z] for [ð] _____

Other substitutions:

Additional comments or suggestions:

Glides (Semivowels)

There are four glides in English:

[l]
[r]
[w]
[j] y

(You will remember that [j] symbolizes the initial sound in "yet, yell, and your." These four sounds defy strict classification, [l], for example, being described by some as a lateral consonant or semivowel rather than a glide.)

A glide is a sound produced by a continuous, gliding movement of the articulatory organs from the position of one sound to that of another. When you make [r w or j], for example, the tongue is in motion as these sounds are being formed. The glides have been described as vowels in motion.

To demonstrate: Consider the initial sound in "well." Hold it briefly, as if you were going to say the word in slow motion. You will discover that it sounds like the *oo* [u] in moon [mun]. Then move into the second sound in the word. As the mechanisms begin moving, you will identify the resulting sound as [w].

Place of
Articulation: tongue and upper gum ridge.

Classification: voiced.

Example: Lena allowed Leslie to fill the pickle barrel with plump apples.

Typical Production:

Place the tip of the tongue lightly against the upper gum ridge. One or both sides of the tongue are lowered to allow the voiced breath stream to be emitted laterally, that is, over the sides. The positions of the lips and the body of the tongue vary considerably, depending upon the sounds that precede or follow the [l].

If [l] is found in an initial position or immediately after an initial consonant, as in "like, clad, sleet," it is described as a clear or front [l]. The back of the tongue is relatively low.

If [l] is found in a final position or immediately before a final consonant, as in "fall, sulk, cold," it may be described as a dark [l]. The back of the tongue is slightly raised.

Faults or Problems:

43. The varying shades of clearness and darkness of [l] sounds depend in part on the subjective judgment of the listener. A dark [l], in itself, is certainly not incorrect, but if it is so dark that it is muffled, it will probably hinder intelligibility. This type of [l] may occur if the tongue tip does not contact the gum ridge.

To help you hear as well as feel the difference between a clear [l] and a dark [l], read the following pairs of words. The first word of each pair begins with a clear [l]. Be sure that the back of the tongue is held relatively low.

The second word of each pair ends with dark [l]. The entire tongue should be pulled farther back in the mouth than it is for clear [l]. The back portion of the tongue is also higher for the dark sound than for the clear one.

lean-seal	lag-gal	lock-call
let-fell	lot-tall	lime-mile
lid-dill	lip-pill	lead-deal
late-tale	loot-tool	lost-stall

44. If [l] is followed by another consonant, as in the word "help," the [l] sound is frequently distorted or swallowed.

Result: *help* [hɛlp] may sound like *hep* [hɛp]

If this occurs, it is entirely possible that the speaker is lifting the back of the tongue as he should, but is failing to touch the gum ridge with the tip of the tongue.

In some cases, a sound resembling the neutral [ə] will be substituted.

Result: *silk* [sɪlk] may resemble *si-uk* [sɪək]
wolf [wʊlf] may resemble *woo-uf* [wʊəf]

Not infrequently we hear individuals who omit final [l] sounds altogether.

Result: *all right* [ɔl ˈraɪt] becomes *aw right* [ɔ ˈraɪt]
baseball [ˈbesbɔl] becomes *baseba* [ˈbesbɔ]

Be certain that the tongue tip is making the proper contact with the gum ridge as you articulate [l], regardless of its position, while practicing the following:

a.
helm	billion	Ralph	awl
dial	shelve	talcum	film
twelve	alb	pelvis	yelp
help	alm	scald	bulb
Paul	already	dolphin	malt
self	pall-mall	whelp	pelf
revolve	kelp	lollipop	solve

b. Nell told Sal not to gulp the pill.
c. Do not broil lamb or fowl on the grill.
d. Shall I place the small hotel stool on the tile shelf?
e. The cold, gold bells of the realm were worth twelve billion in the bulk.
f. O Lord—if there is a Lord; save my soul—if I have a soul.
g. He knows little who will tell his wife all he knows.
h. Is Melville's *Moby Dick* a tale about a real whale?
i. One must never rely on miracles.
j. Most men are like eggs: too full of themselves to hold anything else.
k. All the world may not love a lover but all the world watches him.
l. If fifty million people say a foolish thing, it is still a foolish thing.
m. A lady is a woman who makes a man behave like a gentleman.
n. Drunkard: A person who tries to pull himself out of trouble with a corkscrew.
o. There is nothing will kill a man so soon as having nobody to find fault with except himself.

45. Such types as the Chinese laundryman and the Japanese gardener or houseboy seem to be disappearing from the TV comedians' repertory of dialect jokes. A reason for their one-time popularity is that Oriental accents are relatively easy to mimic. A singsong pitch pattern and the substitution of [l] for [r], or [r] for [l] will generally result in a reasonably convincing accent. The Oriental allegedly says *velly good laundly* for *very good laundry* or *flied lice* for *fried rice.*

These are exaggerations, of course, but it is true that the individual whose first language was Oriental rather than English may confuse [l and r]. Most Oriental languages do not contain sounds which are exactly like our [l] and [r]. They do, however, contain a consonant which resembles and has some characteristics of both, hence the confusion.

For those who need to work on this problem: Remember that for [l] the tip of the tongue must touch the upper gum ridge. For [r]: the central portion of the tongue is raised, and the tip is pointed upward but should not contact either the gum ridge or the hard palate immediately above the gum ridge. With these differences in mind, practice the following:

a.
lamb-ram	lack-wrack	blink-brink
lope-rope	loan-roan	blat-brat
lip-rip	limb-rim	glimmer-grimmer
lag-rag	lock-rock	plank-prank
lung-rung	lewd-rude	fly-fry
list-wrist	Lyle-rile	climb-crime
line-Rhine	leap-reap	plate-prate

b. Do not cram the clams into the crock near the clock.
c. He hauled the long load of blue brew down the wrong road.
d. The rain fell on the lane as the leak in the ramp lamp began to reek.
e. Mr. Ringling arrived alive even though he had ripped the lid.
f. The heated lead turned red as the glow began to grow.

46. [l] is a troublesome consonant, and articulatory problems involving this sound are by no means uncommon. It is also one of the sounds to be acquired last by children. A small child will quite often substitute [w and j] and, less frequently, [r] for the [l] sound.

Result: *like* [laɪk] becomes *yike* [jaɪk] or *wike* [waɪk]
            look [lʊk] becomes *yook* [jʊk] or *wook* [wʊk]

Well-meaning parents sometimes find these substitutions "cute," and if the child is encouraged to continue his baby talk, a defective [l] may carry over into adulthood.

As we shall presently see [w] requires a fairly lively activity of the lips rather than the tongue. Thus, if it is being substituted for [l], lip movements must be minimized and the tongue tip must be touching the upper gum ridge.

If [j] is being substituted, compare its articulation with that of [l].

     For [j]:   Raise the front part of the tongue toward the hard palate. The position is almost the same as the one for *ee* as in *meet*.

If [r] is being substituted, compare its articulation with that of [l].

     For [r]:   The central portion of the tongue is raised toward the palate; the tip may be close to the gum ridge, but contact should be avoided.

For [l], of course, the tip of the tongue must touch the upper gum ridge.

a.
way-lay	yank-lank	rot-lot
wake-lake	yet-let	rung-lung
wick-lick	year-leer	rip-lip
wore-lore	yard-lard	rap-lap
week-leak	yore-lore	Ross-loss
wire-liar	yam-lamb	rain-lain
wink-link	yeast-least	ram-lamb
wilt-lilt	yawn-lawn	rhyme-lime
wax-lax	Ute-lute	raid-laid

b. Will Lillian wed Larry Wilson or will she elope with Leslie Williams?

c. Leah yelled at Louis and Liz Young yesterday.

d. Let's lug the large Yule log to the yellow lodge on Yankee lake.

e. Larry Larson yawned as the Weber youth lost his place while reading *All's Well That Ends Well.*

f. "Yes," said Les, "Yang Lang failed Chinese at Yale."

47. Less frequently encountered are three other faults involving the production of [l].

Foreigners may dentalize [l], that is, allow the tongue tip to contact the edges of the teeth and, in some cases, to protrude between the teeth. The so-called dental [l] is permissible when it is combined with [θ], as in "athlete" and "wealth" [ˈæθlit, wɛlθ]. Otherwise, this type of [l] may tend to distort the sounds preceding or following it.

In careless speech, the schwa [ə] is occasionally inserted between [l] and a preceding initial consonant. Thus, *clean* [klin] becomes *cuh-lean* [kəˈlin] and *plenty* [ˈplɛntɪ] becomes *puh-lenty* [pəˈlɛntɪ].

Syllabic [l] is generally found in or near final positions in words, such as "kettle, ladle, petal." You will notice that in such cases the [l] forms a syllable by itself without the help of any other vowel sound. Syllabic [l] causes little difficulty unless the [l] is preceded by [t or d]. In this type of combination, some speakers will omit the [t or d].

Result: *little* [ˈlɪtl̩] sounds like *li-ul* or *li'l* [ˈlɪəl / lɪl]

           saddle [ˈsædl̩] sounds like *sa-ul* or *sa'l* [ˈsæəl / sæl]

Careful ear training, as always, is essential to correct these faults. Again, check the position of the tongue, especially the tip. It is also imperative that the breath stream not escape centrally, but over one or both sides of the tongue. Try to articulate satisfactory and acceptable [l] sounds as you practice the following:

a. When all candles are out, all cats are gray.

b. The Promised Land always lies on the other side of a wilderness.

c. Maybe if we could all laugh alike, and laugh at the same time, this world of ours wouldn't be able to find so many things to squabble about.

d. Love is like the measles, all the worse when it comes late in life.

e. Conscience is the still small voice that makes us feel still smaller.

f. Learn a new language and get a new soul.

g. All the things I really like to do are immoral, illegal, or fattening.

h. Smile, and they'll call you silly; frown, and they'll call you gruff.

i. A drunkard is like a whiskey bottle, all neck and belly and no head.

j. We are cold to others only when we are dull in ourselves.

k. Flattery is telling the other fellow what he already thinks of himself.

l. The man who is too old to learn was probably always too old to learn.

m. There is only one rule for being a good talker: learn to listen.

n. Weep, and you're called a baby; laugh, and you're called a fool.

o. *Hamlet* is the tragedy of tackling a family problem too soon after college.

p. What is moral is what you feel good after, and what is immoral is what you feel bad after.

q. I do not believe today everything I believed yesterday; I wonder, will I believe tomorrow everything I believe today?

r. I've never met a healthy person who worried much about his health, or a good person who worried much about his soul.

s. An excellent teacher has three rules in teaching: He talks realistically, he convinces students that he is genuinely interested in them, and he makes it clear that he'll break their blooming necks if they don't work.

Place of
Articulation: tip or blade of tongue behind upper gum ridge.

Classification: voiced.

Example: Raymond could not bear rock and roll music so Gertrude wrote an opera for him.

[r] is one of the most interesting and controversial sounds in the English language. It is also the chameleon of the language, a highly variable and fickle sound. Individual differences result in different [r] sounds, and the section of the country in which you live may strongly influence certain of your [r] sounds.

There are several ways of producing an acceptable [r]. Two of them will be described here, and a few variations will be included with exercises and drill material found later in this section.

One Manner of Production:
The central portion of the tongue is tensed slightly and raised toward the hard palate (the roof of the mouth). The tip of the tongue may be lowered and drawn back somewhat from the lower teeth.

Another Manner of Production:
The tip of the tongue may be brought close to the gum ridge and turned back slightly toward the middle of the hard palate.

Both of these are starting positions. As soon as the sound is begun, the tongue glides or moves to the position necessary to make the following sound. The exact position of the lips and the jaw also depends largely upon the sound that follows.

Faults or Problems:
48. A lazy tongue will do much to destroy a clear and recognizable [r]. Lip activity is present but it is minimal, for it is the position and the activity of the tongue which are chiefly responsible for producing this sound.
    a. Review Exercises 8-11 at the beginning of this chapter.
    b. Say *a* as it is pronounced in *are* [ar]. Then raise the tongue slowly to the [r] position, connecting the two sounds, but do not permit the lips to move. Repeat.
    c. Pronounce *are* backwards: [ra]. Place your tongue in the position for [r] while maintaining the [a] position with your lips and jaw. Again, avoid lip movement. Repeat.
49. Another approach which will help you produce a satisfactory [r] sound requires a little bit of exaggeration. Before you sound the initial [r] in such words as "red, right," make the sound of *er* [ɝ] as in "ermine, fern."

    To make *er:* Raise the middle portion of the tongue toward the roof of the mouth. If this seems unnatural to you, simply make sure that the front of the tongue is higher than the back. Some individuals point the tip of the tongue upwards; others curl it slightly backwards.

    Each of the following words and sentences is to be read twice. In the first reading exaggerate by articulating an *er* sound before the initial [r], thusly:

    er-red   er-right   er-rake   er-rid

    er-round the er-rough and er-rugged er-rock the er-ragged er-rascal er-ran.

As you read the material the second time, keep the same tongue position on the initial [r] which you used on the *er* sounds, but cut the preliminary *er* quite short.

a.

rent	rim	rail	ripe
rift	wren	rant	rock
raw	wrack	run	rink
rabbit	road	ride	wrought
rain	rhyme	royal	root

b. Round the rough and rugged rock the ragged rascal ran.
c. Richard Riley reeled when he ripped the rope from his wrist.
d. Ralph removed the ripped, red robe in the run-down room.
e. The robin raced the red fox along the rim of the range road.
f. The roadrunner is a racy rodent that likes to raid carrot patches.
g. Rex became rich from making red wine from ripe grapes.
h. Roger rolled the ruby ring toward the road.
i. The Russian threw the rice and roses into the rut.
j. The rip in the roof is the real reason he ran in the wrong direction.

50. If [r] is preceded by another consonant and occurs at the beginning of a syllable or word, it is described as an [r] cluster.

    Examples: <u>pr</u>oud, <u>fr</u>ee, <u>br</u>ake, <u>tr</u>uth, <u>str</u>eak, <u>cr</u>owd, <u>gr</u>in, <u>dr</u>ink

[pr, br, fr] Clusters

[p and b], as we have noticed, require rather strong lip activity. [f] requires less. As the articulators adjust from the initial consonant to the [r], a sound much like [w] may be heard.

Result: *pride* [praɪd] becomes *pwide* [pwaɪd]
         brim [brɪm] becomes *bwim* [bwɪm]
         fry [fraɪ] becomes *fwy* [fwaɪ]

The [w] substitution is to be avoided, of course. Remember—and this is not as tricky as it may seem—the tongue articulates [r] in these clusters at the same time that the lips articulate [p, b, and f]. In other words, before you have finished making [p, b, and f], the [r] sound has already begun. Try the following:

a.

pride	brought	freak
prank	brick	frill
prod	brunt	fright
prattle	broom	from
prawn	brute	froze

b. The proud prince brought the broken freezer to his frightened friend.
c. The frozen fruit was prepared as a present for the grieving bride.
d. The brown bricks pressed against the pretty grass frame.
e. "Are you proud of the prank?" asked the bragging friar.

[kr, gr] Clusters

Again, the initial consonant must virtually overlap with the [r]. This very close blend is not difficult to form if the [r] is articulated with the tongue pulled back as it would be if [k and g] were being articulated. Do not hold the initial sounds too long as you practice these:

f.

cross	crate	grill	grace
crust	crack	grim	groom
crude	creek	grade	gripe
croak	cry	grant	Greek
crepe	crib	grog	gruff

176

g. The crude crook ground the green grapes into the cramped cradle.
h. Greta Gray crams for her courses but Craig Crockett is a grind.
i. The grim groom groaned as the crowd crawled toward the crumbs.
j. Mr. Cromwell crept into the grass-covered grotto when his craft crashed.

[tr, dr, thr] Clusters

The [r] that most of us produce in words such as "try, drip, throw" is still another kind of [r] and with a personality of its own. Friction noises can be heard with this sound and, as a matter-of-fact, in its manner of production, it is somewhat similar to the fricative family.

For [tr and dr] Combinations

Lower the tip of the tongue just enough to produce the [t or d]. Then retract it quickly with the tip of the tongue near but not in actual contact with the gum ridge. Incidentally, many individuals find it easy to produce a successful [r] if the tongue touches the gum ridge lightly.

For [thr] Combinations

The pattern used to articulate [tr and dr] is basically applied here. In other words, in starting the [thr] combination, the tip of the tongue makes a light contact with the upper front teeth and then retracts, as described above.

As you drill with this material, avoid two fairly common faults:

Do not make the [r] clusters conspicuous because they are too noisy or sustained.

Do not insert a sound resembling *uh*— the schwa [ə]—between an initial consonant and the [r]. When this is done, we hear such words as *tuh-ry, thuh-ree, and duh-ream* [tə'raɪ, θə'ri, də'rim] for *try, three,* and *dream.*

k.	trim	dram	throw
	trod	dreary	thread
	trout	draft	thrust
	trek	drink	thrill
	treat	droop	thrush
	trail	drew	thrash
	trap	dray	thrive
	troll	drawl	throng

l. Troy would not trade the drawn trout for the trapped thrush.
m. Drew Draper felt a throb in his throat when the troops told the truth.
n. She draped the three trinkets over the tree throne.
o. The trapped troops drilled until they drooped and dropped.
p. The tropical thrush fell into the trash trap.
q. The throng threatened to drench the drake.
r. The drab train collided with the drafty tram.
s. Is it true that the truce triggered more trouble in the Tropics?

51. In infantile speech [w and l] are often substituted for [r], a trait which, if carried over into adulthood, may label the speech of the offender as immature. (See also Exercise 46.)

To help you eliminate the [w] substitute, keep the lips relatively immobile, avoid raising the back of the tongue, and emphasize, instead, movements of the front of the tongue as you sound the [r]. If you are substituting [l] for [r] carefully contrast and compare the two sounds. The [l] sound, you will recall, is emitted laterally over the sides of the tongue. [r], however, requires a central emission of sound waves.

a.	wad-rod	way-ray	wide-ride
	wade-raid	wane-rain	woo-rue
	wine-Rhine	week-reek	will-rill
	won-run	woe-row	wing-ring
	weep-reap	went-rent	wore-roar
b.	lay-ray	lump-rump	lam-ram
	lap-rap	lane-rain	light-right
	list-wrist	lit-rit	lock-rock
	look-rook	leap-reap	loss-Ross
	lot-rot	lewd-rude	lamp-ramp

c. Wright wiggled as Rollin Waldo and Wanda Ronson were wed.
d. Rhea liked to race around the worn loom.
e. Rory wailed after the wild ride through the waning rain.
f. Are there reeds or weeds on the leafy reef near the river?
g. Ryan and Will sang loud songs as they went to pay the rent.
h. As it rained in the lane, Larry Ware tried to throw the rake into the lake.
i. The rich witch raved when the wave wrecked the rock.
j. "Row the low boat before you get rid of the lid," Ray wailed.

52. In American English today [r] is not trilled, although persons whose language background is German, Russian, French, Spanish, Slavic, Scottish, or Irish may trill an occasional [r]. There are several varieties of trills. In one of them, the back of the tongue is raised toward the soft palate in such a manner that the outgoing breath stream causes the uvula to flutter. In another variety of trill, the tongue is tensed and the tip is allowed to strike in rapid succession the upper teeth or gum ridge.

If you trill your [r] sounds, you probably regard the American untrilled [r] as rather pallid and nondescript. You will have to train yourself to consider it as an entirely different type of sound, one which is more like a vowel than a consonant. The *uh* [ə] approach may be helpful.

Say *uh*, prolong it, and try to curl back the tip of the tongue. With a little practice you should be able to produce a satisfactory [r]:

a.	rot	trap	forest
	ran	drop	foundry
	rail	crop	Lorna
	rue	grade	wearing
	rise	prim	Jordan
	rip	brake	barred

b. Robert wrote that the rates on the royal road were wrong.
c. "Really, Ronald!" Rhea remarked. "Did Roberta run away with Ricky?"
d. The rabbit and the parrot roamed around the wrecked rail.
e. The Rolls-Royce ran into the broad rock in the drizzling rain.
f. Tracy caught her foot near the ruined reef.

53. Every four years we have the chance to watch and hear the two major political parties in the United States as they participate in mammoth conventions to nominate candidates for the offices of president and vice-president. There is enough hell-bubbling activity, pageantry, and speech-making for almost everybody. Most interesting to some of us, however, is the wonderful conglomeration of dialects or "accents," as we often like to say.

The delegate from Boston who compared the war in Viet Nam with the *wa' in Korear* [wɔɪn ko 'rɪr] is just as interesting as the senator from South Carolina who told the convention about his great *feah of wah* [fɛə ʌv wɔə]. Or when the chairman, who hails from New York City, uses such a phrase as *dawk* [dɑk] *spots,* is he saying *dock* or *dark?* The visiting governor of Iowa, however, may hang onto the *r* in *bar* as though his life depended on it.

Who has the correct *r* sound? If intelligibility is not obscured, probably all of them do. The old saw about "When in Rome do as the Romans do" is more applicable to actions than to speech. If your speech is characteristic of a certain section of the United States and you find yourself transplanted to an area in which the speech is markedly different, listen carefully and critically to the speech around you. If it is necessary for you to modify your own speech, let those whose speech is unostentatiously intelligible serve as your guides. "Getting rid of an accent" need not be your major concern.

If [r] follows a vowel and occurs in or near the final position of a word, such as "fa<u>ir</u>" and "ca<u>rt</u>":

> and if the American English you speak is identified with General American dialect, you will probably articulate the [r] with definite [r] coloring.

> and if the American English you speak is identified with Eastern or Southern dialects, you may possibly articulate an [r] which closely resembles *uh* or the schwa [ə].

General American	Eastern and Southern
far = [fɑr]	far = [fɑə]
park = [pɑrk]	park = [pɑək]
beard = [bɪrd]	beard = [bɪəd]

Perhaps you have no problem with this variation of the [r] family. Let your instructor advise you. If you are told that your [r] sound is too hard and prominent or accompanied by unpleasant friction noises, you may be curling the tongue tip back excessively as well as prolonging the sound. As you read the drill material in this section, try to get the feel of the tongue activity and position. The tongue tip should not curl back on itself.

If you are told that your [r] sound lacks [r] coloring, is too close to *uh* [ə], or is otherwise conspicuous for the area in which you live, raise the central portion of the tongue and point the tip of the tongue in the direction of the gum ridge. It may help you to prolong the [r] sound momentarily as you read aloud:

a.	fear	queer	leer	bare
	rare	mar	poor	floor
	liar	start	port	mire
	air	bored	barn	sire
	more	Bart	ear	war
	bar	fork	short	card

b. Did the pair from Newark carve the warm pork?

c. The bear felt fear in his heart when he faced the barn door.

d. You cannot wear your fire-colored beard any more this year.

e. The worn gear fell into the moor near the tar pit.

f. The fire near the wire chair was put out with warm beer.

The use of the intrusive [r] common in parts of New England and in the New York City area, is hardly a dastardly offense, although it often provides amusement for outsiders. This [r] is inserted between two words if the first one ends with a vowel and the second one begins with a vowel. This seems to ease the transition between consecutive vowels. Thus, we hear *sofa-r in the living room, idea-r of his, law-r of the state.* Speakers who use the intrusive [r] may also hook it on to the end of a single word: *potater* [pə'tetɚ] for *potato* and *arear* ['ɛriɚ] for *area.*

Those who use General American or Southern dialect will rarely use the intrusive [r]. If you use Eastern dialect, you may be inserting this extra [r] sound. If you feel that it is necessary for you to eliminate it, practice with the following. Let somebody listen to you and work until the intrusive sound has disappeared.

a. Maria saw a car hit a sofa and a chair.
b. The President said, "America is a land of law and order and we shall abide by the law of the state."
c. Hannah Adams and Papa ought to dance the polka all day.
d. The gorilla understood how to eat a banana in the arena.
e. "The idea of doing a drama in an Alabama open-air theater is great," Anna answered.
f. Ole ate raw oysters in Alaska and Canada.
g. Georgia Upton wore the toga in the plaza in Cuba.
h. Eva bought the china in Vienna after the tourists went to Russia.

54. Whatever the nature of your [r] sounds, be certain that they are not so spectacularly nonconformist as to interfere with the general understandability of your speech. In general it is safe to say that the sound should not be lengthened or noisy. If you are inserting or adding it, especially where spelling does not indicate its presence, you may want to eliminate it. If you are a foreign student and are trilling the sound, you may find it desirable to modify your way of making [r]. If you have been substituting [l or w] for this sound, you should always try to avoid these undesirable substitutions. Most importantly, if your manner of articulating [r] calls too much attention to you, the speaker, or if others find your speech difficult to understand, strive for an acceptable [r] sound.

The material below contains [r] in many combinations and positions:

a.
shop-sharp	code-cord	load-lord
Don-darn	pock-park	ought-art
hod-hard	toe-tore	mock-mark
bought-Bart	show-shore	fa-far
saw-a-car	foe-fore	tomato-and-corn
era-of-war	Moe-more	radio-in-there
hello-out-there	low-lore	rodeo-in-December
go-gore	henna-her-hair	Dora-asked-Cora

b. When Anita is singing the aria, will Leona assist on the cello?
c. The cop caught the carp off the dock after dark.
d. Bob and Barbara saw the lark break the lock and eat the corn pone.
e. "Here," said King Lear. "Put the rare deer on the chair near the fire."
f. A clever man commits no minor blunders.
g. The secret of being tiresome is to tell everything.
h. Life is short, but it is long enough to ruin any man who wants to be ruined.
i. We are terrified by the idea of being terrified.
j. "My country, right or wrong," is like saying, "My mother, drunk or sober."
k. The man who first invented the art of supporting beggars made many wretched.
l. Learn all the rules, every one of them, so that you will know how to break them.
m. Don't believe the world owes you a living; the world owes you nothing—it was here first.
n. A friend who is very near and dear may in time become as useless as a relative.
o. Some act first, think afterward, and then repent forever.
p. The hardest job of all is trying to look busy when you're not.
q. Lettuce is like conversation: it must be fresh and crisp, so sparkling that you scarcely notice the bitter in it.
r. Both tigers and zebras have striped skins, but under the skin they stop being brothers.
s. I divide all readers into two classes: those who read to remember and those who read to forget.

$\left[\text{W}\right]$

Place of
Articulation: lips.

Classification: voiced.

Example: <u>W</u>ilma <u>w</u>ailed q<u>u</u>ietly as <u>o</u>ne tear <u>w</u>obbled down her q<u>u</u>ivering cheek.

Typical Production:

Round and protrude your lips as if you were going to produce a sound similar to the vowel *oo* in *moon* [mun]. The back of the tongue should be arched toward the soft palate. The tip of the tongue is down, touching the back of the lower front teeth. As the sound begins, the lips and tongue move rapidly into the position of the vowel which follows. (The *w* sound under discussion always precedes a vowel sound.) It is the rapid widening of the lips which gives [w] its characters. An excellent [w] can be produced with little or no movement of the tongue.

Faults or Problems:

55. In childish speech [w and r] are frequently confused with each other. Review Exercise 51, if necessary.

56. If you are having a problem with the [w] phoneme, and this might be the case if English is not your native language, try this: Attack the [w] sound as though it were *oo* [u] in *moon* [mun]. Protrude and round the lips, and for practice purposes only, exaggerate the lip movements, and hold the sound for two or three seconds.

    Example: Say the word *way* as though it were spelled *oo-ay*, but emphasize and prolong the *oo*.

    Use this procedure as you read the following. As soon as you have an acceptable [w], repeat this material without the exaggerated *oo*.

    a.

wide	wing	will	wow
wake	want	weep	won
wart	once	work	waist
wine	waffle	wean	wood

    b. Was Willy weak as he watched the witness at the wedding?
    c. One should not waste water by washing waxed wire.
    d. Wanda winked at Wilbert because he wore a woolen, Western windbreaker.
    e. The wise widow added a wooden wing to the warehouse.
    f. "Well," said Wayne Wilson, "the wild woman tossed the whip through the window."

57. Individuals with a Germanic language background, and occasionally other foreign languages, often confuse [w] with [v or f]. It is actually easy to see the difference between the two. Note and compare the rounded lip position we use for [w] with the position for [v or f]: the lower lip is held lightly against the edges of the upper front teeth. For [w]: the lips must not touch the teeth. Watch yourself in a mirror as you say the following:

    a.

vail-wail	vary-wary	vest-west	fade-wade
veal-weal	vault-Walt	vine-wine	fin-win
vane-wane	veld-weld	vaunt-want	food-wooed
vet-wet	vent-went	vee-we	fell-well
viper-wiper	visor-wiser	vend-wend	fate-wait

   b.   Will Velma Weems give Wilbur West's vest to the vet?

   c.   Why did Violet weigh Warren Vernon and Vesta Watson?

   d.   Van weeps when vines and weeds are watered in winter.

   e.   Verna Winston whispered, "We must wander with Wendy toward Venice."

   f.   Was the valley of waves in the west visible from Waterloo Valley?

58. The *qu* spelling in such words as "quit, Quaker, queen" does not indicate the presence of the [w] phoneme, but the sound is present in every English word which begins with *qu*. Notice the phonetic spelling of these words:

     [kwɪt   'kwekɚ   kwin]

There is a tendency in careless speech to weaken the [w] sound in [kw] clusters. Be sure that the sound is firm as you practice the following. Do not forget to protrude and round the lips for [w]:

   a.

quad	quilt	quick
quaint	quart	quantity
quality	quite	quell
quarter	quest	quitter

   b.   The quintet played before the queen in Quebec.

   c.   He quivered as he quietly paid a quarter for the quilt.

   d.   I have no qualms about quickening our quest and quelling the quarantine.

   e.   The duck quaked and quacked as it fell into the quicksand.

   f.   Quakers will not quarrel and quibble while quizzed.

59. Chronic mumblers will generally produce weak and flabby [w] sounds. If the lips are allowed to hang like two pieces of inanimate liver, a clear [w] cannot be produced. Lip movement must be vigorous, rapid, and forceful. Read each of the following twice. The first time, exaggerate lip rounding and protruding, and prolong [w] sounds slightly. The second time, avoid exaggeration, but work for distinctness and sharpness of articulation.

   a.   The wind wiggled the wigwam as he watched for water in the wilds.

   b.   They wondered if the wagon had blown away to Wichita.

   c.   The wistful woman always wanted to waltz backward rather than forward.

   d.   Will Wordsworth, the weaver, waved to Woodrow Wilson.

   e.   After one quick swim at twelve o'clock, the quiet squire was quite queasy.

   f.   Sir Wilfred wouldn't walk to Walla Walla, Washington.

   g.   Walter Wallace wondered who would waste the well-flavored wines.

   h.   Warren watched the warriors on the Wyoming warpath.

   i.   The unwise widow wouldn't wed Wilbur Wells.

   j.   We were awakened when the wind blew the willow into the windmill.

   k.   A boy's will is the wind's will.

   l.   The wasp wiggled up the wide, wet wall.

   m.   The wilted watermelon was washed with warm water.

   n.   The waif waddled toward the warped wall in Walden.

   o.   Whatever is worth doing at all, is worth doing well.

   p.   The quarrelsome choir was persuaded to switch plans quickly.

   q.   Queen Wendy was unaware that it would be awkward to quit in Wessex.

   r.   You never miss water till the well runs dry.

   s.   Those who work much do not work hard.

   t.   Those who are wise have no wide range of learning; those who range most widely are not wise.

   u.   There is no need to worry, because the only thing to worry about is whether you are rich or poor. If you are rich, there is nothing to worry about. If you are poor, all there is to worry about is whether you are sick or well. If you are well, there is nothing to worry about. If you are sick all you have to worry about is if you are going to get well or die. If you get well, there is no need to worry. If you die, all you have to worry about is if you go to heaven or hell. If you go to heaven, there is nothing to worry about. If you go to hell, you will be so busy shaking hands with your friends that you won't have time to worry.

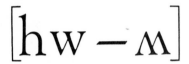

<u>Place of
Articulation</u>:   lips.

<u>Classification</u>:   an [h] approach to [w]; a fricative-glide.

<u>Example</u>:   <u>Why</u> did the <u>white</u> <u>whale</u> <u>whirl</u> around <u>when</u> fed <u>whitefish</u>?

<u>Typical Production</u>:
The lips assume the rounded position for [w], but the initial part of the following gliding movement is accompanied by the voiceless [h].

<u>Faults or Problems</u>:

60.   In Old English, most of our present-day words beginning with *wh* were spelled with the two letters reversed: *hw*. Thus, *where* was spelled *hwaer* and *why* was spelled *hwi*. If this seems quaint, it is perhaps a more accurate indication of pronunciation than the current *wh* spelling.

The point is this: if you choose to sound [h] in words beginning with *wh* combinations, you will have to sound it before, not after, the [w]. However, the necessity of using the [h] is largely a matter of choice. Some textbooks insist that the [h] in such words as *where, while, when, whim* [hwɛr, hwaɪl, hwɛn, hwɪm] be sounded.

"How else," they inquire, "can we tell the difference between *wear* [wɛr] and *where* [hwɛr], or between *wet* [wɛt] and *whet* [hwɛt]?"

The answer: We can generally tell one from the other by considering them in context. We have little trouble distinguishing between them in such sentences as:

"What will you <u>wear</u>?"	and	"<u>Where</u> are you going?"
"<u>Which</u> one is his?"	and	"He thought he saw a <u>witch</u>."
"She likes red <u>wine</u>."	and	"Did the dog <u>whine</u>?"

Should we pronounce the [h] under consideration in careful, precise speech? In rapid conversational speech probably a majority of us do not articulate the [h] in *wh* combinations. Yet, one occasionally hears speakers, readers, and actors who are concerned with finesse and precision in their articulation who do use it. The immediate impulse, therefore, might be to insist that [h] not be omitted. Nevertheless, if we listen carefully to good speakers and well-trained voices—and radio and TV have many fine examples—we might inevitably come to the conclusion that the [h] in [hw] combinations is disappearing from pronunciation rather rapidly. Perhaps, then, the only reasonable conclusion to be presented is this: it is neither incorrect to use it nor is it incorrect to drop it. Use it if you will. For those who will:

Differentiate between the *wh* combinations and the single *w* in the following:

a.

whether-weather	where-wear	whet-wet
wheel-weal	whale-wail	whir-were
when-wen	what-watt	whey-way
whine-wine	whish-wish	why-y
whit-wit	whin-win	whig-wig
whirled-world	whoa-woe	while-wile

b. Why does Mr. Wye whack the wax?

c. Where did the white wight wear the wispy whiskers?

d. Which witch whined when the wine was spilled on the wheel?

e. "I don't care a whit for your wit or whims," said Will White.

f. Do not whimper if you do not win the whippet.

g. The wire wheel whirled somewhere around the wheat field.

h. Just because a person is listed in "Who's Who" doesn't mean he always knows "What's What."

Place of
Articulation: front of tongue-hard palate.

Classification: voiced.

Example: Yank York, the valiant young champion, sailed the yellow yacht which was loaded with bullion.

Typical Production:

Raise the front of the tongue toward the front of the hard palate. The position is quite similar to the one used for the vowel sounds in *fee* [fi]. The lips may be slightly parted and retracted as the sound is begun. The tongue shifts rapidly into the position for whatever vowel follows.

Faults or Problems:

61. By itself [j] presents no special difficulties. We have noted previously that some foreigners, commonly those with Scandinavian backgrounds, confuse [j] with [dʒ]. In all four Scandinavian languages, the "j" spelling is used to represent [j]. Thus, a Norwegian may say "yoke" [jok] for "joke" [dʒok]; "Yune" [jun] for "June" [dʒun]. It will help to remember that for [j] the front part of the tongue is raised high toward, but not in actual contact with, the hard palate. For [dʒ] the tip of the tongue is pressed rather firmly against the gum ridge and then moves downward rapidly. (See also Exercise 41.)

a.

yak-Jack	year-jeer	yap-Jap	yet-jet
yoke-joke	yaws-jaws	yip-gyp	yard-jarred
yam-jam	yell-jell	yowl-jowl	yea-jay

b. Joe dropped the yo-yo into the yam-flavored jam.

c. She will yell if the youth drops the yolk on the jacket.

d. Jack yawns whenever Jane yearns for Jerry.

e. Yesterday, Yorick the Jester said that the jet from Yale had not yet arrived.

f. He did not care a jot if the yellow jewels fell off Jock's yacht.

g. Jay, the talking yardbird, learned to say "yea" and puff its jowls.

62. What differences in pronunciation do you note between the vowel sounds in each of the following pairs of words?

food-feud
boot-butte
who-hue
ooze-use

You can hear *oo* [u] in all of the words. But in the words in the right-hand column you hear an extra sound inserted just before the [u], this, of course, being [j] or a sound closely resembling it. Together [j and u] form a combination sound which is pronounced exactly like the common pronoun: *you.* At the risk of being extremely obvious, we will list again the words in the right-hand column along with the equivalent nonphonetic spelling:

feud—f-you-d   butte—b-you-t

hue—h-you   use—you-z

When do we use [u] and when do we use [ju]? As a rule when the spelling of a word uses "o," such as in "boot, loot, food, mood," do not use [ju]. Also the simple vowel [u] when preceded by [s], [z], [l], or [θ] is generally used.

[ju] is used after [p, b, k, g, f, v, m]. Should one memorize these consonants? It isn't necessary. Nine times out of ten your familiarity with the word in question will guide your pronunciation. Examples:

pure	butte	cubic
ague	fuse	review
mute	beauty	cure
argue	fume	view

When [u] follows other consonants, however, there is almost as much inconsistency as there is controversy about preference. The person who declares that "It is the duty [d-you-ty] of each student [st-you-dent] to read the newspaper [n-youz-paper] on Tuesday [t-youz-day]" is, it seems to us, working rather hard to achieve precision and finesse. Of course, if one's education or environment dictates the use of [ju] in such words, there is probably nothing wrong with doing so. The conclusion that can be made about [ju], when its use is optional, is probably the same conclusion we have reached about the *h* in certain *wh* combinations. It seems to be disappearing.

In the following, when [ju] is required, pronounce it accordingly. When it is not required, let your own personal sincerity be your guide.

a. The new steward placed the beautiful bureau in front of the music stand.

b. In the future he will resume singing the cute tune with enthusiasm.

c. As a rule, June roses are covered with dew.

d. The puny student was aroused to fury when the icecube was dropped on the new uniform.

e. He knew that it was his duty to cut coupons out of the duke's newspaper.

f. Is it stupid to muse and view the future of curfews with amusement?

g. The union said that the barbecue was useless and confusing.

h. The pure air in the large fuel tube was humid.

i. Were the unique lute and tuba part of the loot?

j. He brewed the blue mixture and then blew out the fire in the flue.

63. The following material contains all of the glides in a variety of positions and sound combinations. Practice for clear and accurate articulation of sounds, but avoid exaggeration.

    a. Youth is a wonderful thing. What a crime to waste it on children.

    b. A puritan is a person who pours righteous indignation into the wrong things.

    c. He who will not reason is a bigot; he who cannot is a fool; he who dares not is a slave.

    d. The battle of Waterloo was won on the playing fields of Eton.

    e. Winter lingered so long in the lap of spring that it occasioned a great deal of talk.

    f. Wonder is the feeling of a philosopher, and philosophy begins in wonder.

    g. Wrinkles should merely indicate where smiles have been.

    h. Your old men shall dream dreams; your young men shall see visions.

    i. At the Day of Judgment we shall not be asked what we have read but what we have done.

    j. A university should be a place of light, of liberty, and of learning.

    k. We worry as though we had a thousand years to live.

    l. The most lost day of all is the day on which we do not laugh.

    m. To the being fully alive, the future surrounds the present like a halo.

    n. "Into every life a little rain must fall," Noah told his family.

    o. The true laws of God are the laws of our own well-being.

    p. People would rather help those who don't need help than those who do.

    q. All good maxims are in the world. We only need to apply them.

    r. If wise men were hairs, the world would need a wig.

    s. Life would not be worth living if we didn't keep our enemies.

    t. What you long for in youth, you get aplenty in old age.

    u. The word yes brings trouble; the word no leads to no evil.

    v. A quorum means enough people are there to start a quarrel.

    w. Girls we love for what they are; young men for what they promise to be.

    x. We often read with as much talent as we write.

    y. If you bow at all, bow low.

    z. When I was young, I pitied the old. Now old, it is the young I pity.

    aa. Lord! I wonder what fool it was that first invented kissing.

    bb. A fairy tale is a horror story to prepare children for the newspapers.

    cc. It is only the people with push who have pull.

    dd. If men are so wicked with religion, what would they be without it?

    ee. There is no such thing as a moral or an immoral book. Books are well written or badly written. That is all.

    ff. Brotherhood is not just a Bible word. Out of comradeship can come and will come the happy life for all. The underdog can and will lick his weight in the wildcats of the world.

Assignment 16 (See suggested Checklist for this assignment)

Prepare material which contains all of the glides and in various positions. (Remember that [w and j] do not occur as glides in final positions.) Be certain that there is an abundance of those glides which you may have found troublesome. [l and r], you will recall, are two of the trickiest sounds in the English language. [w] is a relatively easy sound for most people, but if you have been criticized for having flabby articulation, it would be a particularly good sound for you to emphasize in this assignment. Work for glide sounds which are accurate, natural, and not unnecessarily noticeable.

Suggested Checklist for Assignment 16

As you practice by yourself you may want to work with this checklist. Listen carefully to yourself. If it is feasible record the assignment or get a classmate or friend to listen to you as you read the material. Eventually your goal will be to have a check mark in the Yes column for each category. (Optional: Perhaps your instructor will want to use the checklist to evaluate you during your classroom presentation.)

	Yes	No
Articulates glides which are accurate, natural, and not unduly conspicuous.		
Avoids substituting [l] for [r].		
Avoids substituting [l] for [w].		
Avoids inserting the schwa [ə] before [l].		
Avoids omitting or distorting [l].		
Avoids harsh, overprominent [r].		
Avoids intrusive [r].		
Avoids trilled production of [r].		
Avoids weakening or distorting [r] in clusters: [br dr fr gr kr pr thr tr].		
Avoids substituting [r or l] for [j].		
Avoids inserting the schwa [ə] before [r].		
Produces sharp, clear, and distinct [w] sounds.		
Avoids weakening [w] in [kw] clusters.		
Avoids substituting [w or j] for [l].		
Avoids substituting [w] for [r].		
Avoids substituting [v or f] for [w].		
Avoids confusing [j] with [dʒ].		
Avoids intrusive [j].		
Avoids substituting [j] for [l].		
Avoids substituting [u] for [ju].		

Additional comments or suggestions:

Nasals

[m, n, and ŋ] *are described as nasals because the sounds are directed primarily through the nasal passages rather than the oral cavity. All other sounds in American English, however, are resonated and articulated largely in the oral cavity. In the production of the nasals, the oral cavity must be blocked at some point, the velum (soft palate) must be relaxed and lowered and the vocalized breath stream must be diverted through the nasal cavities.*

As a simple illustration of a basic difference in the production of nonnasal sounds and nasal sounds, try this:

Sustain the vowel [ɑ] as in c<u>a</u>lm for a few seconds and then pinch both of your nostrils quite firmly. You will note that you can continue [ɑ] as long as you wish, even with the nasal passages blocked off.

Now, prolong [m] as in the word <u>hum</u> for a few seconds and then pinch both of your nostrils. You will not be able to make the sound, once the nasal passages are stopped.

The three nasals are not extremely difficult sounds, and as you work on them, you will discover that the manner in which they are articulated resembles the articulation of three of the plosives. Except for the position of the velum which must be lowered for the nasals—

[m] in its production is similar to [b]

[n] in its production is similar to [d]

[ŋ] in its production is similar to [g]

[m]

<u>Place of</u>
<u>Articulation</u>:   lips.

<u>Classification</u>:   voiced.

<u>Example</u>:   <u>M</u>any ta<u>m</u>e la<u>m</u>bs ca<u>m</u>e ho<u>m</u>e when <u>Em</u>ma s<u>m</u>iled at the<u>m</u>.

<u>Typical Production</u>:
Close the lips firmly as if you were going to make a [b] sound. The lower teeth should be close to the upper. The tongue is generally relaxed on the floor of the mouth, although its position may vary somewhat, depending on the sound which follows the [m]. The vocal tone is emitted through the nasal passages.

<u>Faults or Problems</u>:

64. [m] is by no means as troublesome as [r], the most fickle sound in the language. Now and then, however, and especially in careless and hurried speech, the [m] may lose its identity or disappear. This happens most commonly when [m] is followed by another consonant.

Result: *lamp* [læmp] may sound something like *lap* [læp]
    humble [ˈhʌmbl̩] may sound something like *hu′bl̩* [hʌbl̩]

If the consonant following [m] is one of those which is made with the tip of the tongue against the teeth or gum ridge—[t, d, θ, l, n]—the [m] sound may lose its identity, and a sound which closely resembles [n] may be substituted.

Result: *I'm taller* may be distorted to *I'n taller*
    warmed may be distorted to *warned*
    same thing may be distorted to *sane thing*
    Hamlet may be distorted to *Hanlet*
    amnesty may be distorted to *anesty*

Most of these distortions can be avoided if you are careful to make a firm and complete closure of the lips as you articulate the [m] sound in the following:

a.
seemly	doomlike	hymnal
sometime	rammed	same theory
I'm trying	gemlike	climbed
simple	lumber	clamp
umbrella	aimless	employ
whimper	something	trimmed
champ	company	I'm tired

b.   I'm leaving the number of the lumber company with Mr. Compton.
c.   They seemed to have aimed the empty pumpkin at the blimp.
d.   Some think that I'm taking some things for granted.
e.   Romney grumbled about the rumlike drink and the clam dip.
f.   Jim took a look at the emblem on the hymnal and exclaimed, "I'm through with this composing."
g.   He tramped through the campus for a glimpse of the amber umbrella.
h.   Mr. Hamner was covered with lumps and bumps when the timber fell on him.
i.   Tim knew that Miss Wimple had a pompous personality.

> *j.* The amnesty gave the doomed enemy camps little comfort.
>
> *k.* Sam tried to hide the time bomb among the elm trees.

65. Other troublesome [m] clusters:

    If [m] occurs at the end of a syllable or word and is followed by certain consonants at the beginning of the next syllable or word, a murky or distorted [m] sometimes results. Here are some of the awkward clusters:

[m-f]:	brimful	[m-v]:	Amvet
[m-k]:	tomcat	[m-g]:	dream girl
[m-s]:	crimson	[m-w]:	homework

    Again, as you practice the following, make sure that the lips meet with a firm contact as you make the [m] sound.

    a. Tom felt that Pam Frank wasn't comfortable in the roomful of people.

    b. I'm cutting comb caps and drum covers.

    c. Is Jim Samson homesick for the clumsy seamstress?

    d. The team veered toward the lame vet.

    e. Some good ham gravy would make Lem very happy.

    f. Sam Wilmer wanted someone to do his homework.

66. If the nasal passage is congested as the result of a cold, by enlarged adenoids, or other growths, the [m] is apt to sound more like a [b]. The cold is temporary, of course, but individuals with adenoids who wait until adulthood to have them removed may still produce a muffled [m]. In such cases voice retraining is generally necessary. To produce a good [m], the individual should try to gain conscious control of the velum and should keep the lips closed as the sound is being produced. Differentiate carefully between [b and m] in the following:

    a.

boast-most	be-me	boor-Moor
bore-more	bill-mill	rib-rim
bike-Mike	bound-mound	cub-come
bop-mop	bare-mare	bock-mock
bad-mad	bent-meant	sub-sum

    b. The men watched Ben back the Mack truck into the marble quarry.

    c. Bess dropped the mess and the mash into the boat.

    d. Mark barked a command when Bob led the mob by the moat.

    e. If you give me the bees, I'll give money to Benny.

    f. Berle and Merle felt mellow as Bert gave the pin to Ben Mennon.

    g. The Barton, Morton, Meyer, and Beyer Corporation hired Bim to run the mart.

    h. Mary and Barry paid the bill to Mr. Miller before eating the meat and beets.

67. Singers in the small "pop" ensembles as well as those in glee clubs and other choral groups have often been partial to [m] as well as other nasals. When the sound occurs at the end of a word, phrase, or line, it can easily be prolonged. It goes without saying that it is also the sound most frequently used in humming. Obviously in conversational or even more formal speech, prolonged [m] sounds would be ridiculously theatrical, but on the other hand, speakers often tend to cut the sound extremely short. It is basically a rather pleasant sound, and to give it at least its full value is to enrich the sound of our speech. Read each of the following sentences twice. The first time exaggerate the [m] sounds slightly. Prolong the sound for two or three seconds. On your second reading avoid obvious exaggeration, but be sure that the sound is not neglected. Don't forget: The lips must be tightly closed as you articulate [m].

    a. Mickey dumped lemon blossoms on the moving ramp.

    b. The comely miss swam from Tampa to Miami Beach last summer.

    c. An American thinks he is moral only when he is uncomfortable.

d. Imagination is as good as many voyages—and how much cheaper.
e. Every man is a volume, if you know how to read him.
f. Spank: To impress upon the mind from the bottom up.
g. Every tooth in a man's head is more valuable than a diamond.
h. Man should go out of the world as he came in—chiefly on milk.
i. It is maintained that married men live longer than single men.
j. The perfect man uses his mind like a mirror.
k. If you are a master, be sometimes blind. If a servant, sometimes deaf.
l. God said: "Let us make man in our image"; and Man said: "Let us make God in our image."
m. Every man is a fool for at least five minutes every day; wisdom consists in not exceeding the limit.
n. My prayer to God is a very short one: "O Lord, make my enemies most ridiculous!" God has granted it.

Place of
Articulation: tongue tip, upper gum ridge.

Classification: voiced.

Example: <u>N</u>ewto<u>n</u> was <u>kn</u>ighted by Quee<u>n</u> A<u>nn</u>e a<u>nd</u> prese<u>nt</u>ed with a golde<u>n</u> <u>n</u>iform.

Typical Production:

The tongue is raised and the tip should be placed against the upper gum ridge. The sides of the tongue may touch the inner edges of the teeth. The lower jaw is slightly depressed. The lips and teeth are generally parted. The articulatory positions are similar to those for [t or d]. The nasal port is open, of course, which permits a continuous flow of vocalized sound to pass through the nose.

Faults or Problems:

68. Like [m], [n] may lose its identity or disappear before another consonant. What happens in such cases is that the articulatory position for [n] is apt to be the position for the sound which follows instead of for the [n] itself.

    Awkward [n] Clusters:
    [n-k, n-p, n-s, n-sh]: In these combinations, the sound is mangled and the resulting sound may be close to *ng* [ŋ] as in sing.
    Result: For words such as co<u>nc</u>rete, u<u>ng</u>lue, co<u>ns</u>ist, <u>ins</u>ure we get:

               cong-crete, ung-glue, cong-sist, ing-sure

    [n-b, n-p, n-f, n-v, n-m]: In these combinations, the [n] is transformed to a sound which resembles [m].

Result: *inbred* becomes *imbred*   *unpressed* becomes *umpressed*
           infantry becomes *imfantry*   *invalid* becomes *imvalid*
           inmate becomes *immate*   *government* becomes *govermment*
           earn more becomes *earmore*   *can meet* becomes *cameet*

[n] is a tongue tip-upper gum ridge sound. This means that the tongue is to be placed against the upper gum ridge. Bear this in mind as you articulate [n] in the following:

a.

stand	tenth	lunch	knit
happen	Sunday	ninety	knave
concoct	ungainly	consider	taint
tension	unbound	unpeg	nude
infer	invade	unmask	unpin

b. The bonfire consumed the ungainly, unpleasant fence.
c. Norton Knapp was inclined to invent sinful tales about his income.
d. It is unbelievable that the knife and the knob are unbent and unbroken.
e. The colonel insisted that he would inspect the run-down mansion once more.
f. The unmanly inmate was unsure of himself when confined in the unclean compound.
g. The ungodly noise almost unbalanced Norman's mind.
h. The unguarded insect with ninety-nine legs uncoiled and fell into the canyon.
i. It is unfair to insist that the infantry captain unpin the unfit gunner's uniform.
j. I can make more money because I learn more.
k. The Yankee infielder unpacked his man-made overnight case when he heard about the pennies.

69. [n], too, may be distorted or muffled by a cold or adenoids, and a sound approximating [d] may be substituted. If the adenoids are removed and voice training is indicated, the following material may be of help. Again, the individual should be certain that the velum is lowered for the nasal sound, but raised for the plosive.

a.

dew-new	down-noun	dud-done
dough-know	dip-nip	id-in
deed-need	dock-knock	Ted-ten
dice-nice	day-nay	Dan-Nan

b. At nine we will dine on the deck near Deer Neck Lodge.
c. When Dora saw Nora wed Ben, she knew that Dewey had won his bet.
d. Nell Dell and Nancy Dan knew that there was dew on the damp net.
e. He soon sued Lanny and Hatty for knocking down the dock.
f. When Dee fell on her knees, she cracked her neck on the deck.
g. Dale dipped the nails into the padded pan.
h. Donna and Lonny gnawed the beans and the beads.

70. Like its cousin [m], [n] is often neglected in final positions by being cut extremely short. It is also an agreeable sound, and its presence further enriches the sound of our speech. As you practice these, avoid extremes, but try to give [n] its maximum rather than its minimum value:

a. A portion of the fine Rhine wine had turned brown.
b. John and Jan put the lemon-covered chicken in the broken oven.
c. A dozen keen-eyed diners detected one rotten pumpkin in the gardener's pan.
d. Does the well-trained hound, Rin-Tin-Tin, know how to stay nimble?
e. In June the rain falls in vain on the plains of Spain.
f. The green and tan train broke down at ten and then again at eleven.
g. Nan and Dan had fun soaking the raisins in the champagne.
h. For the lonely one even noise is a comfort.
i. Nothing matters to a man who says nothing matters.

j. When the need is highest, God is nighest.

k. Two pieces of coin in a bag make more noise than a hundred.

l. We read a good novel not in order to know more people, but in order to know fewer.

m. The newspapers are full of what we would like to happen to us and what we hope will never happen to us.

n. Have as many enemies in front of you as you can tackle, but never leave one behind you if you can help it.

o. The fence around a cemetery is foolish, for those inside can't come out and those outside don't want to get in.

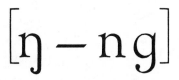

Place of
Articulation: back of the tongue, soft palate.

Classification: voiced.

Example: U<u>n</u>cle Bi<u>ng</u> sa<u>ng</u> the dri<u>n</u>ki<u>ng</u> song on the ba<u>n</u>k of the Li<u>n</u>coln river.

Typical Production:

Raise the rear portion of the tongue so that it makes contact with the lowered soft palate. The vocalized breath stream is directed through the nose. Openness of mouth and the position of the lips depend upon the sounds that precede or follow [ŋ]. The position of the tongue for this nasal sound is quite similar to that used for [k and g].

Faults or Problems:

71. If the nasal passageway is blocked, a type of [g] sound may be substituted for [ŋ]. If the obstruction is of such a nature that it may be removed, the substitution may still persist. Try the material below, raising the back of the tongue against the lowered velum for [ŋ], but keeping the velum raised for [g]:

a.

tag-tang	bog-bong	big-bing
rag-rang	hug-hung	fag-fang
wig-wing	sprig-spring	lag-Lang
log-long	gog-gong	pig-ping
lug-lung	sag-sang	rug-rung

b. After he had wrung out the rag rug, he ran to the register and rang up the sale.

c. As a gag the gang played tag in the tang of the sea air.

d. The old hag tried to hang the wig on the swing.

e. Mr. Bing is too big to stay lost behind the log for very long.

f. Did the brig or the tug bring the cargo of beef tongue?

g. "Kid" King found the toy pink pig in the jug near the junk.

h. She banged the old cloth bag against the rag as she rang the bell.

72. Like [m and n], [ŋ] may weaken and virtually disappear in a medial or final position. Sound [ŋ] firmly as you read the following, but do not emphasize it excessively:

   a. Did the king swing the gong around the long trunk?
   b. Mr. Ringling sang a song about Wild Fang, the amazing dog from Bingham.
   c. Baked beef tongue dressing is appetizing when served in a chafing dish.
   d. The strength of King Kong amazed the shouting gang.
   e. He flung the wrong thing through the throng.
   f. Mr. Young said, "It is wrong to use slang in songs."
   g. The ringleader decided to hang the tongs with strong string.
   h. The gang from the Bronx sprang toward the boxing ring.

73. The individual who says:

   "As I was standin' on the corner, I saw the mob comin' down the street shoutin' and jumpin'."

is guilty of a very common fault. Substituting [n] as in sin for final [ŋ] as in sing will not always make our speech unintelligible, but it will label our speech behavior as careless.

Educated and cultured people may pronounce *Tuesday* as *tooz-day* ['tuzdɪ] instead of *t-youz-day* ['tjuzdɪ]. And they may pronounce *when* as *wen* [wɛn] instead of *hwen* [hwɛn]. Very few intelligent listeners will criticize unfavorably. But those who insist on saying: *comin', goin', thinkin', studyin', datin', sleepin'* will generally attract the wrong kind of attention to their speech, not to mention unfavorable criticism. College graduate job-seekers, otherwise well qualified, have been rejected in interviews because their speech was marred by this particular mannerism.

This fault is often described as "dropping the g"—an inaccurate description, of course, because there is no g in [ŋ].

If you will articulate slowly [n-ŋ-n-ŋ-n-ŋ] you will notice a basic difference in tongue position between the two sounds. The [n] is formed with the front part, the tip, or the point of the tongue. [ŋ] is formed with the back of the tongue. Remember this distinction as you practice the following:

a.

sin-sing	lawn-long	gun-gung	tan-tang
run-rung	hun-hung	gone-gong	ton-tongue
sun-sung	thin-thing	pin-ping	win-wing
ban-bang	bin-bing	pan-pang	ran-rang
Ron-wrong	fan-fang	kin-king	bun-bung

Read the following nonsense material very slowly, concentrating on the difference between the articulation of [n and ŋ]. Get the feel of [n] as a tip-of-the-tongue sound, and of [ŋ] as a back-of-the-tongue sound. (Note: Read across the columns, from left to right.)

b.

fan	fang	fan-in	fang-in	fang-ing
sin	sing	sin-in	sing-in	sing-ing
ban	bang	ban-in	bang-in	bang-ing
gon	gong	gon-in	gong-in	gong-ing
lin	ling	lin-in	ling-in	ling-ing
wen	weng	wen-in	weng-in	weng-ing
pan	pang	pan-in	pang-in	pang-ing
lon	long	lon-in	long-in	long-ing
chin	ching	chin-in	ching-in	ching-ing
shun	shung	shun-in	shung-in	shung-ing

The person who insists on saying *wearin'* for *wearing* would have no problem at all if he were asked to pronounce only the last four letters of the word. He would certainly say *ring* rather than *rin*.

Exaggerate as you practice the following. The words are divided in a purely mechanical fashion. Wherever you see a double diagonal line, pause for a second or two, eliminating any kind of vocal sound.

c. ring / / ring / / ring / / ring:

fear / / ring, soar / / ring, hear / / ring
bar / / ring, sour / / ring, pour / / ring
mar / / ring, stir / / ring, star / / ring

d. Now, eliminating the pause that divides the word, connect the two syllables and say them rather rapidly. Are you able to make a firm [ŋ] at the end of each word?

fearing,	soaring,	hearing
barring,	souring,	pouring
marring,	stirring,	starring

e. Repeat the procedure suggested for Exercise c as you practice these:

king / / king / / king / / king:

kick / / king, talk / / king, hook / / king
speak / / king, pick / / king, back / / king
knock / / king, work / / king, stock / / king

f. Repeat the procedure suggested for Exercise d eliminating the pause in each word.

kicking,	talking,	hooking
speaking,	picking,	backing
knocking,	working,	stocking

g. with pauses:

sing / / sing / / sing / / sing:

kiss / / sing, pass / / sing, fuss / / sing
toss / / sing, dress / / sing, cross / / sing
sass / / sing, toss / / sing, bless / / sing

h. no pauses:

kissing,	passing,	fussing
tossing,	dressing,	crossing
sassing,	tossing,	blessing

74. [ŋ] occurs only in medial and final positions. As you practice the following, make certain that you are not substituting [n for ŋ]:

a. Peter Pan pinned the swinging gong on the laughing king.
b. Is going to a songfest the same thing as going to a surfing party?
c. Arriving in Washington, the blustering senator faced the jeering, shouting mob.
d. The snickering and giggling twins were last seen going toward the skating rink.
e. Boxing, wrestling, and swimming are more fun than pitching a baseball.
f. Flinging the swinging bell to the ground, the groaning man saw us leaving.
g. The banging, clanging motor was annoying the perspiring man who was standing there wringing his glowing hands.
h. Some people spend the day in complaining of a headache, and the night in drinking the wine that gives it.
i. Worth seeing? Yes, but not worth going to see.
j. When a woman is speaking to you, you should be listening to what she is saying with her eyes.
k. I'm living so far beyond my income that we may almost be said to be living apart.
l. The art of writing is the art of applying the seat of the pants to the seat of the chair.
m. Some folks get what's coming to them by waiting, others while crossing the street.
n. Whenever a man's friends begin complimenting him about looking young, he may be sure that what they are really thinking about is that he is growing old.

o.   It was as helpful as throwing a drowning man both ends of a rope.

p.   Everything is not known, but everything is said.

q.   The waking have one common world, but the sleeping turn aside each into a world of his own.

r.   In teaching, the greatest sin is to be boring.

s.   Many a man is saved from being a thief by finding everything locked up.

t.   Taking something from a man and making it worse is plagiarism.

u.   When children are doing nothing, they are doing mischief.

v.   There are more ways of killing a cat than choking her with cream.

w.   In much of your talking, thinking is half murdered.

x.   Gardens are not made by singing "Oh, how beautiful," and sitting in the shade.

y.   Retreating and beating and meeting and sheeting,
Delaying and straying and playing and spraying,
Advancing and prancing and glancing and dancing,
Recoiling, turmoiling, toiling, and boiling,
And gleaming and steaming and streaming and beaming,
And rushing and flushing and brushing and gushing,
And flapping and rapping and clapping and slapping,
And curling and whirling and purling and twirling,
And thumping and plumping and bumping and jumping;
And dashing and flashing and splashing and clashing;
And is never ending, but always descending,
All at once and all o'er, with a mighty uproar,
And this way the water comes down at Lodore.   [Southey]

75. If you say *stinger* and *linger* you will note that the *ng* is not pronounced the same in both words. *Stinger* is pronounced *sting-er* [ˈstɪŋɚ]. The [ŋ] is simply the nasal sound we are presently considering. There is no plosive *hard g* [g] in the word.

Linger, however, is pronounced *ling-ger* [ˈlɪŋgɚ]. Here, the *ng* represents a combination of the nasal [ŋ] and the plosive [g].

No wonder, then, that we occasionally have trouble with *ng*. Once again we might note that English spelling is of very little help. To add to the confusion, in certain foreign languages and dialects [ŋ] is almost invariably followed by a [g or k]. Thus, individuals whose language background includes Yiddish, Slavic, Spanish, Hungarian, or Italian, even though the speaker may be native born, are often prone to add the so-called *ng-click*. Characteristically, *sing* then becomes *sing-g* or *sing-k* [sɪŋg-sɪŋk] and *hang* becomes *hang-g* or *hang-k* [hæg-hæk].

How can the *hard g* be eliminated? Your sense of hearing and feeling will help. You will remember that the back of the tongue is raised against the velum or soft palate to make *ng* [ŋ]. If you will say *sing* [sɪŋ] you will be able to feel the contact.

Say *sing* again, but this time, listen quite carefully to the nasal sound, prolong it slightly, and as you are prolonging the [ŋ], pull your tongue away from the velum. If this is done, you will not add the *hard g*.

Read the following with exaggerated slowness, always prolonging the *ng* [ŋ]. Pull the tongue away from the velum during the production of the nasal rather than after, and you will probably be able to eliminate the *after-click*.

thing	sing	ring
bang	long	bong
wrong	rang	clang
lung	wing	young
spring	gong	rung
going	hang	king
pang	sung	tong

The following nonsense material will help you distinguish between the *ng* [ŋ] we use in "sing, ring, thing" and the *ng-g* [ŋ-g] which has the *hard g* tacked onto it.

As you read Column 1, deliberately add the *hard g* (and this is the *g* which you use in a word like <u>g</u>a<u>g</u>) to the previous *ing* syllable.

As you read Column 2, eliminate the *hard g*.

In Column 3, deliberately add the *g* as indicated, and in Column 4, drop it. Pause briefly at the double diagonal lines.

b.

1. add [g]	2. drop [g]	3. add [g]	4. drop [g]
ting / / g	ting	ting / / ging / / g	ting / / ing
ling / / g	ling	ling / / ging / / g	ling / / ing
ming / / g	ming	ming / / ging / / g	ming / / ing
shing / / g	shing	shing / / ging / / g	shing / / ing
ving / / g	ving	ving / / ging / / g	ving / / ing
king / / g	king	king / / ging / / g	king / / ing
zing / / g	zing	zing / / ging / / g	zing / / ing
ning / / g	ning	ning / / ging / / g	ning / / ing

c.   If a word ends in the spelling *ng* or *ngue* the sound is always [ŋ]:

strong	sighing	harangue	gang
tongue	bring	fang	zing
feeding	meringue	ping-pong	wing
sang	slung	boating	going

d.   If a suffix (-ing, -er, -ly, -ish) is added to a word ending in *ng* the *ng* is, with a few exceptions, almost always pronounced as [ŋ]:

thronging	stinger	tongues	longish
ringer	springish	haranguing	Washington
kingly	cliff-hanger	singer	Springfield
longish	swinger	youngster	youngish

Exceptions to the rule include the comparative and superlative forms of a few adjectives:

long	longer	longest
young	younger	youngest
strong	stronger	strongest

[ŋ g] is also used in "elongate, elongation, and prolongation."

e. If the spelling *ng* occurs within the root or stem of a word, it is generally pronounced as [ŋg]:

linger	single	mingle	anguish
fungus	anger	kangaroo	tangle
hunger	extinguish	angle	language
jingle	jungle	angry	distinguish
finger	English	bungle	tingle

(A few exceptions: "gingham, Bingham, Washington, hangar, strength, length, clangor.")

f. *nge* in the final position may represent the sounds [ndʒ]:

singe	strange	fringe	orange
change	lunge	mange	range
plunge	lounge	avenge	sponge

g. If [n] is followed in the same syllable by *c*, *k*, or *x* the pronunciation will be *ng-k* [ŋk]:

zinc	thank	think	larynx
bank	distinct	sphinx	dank
anxious	uncle	mink	Bronx
instinct	crank	tincture	clink

76. As we have seen [ŋ] appears in combinations which are often troublesome. Even experienced speakers, if they attempt to let English spelling indicate correct pronunciation, will frequently "slip" on certain rather common words containing the [ŋ] sound. All the rules and the annoying exceptions stated in Exercise 75 will do you no good unless you can put them into practice.

The following material contains all of the [ŋ] combinations previously discussed. Be cautious as you practice them, and if you are in doubt, you may wish to consult a dictionary.

a. "Thanks," said Hank, "for mingling with the monkies and kangaroos."
b. The angry young singer from Birmingham lingered too long in the bank.
c. During the wedding the gangly bride was clinging to the spangled ring.
d. The hungry youngster with the longest arm won the meringue pie.
e. You may put your longest finger on the pink sponge.
f. The youngish Miss Kingston sang the strange Song of Songs in a Long Island lounge.
g. The strongest youngster from Bingham was mangled in the zinc wringer.
h. Ed Long, the anxious gangster from Washington, lingered near his hangout.
i. Did the Singapore strong man tangle with the single kangaroo?
j. Was it fun training the singing monk to be a bell ringer?
k. He was flinging the coin into the bubbling fountain when the gong rang.
l. The humming singer was running his fingers through the long wings of the penguin.
m. The strange sound of the Mongolian language gave Uncle Hank a sinking feeling.

Practice Material for the Nasals

77. The following drill material is saturated with the three nasals. Do not permit the sounds to weaken, and strive for accuracy.

[m]: you will remember, requires the lips to be firmly closed.
[n]: the tip of the tongue is placed against the upper gum ridge.
[ŋ]: the rear of the tongue makes contact with the velum.

a. At feeding time, the meowing lynx clung to the swing.
b. Certain English singers with long hair have angered anxious throngs.
c. She felt a tingle in her finger as she touched the gingham fringe.
d. The sighing tinker hung the shingle on the hangar.
e. The worst tempered people I've ever met were people who knew they were wrong.

f. There are many paths to the top of the mountain, but the view is always the same.

g. To most people nothing is more troublesome than the effort of thinking.

h. Commonly, physicians, like beer, are best when they are old, and lawyers, like bread, when they are young and new.

i. If a mosquito bites you on one hand, give him the other—palm downward.

j. Yankee: In Europe, an American. In the northern states of our Union, a New Englander. In the southern states, the word is unknown.

k. If you drive with one arm, you end up either walking up a church aisle or being carried up it.

l. Oysters must not be eaten in those months which, in pronouncing, want the letter R.

m. There may come a time when the lion and the lamb will lie down together, but I am still betting on the lion.

n. Ulysses: A man whose adventures should have been a warning to wandering husbands.

o. Those who bring sunshine to the lives of others cannot keep it from themselves.

p. To be ignorant of one's ignorance is the malady of the ignorant.

q. A guitar is a missing link between music and noise.

r. The naked man never mislays his wallet.

s. Our enemies come nearer the truth in their opinions of us than we do in our opinions of ourselves.

t. One machine can do the work of fifty ordinary men. No machine can do the work of one extraordinary man.

u. To write a good love letter you ought to begin without knowing what you mean to say, and to finish without knowing what you have written.

v. Better do a kidness near home than go far to burn incense.

w. To see something new, we must make something new.

x. A vacation is time off to remind employees that the business can get along without them.

y. The Great Author of all made everything out of nothing, but many a human author makes nothing out of everything.

z. Hating people is like burning down your house to get rid of a rat.

aa. What this country needs is a good five second television commercial.

bb. A university is a college with a stadium seating more than 40,000.

cc. You are never so easily fooled as when you are trying to fool someone else.

dd. If you can't say no, you can't expect to live within your income.

ee. He who is most slow in making a promise is the most faithful in the performance of it.

ff. The ten most beautiful words in the English language: dawn, hush, lullaby, murmuring, tranquil, mist, luminous, chimes, melody, golden.

gg. A bore is a man who spends so much time talking about himself that you can't talk about yourself.

Assignment 17 (See suggested Checklist for this assignment)

Prepare material containing numerous nasal consonants: [m n ŋ]. If you have had no special difficulty with these sounds, stress them slightly to bring out their pleasant quality as you practice, but avoid gross exaggeration. If you have found any of them troublesome—and [n and ŋ] in certain words, especially the latter as a final sound, are often faulty—work for sounds which are accurate and correct.

Suggested Checklist for Assignment 17

As you practice by yourself you may want to work with this checklist. Listen carefully to yourself. If it is feasible record the assignment or get a classmate or friend to listen to you as you read the material. Eventually your goal will be to have a check mark in the Yes column for each category. (Optional: Perhaps your instructor will want to use the checklist to evaluate you during your classroom presentation.)

	Yes	No
Avoids exaggerating [m n or ŋ].		
Avoids omitting [m].		
Avoids weak production of [m] in medial or final position.		
Avoids substituting [b] for [m].		
Avoids substituting [n or ŋ] for [m].		
Avoids omitting [n].		
Avoids weak production of [n] in medial or final position.		
Avoids substituting [d] for [n].		
Avoids substituting [m or ŋ] for [n].		
Avoids omitting [ŋ].		
Avoids weak production of [ŋ] in medial or final position.		
Avoids substituting [g] for [ŋ].		
Avoids substituting [m or n] for [ŋ].		
Avoids confusing [g or k] with [ŋ].		

Additional comments or suggestions:

78. **Bilabial Sounds:** *The material in this section emphasizes sounds which are articulated primarily by the activity of the two lips:*

[p b m w hw]

a. Born poor, but of honored and humble people, I am particularly proud to die poor. [Pope John XXIII]
b. One of the quickest ways to learn how to think on your feet is to become a pedestrian.
c. I chose my wife, as she did her wedding gown, for qualities that would wear well.
d. The power that produced man when the monkey was not up to mark can produce a higher creature than man if man does not come up to the mark.
e. It is folly to borrow when there is no prospect of or ability to pay back.
f. The proud are ever most provoked by pride.
g. Heartbreak: The end of happiness and the beginning of peace.
h. Be brief when you cannot be good.
i. If you will please people, you must please them in their own way.
j. A bank is a place where they lend you an umbrella in fair weather and ask for it back again when it begins to rain.

79. **Labiodental Sounds:** *The material in this section emphasizes sounds which are articulated primarily by the activity of the lower lip being placed against the upper teeth:*

[f v]

a. It costs more to satisfy a vice than to feed a family.
b. One of the strangest things about life is that the poor, who need money the most, are the very ones that never have it.
c. Fog: Stuff that is dangerous to drive in—especially if it's mental.
d. The heart of man is the place the devil dwells in: I feel sometimes a hell within myself.
e. Vocation is the spine of life.
f. Furthermore is much farther than further.
g. There are three things I have always loved and never understood—art, music, and women.
h. Fancy Free: A fancy way to say "Playing the field."
i. A wife is to thank God that her husband has faults; a husband without faults is a dangerous observer.
j. Don't tell your friends their social faults; they will cure the fault and never forgive you.

80. **Linguadental Sounds:** *The material in this section emphasizes sounds which are articulated primarily by the activity of placing the tip of the tongue against the back or underneath the front teeth:*

[θ ð] th — th̸

a. The art of taxation consists in so plucking the goose as to obtain the largest amount of feathers with the least amount of hissing.
b. The afternoon: That part of the day we spend thinking about how we wasted the morning.
c. Take care of the sense and the sounds will take care of themselves.
d. People always say that they are not themselves when tempted by anger into betraying what they really are.
e. Some people study all their life, and at their death they have learned everything except to think.
f. Sending a son through college these days is very educational. It teaches both the mother and the father how to do without a lot of things.
g. God is a thing that thinks.
h. There are mighty few people who think what they think they think.

i. All that we are is the result of what we have thought.

j. The man who is always worrying whether or not his soul would be damned generally has a soul that isn't worth a damn.

81. **Lingua-Alveolar Sounds:** *The material in this section emphasizes sounds which are articulated primarily by the activity of placing the tip or the blade of the tongue on or near the upper (sometimes the lower) gum ridge:*

[t d l s z n]

a. Death is for many of us the gate of hell, but we are inside on the way out, not outside on the way in.

b. The art of medicine consists of amusing the patient while nature cures the disease.

c. Mankind must put an end to war or war will put an end to mankind.

d. Man can climb to the highest summits, but he cannot stay there long.

e. The learned fool writes his nonsense in better language than the unlearned, but it is still nonsense.

f. Do not stand in a place of danger trusting in miracles.

g. There are three kinds of lies: lies, damned lies, and statistics.

h. What grace is to the body, good sense is to the mind.

i. I get my exercise acting as a pallbearer to my friends who exercise.

j. The world, like an accomplished hostess, pays most attention to those whom it will soonest forget.

82. **Linguapalatal Sounds:** *The material in this section emphasizes sounds which are articulated primarily by the activity of the tip or the blade of the tongue on or near the hard palate:*

[ʃ ʒ j r] sh zh y r

a. One of the finest accomplishments is making a long story short.

b. Aviation: Bird imitations on a commercial scale.

c. What is liberty? Leisure. What is leisure? Liberty.

d. A wrong reason is worse than no reason at all.

e. Pleasure is more trouble than trouble.

f. There is only one religion, though there are a hundred versions of it.

g. Rejoice, young man, in your youth; and let your heart cheer you in the days of your youth.

h. No wise man ever wished to be younger.

i. To establish oneself in the world, one does all one can to seem established there.

j. Nothing beats a cold shower before breakfast except no cold shower before breakfast.

83. **Linguavelar Sounds:** *The material in this section emphasizes sounds which are articulated primarily by the activity of raising the back portion of the tongue so that it contacts the soft palate or velum:*

[k g ŋ]

a. The saying that beauty is but skin-deep is but a skin-deep saying.

b. In the kingdom of the deaf, the man with one ear is king.

c. There are books of which the backs and covers are by far the best parts.

d. Almost everything comes from almost nothing.

e. The proof of the pudding is in the eating.

f. Escapist: A person who looks the facts of life in the back of the neck.

g. If I cannot brag of knowing something, then I brag of not knowing it. At any rate—brag!

h. A secret may be sometimes best kept by keeping the secret of its being a secret.

i. Good breeding consists in concealing how much we think of ourselves and how little we think of the other person.

j. The brain is a wonderful organ; it starts working the moment you get up in the morning, and doesn't stop until you get to the office.

84. **Glottal Sounds:** *The material in this section emphasizes a sound which is produced at the glottis, or opening between the vocal folds. The folds are open just enough so that the air in passing through the glottis produces a frictionlike sound:*

[h]

a. Many might go to heaven with half the labor they go to hell.
b. An honest man's word is as good as his bond.
c. While the sick man has life there is hope.
d. Heaven's help is better than early rising.
e. Hand: A grappling hook attached to the human arm.
f. It has been my experience that folks who have no vices have very few virtues.
g. Many a man does not find his heart until he has lost his head.
h. A sight of happiness is happiness.
i. Horse Sense: That rare intelligence that keeps horses from betting on human beings.
j. Down in their hearts, wise men know this truth: the only way to help yourself is to help others.

Vowels

Consonants have been described as consisting of "buzzings, gruntings, hummings, and explosions." Such a description, however, does not accurately fit the seventeen vowels in American English. The "buzzings and explosions," for example, are produced by obstructing the breath stream. A closure or a partial closure must occur at some point in the mouth. Compare the consonants [p] and [z] with the vowels [ɔ] *"awe"* and [ʌ] *"uh."* You will note that as you sound the vowels, there is relatively little obstruction.

Vowels may be defined as relatively open and continuous sounds which are sonorous and free of friction noises. In normal utterance—nonwhispered speech—all vowels are voiced. They result from vocal tone created by the vibration of the vocal folds.

Vowels can be sung. (You cannot sing the plosives, for example.) The consonants may provide beginnings, middles, and endings of words. They are often the boundary markers of speech. When we talk about intelligibility, crispness, and distinctness of speech, we are primarily concerned with consonants. "Consonants," said Alexander Graham Bell, "constitute the back-bone of spoken language—vowels, the flesh and blood."

Voice quality, however, is more closely related to the vowels than to the consonants. Even when we use extremely general terms to describe the sound of someone's voice: "nasal," "husky," "edgy," "rich," "resonant"—we are basing our judgment largely on the speaker's vowel sounds rather than the consonants. Pitch changes, variations in loudness, and sound duration are also more obvious in vowels than in consonants.

We may classify vowels on the following bases:

Place of Articulation
There are front, mid- or central, and back vowels, depending on which part of the tongue is most actively involved in producing the particular vowel.

Height of Tongue
If you say "m<u>ee</u>t," you will be aware that the front of the tongue is high in the mouth as you produce the vowel sound.

"m<u>a</u>te": the front of the tongue is in a midhigh position on the vowel sound.

"m<u>a</u>t": the front of the tongue is almost flat on the floor of the mouth on the vowel sound.

Contrast also: "f<u>ee</u>t" with "f<u>a</u>te"; "w<u>ay</u>" with "w<u>oe</u>."

Tension of Tongue Muscles

The tongue muscles are more tense for the vowel in "m<u>ee</u>t" than in "m<u>e</u>t." More tension is present for the vowel in "m<u>oo</u>n" than in "m<u>oa</u>n."

Shape and Degree of Lip Rounding

The vowel sounds in "m<u>oo</u>n, l<u>oo</u>k, m<u>oa</u>n, b<u>ou</u>ght" require various degrees of lip rounding. The other vowel sounds are produced with little or no lip rounding.

Charts and diagrams are almost always a little bit suspect. They tend to fix or set things in place rather permanently. Permanency suggests standing still, unchangeability, immovability. Vowels are notably fickle and to put them in a chart is almost akin to charting the ocean surf. (Obviously, too, the mouth cavity is not shaped like a cup or a mug which a vowel chart suggests.) However, some kind of vowel chart or diagram may be of use to us if we understand that the various positions represented are relative and not fixed.

We must also understand that there is no such thing as a pure vowel sound, meaning one sound and one sound only for each phonetic symbol. Consider [ɑ] in this sentence:

"<u>F</u>ather said '<u>ah</u>' as he dr<u>o</u>pped his <u>a</u>rms from the r<u>o</u>d and h<u>o</u>pped onto the c<u>o</u>t."

Is the same [ɑ] used for each of the underlined vowels? A keen ear will tell you no. Nevertheless, we recognize them as [ɑ] or close relatives of [ɑ]. Therefore, the closely related sounds constitute a kind of sound family, or, as we have previously pointed out, a "phoneme."

If you will remember that a vowel diagram suggests typical but not exact positions and that the differences in tongue positions from one vowel to another are comparatively slight, we may experiment with the diagram. The top of the diagram suggests the roof of the mouth; the bottom suggests the floor of the mouth.

The left side of the diagram represents the front part of the mouth. The sounds are referred to as front vowels. To produce these sounds, the front portion of the tongue is most active.

Beginning with [i] say the front vowels and note what takes place. The tongue is arched high and far forward, but as you move down through the others, you will feel the front of the tongue and the jaw dropping and the mouth gradually opening more widely. The lips for [i] suggest a narrow rectangle, but as you say the others, the lips tend to change from a narrow slit to a more relaxed and open position.

The right side of the diagram represents the back part of the mouth. The sounds are referred to as back vowels. To produce these sounds, the back portion of the tongue is most active.

As you proceed from [u] down through [ɑ], note how the back of the tongue and the jaw gradually lower. The lips are protruded and rounded for [u], but by the time you reach [ɑ] they are relatively open and relaxed.

The central portion of the diagram represents the middle of the mouth. The sounds are referred to as mid- or central vowels. To produce these sounds, the middle portion of the tongue is most active.

As you begin with [ɝ], you will note that the tongue may be arched relatively high in the middle of the oral cavity. With the other sounds the tongue generally drops slightly. When you reach [ə and ʌ] you will be aware that the tongue, lips, and jaw are in quite relaxed positions.

(In figure 6.2, phonetic symbols are placed to the left of the key word. Dictionary symbols are placed to the right.)

	Front Part of Tongue	Central Part of Tongue	Back Part of Tongue	
Position of Tongue	Roof of Mouth Cavity			
HIGH	i (m<u>e</u>) ē ɪ (<u>i</u>t) i or ĭ		u (c<u>oo</u>l) o͞o U (l<u>oo</u>k) o͝o	Most closed position
MID	e (d<u>a</u>te) ā ɛ (<u>e</u>gg) e or ĕ	ɝ - ɜ (b<u>ir</u>d) ûr ɚ (nev<u>er</u>) ər ə (sof<u>a</u>) ə	o (<u>o</u>bey) ō	
LOW	æ (h<u>a</u>t) a or ă a (p<u>a</u>th) ȧ or ă	ʌ (c<u>u</u>t) u or ŭ	ɔ (<u>a</u>ll) ô ɒ (n<u>o</u>t) o or ŏ ɑ (c<u>a</u>lm) ä	Most open position
	Floor of Mouth Cavity			

Figure 6.2

Front Vowels

$[\,i\,]$

$[\,\bar{e}\,]$

Example: St<u>e</u>ve and K<u>ei</u>th b<u>e</u>l<u>ie</u>ve that C<u>ae</u>sar f<u>ea</u>sted in the d<u>ee</u>p rav<u>i</u>ne near Ph<u>oe</u>nix.

Typical Production:
Arch the front of the tongue high and far forward so that it almost touches the hard palate. The tongue should be tensed. The lips are spread slightly and the upper and lower teeth are quite close together.

Faults or Problems:
85. [i] is often described as a tense and brilliant sound. Too much tension of the tongue or lips, however, may distort the sound and make it unpleasantly shrill. Try this experiment:

As you read the following, deliberately make the tongue and lips as tense as possible on the large <u>EE</u> combinations. Then relax the mechanisms somewhat for the small <u>ee</u> combinations, and see if you can produce a clear but less piercing sound. You should be able to hear and feel the difference.

a. EE ee EE ee EE ee EE ee

b.
h<u>EE</u>l-heel	k<u>EE</u>p-keep	p<u>EE</u>t-peet
b<u>EE</u>t-beet	s<u>EE</u>n-seen	k<u>EE</u>n-keen
f<u>EE</u>t-feet	tr<u>EE</u>-tree	r<u>EE</u>d-reed
m<u>EE</u>t-meet	<u>EE</u>l-eel	gr<u>EE</u>t-greet

Read these sentences, trying to use the relatively less tense <u>ee</u> for all [i] sounds:

c. The mean weasel had eaten three eagles under the tree.
d. Marie agreed to please the people and repeat her dream.
e. The greedy sheep crossed the eastern stream and ate the green leaves.
f. Phoebe, eager to tease, seized the ski from Eva and dropped it on the wheel.
g. We had seen the meek thief hide the tea and the wheat on the beach.

86. Occasionally one hears an extra sound inserted before or after [i]. The added sound is referred to as an on-glide, an off-glide, or a schwa [ə].

Result: *meet* [mit] may sound something like:

  mee-it—[miɪt]
  mi-eet—[mɪit]
  me-uht—[miət]

This fault seems to be the most apparent when [i] is followed by [l], as in *peel.* Read the following word pairs. You will probably have no difficulty producing the [i] in the first word of each pair. Try to carry the same [i] over to the second word without any kind of on-, off-glide, or a schwa inserted.

keen-keel	read-real	eke-eel
peek-peel	seen-seal	teak-teal
feed-feel	dean-deal	heat-heel
mean-meal	wheat-wheel	Zeke-zeal
creed-creel	repeat-repeal	need-kneel

87. People with certain foreign language backgrounds may confuse [i] as in b<u>ee</u>t with the [ɪ] as in b<u>i</u>t.

Result: *feet* [fit] may sound more like *fit* [fɪt]
     meat [mit] may sound more like *mit* [mɪt]

For [i], the tongue is high and far forward, but for [ɪ] it is slightly lower and further back in the mouth. Try to feel and hear the difference as you read the following:

a.
reap-rip	sheen-shin	heap-hip	leap-lip
seep-sip	deal-dill	seat-sit	beet-bit
deep-dip	feel-fill	ream-rim	leak-lick
bean-bin	seek-sick	seen-sin	wheat-wit
peel-pill	keen-kin	dean-din	steal-still

Practice the following. Avoid inserting an extra, unwanted sound before or after [i], and distinguish carefully between [i and ɪ].

b. A man always has two reasons for doing anything—a good reason and the real reason.
c. Little Lee dipped the green pill into the deep teal-colored till.
d. Wee Willie weeps when he slips on his skis.
e. Tim seemed to leap over ditches and peaks.
f. The eager kitten slid down the sleet-covered hill on its heels.
g. Lizzie found it easy to tease simple, meek people.
h. He grinned even though his skinned shin turned green.
i. Gene concealed the rim of the steel wheel.
j. Did the Sea-Bees feed pills to the sick seals?
k. Zest: The peel of an orange squeezed into wine.
l. He who will not be meek below will be a footstool for God's feet above.
m. It has been said that there is no grief like the grief which does not speak.
n. Flirting: The art of making a man feel pleased with himself.

o. We are both great men, but I have succeeded better in keeping it a profound secret than he has.

p. Be nice to people on your way up, because you'll meet them on your way down.

q. The chief knowledge that a man gets from reading books is the knowledge that very few of them are worth reading.

$[\text{I}]$ $[\text{i} - \bar{\text{i}}]$

Example: Is Bill's pretty sister guilty of singing English hymns in business buildings?

Typical Production:

Lower the tongue slightly from the [i] position and pull it farther back as you sound [ɪ]. The teeth are wider apart than for [i] and, in general, the lips and tongue are somewhat more relaxed. It is almost always shorter in duration than [i].

Faults or Problems:

88. The confusion between [i and ɪ], a fairly common fault among those whose native language background is not English, has already been discussed. Review Exercise 87.

89. Careless individuals often substitute the [ɛ] of _egg_ for [ɪ]. The tongue positions for the two sounds are somewhat alike, but if you say _sit-set_, _bit-bet_, _mitt-met_ you will discover that the tongue is higher and further forward for [ɪ] than for [ɛ]. Do not confuse the two sounds as you read:

a.
did-dead	rid-read	kin-Ken
itch-etch	lid-led	pit-pet
bit-bet	sill-sell	hid-head
gym-gem	limb-Lem	pick-peck

b. Ben sits in the bin to watch the sun set.

c. Lil and her sister, Nell, picked a peck of dill pickles.

d. Bill, the little pig, learned the trick of hitting the peg and ringing the bell.

e. Sid said that Milt ran pell-mell toward the tin mill.

f. The red chicken hid its head under the lead lid.

90. How does one pronounce the word _begin?_ There are two standard pronunciations:

bee-gin [bi'gɪn] or _bi-gin_ [bɪ'gɪn]

This applies to most words containing prefixes spelled with _e._ To pronounce the word as: _buh-gin_ [bə'gɪn], however, substituting the schwa [ə] for [i or ɪ] is considered incorrect by some.

Avoid the schwa substitution as you practice these:

a.
receive	believe	prevent
behalf	behave	begone
beget	behold	decrease
demand	prefer	decree

b. He decided to sit beside rather than behind the decoy.

c. She preferred not to predict what would become of the prefab building.

d.   Cindy could not describe the details of the design of the new destroyer.

e.   Judge Smith demanded that the deserter be defended.

f.   Kitty pretended to behave badly when the band played "Begin the Beguine."

91.   Do we use [ɪ or i] in unstressed, final positions?

funn<u>y</u>   happ<u>y</u>   monk<u>ey</u>

prett<u>y</u>   coff<u>ee</u>   brown<u>ie</u>

If you will say *funny* quite slowly, it is true that you may pronounce it as *funee* [ˈfʌni]. However, in most conversational speaking we do not say the word with such exaggerated slowness. Thus, it is doubtful that we invariably use [i].

On the other hand, is the final sound the same as the [ɪ] in <u>sit</u> [sɪt]? Not exactly, regardless of the speed at which we say the word. The sound most of us use probably falls some place between [ɪ and i], having not quite the comparative dullness of the former or the comparative brilliance of the latter.

(In the South, this unstressed and final sound is often closer to [ɪ] than [i]. In the North and in areas of the East, the sound is often closer to [i] than to [ɪ].)

In reading the drill material determine which sound or which variation you use in final and unstressed positions and try to be reasonably consistent in its usage. Avoid the tendency to exaggerate <u>y</u>, <u>ey</u>, <u>ee</u>, <u>ie</u> endings.

a.   city   kitty   ditty   simply

flighty   family   donkey   lumpy

Polly   duty   dummy   orgy

Betty   rummy   merry   filly

b.   Jimmy and Mary gave the tiny puppy to Lily, the Brownie scout.

c.   Lassie, a highly-trained collie, has saved many children from nasty disasters.

d.   The owly Indian traded toffee and coffee for the taffy-flavored honey.

e.   Benny gave the tiny merry-go-round to Mary and Tillie.

f.   Billy fitted the wobbly jalopy with a pretty canopy.

92.   In some Southern speech the off-glide is added, with the result that *pit* [pɪt] sounds something like *pi-uht* [pɪət] and *bit* [bɪt] becomes *bi-uht* [bɪət].

At times [ɪ] is permitted to sound muffled or swallowed. This may happen if the speaker pulls the tongue too far back toward a central position and rounds the lips on the vowel. This is most apt to occur if [ɪ] is preceded or followed by [r or l] or by the lip and lip-teeth consonants: [m, w, f, v, p, b].

Work for an [ɪ] sound which is free of the off-glide and which retains the [ɪ] quality, avoiding the muffled or swallowed distortions.

a.   pill   bitter   risk   mitten

hip   fib   lip   brim

fifty   vim   hill   will

live   sniff   wind   sieve

b.   Will Bill kiss Wilma Mills under the wispy mistletoe?

c.   Lily Brill saw the villain fill the bin with mixed mint.

d.   Tim hid the dill in the thin grill in the ditch.

e.   The hills of Illinois drift inch by inch toward the river.

f.   Trim the gristle from the liver before you let the fish and chips simmer.

g.   Bim flipped the big lid off the wishing well with the kickpin.

h.   Will the missing gypsy jilt the prince in Finland?

i.   Do God's will as if it were your will, and He will accomplish your will as if it were His own.

j.   Income: Something that you can't live without or within.

k. An egotist is a person of low taste, more interested in himself than me.
l. Rick and Mick were silly, not witty.
m. The man who leaves no will after his death had little will before his death.

[e]

[ā]

Example: Kate and the eight apes from Asia ate the steak in April.

Typical Production:

Lower the tongue slightly from the [ɪ] position to a midhigh position and pull it farther back as you sound [e]. The mouth should be open somewhat wider; the lips are more relaxed. In unaccented positions [e] is often considered to be a relatively pure vowel. In certain accented positions, however, it may become a diphthong—a rapid blending of two vowel sounds in the same syllable. (See page 239 for a discussion of the diphthong [eɪ].)

Faults or Problems:

93. Perhaps the most common fault involving [e] is the tendency to nasalize it in words in which it is preceded or followed by [m, n, or ŋ]. The velum must be raised for correct pronunciation of [e], and excessive tension in the throat and tongue is to be avoided.

The [e] in the second word of the following pairs should be as free of undesirable nasality as the [e] in the first word of each pair:

a.
day-dame	fray-frame	gay-game	day-Dane
ade-made	Kay-came	pay-pain	ail-nail
ape-nape	ray-rain	shay-shame	say-same
ate-mate	air-mare	ale-male	ache-make

Guard against excessively nasalized and strident [e] sounds as you practice this material:

b. *Two Danes and a Dame* is a maimed version of Shakespeare's famous *Hamlet*.
c. Mamie was ashamed to say that her vacation in Maine was tame.
d. Did the lame male impress his mate with a feigned ailment?
e. Jane maintained that Mason Lane should not blame Spain.
f. The ancient frame was not the same as the one the painter made.
g. After she ate the grain, the pain began to wane.
h. Zane nailed the main crane to the wooden pane.

94. In some Southern speech, the schwa [ə] is inserted after [e].

Result: *mail* [mel] becomes *may-uhl* [meəl]
trail [trel] becomes *tray-uhl* [treəl]

Work for a clear, pure [e] vowel as you read these:

a. Ray placed the pale ale near the cane and the railing.
b. Abe strafed the freight train at the station.
c. They gave great help to their neighbors during the rain.
d. Liberty is always dangerous, but it is the safest thing we have.
e. Is life a fairy tale, a flame, a one-way street, or a state of war?

f. Kate was too lazy to praise "The Lady of the Lake."

g. Civilization is, after all, but a coat of paint that washes away when the rain falls.

h. Good painting is like good cooking—it can be tasted but not explained.

i. Will Rogers used to say: "Maybe 'ain't' ain't so correct, but I notice that lots of folks who ain't using 'ain't' ain't eating."

j. The veiled player obeyed the waiter and gauged his appetite before ordering the entrée.

 [ɛ]   [e – ĕ]

Example: Ed and his friend found an empty treasure chest buried next to the chemistry lab.

Typical Production:

The tongue should be lower and more relaxed than for [e]. It may also be farther back in the mouth. The jaw has dropped; the mouth is wider open.

Faults or Problems:

95. In careless or provincial speech [ɛ] is often confused with other sounds, notably [e, ɪ, and æ].

Result: *egg* [ɛg] becomes *aig* [eg]
             been [bɛn] becomes *bin* [bɪn]
             shell [ʃɛl] becomes *shall* [ʃæl]

Differentiate carefully between these sounds and be as consistent as you can in pronouncing [ɛ] in the following:

a.

Ben-bane	pen-pin	pen-pan	sell-sale	beg-big
lend-land	fed-fade	set-sit	set-sat	met-mate
head-hid	pled-plaid	bet-bait	pell-pill	Ed-add
bed-bad	Meg-Mag	pen-pain	net-nit	lead-lid
den-Dane	welt-wilt	met-mat	yell-Yale	sell-sill
ten-tan	wet-wait	peck-pick	leg-lag	mess-mace
check-chick	pent-pant	fen-feign	ten-tin	send-sand

b. Jenny and Peggy were very merry with the ten men at the wedding.

c. Ellen Dane hid the eggs in the den and yelled.

d. Kent can't wait to pat his pet duck on the deck.

e. Ted and Tad guessed that Gus would put Bud to bed.

f. Ben and Meg filled twenty kegs with eggnog.

g. The welt on Mary's neck began to wilt in the nick of time.

h. Let the Latvian pen ten letters not later than Wednesday.

i. Is it just to jest at Sally for selling shells to shills?

j. Did Ben beg his big brother to give him the tinted tent to hem?

96. In drawled speech the schwa vowel may be unnecessarily added to [ɛ].

Result: *head* [hɛd] becomes *he-uhd* [hɛəd]
             fed [fɛd] becomes *fe-uhd* [fɛəd]

Like [e], [ɛ] may also become unduly nasalized if preceded or followed by [m, n, or ŋ].

If you have a tendency toward drawling your speech, try to eliminate the [ə] addition to [ε] as you practice the following. Be certain, too, that [ε], when adjacent to a nasal consonant, is not nasalized excessively.

a. Everywhere in America men are in quest of pleasure.
b. Many of the men pair pennies for the emory and the ebony.
c. He bet that Meg could eat twelve eggs while standing on her head.
d. The elephant boy fell off the red shelf.
e. It was a genuine pleasure to see Helen Heller act so well in *Measure for Measure*.
f. Running into debt isn't so bad; it's running into your creditors that hurts.
g. Engagement ring: A test band.
h. A bachelor never quite gets over the idea that he is a thing of beauty and a boy forever.
i. God helps them that help themselves.
j. Headlines are frequently twice the size of the events.
k. Education: The development of the memory at the expense of the imagination.
l. Obscenity can be found in every book except the telephone directory.
m. Why fear death? Death is only a beautiful adventure.
n. Egg: A day's adventure for a hen.
o. Men like conventions because men made them.
p. Early to bed and early to rise,
   Makes a man healthy, wealthy, and wise.
q. Leonard said to his friend that the leather collar would never check the leopard.

 $$[æ] \qquad\qquad [a - \breve{a}]$$

Example: The angry man slammed the plaid basket of trash into the can.

Typical Production:

The tongue is lower in position, lying almost flat on the floor of the mouth, but there may be a slight elevation of the front part of the tongue. The mouth is wider open for [æ] than for [ε]. The tongue muscles should be quite lax, and the tongue itself should be kept well forward in the mouth.

Faults or Problems:

97. In some careless speech [ε, ʌ, or ɪ] are often substituted for [æ].

Result: *had* [hæd] sounds like *head* [hεd]
            rather [ˈræðɚ] sounds like *ruther* [ˈrʌðɚ]
            can [kæn] sounds like *kin* [kɪn]

Distinguish carefully between [æ-ε, æ-ʌ] and [æ-ɪ]:

a.
Dan-den	Sam-some	sack-sick
bat-bet	dam-dumb	mat-mit
sand-send	fan-fun	had-hid
dack-deck	bad-bud	dapper-dipper
fan-fen	rag-rug	salve-sieve
chat-chet	clack-cluck	flam-flim
ham-hem	ram-rum	dad-did
sat-set	cram-crumb	fan-fit

211

b. Hal Henry asked the Eskimo not to drop the butter and the batter on the rag rug.

c. Aunt Addie can remember the anniversaries of all her kinfolk.

d. Chad had hidden Chet's chickens in the smashed shack.

e. Skip Capper crammed the salmon into the bent tank.

f. Pat Pitt gave Sam and Ed some lumps of lamb stew.

g. Hank hid the bass after he had packed the peck of yams into the van.

h. "Hush," said the laughing lad as he passed the cash to Andy.

i. The mad men could not catch the ketch before it rammed the craft.

j. Stubby stabbed the stack of plastic sticks with a dagger.

98. The most common problem involving [æ] is a tendency to produce it with an unpleasant, tense, and nasal quality. This is especially true in some of the speech one hears in the Eastern United States. Not a few citizens of New York, Philadelphia, and Baltimore, for example, are apt to articulate a very taut and displeasing sound. Typically, they might utter such a sentence as:

Ask the man about the tan cat

[æsk ðə mæn ə'baʊt ðə tæn kæt]

so that it resembles instead:

Eh-usk the meh-un about the teh-un ceh-ut

[ɛ-əsk ðə mɛ-ən ə'baʊt ðə tɛ-ən kɛ-ət]

This type of flat, dry, and disagreeable distortion often results from a tongue which is not only over-tense but is raised too high. A tight and closed jaw will also add to the undesirable quality. Speakers in other sections of the country must also be careful with this sound. If [æ] is near a nasal consonant or a plosive, it can easily slip into a hard, metallic distortion.

Try this experiment with the following word pairs:

On the first word of each pair, deliberately tense the tongue, tighten and close the jaw somewhat, and be as nasal as you can. As you pounce on each of the [ɛ] sounds, think of saying the word *egg* [ɛg] between clenched teeth.

On the second member of the pair, work for a relaxed, almost-lazy tongue, open the jaw, and guard carefully against nasality:

a.
[bɛən-bæn]	[dɛən-dæn]	[mɛəd-mæd]
[fɛən-fæn]	[rɛən-ræn]	[rɛəm-ræm]
[tɛən-tæn]	[hɛəd-hæd]	[tɛəŋ-tæŋ]
[mɛən-mæn]	[fɛəd-fæd]	[grɛənd-grænd]
[klɛəm-klæm]	[sɛət-sæt]	[slɛəŋ-slæŋ]
[bɛəd-bæd]	[ʃɛəd-ʃæd]	[bɛəθ-bæθ]
[pɛət-pæt]	[skɛən-skæn]	[mɛəst-mæst]

b. Using the more agreeable, relaxed, and pleasant [æ] of the second word in each pair, say the following rapidly:

ban-shan-han-van-can-lamb-tram
jam-jab-sap-tab-Ann-sack-hack
add-mad-scram-bat-map-lass-lab
lag-dad-crab-Nan-and-prance-an
lack-sack-back-wrack-crack-tack-jack
ma'm-map-mack-mass-mab-man-mat
staff-stamp-stab-stand-stack-stag-stanza
Sam-ram-cram-bam-ham-lamb-dam

Again, avoiding any kind of distortion of [æ] which results from undue tongue or jaw tensions or nasality, read the following until you are able to produce a desirable sound:

   c. The mad man ran rapidly over the sand-sacks.
   d. Did Randy Anderson's mantle hang on a hat rack near the dank attic?
   e. Harry carried the basket of arrows in the handsome wheelbarrow.
   f. The lanky lass grabbed the candied apple from the frantic lad.
   g. That handsome actor, Tab Anthony, has a hankering to play *Macbeth* in France.
   h. Half the band was crammed into the grandstand near the shanty.
   i. Janet sang the national anthem in a sad manner.
   j. Man is a social animal; suit your manner to the man.
   k. When angry, count four; when very angry, swear.
   l. One shabby camel carries the burdens of many donkeys.
   m. One can't go half way around the world to count the cats in Zanzibar.
   n. Nothing happens to you that hasn't happened to someone else.
   o. Anger: A slashing wind which blows out the lamp of man's mind.

99. [æ] does not occur in some foreign languages, so if English is your second language, you may possibly be substituting [ɑ] for [æ]. In this case you would say *shock, cot* [ʃɑk, kɑt] for *shack, cat* [ʃæk, kæt].

For [ɑ]:   the tongue should be low, flat, and relaxed on the floor of the mouth.

For [æ]:   the tongue is low, but there may be a slight elevation of the front part.

Contrast the following:

   a. [ɑ - æ]   [ɑ - æ]   [ɑ - æ]
       mop-map   ox-ax   flog-flag
       sock-sack   rock-rack   not-gnat
       clod-clad   rot-rat   cop-cap
       pod-pad   mod-mad   bottle-battle
       flop-flap   con-can   bond-band

Do not substitute [ɑ] for [æ] as you read the following:

   b. Do not knock the odd clothes that the mad characters wore in *The Knack*.
   c. The cad tossed the cod to the cat under the cot.
   d. The clod who led the band was clad in Bond Street clothes.
   e. Don told Dan that the packet in his pocket contained only a sack of socks.
   f. The odd soldiers added tags to their togs before the volley of shots rang through the valley.

100. Even if [æ] is produced without undesirable nasality or tension, it is occasionally heard as a type of diphthong and an [ə] is added to the [æ] sound.

   Result: *bad* [bæd] becomes *ba-uhd* [bæəd]
             mat [mæt] becomes *ma-uht* [mæət]

This fault is especially evident in drawled speech in which the [æ] may be more prolonged than needed. As you practice, try to keep the vowel as short and pure as possible.

   a. The fat cat will catch the black rabbit on Saturday.
   b. Grab Sam's hand and ask him to pat the damp mattress.
   c. The masked bandit grabbed the calf in the last shaft.
   d. Half measures and half desires only show half men.
   e. God will not give any soldier ammunition who is not willing to go into battle.
   f. Half the world knows not how the other half lives.
   g. Happiness is that it happens to me.
   h. Death rides a fast camel.

i.   Man is the only animal that can be a fool.
j.   The higher taxes go, the sharper the voter grinds his ax.
k.   What really flatters a man is that you think him worth flattering.
l.   Man has almost mastered the elements—provided nothing happens.
m.   Adam was human; he didn't want the apple for the apple's sake. He wanted it because it was forbidden.

$[\dot{a} - \breve{a}]$

Example: He asked his aunt to do a fast dance on the grassy path.

Typical Production:
The tongue is slightly lower and more retracted than for [æ]. The mouth is open wider and the jaw is more relaxed.

Faults or Problems:
[a] is frequently described as the "intermediate A" which means that this vowel lies midway, theoretically speaking, between [æ] as in *ask* and [ɑ] as in *arm*.

As an experiment, try [æ, a, and ɑ] with the word *aunt:*

  [ænt   ant   ɑnt]

You will note that the middle [a] differs from the first [æ] and the last [ɑ]. Which is correct?

The truth is that a majority of us probably say [ænt]. [ɑnt] sounds somewhat affected and unnatural. Some authorities, however, suggest the "in-between" [a] as a compromise in certain words. There is no harm in the suggestion, but its general use in American speech is rather limited, although some feel that its use is growing. It is, as a matter of fact, a pleasant sound. It is most commonly heard in Eastern New England. However, unless [a] is natural to the speech of an individual it is rarely necessary for him to acquire it. It is a matter of interest to note that [a] often occurs in words in which it is followed by certain voiceless fricatives [f, θ] and such combinations as [nt, ns].

101. For those who favor the intermediate [a], one word of caution. Try to be reasonably consistent. Avoid such garbled confusions as:

[hɚ   ænt   tʊk   ə   baθ   æftɚ   ðə   dɑns]

Her aunt took a bath after the dance.

Use [æ or a] in the underlined words in the following. Be consistent.

a.   The mast in the craft fell on the class.
b.   Laughing, she pranced down the path.
c.   Half of the branch is under glass.
d.   The class gave the answer as an example.
e.   Aunt Frances said that the draft in France has been a disaster.
f.   Vance raised his brass lance and advanced toward the castle.
g.   Is there a chance that Hanson will not be able to grasp the vastness of the task?
h.   The first half of our lives is ruined by our parents and the second half by our children.
i.   Half the world is composed of people who have something to say and can't, and the other half who have nothing to say and keep on saying it.

214

Assignment 18 (See suggested Checklist for this assignment)

Prepare material containing many examples of the front vowels with which you particularly need practice. As a reminder, here is a key:

[i] ē be

[ɪ] i or ĭ hit

[e] ā cake

[ɛ] e or ĕ led

[æ] a or ă ask

[a] à or ă bath

Suggested Checklist for Assignment 18

As you practice by yourself you may want to work with this checklist. Listen carefully to yourself. If it is feasible record the assignment or get a classmate or friend to listen to you as you read the material. Eventually your goal will be to have a check mark in the **Yes** column for each category. (Optional: Perhaps your instructor will want to use the checklist to evaluate you during your classroom presentation.)

	Yes	No
Avoids inserting an on-glide, off-glide, or a schwa [ə] before or after a front vowel.		
Avoids nasalized production of front vowels especially when preceded or followed by [m n ŋ].		
Avoids producing an unpleasantly shrill [i].		
Avoids substituting schwa [ə] for [i].		
Avoids substituting [ɪ] for [i] or [i] for [ɪ].		
Avoids substituting [ɛ] for [ɪ].		
Avoids substituting schwa [ə] for [ɪ].		
Avoids articulating exaggerated "ye, ey, ee, ie" endings.		
Avoids substituting [ɛ] for [e].		
Avoids substituting [æ e ɪ] for [ɛ].		
Avoids substituting [ɑ ɛ ʌ ɪ] for [æ].		

Additional comments or suggestions:

Example: Ruth saw the gloomy crew loot the blue room.

Typical Production:

Raise the back of the tongue high toward the palate. The front of the tongue should be depressed and retracted. The lips are more protruded and rounded for this sound than any other vowel.

Faults or Problems:

102. A fairly common fault is to make a diphthong out of [u]. Words such as *moon* and *tool* sound something like *moo-uhn* [muən] and *too-uhl* [tuəl]. Be sure that your [u] is not diphthongized.

a.
cool	rude	pool	stoop
boot	coo	grew	prove
bloom	June	noon	wooed
whose	woo	boost	snoop
shoot	flew	toot	fruit

b.   Luke was tattooed in the school room during the noon hour.
c.   Lou swooped down onto the goose which was roosting in the booth.
d.   The Duke was rude to Sue, booing her as she swam in the pool.
e.   The fool soon drew the shoe from the boot.
f.   Hugh Steward said, "The root will push the booth off the roof."
g.   The cool moonlight made the crude room look like a tomb.
h.   Lou will rue the day she glued the bamboo to the canoe.
i.   June likes the fruit trees blooming in the New York zoo.

103. There is some controversy over a handful of *oo* words. How should we pronounce *roof*, *room*, and *root*, for example?

   roof [ruf] or [rʊf][2]
   room [rum] or [rʊm]
   root [rut] or [rʊt]

The Random House Dictionary and *Webster's Third New International Dictionary* list [ruf, rum, and rut] as first choices, and [rʊf, rʊm, and rʊt] as second choices. This simply means that both choices are standard.

As you pronounce the following, perhaps you will have to let your own ears serve as your guide. Try both of the sounds in question, but if one of them sounds strange to you, use the other one.

a.
room	roof	root	broom
groom	hoof	coop	hoop
soot	rooster	soon	hooves

With a large majority of *oo* words, however, there is no disagreement regarding pronunciation.

---

2. [U] is the sound generally used in the word *book*.

To use [ʊ], the *oo* in *look* for example, in such words as these would be completely nonstandard.

mood	whom	shoe
tool	moon	boom
move	grew	tooth

If you have a foreign language background, however, you may confuse [u] and [ʊ]. Remember that if the lips are insufficiently rounded or if the tongue is allowed to become too lax [u] will sound more like [ʊ], the vowel sound in *took*. The tongue and lips are relatively tense for [u], but more relaxed for [ʊ].

b.

[u]	[ʊ]	[u]	[ʊ]
fool	full	Luke	look
wooed	wood	pool	pull
stewed	stood	cooed	could
shooed	should	who'd	hood

c.　She tried to pull the duelist into the full pool.
d.　He would have wooed her if he had not seen her looking at the nook full of loot.
e.　The rude group put the rulebook at the foot of the boom.
f.　Sue hooted when the flute-playing crook pushed the goose into the room.
g.　The bush looked as if it would bloom by noon.
h.　Luke looked at the hood who'd wooed Lucy Cook.
i.　He took the poodle's loot and put it in the pool.
j.　The fool said the woods are full of blooming fruit trees.
k.　The troop of Sioux threw two bouquets and plumes to the crew.

<u>Example:</u>　　　　Sh<u>ou</u>ld she p<u>u</u>t the p<u>u</u>dding and the c<u>oo</u>kies on the s<u>oo</u>ty c<u>u</u>shion?

<u>Typical Production:</u>

In comparison with the position for [u], the tongue should be relatively lax and the lips should be slightly less tense and somewhat less rounded for [ʊ]. The back of the tongue is a bit lower and the jaw drops slightly.

<u>Faults or Problems:</u>

104. In Exercise 103, it was indicated that [ʊ] is often substituted for [u]. The exercises below will help make the differences clear. Another fault is that of weakening [ʊ] to [ʌ or ə].

If this occurs—

　　would may sound something like *wuhd* [wʌd]

or note what may happen in a sentence such as this:

　　If I had known, I <u>would</u> have been there.

　　would may sound something like [wəd]

Do not substitute [u, ʌ, or ə] for [ʊ] as you read this material. You will be able to avoid such substitutions if you keep the lips rounded for [ʊ].

a. He would have wooed Sue Cooper, but she pushed him into the pool.
b. The poor little pullet stood in the soot-covered shoes.
c. Huck saw the wolves chew the buck's hoof.
d. Ruth looked at the wool hood on the toothless football player.
e. The cook and the butcher could have pulled the goose out of the bushel basket.
f. He took the crude hook out of the bullet-riddled book.
g. "Good!" said Lou Wood as he took the sugar to the breakfast nook.
h. Could the bull push Butch's hook off the crooked path?
i. Mr. Brooks would have to put the bulletin on the pulpit in Cooperstown.

105. In some regional speech, and especially in areas where there is a tendency to drawl, a schwa [ə], or an [ɪ] vowel may be inserted before or after the oo [ʊ] sound under discussion.

Result: Put the good book near the bush.

[pʊt ðə gʊd bʊk nɪr ðə bʊʃ]

may come closer to:

Pu-uht the gi-ood boo-uhk near the bu-ish.

[pʊət ðə gɪud bʊək nɪr ðə bʊɪʃ]

In most American speech this is nonstandard pronunciation. The individual with this problem needs to be reminded that the lips must be well rounded for [ʊ]. Also, if the tongue is pulled far enough back in the mouth there will be little danger of inserting [ɪ] or [ə] before or after [ʊ].

Be certain that your [ʊ] is satisfactory as you practice these sentences:

a. A good cook would not put sugar cookies in the pudding.
b. The wolf mistook the neighborhood moor for the wooded nook.
c. The tourist shook as he saw the bullet push through the wool.
d. The crook's good looks did not save him from the hook in the butcher shop.
e. Miss Cook said that the push and pull method would help poor writing.
f. The hood said, "Sure, I pushed the book into the footlocker."
g. The roof fell on the poor wolf in Little Red Riding Hood.
h. The sure-footed pussy cat slipped on the hooked wool rug.
i. Woody Goodson took a good look at the cook books.
j. The football player's right foot was fully insured.
k. What a good thing Adam had—when he said a good thing, he knew nobody had said it before.
l. Ginger Ale: A good, sugary drink that tastes like your foot feels when it's asleep.
m. This was a good dinner enough, to be sure; but it was not a good enough dinner to ask a man to.
n. Success would not be so misunderstood if successful men looked a little happier.
o. The punishment of criminals should be of use; when a man is hanged he is good for nothing.
p. It surely would be a good world if everybody was as pleasant as the fellow who's trying to rook you.
q. Oh, give thanks unto the Lord, for he is good, for his mercy endureth forever.
r. Cooking: A process of preparing food which would be pushed along fifty years by the use of zippers on canned goods and frozen foods.
s. Any young man with good health and a poor appetite can save up bushels of money.
t. The cook was a good cook, as cooks go: and as cooks go, she went.

Example: Most of the boats floated in the ocean near the hotel.

Typical Production:

Round and protrude the lips. Drop the jaw to a position lower than it was for [ʊ]. Lower the relatively tense tongue slightly from the [ʊ] position. It should now be in a midhigh position.

Generally speaking, this sound is most likely to be found in unaccented or lightly stressed positions: "opinion, obey, omit." Occasionally it may be heard as a simple vowel when followed by a voiceless consonant: "lotion, bloated, coach," or by [r]: "door, core."

Most often, however, the sound is diphthongized to [oʊ]. (See Exercise 126.)

Faults or Problems:

106. [ə or ʌ] are sometimes substituted for [o].

In connected speech—

uh-pinion [ə ˈpɪnjən] and uh-bey [ə ˈbe]

are probably just as intelligible as

opinion [o ˈpɪnjən] and obey [o ˈbe]

The word goal, however, pronounced as gull [gʌl] instead of [gol] would be nonstandard.

In unaccented or lightly accented syllables, the pronunciation of [o] is, again, subject to some variation, as well as a matter of individual taste.

In everyday conversation, do we say—

seven o'clock [o ˈklɑk] or seven uh-clock [ə ˈklɑk]?

Most of us use the latter, with the schwa [ə] substituted for the initial [o]. It has been argued that to say o'clock [o ˈklɑk] is a case of overpronunciation.

On the other hand, we are told that we should not use the schwa in such words as omit and location. The preferred pronunciations:

[o ˈmɪt, lo ˈkeʃʌn]

To say something which sounds like uh-mit [ə ˈmɪt] and luh-cation [lə ˈkeʃʌn] is wrong.

As far as the unaccented [o] is concerned, in some cases you may have to consult a dictionary. In other cases, your better judgment will tell you that fell-uh for fellow and pianuh for piano would be unsatisfactory under any circumstances.

[o] is required in most of the o words in the material below. Keep the lips well rounded and protruded for this sound.

a.   The obedient oaf hid both bars of soap near the oak.
b.   I hope that Joe will not choke on the bone.
c.   Post the oath of rotation on the post.
d.   He was hoping that both ghosts would float away.
e.   The host gloated mostly over the unopened toaster.
f.   The official could not tell Goldie the location of the old yellow hotel.
g.   In Joe Jones' opinion the ovation should have been omitted after the oration.

h. *The Shadow*, an old program on radio, often dealt with bones, moans, and groans.

i. *Oklahoma*, a Broadway show, is the mellow story of a lonesome cowpoke.

j. The bold soldier from Ohio gloated when he won at poker.

107. Now and then we hear the schwa [ə] inserted before or after [o].

Result: *go* changes to *guh-o* [g əo]

                gold changes to *go-uhld* [g oəld]

The intrusive schwa should be eliminated. If [o] follows another consonant, start rounding the lips as you make the initial consonant. If [o] precedes another consonant, continue the lip rounding through the production of the other consonant.

Avoid making [ə-o] or [o- ə] as you practice these:

a. He scolded the cold foal for falling into the hole.

b. He sold the whole roll for a piece of gold soap.

c. The open boat was towed to the ocean coast.

d. When Joe felt the blow, he hit his foe with a lump of frozen coal.

e. The golden rule is that there are no golden rules.

f. A man of no conversation should smoke.

g. Gold! Gold! Gold! Gold! Bright and yellow, hard and cold.

h. A man never goes so far as when he does not know where he is going.

i. Ghosts were created when the first man woke at night.

j. As soon as people are old enough to know better, they don't know anything at all.

Example: The outlaw's scalded jaw looked rather raw to Paul in the morning.

Typical Production:

The tongue should be relatively low, although the back of the tongue may be partially elevated. The lips are slightly rounded; they may or may not be somewhat protruded. The muscles of both the tongue and the lips are a little bit less tense than for [o].

Faults or Problems:

108. [ɔ] is a notoriously fickle sound. The area of the country in which you live will have some influence on your pronunciation of this unstable vowel. To add a little more confusion: if you were to ask each member of your class to say *Paul*, you might hear at least three different vowel sounds. Obviously, even within geographical areas, there will still be individual differences.

Some individuals will frequently use [ɒ or ɑ], the next two vowels to be discussed, in place of [ɔ]. A few persons do not seem to use [ɔ] at all. Fortunately, [ɔ] does not involve too many major problems.

In certain sections of the East, it is not uncommon to hear [ɚ] added to [ɔ].

Result: *law* [lɔ] may become *law-r* [lɔɚ]

                jaw [dʒɔ] may become *jaw-r* [dʒɔɚ]

(This problem is discussed in greater detail in Exercise 53 of this chapter.) Occasionally [ə or ʊ] may be added to [ɔ].

Result: *ball* [bɔl] may become *ba-uhl* [bɔəl]
 daughter [ˈdɔtɚ] may become *da-ooter* [ˈdɔutɚ]

Those whose speech is Southern should be careful to avoid inserting [w] as well as the schwa [ə]. If this is done:

 tall [tɔl] becomes *ta-wuhl* [tɔwəl]
 taught [tɔt] becomes *ta-wuht* [tɔwət]

Less commonly, [o] may be inserted after [ɔ].

 talk [tɔlk] becomes *ta-ohk* [tɔok]
 chalk [tʃɔlk] becomes *cha-ohk* [tʃɔok]

Such additions as these are generally considered incorrect. Be sure that they are not present in your speech as you read the following:

a.

wash	shawl	thought	moth
gone	caught	squaw	cough
maw	Saul	falcon	morgue
awl	yawn	loss	wrong
loud	brawl	lorry	broad

b. George guffawed when Morse caught the ball on the wall.
c. The thoughtful foreman ate the morsel of warm sauce.
d. The author saw the flaw in Shaw's play about the Indian squaw.
e. The hawk often gnawed the awning on the auburn halter.
f. Mort and his auto were caught in the squall last August.
g. Paul crawled and pawed his way across the broad sidewalk.
h. Maud fed the hawk corn, sauce, and pork.
i. At dawn, Ross honked the horn and hauled away the straw.
j. Saul faltered but then blew the horn to call the fawn.

$$[\mathrm{o} - \breve{\mathrm{o}}]$$

Example: Odd moths hide in soft moss under frosty logs.

Typical Production:

The tongue muscles are relaxed and the back of the tongue and the jaw drop slightly from the [ɔ] position. The lips are less rounded and the lip opening is wider than for [ɔ].

[ɒ] is often described as being midway between the [ɔ] sound we hear in <u>all</u> and the [ɒ] sound we hear in <u>palm</u>. The sound appears in American English somewhat sporadically, and it is by no means consistent. It is occasionally present in the speech of eastern New England, New York, and western Pennsylvania. In General American speech, the use of [ɒ] is not common. Yet it must not be branded as nonexistent wherever General American is used, for it can and does appear in the speech of some individuals.

109. Try to use [ɔ] in each of the following words. Then pronounce them again, using [ɒ]. Finally, see if you can approximate [ɑ]:

a.
stop	odd	doll	got
loss	toss	water	off
often	moth	coffee	mock
watch	golf	gloss	frost
hog	cost	wander	scoff
mop	job	fodder	offer
soft	opera	profit	dog

Which of the three sounds seems to be the most natural to you? Practice saying them until you are quite certain. Then read the following. Regardless of which sound you may use, and you may possibly use all three of them in one sentence, avoid exaggerated lip rounding:

b. Honesty is often the best policy.

c. She sang softly the long song about the moth which fell off the coffee cup.

d. Don sobbed as the chocolate shop was robbed while he watched.

e. Olive Wallace wandered about oddly from job to job.

f. Olga poured the watered broth on the popcorn.

g. The dog often wandered around on the glossy golf course.

h. It is wrong for audiences to scoff at opera.

i. Miss Moss offered the frosted chocolate to her father.

j. The lost ox ate the moss in the forest.

k. It isn't the cough
That carries you off;
It's the coffin
They carry you off in.

[ɑ]   [ä]

Example: Father calmly carted Tom's ominous looking bomb into the barn.

Typical Production:

The tongue should be low, relatively flat, and relaxed on the floor of the mouth. Some individuals produce this sound with the back of the tongue slightly raised. The lips are rather far apart and unrounded. The jaw is dropped to the lowest point possible for any of the vowels.

Faults or Problems:

110. [ɑ] is a widely used and pleasant sound. American English has many so-called "short o" words, such as "cot, not, dot, hot," and a majority of us pronounce these words with [ɑ].

Similarly, we have an abundance of common words in which the letter a is followed by r: "warm, car, part, large," and with many of these, too, the [ɑ] is generally used.

Easterners, especially New Englanders, may use [ɔ and ɒ] in "short o" words. [a] is often favored over [ɑ] in the ar words listed above. These are quite standard variations.

Many foreign languages lack the [æ] of *and*. Thus, in learning English, foreigners will often substitute a sound close to [ɑ] where the [æ] is required.

Result: *cat* will be pronounced something like *cot* [kɑt] instead of [kæt].

Say [æ and ɑ] and feel the obvious difference in tongue position. For [æ], the tongue will be thrust forward, but for [ɑ] it will be thrust back.

[ɑ] is an easily made sound. Avoid confusing it with [æ]:

a.

sot-sat	pod-pad	knock-knack
stock-stack	mop-map	bond-band
lock-lack	Don-Dan	pot-pat
hot-hat	chop-chap	hock-hack

b.   Dan guarded the yarn mop as Don pointed to the map.
c.   Did Tom's partner hock the hacksaw in the shack on the dock?
d.   The lad caught the cod but not the gnawing rat.
e.   The barge man with the badge tacked the lock onto the sack.
f.   The ox backed into the axe on the box.
g.   Pat gave the pot of lard to the lad who had argued with the sergeant.
h.   He put the patch on the smashed cot in the parched marsh.

111.   If [ɑ] is near a nasal sound: [m, n, ŋ] there is frequently a tendency to "push the vowel through the nose"—in other words, to produce an unpleasantly nasalized [ɑ]. If you will remember that the velum must be lowered for the production of the nasal consonants, but not for other sounds, you should be able to avoid an unpleasant quality with this vowel.

As is the case with several other vowels, the schwa [ə] can be inserted after [ɑ], but this may label your speech as provincial. Do not say *ho-uht* [hɑət] for *hot* [hɑt] or *cho-uhp* [tʃɑəp] for *chop* [tʃɑp].

Check for nasalization and schwa insertions as you read these:

a.   She saw Ronald sing the psalm with calm and charm.
b.   Carl called to the cawing crow from the worn-out car.
c.   The auk yawned as it pushed the shark into the rock.
d.   Lottie taught the little tot to saw the sod.
e.   The star, Robert Arthur, was alarmed when his partner marred the armor.
f.   Father argued calmly with the farmer in the park.
g.   Otters and larks were part of the cargo of Noah's Ark.
h.   Polly Martin said, "Let us honor the army from Oz."
i.   The sharkskin scarf was a bargain in Charleston.

Assignment 19 (See suggested Checklist for this assignment)

Prepare material containing many examples of the back vowels with which you particularly need practice. As a reminder, here is a key:

[u]	o͞o b<u>oo</u>t	[ɔ]	ô <u>a</u>ll
[ʊ]	o͝o b<u>oo</u>k	[ɒ]	o or ŏ <u>o</u>dd
[o]	ō h<u>o</u>pe	[ɑ]	ä <u>a</u>lms

224

Suggested Checklist for Assignment 19

As you practice by yourself you may want to work with this checklist. Listen carefully to yourself. It if is feasible record the assignment or get a classmate or friend to listen to you as you read the material. Eventually your goal will be to have a check mark in the Yes column for each category. (Optional: Perhaps your instructor will want to use the checklist to evaluate you during your classroom presentation.)

	Yes	No
Avoids inserting [ɪ] or the schwa [ə] before or after back vowels.		
Avoids addition of [ʊ] to back vowels.		
Avoids addition of [r] to back vowels.		
Avoids nasalized production of back vowels especially when they are preceded or followed by [m n or ŋ].		
Avoids substituting [ə or ʌ] for [ʊ or u].		
Avoids substituting [ʊ] for [u] or [u] for [ʊ].		
Avoids confusing [o and ʊ] especially when [r] follows.		
Avoids substituting [ə or ʌ] for [o].		
Avoids addition of [ɚ] to [ɔ or ɑ].		
Avoids substituting [æ or ʌ] for [ɑ].		

Additional comments or suggestions:

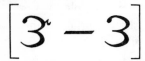

[ûr]

Classification: [ɝ]:   "r coloring" is present. Characteristic of most General American speech.

[ɜ]:   "r coloring" is absent. Characteristic of Eastern New England, large areas of the South and many individuals in New York City.

Examples: [ɝ]:   Early birds who chirp in fir trees do not catch emerging worms.

[ɜ]:   Murphy, the stern attorney, turned down her urgent plea.

Typical Production:

[ɝ]: The tongue should be slightly retracted and the central portion of it should be raised midhigh toward the palate. The tongue tip may be raised toward the front part of the palate. Generally the lips are unrounded and open.

[ɜ]: The lips and the jaw are approximately in the same position as for [ɝ], but the tip of the tongue is somewhat spread and rests behind the lower front teeth. [ɝ-ɜ] occur only in accented syllables.

Faults or Problems:

For those who use [ɝ] (with "r coloring"):

112. Some speakers produce a satisfactory [ɝ] curling the front of the tongue backward toward the hard palate. If the degree of tongue-curling is excessive, a rather hard and unpleasant sound may result. This particular kind of [ɝ] is not uncommon among Midwesterners, but in many other areas of the United States it may attract unfavorable attention to itself. Nor should the sound be prolonged, the tongue held too tensely or retracted too far. The hillbilly type of comedian, so popular on TV, does this purely for comic effect when he says, "Gol durrrrrn it!"

Avoid an unduly conspicuous, hard, or prolonged [ɝ] as you read:

a.   The Earl of Burton purchased the ermine furs for Myrtle and Irma.
b.   Shirley was certain that she would smirk during the sermon.
c.   Colonel Virgil journeyed around the world in his purring whirlybird.
d.   The third girl was irked when her purse fell into the furnace.
e.   Burt learned to herd furry squirrels through the birches.
f.   He referred to the murder which occurred in Jersey.
g.   The dirty shirts were a burden to the suburban merchant.
h.   Is it urgent for the girls to search for the spurned urchin?
i.   Ernest urged Verna not to hurl the pearl from the fir tree.

113. English spelling, as we have noted several times, is not always helpful as far as pronunciation is concerned. Now and then, however, it is an excellent guide. What is the problem with the salesman who says:

"A hunderd pre cent perfer our product."

when he means:

"A hundred per cent prefer our product."

His problem is not primarily that of an incorrect tongue position, for example. He is simply guilty of ignoring the spelling of certain words with *re* and *er* combinations.

Contrast the following nonstandard with the standard pronunciations. Nonstandard pronunciations are in the left-hand columns; standard, in the right.

a.
childern-children	prefect-perfect
pertend-pretend	kinderd-kindred
preform-perform	pervail-prevail
modren-modern	preplex-perplex

As far as the *re, ra, ro,* and *er* combinations in the underlined words are concerned, let the spelling guide you as you read:

b. The organist perspired as he performed the "Prelude to the Afternoon of a Faun."

c. "Perhaps this prescription will prevent you from dying," said Dr. Preston.

d. The weather man, who is one hundred per cent right, says to prepare for precipitation.

e. She tried to preserve the perfume which spoiled the pattern on the apron.

f. The Presbyterian preferred the preliminary performance.

g. In modern times, the per capita income is higher in eastern and western countries.

h. The perverse Persian made his entrance banging the percussion instrument.

i. It was predictable that the Southerner would attend the premiere of the movie.

For those who use [ɜ] (without "r coloring"):

114. Do not make a diphthong out of [ɜ]. In other words, do not insert an extra and unwanted sound before or after the vowel in question. Easterners, and especially those in the New York City area, should avoid saying *bird* [bɜd] so that it sounds like:

> *be-id* [bɜɪd]
>
> *be-uhd* [bɜəd]
>
> *buh-id* [bʌɪd]

Avoid adding an unnecessary sound before or after [ɜ]:

a.
heard	gird	Bert
whirl	jerk	earth
dirt	curl	fur
third	burn	curse
pearl	were	lurk
girl	search	verse

b. Mr. Earl boiled the herbs and burrs over the turf.

c. The nurse was irked as she read the terse verse in a girlish voice.

d. To earn while you learn is worthy; to learn while you earn is perfect.

e. A bird in the hand is worth what it will bring.

f. The service we render to others is really the rent we pay for our room on this earth.

g. Perfume: Any smell that is used to drown a worse one.

h. If a little bird whispers some gossip in your ear, be sure it isn't a cuckoo bird.

i. Her capacity for affection is superb; when her third husband died, her hair turned quite gold from grief.

Example: Robert Baker, the other actor, played the killer better in "Murder in Amsterdam."

Typical Production:

Approximately the same as for [ɝ], but it has a more relaxed production. The tongue position may be lower.

The principal difference between [ɝ and ɚ] is this:

> [ɚ] occurs in unstressed syllables. [ɚ] is shorter in duration than [ɝ].
> [ɝ] occurs only in stressed syllables.

The word *further,* for example, contains both sounds: [ˈf ɝ ð ɚ]

[ɚ] occurs mostly in General American speech. Speakers from Eastern New England, large areas of the South and sections of New York City tend to use [ə]—without "r coloring."

Faults or Problems:

115. [ɚ] should never be stressed or prolonged. It is shorter and weaker than [ɝ]. As you practice the following, do not neglect the sound but be certain that it is not emphasized or drawn out:
>   *a.*   The dancer lost her feathers after she was deserted by her manager.
>   *b.*   The rainmaker tried to measure the waterfall at his leisure.
>   *c.*   Faces of hunters and sailors never appear on picture posters.
>   *d.*   I wonder if Dr. Miller blundered by tacking the roster on the pillar.
>   *e.*   Herbert murmured that the dollar mirror had been tossed into the harbor.
>   *f.*   The baton twirler threw the copper ringer at the welder.
>   *g.*   Yesterday, Mother and Father had a wonderful time making butter.
>   *h.*   An elephant never forgets—but after all, what has it got to remember?
>   *i.*   Poverty is the stepmother of genius.
>   *j.*   A nightingale dies for shame if another bird sings better.
>   *k.*   Go to your business, pleasure, while I go to my pleasure, business.
>   *l.*   The singer was a better letter writer than the teacher.
>   *m.*   The actor treasured the first dollar he had made in the Zephyr Theatre.

Example: Anita was amazed to find Eva, the adult gorilla, eating bananas in the arena.

Typical Production:

The tongue should be relatively low and relaxed. The central portion of the tongue may be very slightly arched. The lips are not rounded, the jaw is relaxed and the mouth is slightly open. [ə] can appear only in unstressed positions.

[ə] is too interesting a sound to deserve entirely the descriptions it frequently receives: "dull," "gray," "colorless." A more accurate description might be "neutral."

Theoretically, if one were to mix every conceivable color of paint, the result would be an off-shade of black. If it were possible to mix all the vowels together, the result might possibly be the schwa: [ə]. It is possibly the most commonly used vowel in our language. English spelling by no means indicates the frequency with which we use it.

For example, note the underlined vowel in the word *about*. If we pronounce the word by itself, slowly and carefully, it is possibly true that we might pronounce the initial *a* with the same sound we use in *ask* [æsk]: [ˈæbaʊt].

But everyday conversation or even formal speech is generally connected speech; it moves rather rapidly, and most of us will follow the path of least resistance and use the [ə]. It is an easier sound to make than [æ]; it is perhaps the easiest of all vowel sounds to produce.

A large majority of us, therefore, will pronounce *about* this way: [əˈbaʊt].

How do we pronounce the underlined *o* in *welcome?* To use the *o* that we use in *go* or *not* would make the pronunciation absurdly stilted. Again, the unstressed vowel becomes [ə: ˈwɛlkəm].

The final *a* in *idea?* For most of us: [aɪˈdiə].

As it can be seen, there is a very definite tendency for vowel sounds in unaccented positions to lose their individual coloring and identities and become [ə].

Faults or Problems:

116. There are two problems involving [ə]:

Speakers with slovenly diction often omit or swallow the sound. There is no reason whatsoever for eliminating this helpful little sound. When its presence is called for, however, we should remember that the schwa is always short and unstressed.

The sound is unnecessarily "tacked on" to the beginnings of many verbs.

One of the speech mannerisms of those who try to create an impression of being "folksy" or quaint is the insertion of [ə] before a verb. In certain "folksy" speech we hear:

"I'm a-comin' and then we're a-goin' a-fishin'."

(It almost goes without saying that these people will also substitute [n] for final [ŋ].)

If there is such a thing as "small town" General American dialect, this is certainly one of its characteristics. The intruded [ə] is heard frequently not only in the Mid-West, but it is widely heard in certain areas of the South and Southwest. This mannerism should be eliminated.

Watch for unaccented vowels as you read the material below. If the schwa substitution is acceptable, use it, but do not emphasize or lengthen it. A "tap," a short vocal grunt, will do. Avoid using it as a prefix to certain verbs.

a. Rita adores dancing around when the orchestra plays.
b. Howard and Ella read quiet poems to one another.
c. Nora admitted that the breakfast chocolate was terrible.
d. Martin, the solemn postman, had a mania for violent accidents.
e. The audience fell asleep while awaiting the appearance of the tuba player.
f. The police agreed that the cruel riot would have to be suppressed.
g. Christians and zebras were fed to savage lions in the arena.
h. The president did not allow the American editor to annoy the police.
i. Greta and Amanda drank the vanilla soda at the circus.
j. The visitor was amazed at the jewels hidden in the camera.
k. Mom was sitting under the umbrella, washing and peeling potatoes.

Example: Uncle Chuck discovered the lucky buck buried under a ton of mud.

Typical Production:

Open the mouth, relax the jaw and tongue. The tongue plays a rather passive role, but the central part of it may be raised slightly. The lips are unrounded. [ʌ] occurs most frequently in syllables which carry some accent or stress; it occurs infrequently in unstressed syllables.

117. [ɪ or ɛ] are sometimes erroneously substituted for [ʌ].

Result: *just* [dʒʌst]

will then be mispronounced as

jist [dʒɪst] or *jest* [dʒɛst]

There are many [ʌ] sounds in the following. Be careful to articulate that sound rather than [ɪ or ɛ]:

a. "Just think," said Judge Dunn, "such judgment as this is indeed unjust."
b. Mr. Munn ducked when the bunny jumped from the brush.
c. Mother clutched the big jug which was full of nuts and onions.
d. "Shucks," muttered Sonny, "I can jump up there and touch the skull."
e. Buck just did not enjoy much of his lunch after he had drunk the punch.
f. It was a blunder for the thug to pour honey on the bun.
g. The hungry monkey lunged at the supper in the oven.
h. The usher mumbled as they hovered over the young umpire.
i. Suburbs are things to come into the city from.
j. The old-time mother, who used to wonder where her boy was, now has a grandson who wonders where his mother is.

118. Those with foreign language backgrounds are prone to substitute other vowels for [ʌ]:

Do not substitute $\begin{cases} [u] \text{ as in } cool \\ [ɔ] \text{ as in } all \\ [ɑ] \text{ as in } calm \end{cases}$ for [ʌ].

[u and ɔ] have been described, and you will remember that they require for their production some activity of the back of the tongue, while [ʌ] is a relaxed central vowel which may need a slight raising of the central portion of the tongue. Too, the tongue should be raised higher for [ʌ] than for [ɑ].

Distinguish carefully among them:

a. | [u-ʌ] | [ɔ-ʌ] | [ɑ-ʌ] |
    |---|---|---|
    | boot-but | Gaul-gull | sop-sup |
    | shoot-shut | pawn-pun | knot-nut |
    | goose-Gus | call-cull | cob-cub |
    | coot-cut | gone-gun | calm-come |
    | room-rum | moss-muss | mock-muck |

b. Tom Thumb was fond of putting funds in the hot hut.
c. Maude caught Hud's hawk tucking mud under the cot.
d. The dog dug in the sod and gnawed under the nut tree before Don was done.
e. Middle age occurs when you are too young to take up golf and too old to rush up to the net.
f. The Cooper couple was unable to put the mutton and the duck on the other dock.

Assignment 20 (See suggested Checklist for this assignment)

Prepare material containing many examples of the central vowels with which you particularly need practice. As a reminder, here is a key:

[ɝ — ɜ] ûr f<u>ir</u> [ɚ] ər ev<u>er</u>

[ə] ə ide<u>a</u> [ʌ] u or ŭ <u>u</u>p

Suggested Checklist for Assignment 20

As you practice by yourself you may want to work with this checklist. Listen carefully to yourself. If it is feasible record the assignment or get a classmate or friend to listen to you as you read the material. Eventually your goal will be to have a check mark in the **Yes** column for each category. (Optional: Perhaps your instructor will want to use the checklist to evaluate you during your classroom presentation.)

	Yes	No
Avoids a tense, conspicuous [ɝ].		
Avoids a stressed, prolonged [ɚ].		
Avoids emphasizing the schwa [ə].		
Avoids overuse of the schwa [ə] or inserting it where it does not belong.		
Avoids omitting the schwa [ə].		
Avoids inserting an off-glide [ɪ] or the schwa [ə] before or after middle vowels.		
Avoids substituting [ɔ ɪ] for [ɝ or ɜ].		
Avoids confusing [ɝ] and [ɜ].		
Avoids mispronunciations in words containing *re, ra, ro, er* spellings.		
Avoids substituting [ɪ or ɛ] for [ʌ].		
Avoids substituting [u ɔ or ɑ] for [ʌ].		

Additional comments or suggestions:

Review Material for All the Vowels

119. Front Vowels: *The material in this section emphasizes vowels in which the front part of the tongue is most active:*

[i] ē	[ɛ] e or ĕ
[ɪ] i or ĭ	[æ] a or ă
[e] ā	[a] ȧ or ă

a. A thief is never the one who steals but the one who gets caught.
b. The greatest joy a petty soul can taste is to dupe a great soul and catch it in a snare.
c. The ailing women found the key to the bicycle and then handed the subpoena to the friendly people.
d. In eating, a third of the stomach should be filled with food, a third with drink, and the rest left empty.
e. Hell is truth seen too late.
f. A man who is a master of patience is master of everything else.
g. The worst men often give the best advice.
h. Military Fame: To be killed in the field of battle and have our names spelled wrong in the newspapers.
i. There are many people who think that Sunday is a sponge to wipe out all the other sins of the week.
j. Every man should have a fair-sized cemetery in which to bury the faults of his friends.

120. Back Vowels: *The material in this section emphasizes vowels in which the back part of the tongue is most active:*

[u] o͞o	[ɔ] ô
[ʊ] o͝o	[ɒ] o or ŏ
[o] ō	[ɑ] ä

a. Moonshine is all moonshine to me.
b. Modern Art: Oodles of doodles.
c. An old man in a house is a good sign.
d. There are more books upon books than all other subjects.
e. Let us be thankful for fools; but for them the rest of us could not succeed.
f. It was hot on the open range, of course, and many good foods were cooked there.
g. It was the old notion that justice should not arise from laws, but laws from justice.
h. Men are called fools in one age for not knowing what they were called fools for in the age before.
i. Some people are so dry that you might soak them in a joke for a month and it would not get through their skins.
j. All work, even cotton-spinning, is noble; work is alone noble. A life of ease is not for any man, for any god.

121. Mid- or Central Vowels: *The material in this section emphasizes vowels in which the central part of the tongue is most active:*

[ɝ — ɜ] ûr	[ɚ] ər
[ə] ə	[ʌ] u or ŭ

a. We are franker towards others than towards ourselves.
b. The drummer and the tuba player earned and deserved the award.
c. Good luck is a lazy man's estimate of a worker's success.
d. He is old enough to know better—or worse.

e. A dog is the only thing on earth that loves you more than he loves himself.
f. California is a fine place to live in—if you happen to be an orange.
g. Everyone is crazy but me and thee, and sometimes I suspect thee a little.
h. If it were not for the presents, an elopement would be preferable.
i. The worst of enemies are flatterers, and the worst of flatterers are pleasures.
j. I am never less at leisure than when at leisure, nor less alone than when I am alone.

Diphthongs

A diphthong is a continuous, gliding, and rapid blending together of two vowel sounds within the same syllable. There is no interruption or breaking-off as the articulators move from the position of the first vowel to that of the second. A diphthong changes quality during its production. The first vowel element receives greater stress than the second vowel element.

As an example, consider the diphthong *ou* [aʊ] in the oft-quoted *How now, brown cow?* [haʊ naʊ braʊn kaʊ]. Say the words slowly and you will discover that the two vowel elements you are blending together in each word consist of:

[a] as in *path* + [ʊ] as in *book*

Blend [a] rapidly with [ʊ] and you will make the diphthong *ou* [aʊ]. (Many speakers start the diphthong with another vowel: [a] as in *c<u>a</u>lm*, a quite acceptable variation.)

However, a diphthong is not always represented by two letters in conventional spelling. The *i* in *night* [naɪt] is also a diphthong. Say the sound by itself and prolong it. You will hear both vowel elements:

[a] as in *path* + [ɪ] as in *it*

Blend the two rapidly and you will produce [aɪ].

[aɪ]   [ī]

Example: M<u>i</u>ke g<u>ui</u>ded the f<u>i</u>ve sk<u>y</u> d<u>i</u>vers down the <u>ai</u>sle to the h<u>i</u>gh w<u>i</u>re.

Typical Production:

The [aɪ] diphthong begins with the front of the relaxed tongue relatively low, the lips unrounded, and the jaw dropped quite far. It glides to a position in which the front of the tongue is raised relatively high and far forward.

Faults or Problems:

122. Quite commonly in Southern speech the first vowel element is overstressed and overprolonged. As a result, the second vowel element may be weakened to [ə].

Result: *I like to dine* may sound like *Ah lah-uhk to dah-uhn* [a laək tə daən].

In other cases, the second vowel element is virtually allowed to disappear. We hear: *Ah lahk to dahn* [a lak tə dan].

Overstress of the second vowel element, and this is often characteristic of labored or pedantic speech, may result in the substitution of [i] for [ɪ].

high [haɪ] may sound something like *ha-ee* [hai]
rice [raɪs] may sound something like *ra-ees* [rais]

234

Avoid overstressing or dropping either element of [aɪ] as you practice this material:

a.

sigh	buy	geyser	lime
height	lie	rhyme	alive
kite	isle	eye	Ida
try	icicle	miser	guile
icon	dye	cried	bison

b.   Why did I hide Mr. Niles' pineapple pie in the untidy icebox?

c.   To decline life is to decline God.

d.   The ivy and the iris were piled high in the rye.

e.   The pilot cut the tricycle tires with my ivory-handled knife.

f.   The sky is the daily bread of the eyes.

g.   A lie in time saves nine.

h.   I think true love is never blind, but instead, brings an added light.

i.   I do not mind lying, but I hate inaccuracy.

j.   There's a time for some things, and a time for all things; a time for great things, and a time for small things.

k.   I am poor, and I am glad that I am, for I find that wealth makes people more mean and unkind than it does generous.

l.   He who says, what is mine is yours and what is yours is yours, is a saint. He who says, what is yours is mine and what is mine is mine, is a wicked man.

$$[\text{ɔɪ}] \qquad\qquad\qquad [\text{oi}]$$

<u>Example:</u>   The n<u>oi</u>sy b<u>oy</u>s br<u>oi</u>led R<u>oy</u>'s sirl<u>oi</u>n in the s<u>oy</u> sauce.

<u>Typical Production:</u>

Start the sound from the position for [ɔ] as in *awe:* The back of the tongue is generally elevated, and the lips are slightly rounded. It glides to a position in which the front of the tongue is raised relatively high and far forward.

123. The "beautiful goil on thoity-thoid street" type of speech in the New York City area is not quite as common as non-New Yorkers sometimes like to think. Certain New Yorkers frequently pronounce the word *girl* so that it resembles *ge-il* [gɜɪl]— without the "r coloring."

Occasionally, "New Yorkese" pronounces *oil* as *erl* [ɝl]—with the "r coloring." But here, again, however, *e-il* [ɜɪl]—without the "r coloring" is noted more commonly.

New Yorkers, themselves, do not agree entirely on the acceptability of *goil* for *girl* and *erl* for *oil*, but many of them do find the *goil-erl* type of speech nonstandard.

Some speakers tend to omit the second element of the diphthong, allowing *coil* to become *co'l* [kɔl]. Others, by rounding the lips too much or placing the tongue too far forward, substitute [o] for [ɔ]. *Toy* [tɔɪ] becomes [toɪ]. Either of these practices should be avoided.

In some provincial or old-fashioned speech [aɪ] and [ɔɪ] are confused. The mountain folk of West Virginia, for example, may readily ask you to *jine* [dʒaɪn] instead of *join* [dʒɔɪn] them.

If you have been told that your [ɔɪ] diphthong is quaint, rustic, or otherwise attention-getting, rehearse the following. Approximately the same degree of lip-rounding used to produce [ɔ] by itself is necessary for [ɔɪ]:

a.

coy	void	royal	join	gargoyle
loiter	point	doit	buoy	Troy
toyed	foyer	toil	loin	foil
doily	foist	destroy	choice	convoy
voice	joist	envoy	Roy	embroil

b. What kind of a noise annoys a poised cowboy?
c. Roy adroitly pointed the decoy at the void.
d. The convoy was foiled in its attempt to destroy Troy.
e. In a loud voice the envoy from Savoy said "Ahoy!"
f. Lloyd enjoyed putting the foil on the oiled coil.
g. Hoyle hurled the moist oilskin at Earl Boyd.
h. Joyce toiled to hoist the tile over the side of the soiled oil-burner.
i. Did the boy buy the coiled file from Doyle?
j. Mr. Rice's choice was a nice new Rolls-Royce.
k. There's many a boy here today who looks on war with great joy, but, boys, it is all hell.
l. Boy: A noise with dirt on it.
m. Miss Loy enjoyed toying with the coins.
n. In Detroit, Mr. Royal is employed to toil in the soil.
o. Floyd pointed the coil at the boiler.

[aʊ]   [oʊ]

<u>Example:</u>   H<u>ow</u>ard G<u>ow</u>, the <u>ou</u>tlaw, hid <u>ou</u>r br<u>own</u> s<u>ow</u> s<u>ou</u>th of the m<u>ou</u>nd of fl<u>ow</u>ers.

<u>Typical Production:</u>

This diphthong, like [aɪ] in "M<u>i</u>ke," also begins with the front of the relaxed tongue relatively low and the lips unrounded. [a] is the first vowel element. It then glides to a position in which the back of the tongue is elevated and the lips are definitely rounded. [ʊ] is the second vowel element.

Also acceptable, of course, is a blending of the [ɑ] of "c<u>a</u>lm" with [ʊ]. [ɑ] similarly requires the tongue to be low and relatively flat and relaxed.

<u>Faults or Problems:</u>

124. In certain sections of the East, notably in the New York City, Philadelphia, and the Baltimore areas, as well as scattered regions in the South, [aʊ] is often rendered as an extremely unpleasant sound. Instead of using [a or ɑ] as the first vowel element, some speakers from these areas use the [æ] of *as* or the [ɛ] of *egg*.

A combination of:

$$[\ae + \upsilon]\ \text{or of}\ [\varepsilon + \upsilon]$$

in place of:

$$[a + \upsilon]\ \text{or of}\ [\alpha + \upsilon]$$

generally results in a sound which is exceedingly displeasing. It often happens if the tongue is raised too high or held too tensely. A tight, tense jaw will also give this diphthong a hard edginess. The sound has been likened, with considerable justification, to the "meouw" of an irritable cat. To determine which type of diphthong you use, and to correct an improper substitute, try the following:

		as	book	egg	book	path	book	calm	book
a.	(Separately	æ	ʊ	ɛ	ʊ	a	ʊ	ɑ	ʊ
	and	æ	ʊ	ɛ	ʊ	a	ʊ	ɑ	ʊ
	slowly)	æ	ʊ	ɛ	ʊ	a	ʊ	ɑ	ʊ
b.	(Separately and	æ	ʊ	ɛ	ʊ	a	ʊ	ɑ	ʊ
	moderately	æ	ʊ	ɛ	ʊ	a	ʊ	ɑ	ʊ
	rapid)	æ	ʊ	ɛ	ʊ	a	ʊ	ɑ	ʊ
c.	(Blended	æ	ʊ	ɛ	ʊ	a	ʊ	ɑ	ʊ
	together	æ	ʊ	ɛ	ʊ	a	ʊ	ɑ	ʊ
	rapidly)	æ	ʊ	ɛ	ʊ	a	ʊ	ɑ	ʊ

		path	book	path	book	calm	book	calm	book
d.	(Blended	a	ʊ	a	ʊ	ɑ	ʊ	ɑ	ʊ
	together	a	ʊ	a	ʊ	ɑ	ʊ	ɑ	ʊ
	rapidly)	a	ʊ	a	ʊ	ɑ	ʊ	ɑ	ʊ

Carefully avoid the use of [æ or ɛ] as the first vowel element of the *ou* and *ow* blends in the following:

- *e.* How, now, brown cow?
- *f.* Howard will not allow Mr. Bowers to go downtown now.
- *g.* The hound and the owl dropped the flowers into the cowl.
- *h.* I vow that the shouting outlaw will be found down south.
- *i.* Somehow, the clown chased the routed cow around the plow.
- *j.* Lowbrows pout and raise their eyebrows if highbrows scowl at cowboy movies.
- *k.* The howling chow dog chased the scout around the bow.
- *l.* Although Gower has the gout he won his bout with the huge trout.
- *m.* "How!" said the Indian, as the shower drowned out the powwow.
- *n.* Mr. Crowley's loud howls roused the cowed crowd.
- *o.* He found the hourglass under the lout's outfit.
- *p.* Outer Space: Our largest suburb.
- *q.* Cowards do not count in battle; they are there, but not in it.
- *r.* Better be a devout coward than a corpse.

125. Substituting [æ or ɛ] for [a] is, in itself, generally objectionable, but there is another possible complication. [æ and ɛ] are often unduly nasalized, especially if a nasal sound—[m, n, ŋ]—precedes or follows them. Add excessive nasality to [æʊ or ɛʊ] and a disagreeably metallic and tense diphthong results.

Practice this material, avoiding [æ-ɛ] variations or exaggerated nasality in words containing *ou* or *ow*.

- *a.* The brown mouse ran around the mountain town.
- *b.* His mouth sagged as the hound pounced on the ground behind the mound.
- *c.* "Now, now!" said the clown, "don't flounder when you count nouns."

d. The sound of the old round affected Mr. Downes profoundly.

e. The Count bowed to Mrs. Dow when she found the crown.

f. I swapped my cat and got me a mouse,
His tail caught fire and he burned down the house.

g. The brown, ground meat was stuffed into the hound's mouth.

h. He announced that he would count the crowns in the lounge now.

i. She frowned as the hound trounced the astounded owl.

j. It sounded as if Mr. Mount wished to impound a large amount of beef.

<u>Example</u>: <u>O</u>ld cr<u>o</u>ws do not ride sl<u>o</u>w b<u>o</u>ats on sn<u>o</u>w-c<u>o</u>ated <u>o</u>ceans.

<u>Typical Production</u>:

The tongue, slightly tense, is in a midhigh position. Lips should be rounded and protruded. It glides to a position in which the back of the tongue is raised; lip-rounding continues.

[ou] is most often used in accented syllables. In unstressed positions, the simple vowel [o] is frequently used. (For a discussion of this sound, see Exercises 106-107.)

Go, row the old boat, is entirely acceptable even if the so-called *o* sounds are not diphthongized. There is no block to understanding if one says:

> [go ro ðə old bot]
>
> > instead of
>
> [gou rou ðə ould bout]

<u>Faults or Problems</u>:

126. Very commonly in the East and the Middle Atlantic section of the United States, this diphthong becomes a triphthong. A sound approximating [ɛ] is inserted before the [o], and the resulting conglomeration sounds something like [ɛou]. This distortion is often present in the speech of the same individuals who say [æu] for [au]. Similarly, it may be accompanied by excessive nasality and tenseness.

Strive for relatively simple, uncluttered [o or ou] sounds as you read the following. The degree of diphthongization is highly variable, of course. Protrude and round the lips. Avoid unnecessary tenseness and nasality.

a. The odor of roses hung over the snow in Nome.

b. I know that Mr. Moto dropped the bone in the moat.

c. The moaning tone of the oboe floated through the open window.

d. Joe scrubbed the oval face of the oaf until it shone.

e. "Oh," said Poe, "I left my poem, an ode, at home."

f. A poet in history is divine, but a poet in the next room is a joke.

g. A straw vote only shows which way the hot air blows.

h. Polo: Ping-pong with ponies.

i. He that goes a-borrowing goes a-sorrowing.

j. Oboe: An ill woodwind that nobody blows well.

238

[eɪ]   [ā]

<u>Example:</u>   They m<u>ay</u> del<u>ay</u> st<u>a</u>ging the f<u>a</u>mous pl<u>ay</u> about the l<u>a</u>dy from Sp<u>ai</u>n.

Typical Production:

The slightly retracted tongue is in a midhigh position. It moves without interruption to the position for [ɪ]: the front of the tongue is relatively high and far forward.

The diphthong, rather than the vowel, occurs quite often in accented syllables or if it precedes a voiced consonant, as in *rain* [reɪn], *ladle* [ˈleɪdl̩] or *fable* [ˈfeɪbl̩]. In general, too, it may be used more frequently in slow speech than in rapid speech.

They mailed the plate on May Day is entirely acceptable if the so-called *a* sounds are not diphthongized. There is no block to understanding if one says:

> [ðe meld ðə plet ɔn me de]

> instead of

> [ðeɪ meɪld ðə pleɪt ɔn meɪ deɪ]

127. If excessively prolonged [eɪ] may also become a triphthong.

    Result: *fate* becomes *fa-i-uht* [feɪət]

This practice, not uncommon in some Southern speech, is generally to be discouraged.

a.

fate	dale	ray	pail
Hades	April	slay	mate
mail	bathe	crayon	they
came	bane	same	rein
say	Jane	grate	tame
grey	cage	lake	bail

b.   The grateful agent sold eighty-eight acres to the state.

c.   The maiden veiled her aging face as she skated.

d.   The neighbors failed to drape the sail over the shay today.

e.   Gale railed at Grace when Ray was placed in the frame jail.

[ju]   [ɣo͞o]

<u>Example:</u> <u>U</u>sually it is f<u>u</u>tile to v<u>iew</u> only a f<u>ew</u> <u>u</u>tensils.

Typical Production:

The tongue glides from a high front position to a high back position. Tongue muscles are tense. Lips are rounded for the final portion of the sound. Unlike other diphthongs, the second rather than the first element is stressed.

<u>Faults or Problems:</u>

128. Occasionally the schwa [ə] is inserted before the [ju].

> *few* becomes *fuh-you* [fəju]
> *beauty* becomes *buh-you-ty* [ˈbə ju tɪ]

See also Exercise 62, earlier in this chapter, for a further discussion of [ju]. As you practice the following, eliminate the schwa approach to [ju].

a. The huge mule amused Hubert with the cube.
b. After the funeral eulogy Matthew played music on the bugle.
c. The beautiful puma was accused of mutilating the pugilist.
d. Hugh met the cute ukelele player in the student union.
e. The mute pupil refuses to review his university notes about pewter and uranium.

Review Material for All the Diphthongs

129. *a.* In baiting a mouse-trap with cheese, always leave room for the mouse.
    b. Playboy: A plowboy with a Rolls-Royce.
    c. Fame is the perfume of heroic deeds; to many fame comes too late.
    d. If you really don't care, any reason is good enough.
    e. Whose house is of glass must not throw stones at another.
    f. Satan: The scarecrow in the religious cornfield.
    g. One hour's sleep before midnight is worth three after.
    h. Gain not base gains; base gains are the same as losses.
    i. Home is the place where, when you have to go there, they have to take you in.
    j. A good way to be popular is to listen closely to a lot of things you already know.
    k. Train up a child in the way he should go; and when he is old, he will not depart from it.
    l. A minute is a very short period of time unless you are holding your breath.
    m. You have no idea what a poor opinion I have of myself, and how little I deserve it.
    n. His heart was as great as the world, but there was no room in it to hold the memory of a wrong.
    o. Polite Brush-off: The art of telling a man you don't know what he's talking about when you know very well what he's talking about but don't like what he's saying.
    p. He reminds me of the man who murdered both his parents, and then, when sentence was about to be pronounced, pleaded for mercy on the grounds that he was an orphan.

Assignment 21 (See suggested Checklist for this assignment)

Prepare material containing many examples of those diphthongs with which you particularly need work. As a reminder, here is a key:

[aɪ]	ī m<u>y</u>		[ou]	ō g<u>o</u>
[ɔɪ]	oi <u>oi</u>l		[eɪ]	ā m<u>a</u>te
[au]	ou c<u>ow</u>		[ju]	yo͞o <u>u</u>se

Suggested Checklist for Assignment 21

As you practice by yourself you may want to work with this checklist. Listen carefully to yourself. If it is feasible record the assignment or get a classmate or friend to listen to you as you read the material. Eventually your goal will be to have a check mark in the Yes column for each category. (Optional: Perhaps your instructor will want to use the checklist to evaluate you during your classroom presentation.)

	Yes	No
Avoids undue nasalization of diphthongs.		
Avoids addition of schwa [ə] or [ɪ] to diphthongs.		
Avoids addition of [r] to diphthongs.		
Avoids overstressing, weakening, or dropping either vowel element of [aɪ].		
Avoids substituting [eɪ or ʌ] for [aɪ].		
Avoids confusing [aɪ] and [ɔɪ].		
Avoids overstressing, weakening, or dropping either vowel element of [ɔɪ].		
Avoids substituting [ɜ or ɝ] for [ɔɪ].		
Avoids substituting [ɔ ɑ ɪ or oɪ] for [ɔɪ].		
Avoids overstressing, weakening, or dropping either vowel element of [aʊ].		
Avoids substituting [æʊ or ɛʊ] for [aʊ].		
Avoids substituting [a ɑ or ʌ] for [aʊ].		
Avoids substituting [u] for second vowel element of [aʊ].		
Avoids overstressing, weakening, or dropping either vowel element of [oʊ].		
Avoids inserting [ɛ] before [oʊ].		
Avoids substituting [ɔʊ or ʌ] for [oʊ].		
Avoids overstressing, weakening, or dropping either vowel element of [eɪ].		
Avoids substituting [ɑɪ ɛɪ ɛ or ʌ] for [eɪ].		

Additional comments or suggestions:

(Note: Pronunciation is, of course, related to articulation. A section dealing with *pronunciation and vocabulary* will be found in the Appendixes, pp. 243-53.)

Assignment 22

The final oral assignment may be devoted to a final examination performance. Prepare a minimum of five minutes of interesting and varied material. In your presentation to the class, some of your material may be read, but at least half of it should be "told" from memory and not read. An anecdote, a short, short story, an informal descriptive or expository talk would be especially suitable. Do not attempt to memorize verbatim the material you choose for this section of your performance. Work, instead, for conversational spontaneity.

As you practice your selections, rather than concentrating primarily on a certain aspect, fault, or problem of voice, try to think of the many phases of voice and speech you have dealt with in this course as being integrated and blended together.

Demonstrate to your classmates and instructor to the best of your ability the general improvement you have made.

The criticism chart on page 297 is included largely as a matter of convenience for your instructor in evaluating specifically, if he so desires, various elements of voice and speech. It is not necessarily intended to be used as a guide to practice by you, the student.

Pronunciation and Vocabulary

When we hear such pronunciations as *drownded* ['draʊ ndəd] and *the-AY-ter* [θiˈetɚ] should we accuse the speaker of committing errors in articulation or errors in pronunciation? Strictly speaking, these should not be regarded simply as articulatory mistakes. The sounds might be clearly and distinctly produced, and articulation, we understand, refers to distinctness of speech. Something more than articulation is involved: it is pronunciation.

> *Pronunciation includes the correct production of sounds, but it also includes saying them in the right order (and without adding extra ones) and the proper accent on syllables in words.*

In this section the word *standard* will be used to indicate that the listed pronunciation is widely used by educated and cultured people. *Nonstandard* will indicate that the listed pronunciation is used less frequently by educated and cultured individuals.

How should we pronounce "ration"?

RASH un ['ræʃən] or RAY shun ['reʃən]   Both are standard.

How should we pronounce "cache"? (hiding place)

CATCH [kætʃ] or CASH [kæʃ]   Only the second is standard.

How should we pronounce "preferable"?

PREF erable ['prɛfərəbl̩] or pre FER able [prəˈfɚəbl̩]   Only the first is standard.

Now and then most of us become involved in arguments about pronunciation. Quite often somebody will say, "Let's look it up in the dictionary." If we know how to use the dictionary and do not regard it as divinely inspired, this is an excellent suggestion. Editors of good dictionaries are generally quite specific in stating that their publications attempt to describe and record what people say rather than dictate what they are supposed to say.

In his preface to the 1966 *Random House Dictionary*, Jess Stein, Editor in Chief, says:

> Should the dictionary be an authoritarian guide to "correct" English or should it be so antiseptically free of comment that it may defeat the user by providing him with no guidance at all? There is, we believe, a linguistically sound middle course. Language, most people agree, is never static—except when dead. It has a capacity for constant change and growth that enables it to serve effectively the requirements of the society in which it exists. It is, therefore, the function of a dictionary to provide the user with an exact record of the language he sees and hears. That record must be fully descriptive. Since language is a social institution, the lexicographer must give the user an adequate indication of the attitudes of society toward particular words or expressions, whether he regards those attitudes as linguistically sound or

not. . . . He does not need to express approval or disapproval of a disputed usage, but he does need to report the milieu of words as well as their meanings.

It should be remembered, however, that even the finest dictionaries cannot always keep abreast of the latest trends, changes, or fads in pronunciation. Much of the "Hippie" jargon of the 60s and early 70s, for example, has already faded.

And what about the astonishing number of new words added to the language every year? Nor can a dictionary always take into account all regional variations or modifications in pronunciation.

Professional radio and TV announcers who handle commercials frequently pronounce *caramel* as *CAR-a-mel* (the first *a* sound is like the *a* in a_ct_) or, in *IPA*: [ˈkærəml]. Yet one often hears, especially in the Midwest, CAR-mel (the first syllable rhymes with *tar*) or, in *IPA:* [karml]. Both are standard and widely used by educated people.

Too, the pronunciations listed in the dictionary tend to be formal. Words are considered in isolation. We know, of course, that in connected and rapid speech and especially that which is used in informal situations, the pronunciation of words is influenced by other words which precede or follow them.

Is there a standard pronunciation? No. There is, however, a standard of pronunciation. It is this:

Pronunciation which is standard does not attract undue attention to itself.

If it does, the speaker is either guilty of affectation, "putting on airs," or he is trying out his pronunciation in an unfavorable environment.

Standard pronunciation, like good articulation, is always desirable. The occasional mispronunciations of which many of us are guilty do not necessarily label us as barbarians, but consistent and frequent mispronunciations are apt to label us as careless individuals, lacking in culture and refinement.

How May Pronunciation Be Improved?

Be a good listener. Listen carefully to the speech around you, and especially to the speech of educated and cultured individuals. As often as opportunity permits, listen to recordings of your own speech. Compare your pronunciation with that of established, successful speakers and leaders in your own general region.

Have access to a good dictionary. Even a good one will not be of much help unless you know how to use it. Study the "Guides" and the "Explanatory Notes" which most dictionaries include in their introductory sections. What is meant, for example, when two pronunciations of a word are listed?

In most dictionaries both of the pronunciations are regarded as standard. In some cases the first pronunciation shown is considered to be the one most frequently used. But it must be emphasized that the second choice is also widely used by educated speakers.

Which definition shall we use when two or more are given for a word? In the Merriam-Webster dictionaries, the earliest ascertainable meaning is placed first and more recent and current meanings are placed later in the order shown. The *Random House Dictionary*, however, gives the most frequently encountered meaning as the first definition.

All we can say is, whatever the dictionary of your choice, know how to use it!

Our knowledge of the International Phonetic Alphabet will not invariably help us to determine a standard pronunciation of a word, however. For example, look up the word *ENNUI* in the *Random House Dictionary*. Its first pronunciation is transcribed as: [änwē´] and this bears little resemblance to phonetic transcription. As a matter of fact, a majority of popular dictionaries do not use the IPA. Instead, they use a system whereby—

A mark, a sign, or a symbol is attached to a letter to designate one of several sounds for which the letter might stand. This system is known as the diacritical marking system (DMS).

It is possibly true that the DMS is easier to learn than the IPA. On the other hand, diacritical systems are not as precise as the phonetic alphabet nor are they altogether uniform. The DMS used by the *Random House Dictionary* is not identical to the one used by *Merriam-Webster* or *Webster's New World Dictionary*. They differ, in certain respects, from *Funk and Wagnalls Standard Dictionary* and the *American College Dictionaries*.

In spite of the discrepancies, it is wise to familiarize ourselves with at least one DMS. A brief introduction to diacritics will help us use and understand most dictionaries. The system presented here is derived largely from the *Random House Dictionary* and *Webster's New World Dictionary*, two superior and widely used dictionaries. There have been a few minor simplifications and changes. In each case, the IPA symbol is also listed. The comparison is interesting.

Consonants

	DMS	Key Word	Phonetic Symbol	Key Word
1.	b	bib (bib)	b	bɪb
2.	ch	church (chûrch)	tʃ	tʃɝtʃ
3.	d	dud (dud)	d	dʌd
4.	f	fife (fīf)	f	faɪf
5.	g	gag (gag)	g	gæg
6.	h	hope (hōp)	h	hop
7.	hw	while (hwīl)	hw	hwaɪl
8.	j	jig (jig)	dʒ	dʒ ɪg
9.	k	cake (kāk)	k	kek
10.	l	lull (lul) *a pause*	l	lʌl
11.	m	mate (māt)	m	met
12.	n	nun (nun)	n	nʌn
13.	ŋ	ring (riŋ)	ŋ	rɪŋ
14.	p	pipe (pīp)	p	paɪp
15.	r	rip (rip)	r	rɪp
16.	s	sass (sas) *to be rude*	s	sæs
17.	sh	shall (shal)	ʃ	ʃæl
18.	t	tot (tot) *small child*	t	tɑt
19.	th (voiceless)	thin (thin)	θ	θɪn
20.	th (voiced)	then (then)	ð	ðɛn
21.	v	vat (vat)	v	væt
22.	w	won (wun)	w	wʌn
23.	y	yell (yel)	j	jɛl
24.	z	zip (zip)	z	zɪp
25.	zh	azure (azh′ə r)	ʒ	ˈæʒɚ

Vowels and Diphthongs

1.	a	at (at)	æ	æt
2.	ā	way (wā)	e	we
3.	â	hare (hâr)	ɛ , æ	hɛr, hær
4.	ä	calm (käm)	ɑ	kɑm
5.	e	let (let)	ɛ	lɛt
6.	ē	eat (ēt)	i	it
7.	ê	dear (dêr, dĕr)	ɪ	dɪʀ

8.	i	is (iz)	ɪ	ɪz
9.	ī	ice (īs)	aɪ	aɪs
10.	o	odd (od)	ɑ	ɑd
11.	ō	ode (ōd)	o	od
12.	ô	lord (lôrd)	ɔ	lɔrd
13.	oi	oil (oil)	ɔɪ	ɔɪl
14.	o͞o	too (to͞o)	u	tu
15.	o͝o	book (bo͝ok)	ʊ	bʊk
16.	ou	cow (kou)	aʊ	kaʊ
17.	u	cup (kup)	ʌ	kʌp
18.	û	burn (bûrn)	ɝ	bɝn
19.	ə	a̲bout (əbout′)	ə	ə`baʊt
		vio̲lent (vī′ələnt)		`vaɪələnt
		sani̲ty (san′ətē)		`sænətɪ
		comply (kəm plī′)		kəm`plaɪ
		rump̲u̲s (rum′pəs)		`rʌmpəs
20.	ə (small schwa: occurs before l, n, or r in certain words)	little (lit′ əl)		`lɪtl̩
		pardon (pär′dən)		`pɑrdn̩
		tire (tī ə̄r)		taɪr

In many dictionaries the principal accent of a word is indicated by a heavy mark (′), placed after a syllable which receives the greater stress. In some dictionaries the accent mark is placed before the syllable which receives the greater stress. The secondary accent is indicated by a lighter mark (′).

Examples: mis′ i sip′ ē   Mississippi
           in tûr′ pri tā shən   interpretation
           des′ pə rä′ dō   desperado

Pronunciation and Vocabulary Lists

The following lists contain 250 words. Many of the words are quite commonly mispronounced. Most of the mispronunciations result from one or more factors:

Substitution of one sound for another sound:
Chef is not pronounced the way it looks. It is frequently mispronounced with the substitution of a "ch" sound for the correct "sh"—
    Nonstandard: chef (chef)
    Standard: shef (shef)

Omission of a sound:
The word arctic is frequently mispronounced because the third sound is omitted:
    Nonstandard: är′ tik (är′ tik)
    Standard: ärk′ tik (ärk′ tik)

Addition of a sound:
The word escape is frequently mispronounced with the insertion of an extra sound:
    Nonstandard: eks—kap (eks kāp′)
    Standard: es—kap (es kāp′)

Misplaced Accent:
The word abyss is often mispronounced with the accent incorrectly placed on the first syllable:
    Nonstandard: a bis (ab′ is)
    Standard: uh—bis (ə bis′)

Reversal of two sounds:

The word larynx is commonly mispronounced because the "y—n" are reversed to "n—y."

Nonstandard: lar´ niks (lar´ niks)
Standard: lar i ks (lar´ iŋks)

Sometimes, of course, we may pronounce a certain word correctly, but use it incorrectly in our speech. For example, *guile* (trickery, deception) is pronounced correctly by most people: gīl. But it is not always correctly used as an adjective:

Incorrect: "Henry VIII was a guile ruler."
Correct: "Henry VIII was a ruler who practiced guile."

Obviously, then, pronunciation and usage cannot be completely divorced from each other. An expressive and flexible vocabulary, not to mention correct pronunciation, is the mark of an educated and refined person.

Practice the lists. Consult a reputable dictionary for definitions. Use the words in spoken as well as written English.

Note: Some words have more than one standard pronunciation. In the following lists, however, only one will be given. Standard pronunciations, listed at the left, are unbracketed. Nonstandard pronunciations, enclosed in brackets, are placed on the right. Only the Diacritical Marking System will be used in these lists, because a large majority of the dictionaries you will be consulting transcribe pronunciation with the DMS rather than the IPA.

List A

The words in this list are most frequently mispronounced because *one sound is substituted for another.* Practice the list until you have mastered it.

	Standard Pronunciations	Nonstandard Pronunciations
1. ad infinitum	ad in´ fə nī´ təm	[ad in´ fə nē´ təm]
2. agile	aj´ əl	[āj´ īl]
3. anesthetist	ə nes´ thi tist	[ə nes´ thē ist]
4. architect	är´ ki tekt	[ärch´ i tekt]
5. attache	at´ə shā´	[ə tach´ i]
6. avenue	av´ə noo´	[av´ ə nyə]
7. Beethoven	bā´ tō vən	[bē´ thō vən]
8. beige	bāzh	[bēzh]
9. bestial	bes´ chəl	[bēs´ chəl]
10. blasé	blä zā´	[bla zā´]
11. blatant	blāt´ ənt	[blat´ ənt]
12. brevity	brev´ə tē	[brēv´ ə tē]
13. cache	kash	[kach]
14. censure	sen´ shər	[sen´ sər]
15. chameleon	kə mē´ li ən	[chə me´ liən]
16. charisma	kə riz´ mə	[chə riz´ mə]
17. charlatan	shär´ lə tən	[chär´ lə tən]
18. chasm	kaz´ əm	[chaz´ əm]
19. chef	shef	[chef]
20. chic	shēk	[chik]
21. chiropodist	ki rop´ ə dist	[chī rop´ ə d st]

		Standard Pronunciation	Nonstandard Pronunciation
22.	Chopin *composer*	shō′ pan	[chop′ ən]
23.	coiffure *style of hairdress*	kwä fyŏŏr′	[koi′ fyŏŏr]
24.	coma	kō′ mə	[kom′ ə]
25.	comely *fashionable*	kum′ li	[kōm′ li]
26.	complacent *self satisfied*	kəm plā′ sənt	[kəm pla′ sənt]
27.	conjecture *guesswork*	kən jek′ chər	[kən jək′ tər]
28.	connoisseur *an expert of fine*	kon′ ə sûr′	[kōn′ ə sûr′]
29.	copious *abundant art.*	kō′ pi əs	[ko′ pi əs]
30.	crux *crucial point*	kruks	[krŏŏ ks]
31.	cuisine *style of cooking*	kwi zēn′	[kōō zēn′]
32.	deaf	def	[dēf]
33.	debauched *draw from work*	di bôcht′	[di boucht′]
34.	demise *transfer by will*	di mīz′	[di mēz′]
35.	diary	dī′ ə rē	[dâr′ i]
36.	diphtheria	dif thir′ ē ə	[dip thir′ ē ə]
37.	discotheque	dis′ kō tek′	[dis′ kō tēk′]
38.	discretion	di skresh′ ən	[di skrē′ shən]
39.	disheveled	di shev′ əld	[dis hev′ eld]
40.	docile	dos′ əl	[dos′ īl]
41.	echelon *step like formation*	esh′ ə lon′	[ech′ ə lon′]
42.	elite *size of type of aircraft*	i lēt′	[ē līt′]
43.	ensemble *musicians playing*	än säm′ bəl	[en säm′ bəl]
44.	et cetera *addit. similar things*	et set′ ərə	[ek set′ ərə]
45.	eugenics *science dealing with*	yŏŏ jen′ iks	[yŏŏ jēn′ iks]
46.	facade *improvent of race*	fə säd′	[fə säd′]
47.	facetious	fəsē′ shəs	[fəsi′ shəs]
48.	facile	fas′ il	[fa′ sīl]
49.	faux pas	fō pä′	[foks pas]
50.	filet mignon	fi lā′ min yon′	[fi lā′ mig′ nən]
51.	fungi	fun′ ji	[fun′ gī]
52.	genuine	jen′ yŏŏ in	[jen′ yŏŏ wīn]
53.	gesture	jes′ chər	[ges′ chər]
54.	giblet	jib′ lət	[gib′ lət]
55.	gigantic	jī gan′ tik	[jī jan′ tik]
56.	gist	jist	[gist]
57.	guarantee	gar′ ən tē′	[gar′ ən shē′]
58.	handkerchief	haŋ′ kər chəf	[hand′ kər chəf]
59.	harbinger	här′ bən jər	[här′ biŋ ər]
60.	hearth	härth	[hûrth]
61.	height	hīt	[hīth]
62.	heinous	hā′ nəs	[hī′ nəs]
63.	heroism	her′ ō iz′ əm	[hēr′ ō iz′ əm]
64.	homage	hom′ ij	[hōm′ ij]
65.	hostage	hos′ tij	[hōs′ tij]
66.	hysteria	hi stēr′ iə	[hī stēr′ iə]
67.	indict	in dīt′	[in dikt′]
68.	inflammable	in flam′ ə bəl	[in flām′ ə bəl]
69.	Italian	i tal′ yən	[ī tal′ yən]
70.	laconic	lə kon′ ik	[lə kōn′ ik]

	Standard Pronunciation	Nonstandard Pronunciation
~~71~~. laissez faire	les´ ā fâr´	[las´ ā fâr´]
72. latent	lāt´ ənt	[lat´ ənt]
73. lingerie	län´ zhə rā´	[lin´ zhə rā´]
74. longevity	lon jev´ i ti	[loɲ ev´ i ti]
~~75~~. lozenge	loz´ inj	[lōz´ inj]
76. malignant	mə lig´ nənt	[mə lin´ yənt]
77. malinger	mə liŋ´ gər	[mə līn´ ər]
78. masochist	mas´ ə kist	[mas´ ə chist]
79. memento	mə men´ tō	[mō men´ tō]
80. microscopic	mī´ krə skop´ ik	[mī´ krə skōp´ ik]
81. negligee	neg´ li zhā´	[neg´ li zhē´]
82. niche	nich	[nish]
83. obesity	o bē´ si ti	[ō be´ si ti]
84. orgy	ôr´ ji	[ôr´ gi]
85. pantomime	pan´ tə mīm´	[pan´ tə mīn´]
86. pathos	pā´ thos	[pa´ thos]
~~87~~. pique	pēk	[pik]
88. pitcher	pich´ ər	[pik´ chər]
~~89~~. placard	plak´ ärd	[plāk´ ärd]
90. placid	plas´ əd	[plak´ əd]
91. plagiarism	plā´ jə riz´ əm	[pla´ jə riz´ əm]
92. poignant	poin´ yənt	[poig´ nənt]
93. portentous	pôr ten´ təs	[pôr ten´ shəs]
94. posthumous	pos´ chə məs	[post hyōō´ məs]
95. precocious	pri kō´ shəs	[pri ko´ shəs]
96. pretentious	pri ten´ shəs	[pri ten´ təs]
97. pronunciation	prə nun´ si ā´ shən	[prə noun´ si ā´ shən]
98. propitiate *conciliate*	prə pish´ i āt	[prə pit´ i āt]
~~99~~. pugilist	pyōō´ jə list	[pyōō´ gə list]
100. radiator	rā´ di ā tər	[ra´ di ā´ tər]
101. recalcitrant	ri kal´ si trənt	[ri kal´ kə trənt]
~~102~~. regalia	ri gā´ li ə	[ri ga´ li ə]
103. regime	rə zhēm´	[rə gēm´]
104. robot	rō´ bət	[ro´ bot]
~~105~~. rudiment	rōō´ dəmənt	[ru´ dəmənt]
106. ruthless	rōōth´ lis	[ruth´ lis]
107. sagacious	səgā´ shəs	[sə jā´ shəs]
108. salient	sā´ li ənt	[sa´ liənt]
~~109~~. savory	sā´ və ri	[sa´ və ri]
110. slovenly *dirthy*	sluv´ ən li	[slov´ ən li]
111. strength *power*	streŋth	[strenth]
112. suave *smoothly polite*	swäv	[swäv]
113. taciturn *talkj little*	tas´ ə tùrn	[tak´ ə tùrn]
~~114~~. titular	tich´ ə lər	[tīch´ ə lər]
~~115~~. tremolo	trem´ ə lo´	[trem´ yōō lo´]
116. unscathed *unharmed*	un skāthd´	[un skathd´]
117. vagrant *tramp*	vā´ grənt	[va´ grənt]
118. verbatim *word for word*	vər bā´ tim	[vər ba´ tim]
119. virile *strong masculine*	vir´ əl	[vīr´ əl]

	Standard Pronunciations	Nonstandard Pronunciations
120. visa	vē′ zə	[vī′ zə]
121. Wagner (composer)	väg′ nər	[wag′ nər]
122. zealous *fanatical*	zel′ əs	[zēl′ əs]
123. zoology	zō ol′ ə ji	[zōō ol′ ə ji]

List B

The words in this list are most frequently mispronounced because *one or more sounds have been omitted.*
Practice the list until you have mastered it.

	Standard Pronunciations	Nonstandard Pronunciations
1. accelerate	ak sel′ ə rāt	[ə sel′ ə rāt′]
2. accessory	ak ses′ ə ri	[ə ses′ ə ri]
3. Arctic	ärk′ tik	[är′ tik]
4. asphyxiate	as fik′ siāt	[ə fik′ siāt]
5. banquet	baŋ′ kwit	[ban′ kwit]
6. berserk	bər sûrk′	[bə sûrk′]
7. casualty	kazh′ ōō əl ti	[kazh′ əl ti]
8. champion	cham′ piən	[cham′ pēn]
9. correct	kə rekt′	[krekt]
10. couldn't	koŏd′ ə nt	[koŏnt]
11. cumulus	kyōō′ myə ləs	[kyōō′mə ləs]
12. environment	en vī′ rən mənt	[en vir′ mənt]
13. facsimile	fak sim′ə lē	[fa sim′ ə lē]
14. February	feb′ rōō er′ ē	[feb′ yōō er′ ē]
15. figure	fig′ yər	[fig′ ər]
16. forte (music)	fôr′ tā	[fôrt]
17. incidentally *a part of the main happening*	in′ sə den′ tə li	[in′ sə dent′ li]
18. length	leŋth	[lenth]
19. library	li′ brer i	[lī′ bər i]
20. orange	ôr′ inj	[ôrnj]
21. picture	pik′ chər	[pi′ chər]
22. poem	pō′ əm	[pōm]
23. probably	prob′ə bli	[prob′ li]
24. quixotic *romantic*	kwik sot′ ik	[ki ot′ ik]
25. recognize	rek′ əg nīz′	[rek′ ə nīz]
26. regular	reg′ yə lər	[reg′ lər]
27. scrupulous *straightly*	skrōō′ pyə ləs	[skrōō ′pə ləs]
28. surprise	sər prīz′	[sə prīz′]
29. temperature	tem′ pər ə chər	[tem′ pə chər]
30. terrible	ter′ə bəl	[ter′ bəl]
31. twenty	twen′ tē	[twen′ ē]
32. ubiquitous *always there*	yōō bik′ wit əs	[yōō bik′ ə təs]
33. veterinarian	vet′ ər ə nar′ iən	[vet′ ə nâr′ iən]
34. wouldn't	woŏd′ ənt	[woŏnt]

250

List C

The words in this list are most frequently mispronounced because *one or more sounds have been added.* Practice the list until you have mastered it.

		Standard Pronunciations	Nonstandard Pronunciations
1.	accompanist	ə kum′ pə nist	[ə kum′ pə nē ist]
2.	across	ə kros′	[ə krost′]
3.	aluminum	ə loō′ mənəm	[ə loōm′ ni əm]
4.	ambidextrous *full use of both hands*	am′ bi dek′ strəs	[am′ bi dek′ stûr əs]
5.	anonymous	ə non′ ə məs	[ə non′ yə məs]
✓	6. athlēte	ath′ let	[ath′ ə let]
✓	7. athletics	ath let′ iks	[ath ə let′ iks]
	8. attacked	ə takt′	[ə tak′ tid]
✓	9. Bethlehem	beth′ li əm	[beth′ li ham]
	10. burglar	bûr′ glər	[bûr′ gə lər]
	11. business	biz′ nis	[biz′ ə nis]
	12. chimney	chim′ ni	[chim′ ə ni]
	13. column	kol′ əm	[kol′ yəm]
	14. corps	kôr	[kôrps]
	15. disastrous	di zas′ trəs	[di zas′ tər əs]
	16. drowned	dround	[dround′ əd]
	17. electoral	i lek′ tər əl	[i lik tôr′ i əl]
	18. escape	e skāp′	[eks kāp′]
	19. evening	ēv′ niŋ	[ēv′ ə niŋ]
	20. film	film	[fil′ əm]
	21. forte (strong point)	fôrt	[fôr′ tā]
	22. grievous *nervous*	grē′ vəs	[grēv′ i əs]
	23. heir	âr	[hâr]
	24. hors d'oeuvres	ôr dûrvz′	[ôr doŏv′ ərz]
	25. hurricane	hûr′ ə kān′	[hyoŏr′ ə kān′]
	26. laundry	län′ dri	[län′ də ri]
	27. mayoralty *office of mayor*	mā′ ər əl tē	[mā′ ər al ətē]
	28. monstrous	mon′ strəs	[mon′ stər əs]
	29. often	of′ ən	[of′ tən]
	30. once	wuns	[wunst]
	31. pedantic	pə dan′ tik	[pen dan′ tik]
	32. positively	pos′ ə tiv li	[poz′ ə tiv əli]
	33. psalm	säm	[psäm]
	34. righteous	rī′ chəs	[rī′ chi əs]
	35. salmon	sam′ ən	[sal′ mən]
	36. schism	siz′ əm	[skiz′ əm]
	37. scintillate	sin′ tə lāt′	[skin′ tə lāt′]
	38. scion	sī′ ən	[skī′ ən]
	39. statistics	stə tis′ tiks	[stəs tis′ tiks]
	40. subtle	sut′ əl	[sub′ təl]
	41. sword	sôrd	[swôrd]
	42. tremendous	tri men′ dəs	[tri men′ joō əs]
	43. victual	vit′ əl	[vik′choō əl]
	44. vigilant	vij′ əl ənt	[vij′ əlan′ tē]
	45. Worcestershire	woŏs′ tər shir′	[wôr′ ses tər shir′]

List D

The words in this list are frequently mispronounced because of a *misplaced accent*. Practice the list until you have mastered it:

	Standard Pronunciations	Nonstandard Pronunciations
1. abyss	ə bis′	[a′ bis]
2. admirable	ad′ mər əbəl	[ad mĭr ′ə bəl]
3. alias	ā′ li əs	[əlī′ ə s]
4. alienate	āl′ yə nāt	[əli′ ə nat]
5. amicable	am′ ək əbəl	[əmik′ əbəl]
6. auspices omit	ô′ spi siz	[ô spish′ əs]
7. autopsy	ô′ top si	[ə top′ si]
8. barbarous	bär′ bər əs	[bär bâr′ i əs]
9. bravado	brə vä′ dō	[brāv′ ə dō]
10. brochure	brō shoŏr′	[brō′ shər]
11. chagrin	shə grin′	[sha′ grən]
12. comparable	kom′ pər ə bəl	[kəm pàr′ ə bəl]
13. cupola omit	kyōō′ pələ	[kyōō pōl′ ə]
14. deluge	del′ yōō j	[də lōō j′]
15. epitome	i pit′ə mē	[ep′ ə tōm]
16. gamut omit	gam′ ət	[gə mōōt′]
17. guitar	gi tär′	[gē′ tär]
18. horizon	hə rī′ zən	[hôr′ i zən]
19. ignominious	ig′ nə min′ i əs	[ignom′ i nəs]
20. impotence	im′ pə təns	[im pō′ təns]
21. indolence	in′ də ləns	[in dō′ ləns]
22. infamous	in′ fə məs	[in fām′ əs]
23. irreparable	i rep′ ər ə bəl	[i rə pâr′ ə bəl]
24. jocose omit	jō kōs′	[jok′ os]
25. magnanimous	magnan′ əməs	[magn ə min′ i əs]
26. maintenance	mān′ tə nəns	[mān tān′ əns]
27. maniacal	mə nī′ ə kəl	[mān′ i a kəl]
28. mischievous	mis′ chə vəs	[mis chēv′ i əs]
29. omnipotent	om nip′ ə tənt	[om nə pō′ tənt]
30. perseverance	pûr′ sə ver′ əns	[pər sev′ ər əns]
31. police	pə lēs′	[pō′ lēs]
32. preferable	pref′ ər ə bəl	[prə fûr′ ə bəl]
33. prelude	prel′ yōōd	[prə lōōd′]
34. superfluous	soŏ pûr′ flōō əs	[sōō′ pər flōō′ əs]
35. theater	thē′ ətər	[thē ā′ tər]
36. vehement	vē′ ə mənt	[və hē′ mənt]

List E

The words in this list are frequently mispronounced because *two or more sounds are reversed*. Practice the list until you have mastered it.

	Standard Pronunciations	Nonstandard Pronunciations
1. asterisk	as′ t ə risk	[as′ t ə riks]
2. cavalry	kav ′ə l ri	[kal′ və ri]

	Standard Pronunciation	Nonstandard Pronunciations
3. equanimity *omit*	ē′ kwə nim′ i tē	[ē′ kwə min′ i tē]
4. hundred	hun′ drid	[hun′ ərd]
5. introduction	in′ trə duk′ shən	[in′ tər duk′ shən]
6. irrelevant	i rel′ ə vənt	[i rev′ ə lənt]
7. larynx	lar′ iŋks	[lar′ niks]
8. perspiration	pûr′ spə rā′ shən	[pre′ spə rā′ shən]
9. prescription	pri skrip′ shən	[pûr skrip′ shən]
10. professor	prə fes′ ər	[pûr fes′ ər]
11. solemnity	sə lem′ nə tē	[sə len′ mə tē]
12. voluminous *omit*	və lōom′ ən əs	[və lōom′ ni əs]

Pronunciation Lists

The 250 words you have studied in 5 categories are now listed again, not according to category, but simply alphabetized and divided into 5 lists.

Your instructor will suggest how to use these lists. In general, they will serve for review purposes. You should be able to pronounce each word correctly. You may find it interesting and profitable to transcribe each word phonetically, using the IPA. Then, construct sentences using the word correctly. As far as possible, try to incorporate the word into your vocabulary. Use it in everyday conversation as soon as you can, and use it several times.

The lists may be used for oral reviews or written assignments. "Doing" one list approximately every second or third week during the term is generally most convenient, and your instructor will recommend a specific time schedule.

Pronunciation List 1

1. abyss
2. accelerate
3. accessory
4. accompanist
5. across
6. ad infinitum
7. admirable
8. agile
9. alias
10. alienate
11. aluminum
12. ambidextrous
13. amicable
14. anesthetist
15. anonymous
16. architect
17. Arctic
18. asphyxiate
19. asterisk
20. athlete
21. athletics
22. attache'
23. attacked
24. auspices
25. autopsy

26. avenue

27. banquet

28. barbarous

29. Beethoven

30. beige

31. berserk

32. bestial

33. Bethlehem

34. blase′

35. blatant

36. bravado

37. brevity

38. brochure

39. burglar

40. business

41. cache

42. casualty

43. cavalry

44. censure

45. chagrin

46. chameleon

47. champion

48. charisma

49. charlatan

50. chasm

Pronunciation List 2

1. chef

2. chic

3. chimney

4. chiropodist

5. Chopin

6. coiffure

7. column

8. coma

9. comely

10. comparable

11. complacent

12. conjecture

13. connoisseur

14. copious

15. corps

16. correct

17. couldn't

18. crux

19. cuisine

20. cumulus

21. cupola

22. deaf

23. debauched

24. deluge

25. demise

26. diary

27. diphtheria

28. disastrous

29. discotheque

30. discretion

31. disheveled

32. docile

33. drowned

34. echelon

35. electoral

36. elite

37. ensemble

38. environment

39. epitome

40. equanimity

41. escape

42. et cetera

43. eugenics

44. evening

45. facade

46. facetious

47. facile

48. facsimile

49. faux pas

50. February

Pronunciation List 3

1. figure
2. filet mignon
3. film
4. forte (music)
5. forte (strong point)
6. fungi
7. gamut
8. genuine
9. gesture
10. giblet
11. gigantic
12. gist
13. grievous
14. guarantee
15. guitar
16. handkerchief
17. harbinger
18. hearth
19. height
20. heinous
21. heir
22. heroism
23. homage
24. horizon
25. hors d'oeuvres

26. hostage

27. hundred

28. hurricane

29. hysteria

30. ignominious

31. impotence

32. incidentally

33. indict

34. indolence

35. infamous

36. inflammable

37. introduction

38. irrelevant

39. irreparable

40. Italian

41. jocose

42. laconic

43. laissez faire

44. larynx

45. latent

46. laundry

47. length

48. library

49. lingerie

50. longevity

Pronunciation List 4

1. lozenge

2. magnanimous

3. maintenance

4. malignant

5. malinger

6. maniacal

7. masochist

8. mayoralty

9. memento

10. microscopic

11. mischievous

12. monstrous

13. negligee

14. niche

15. obesity

16. often

17. omnipotent

18. once

19. orange

20. orgy

21. pantomime

22. pathos

23. pedantic

24. perserverance

25. perspiration

26. picture

27. pique

28. pitcher

29. placard

30. placid

31. plagiarism

32. poem

33. poignant

34. police

35. portentous

36. postively

37. posthumous

38. precocious

39. preferable

40. prelude

41. prescription

42. pretentious

43. probably

44. professor

45. pronunciation

46. propitiate

47. psalm

48. pugilist

49. quixotic

50. radiator

Pronunciation List 5

1. recalcitrant
2. recognize
3. regalia
4. regime
5. regular
6. righteous
7. robot
8. rudiment
9. ruthless
10. sagacious
11. salient
12. salmon
13. savory
14. schism
15. scintillate
16. scion
17. scrupulous
18. slovenly
19. solemnity
20. statistics
21. strength
22. suave
23. subtle
24. superfluous
25. surprise

26. sword

27. taciturn

28. temperature

29. terrible

30. theater

31. titular

32. tremendous

33. tremolo

34. twenty

35. ubiquitous

36. unscathed

37. vagrant

38. vehement

39. verbatim

40. veterinarian

41. victual

42. vigilant

43. virile

44. visa

45. voluminous

46. Wagner (composer)

47. Worcestershire

48. wouldn't

49. zealous

50. zoology

Voice and Speech Analysis Charts

Voice Quality Analysis Chart

Present material orally before the class or listen to a recording of your voice. If you listen to a recording, you may use the one you recorded at the beginning of the course, or you may make a new one. With the aid of your instructor and classmates, analyze your voice quality as candidly as you are able to. Use this chart as a guide.

Overall Effectiveness:

    Excellent _____ Good _____ Fair _____ Poor _____

In General, My Voice Quality Is:

    Pleasant _____

    Unpleasant _____

If My Quality Is Unpleasant, It May Be Due to:

    Excessive tension _____   Inefficient breathing habits _____

    Inadequate loudness _____   Improper pitch level _____

    Lazy lips, jaw and tongue _____   Tongue humping _____

    Rigid jaw _____   Excessive relaxation of soft palate _____

If My Voice Quality Needs Improvement, the Following Term(s) Most Accurately Describes the Sound of My Voice:

    Breathy _____   Nasal _____

    Glottal Shock _____   Denasal _____

    Harsh-strident _____   Hoarse-husky _____

    Harsh-throaty _____

Do you think you possess personality traits which might contribute to undesirable voice quality? If so, what are they? (Be frank.)

Note any problems of health or hearing which might have a direct bearing on the quality of your voice:

Suggestions for Improvement:

Loudness Analysis Chart

Present material orally before the class or listen to a recording of your voice. If you listen to a recording, you may use the one you recorded at the beginning of the course, or you may make a new one. With the aid of your instructor and classmates, analyze your loudness as candidly as you are able to. Use this chart as a guide.

Overall Effectiveness:

Excellent _____ Good _____ Fair _____ Poor _____

In General, My Voice Is:

Easily heard _____

Difficult to hear _____

If My Loudness Needs Improvement, the Following Term or Phrase Most Accurately Describes My Problem:

Too loud _____

Too soft _____

Unvaried _____

Lacks emphasis and contrast _____

Patterned _____

If My Loudness Is Unsatisfactory, One or More of the Following Factors May Be Responsible:

Inadequate openness of mouth _____   Unsatisfactory voice quality _____

Improper pitch level _____   Sluggish articulation _____

Excessive muscular
  constrictions of throat _____   Insufficient
  energy and animation _____

Improper control
  of breath pressure _____   Too rapid rate of speaking _____

Do you think you possess personality traits which might contribute to problems of loudness? If so, what are they? (Be frank.)

Note any problems of health or hearing which might have a direct bearing on your loudness:

Suggestions for Improvement:

Voice Expressiveness Analysis Chart

Present material orally before the class or listen to a recording of your voice. If you listen to a recording, you may use the one you recorded at the beginning of the course, or you may make a new one. With the aid of your instructor and classmates, analyze your expressiveness as candidly as you are able to. Use this chart as a guide.

Overall Effectiveness:

    Excellent _____ Good _____ Fair _____ Poor _____

In General, My Voice Is:

    Varied and flexible _____

    Patterned (singsong) _____

    Unvaried and monotonous _____

If My Vocal Expressiveness Needs Improvement, the Following Terms or Phrases Most Accurately Describe My Problem:

Pitch		**Rate**	
Too high _____		Too fast _____	Hesitant _____
Too low _____		Too slow _____	Jerky _____
Monotonous _____		Monotonous _____	Poor phrasing _____
Patterned _____		Patterned _____	Lack of pauses _____
Excessive variation _____			

Personality factors are important in determining vocal variety. What traits do you think you possess which might be responsible for problems of expressiveness? (Be frank.)

Note any problems of health or hearing which might have a direct bearing on your vocal expressiveness:

Suggestions for Improvement:

Articulation Analysis Chart

Present material orally before the class or listen to a recording of your voice. If you listen to a recording, you may use the one you recorded at the beginning of the course, or you may make a new one. With the aid of your instructor and classmates, analyze your articulation as candidly as you are able to. Use this chart as a guide.

Overall Effectiveness:

Excellent _____ Good _____ Fair _____ Poor _____

In General, My Speech Is:

Clear, distinct and accurate _____

Sluggish and indistinct _____

Overly-precise _____

If My Articulation Is Unsatisfactory, It May Be Due to:

Sluggish tongue activity _____

Immobile lips _____

Inaccuracy of tongue position and movement _____

Rigid jaw _____

Inactive velum _____

Specific Errors:

Sounds omitted in words such as: (List examples and circle the sounds you dropped:)

Sounds substituted in words such as: _____

Sounds added in words such as: _____

Sounds distorted in words such as: _____

Sounds inadequate in words such as: _____

Mispronunciations: Regional Dialect:

Foreign Dialect:

Do you think you possess personality traits which might contribute to problems of articulation? If so, what are they? (Be frank.)

Note any problems of health or hearing which might have a direct bearing on your articulation:

Suggestions for Improvement:

Analysis Chart 1

	Yes	No
Quality Was his voice pleasant to listen to? Comments: (If you check **Yes**, elaborate briefly. If you check **No**, give reasons. Follow this procedure below also.)		
Loudness Was his voice easily heard? Comments:		
Expressiveness Was his voice varied and flexible? Comments:		
Articulation Was his speech clear, distinct and easy to understand? Comments:		
Unobtrusiveness and Appropriateness Did his voice, speech and pronunciation seem to be natural, unaffected and generally acceptable? Comments:		

Overall Effectiveness:

Excellent _____ Good _____ Fair _____ Poor _____

What is the most serious fault of your subject's voice or speech? _____

_____

What is the outstanding positive attribute of your subject's voice or speech? _____

_____

Your Name _____   Your Subject's Name _____

Class or Section _____   Subject's Occupation _____

Date _____

Analysis Chart 2

	Yes	No
Quality Was his voice pleasant to listen to? Comments: (If you check **Yes**, elaborate briefly. If you check **No**, give reasons. Follow this procedure below also.)		
Loudness Was his voice easily heard? Comments:		
Expressiveness Was his voice varied and flexible? Comments:		
Articulation Was his speech clear, distinct and easy to understand? Comments:		
Unobtrusiveness and Appropriateness Did his voice, speech and pronunciation seem to be natural, unaffected and generally acceptable? Comments:		

Overall Effectiveness:

Excellent _____ Good _____ Fair _____ Poor _____

What is the most serious fault of your subject's voice or speech? _____

_____

What is the outstanding positive attribute of your subject's voice or speech? _____

Your Name _____ Your Subject's Name _____

Class or Section _____ Subject's Occupation _____

Date _____

Analysis Chart 3

	Yes	No
Quality Was his voice pleasant to listen to? Comments: (If you check **Yes**, elaborate briefly. If you check **No**, give reasons. Follow this procedure below also.)		
Loudness Was his voice easily heard? Comments:		
Expressiveness Was his voice varied and flexible? Comments:		
Articulation Was his speech clear, distinct and easy to understand? Comments:		
Unobtrusiveness and Appropriateness Did his voice, speech and pronunciation seem to be natural, unaffected and generally acceptable? Comments:		

Overall Effectiveness:

Excellent _____ Good _____ Fair _____ Poor _____

What is the most serious fault of your subject's voice or speech? _____

_____

What is the outstanding positive attribute of your subject's voice or speech? _____

_____

Analysis Chart 4

	Yes	No
Quality Was his voice pleasant to listen to? Comments: (If you check **Yes**, elaborate briefly. If you check No, give reasons. Follow this procedure below also.)		
Loudness Was his voice easily heard? Comments:		
Expressiveness Was his voice varied and flexible? Comments:		
Articulation Was his speech clear, distinct and easy to understand? Comments:		
Unobtrusiveness and Appropriateness Did his voice, speech and pronunciation seem to be natural, unaffected and generally acceptable? Comments:		

Overall Effectiveness:

Excellent _____ Good _____ Fair _____ Poor _____

What is the most serious fault of your subject's voice or speech? _____

_____

What is the outstanding positive attribute of your subject's voice or speech? _____

_____

Analysis Chart 5

	Yes	No
Quality Was his voice pleasant to listen to? Comments: (If you check **Yes**, elaborate briefly. If you check **No**, give reasons. Follow this procedure below also.)		
Loudness Was his voice easily heard? Comments:		
Expressiveness Was his voice varied and flexible? Comments:		
Artiuclation Was his speech clear, distinct and easy to understand? Comments:		
Unobtrusiveness and Appropriateness Did his voice, speech and pronunciation seem to be natural, unaffected and generally acceptable? Comments:		

Overall Effectiveness:

Excellent _____ Good _____ Fair _____ Poor _____

What is the most serious fault of your subject's voice or speech? _____

_____

What is the outstanding positive attribute of your subject's voice or speech? _____

_____

Analysis Chart 6

	Yes	No
Quality Was his voice pleasant to listen to? Comments: (If you check **Yes**, elaborate briefly. If you check **No**, give reasons. Follow this procedure below also.)		
Loudness Was his voice easily heard? Comments:		
Expressiveness Was his voice varied and flexible? Comments:		
Articulation Was his speech clear, distinct and easy to understand? Comments:		
Unobtrusiveness and Appropriateness Did his voice, speech and pronunciation seem to be natural, unaffected and generally acceptable? Comments:		

Overall Effectiveness:

Excellent _____ Good _____ Fair _____ Poor _____

What is the most serious fault of your subject's voice or speech? _____

_____

What is the outstanding positive attribute of your subject's voice or speech? _____

_____

Analysis Chart 7

Quality

Is the voice pleasant to listen to?

Yes _____ No _____

If the answer is **No**, which of the following is applicable?

Breathy _____   Nasal _____

Glottal shock _____   Denasal _____

Harsh-strident _____   Hoarse-husky _____

Harsh-throaty _____

Loudness

Is the voice easily heard?

Yes _____ No _____

If the answer is **No**, which of the following is applicable?

Too loud _____   Unvaried _____

Too soft _____   Lacks emphasis _____

Articulation

Is the articulation clear, distinct and accurate?

Yes _____ No _____

If the answer is **No**, which of the following is applicable?

General inaccuracy _____

Sounds omitted or dropped _____

Sounds substituted _____

Sounds added _____

Expressiveness

Is the voice varied and flexible?

Yes _____ No _____

If the answer is **No**, which of the following is applicable?

Pitch

Too high _____

Too low _____

Monotonous _____

Patterned _____

Excessive variation _____

Rate

Too fast _____   Hesitant _____

Too slow _____   Jerky _____

Monotonous _____   Poor phrasing _____

Patterned _____   Lack of pauses _____

Unobtrusiveness and Appropriateness

Are voice, speech and pronunciation natural, unaffected and generally acceptable?

Yes _____ No _____

If the answer is **No**, which of the following is applicable?

Arty (overly-precise articulation)

Affected pronunciation _____

Mispronunciation _____

Regional dialect _____

Foreign dialect _____

Overall Effectiveness:

Excellent _____   Good _____   Fair _____   Poor _____

In which aspects of voice and speech do you need to make the most improvement?

What is your outstanding vocal attribute?

Analysis Chart 8

Quality

Is the voice pleasant to listen to?

Yes _____ No _____

If the answer is **No,** which of the following is applicable?

Breathy_____ Nasal _____

Glottal shock _____ Denasal _____

Harsh-strident _____ Hoarse-husky_____

Harsh-throaty _____

Loudness

Is the voice easily heard?

Yes _____ No _____

If the answer is **No,** which of the following is applicable?

Too loud _____ Unvaried _____

Too soft _____ Lacks emphasis_____

Articulation

Is the articulation clear, distinct and accurate?

Yes _____ No _____

If the answer is No, which of the following is applicable?

General inaccuracy _____

Sounds omitted or dropped _____

Sounds substituted _____

Sounds added _____

Expressiveness

Is the voice varied and flexible?

Yes_____ No _____

If the answer is No, which of the following is applicable?

Pitch

Too high _____

Too low _____

Monotonous _____

Patterned _____

Excessive variation _____

Rate

Too fast _____ Hesitant _____

Too slow _____ Jerky _____

Monotonous _____ Poor phrasing _____

Patterned _____ Lack of pauses _____

Unobtrusiveness and Appropriateness

Are voice, speech and pronunciation natural, unaffected and generally acceptable?

Yes_____ No _____

If the answer is No, which of the following is applicable?

Arty (overly-precise articulation)

Affected pronunciation _____

Mispronunciation _____

Regional dialect _____

Foreign dialect _____

Overall Effectiveness:

Excellent _____ Good _____ Fair _____ Poor _____

In which aspects of voice and speech do you need to make the most improvement?

What is your outstanding vocal attribute?

Analysis Chart 9

Quality

Is the voice pleasant to listen to?

Yes _____ No _____

If the answer is No, which of the following is applicable?

Breathy _____ Nasal _____

Glottal shock _____ Denasal _____

Harsh-strident _____ Hoarse-husky _____

Harsh-throaty _____

Loudness

Is the voice easily heard?

Yes _____ No _____

If the answer is No, which of the following is applicable?

Too loud _____ Unvaried _____

Too soft _____ Lacks emphasis _____

Articulation

Is the articulation clear, distinct and accurate?

Yes _____ No _____

If the answer is No, which of the following is applicable?

General inaccuracy _____

Sounds omitted or dropped _____

Sounds substituted _____

Sounds added _____

Expressiveness

Is the voice varied and flexible?

Yes _____ No _____

If the answer is No, which of the following is applicable?

Pitch

Too high _____

Too low _____

Monotonous _____

Patterned _____

Excessive variation _____

Rate

Too fast _____ Hesitant _____

Too slow _____ Jerky _____

Monotonous _____ Poor phrasing _____

Patterned _____ Lack of pauses _____

Unobtrusiveness and Appropriateness

Are voice, speech and pronunciation natural, unaffected and generally acceptable?

Yes _____ No _____

If the answer is No, which of the following is applicable?

Arty (overly-precise articulation) _____

Affected pronunciation _____

Mispronunciation _____

Regional dialect _____

Foreign dialect _____

Overall Effectiveness:

Excellent _____ Good _____ Fair _____ Poor _____

In which aspects of voice and speech do you need to make the most improvement?

What is your outstanding vocal attribute?

Analysis Chart 10

Quality

Is the voice pleasant to listen to?

Yes _____ No _____

If the answer is No, which of the following is applicable?

Breathy _____ Nasal _____

Glottal shock _____ Denasal _____

Harsh-strident _____ Hoarse-husky _____

Harsh-throaty _____

Loudness

Is the voice easily heard?

Yes _____ No _____

If the answer is No, which of the following is applicable?

Too loud _____ Unvaried _____

Too soft _____ Lacks emphasis _____

Articulation

Is the articulation clear, distinct and accurate?

Yes _____ No _____

If the answer is No, which of the following is applicable?

General inaccuracy _____

Sounds omitted or dropped _____

Sounds substituted _____

Sounds added _____

Expressiveness

Is the voice varied and flexible?

Yes _____ No _____

If the answer is No, which of the following is applicable?

Pitch

Too high _____

Too low _____

Monotonous _____

Patterned _____

Excessive variation _____

Rate

Too fast _____ Hesitant _____

Too slow _____ Jerky _____

Monotonous _____ Poor phrasing _____

Patterned _____ Lack of pauses _____

Unobtrusiveness and Appropriateness

Are voice, speech and pronunciation natural, unaffected and generally acceptable?

Yes _____ No _____

If the answer is No, which of the following is applicable?

Arty (overly-precise articulation)

Affected pronunciation _____

Mispronunciation _____

Regional dialect _____

Foreign dialect _____

Overall Effectiveness:

Excellent _____ Good _____ Fair _____ Poor _____

In which aspects of voice and speech do you need to make the most improvement?

What is your outstanding vocal attribute?

Analysis Chart 11

Quality

Is the voice pleasant to listen to?

Yes _____ No _____

If the answer is No, which of the following is applicable?

Breathy _____ Nasal _____

Glottal shock _____ Denasal _____

Harsh-strident _____ Hoarse-husky _____

Harsh-throaty _____

Loudness

Is the voice easily heard?

Yes _____ No _____

If the answer is No, which of the following is applicable?

Too loud _____ Unvaried _____

Too soft _____ Lacks emphasis _____

Articulation

Is the articulation clear, distinct and accurate?

Yes _____ No _____

If the answer is No, which of the following is applicable?

General inaccuracy _____

Sounds omitted or dropped _____

Sounds substituted _____

Sounds added _____

Expressiveness

Is the voice varied and flexible?

Yes _____ No _____

If the answer is No, which of the following is applicable?

Pitch

Too high _____

Too low _____

Monotonous _____

Patterned _____

Excessive variation _____

Rate

Too fast _____ Hesitant _____

Too slow _____ Jerky _____

Monotonous _____ Poor phrasing _____

Patterned _____ Lack of pauses _____

Unobtrusiveness and Appropriateness

Are voice, speech and pronunciation natural, unaffected and generally acceptable?

Yes _____ No _____

If the answer is No, which of the following is applicable?

Arty (overly-precise articulation)

Affected pronunciation _____

Mispronunciation _____

Regional dialect _____

Foreign dialect _____

Overall Effectiveness:

Excellent _____ Good _____ Fair _____ Poor _____

In which aspects of voice and speech do you need to make the most improvement?

What is your outstanding vocal attribute?

Analysis Chart 12

Quality

Is the voice pleasant to listen to?

Yes _____ No _____

If the answer is No, which of the following is applicable?

Breathy _____ Nasal _____

Glottal shock _____ Denasal _____

Harsh-strident _____ Hoarse-husky _____

Harsh-throaty _____

Loudness

Is the voice easily heard?

Yes _____ No _____

If the answer is No, which of the following is applicable?

Too loud _____ Unvaried _____

Too soft _____ Lacks emphasis _____

Articulation

Is the articulation clear, distinct and accurate?

Yes _____ No _____

If the answer is No, which of the following is applicable?

General inaccuracy _____

Sounds omitted or dropped _____

Sounds substituted _____

Sounds added _____

Expressiveness

Is the voice varied and flexible?

Yes _____ No _____

If the answer is No, which of the following is applicable?

Pitch

Too high _____

Too low _____

Monotonous _____

Patterned _____

Excessive variation _____

Rate

Too fast _____ Hesitant _____

Too slow _____ Jerky _____

Monotonous _____ Poor phrasing _____

Patterned _____ Lack of pauses _____

Unobtrusiveness and Appropriateness

Is voice, speech and pronunciation natural, unaffected and generally acceptable?

Yes _____ No _____

If the answer is No, which of the following is applicable?

Arty (overly-precise articulation)

Affected pronunciation _____

Mispronunciation _____

Regional dialect _____

Foreign dialect _____

Overall Effectiveness:

Excellent _____ Good _____ Fair _____ Poor _____

In which aspects of voice and speech do you need to make the most improvement?

What is your outstanding vocal attribute?

Final Oral Performance

Quality

    Satisfactory improvement _____

    Slight improvement _____

    Needs further improvement _____

    Specific Comments: _____

Expressiveness

Pitch

    Satisfactory improvement _____

    Slight improvement _____

    Needs further improvement _____

    Specific Comments:

Loudness

    Satisfactory improvement _____

    Slight improvement _____

    Needs further improvement _____

    Specific Comments: _____

Rate

    Satisfactory improvement _____

    Slight improvement _____

    Needs further improvement _____

    Specific Comments:

Articulation

    Satisfactory improvement _____

    Slight improvement _____

    Needs further improvement _____

    Specific Comments: _____

Unobtrusiveness and Appropriateness

    Satisfactory improvement _____

    Slight improvement _____

    Needs further improvement _____

    Specific Comments:

Overall Effectiveness

    Excellent _____ Good _____ Fair _____ Poor _____

In what aspect of voice and diction have you made the greatest improvement?

In what aspect of voice and diction do you most need to continue working for additional improvement?

index